Quare
Joyce

Quare Joyce

Edited by
Joseph Valente

Ann Arbor
THE UNIVERSITY OF MICHIGAN PRESS

First paperback edition 2000
Copyright © by the University of Michigan 1998
All rights reserved
Published in the United States of America by
The University of Michigan Press
Manufactured in the United States of America
♾ Printed on acid-free paper

2003   2002   2001   2000   4   3   2

A CIP catalog record for this book is available from the British Library.

Library of Congress Cataloging-in-Publication Data

Quare Joyce / edited by Joseph Valente.
     p.   cm.
  Includes bibliographical references and index.
  ISBN 0-472-10898-0 (alk. paper)
     1. Joyce, James, 1882–1941—Criticism and interpretation.
  2. Homosexuality and literature—Ireland—History—20th century.
  3. English fiction—Irish authors—Greek influences.   4. Hellenism
  in literature.   5. Desire in literature.   6. Gays in literature.
  7. Sex in literature.   I. Valente, Joseph.
  PR6019.09Z7837   1998
  823'.912—dc21   97-45415
                                                    CIP

ISBN 0-472-08689-8 (pbk. : alk. paper)

To the Faithful Departed,
Betty Pritz
and
Tom Yingling

Acknowledgments

I wish to thank the *James Joyce Quarterly*, and particularly its Editor, Robert Spoo, for allowing us to reprint revised versions of four essays from *Joyce and Homosexuality*, volume 31, no. 3 (spring 1994): "On Joycean and Wildean Sodomy"; "Thrilled by His Touch: Homosexual Panic and the Will to Artistry in *A Portrait of the Artist as a Young Man*"; "Père-version and Im-mère-sion: Idealized Corruption in *A Portrait of the Artist as a Young Man* and *The Picture of Dorian Gray*"; "James Joyce: Tattoo Artist: Tracing the Outlines of Homosocial Desire." A special note of gratitude goes to Susan Whitlock for her counsel, her support, and her enthusiasm. Great appreciation, finally, is owed Joanne Slutsky, for both her research assistance and her help in preparing the manuscript.

Joseph Valente

Contents

Abbreviations

Joyce's (Sexual) Choices

A Historical Overview

The present volume builds upon a special issue of the *James Joyce Quarterly* entitled "Joyce and Homosexuality" that I edited in spring 1994. The purpose of that initial offering was threefold: to address and thus redress the compulsory heterosexuality that has encumbered even the most critically astute, theoretically sophisticated, and politically progressive Joyce scholarship; to reconfigure the economy of Joyce studies through the importation of a queer theory perspective, much as that economy was previously reconfigured by the introduction of feminism, Lacanian psychoanalysis, deconstruction, cultural studies, and postcolonialism; and, correlatively, to take up the manifold question of homosexuality—its historicity, its variability, its interaction with and suppression by an equally constructed heterosexuality—as it pertains to the always slippery articulation of Joyce's life and his writing.

The response to the special issue upon its release persuaded me not only that a significant beginning had been made in the achievement of the projected goals, but that the horizons for debate over the status and operation of homoeroticism in Joyce had been greatly enlarged, especially insofar as that homoeroticism inflects and is inflected by other affective and political dynamics. In seeking to build on this discussion, while further interrogating the terms on which it has proceeded to date, the present volume combines four essays revised from the earlier collection (two of them "Thrilled by His Touch" and "On Joycean and Wildean Sodomy," substantially expanded) with ten new essays, staging a critical dialogue among scholars of different generations, differing subspecialties, and diverse professional statures and commitments, who situate the topic across a correspondingly variegated literary and conceptual terrain. Joyce's representation, figuration, and, at times, dissimulation of homoerotic desire are here read in connection with classical scholastic thought and literature (Jean-Michel Rabaté), antecedent Irish literature (Vicki Mahaffey), current popular fiction (Margot Norris and Colleen Lamos), recent events in Irish colonial and British imperial history (Robert Caserio), psychoanalytic, medical, and sexological discourse (Tim Dean, Garry Leonard, Marian Eide, Joseph Valente), subcultural idioms and practices (Jennifer Levine), contemporary feminism (Christy Burns), postcolonial identity formation (Gregory Castle), and gay studies/queer theory in general (Christopher Lane).

At the same time, the essays have been assembled and arranged so that they might speak effectively to one another in their very diversity. This strategy aims at allowing certain issues and problematics to evolve from the interplay of the various arguments as the salient points of their mutual interrogation, contention, and reassessment.

At the methodological level, the reader will discover an implicit debate (made explicit in the afterword) over whether a gay studies or psychoanalytic approach is the more productive in addressing the (homo)sexual dynamics in/of Joyce's texts and whether these paradigms are, finally, compatible or not. More broadly still, the question arises as to whether the homoerotic valences traversing Joyce's narratives should be treated *primarily* in a psychological register—as attaching to the particular, interiorized subjectivities of the characters, the narrator, the author, or the readers—or whether these valences should be treated *primarily* in a cultural register—as engaging the manifold discursive constructions of homosexuality, and of perversity at large, in an act of aesthetic "resignification."[1]

At the hermeneutical level, in turn, a new set of questions, with distinctively political implications, can be seen to derive from these alternatives. A number of these essays ask, for example, what relationship obtains between the homophobia often represented in Joyce's work and the modes of narration in which it is disclosed, and to what degree do these narrative tactics implicate the author or the reader in the attitudes depicted? On the larger cultural scale, a number of the essays ask, what is the burden of Joyce's appropriation of certain received typologies of homosexuality: its supposed origin, secondary characteristics, relation to a complexly delimited heterosexual norm? Does his particular recirculation of certain late Victorian images and associations of homosexuality serve to affirm and reinforce prevailing stereotypes, to reconfigure them through a redistribution of emphases, to transvalue them altogether? Extending this political line of inquiry, several of the essays in this volume also consider how these social currencies of the homosexual interact in Joyce's text with those of other subaltern subject categories such as the feminine or the colonized, and to what ideological effect.

At the theoretical level, finally, many of these controversies and deliberations converge in a multifaceted canvassing of that most conspicuous of queer tropes, the closet, and the matters of secrecy, concealment, misrecognition, and repression that it crystallizes. Ontologically, does the closet, the injunction to secrecy, quarantine and camouflage certain selected transgressions of the sexual norms that it enforces—what Foucault calls the "repressive hypothesis"—or does the closet constitute the modern subject as the very possibility of such transgressive agency—what Foucault terms the implantation of forbidden desire?[2] Epistemologically, does the metaphorics of the closet (a repressed impulse, a latent affect, a concealed orientation) provide sensitive instruments for analyzing the nuanced dynamics of sexual identification and normalization, or does it instead essentialize sexual desire in terms of aims and objects that are themselves, in the last analysis, profoundly contingent? Politically, is the explanatory trope of the closet, for historical reasons, exclusively relevant to homosexuality, and, no less importantly, is it, for historical reasons, properly or automatically relevant to homosexuality? Should the closet be extended and reconfigured to suit other forms or classes of social identity, or should its deployment be resisted altogether?

Beyond giving the collection a dialectical cohesiveness, the emergence of these decisive yet still undecided questions should enhance its pedagogical utility, unfolding a series of cruxes around which to organize class discussion, students' research projects, or even a course schedule. The pedagogical *urgency* of the volume, however, resides in the subject matter itself, specifically in its capacity to alter our present understanding of Joyce's fiction by refocusing the conditions of their production and initial reception. That is to say, the project of queering Joyce enacted in the ensuing essays does something more pedagogically significant than simply locate another layer of cultural import in the highly sedimented texts under consideration, something more than complicate or disturb the strata that have already been mined. This project taps into, prospects, and retrieves a whole other creative and critical history for Joyce's writing, a framework of causes and corollaries, both material and discursive, that supplements, in the strong Derridean sense, the previously established patterns of Joyce's (af)filiations. Instead of offering sketches of the respective essays (substantively treated in Christopher Lane's afterword), I would like to sketch out this double history, which each of the essays inevitably engages.

II

Thanks to the ascendency of feminist perspectives and methodologies, the most innovative and influential work on Joyce over the last decade has been devoted to the study of gender representation, performance, privilege, and anxiety. Prominent books like *Joyce and Feminism, James Joyce: Authorized Reader, Joyce's Anatomy of Culture, Reauthorizing Joyce, Paperspace, James Joyce and Sexuality, James Joyce and the Politics of Desire, Wandering and Return in Finnegans Wake, The Veil of Signs, Reading Dubliners Again, Joyce's Web,* and the forthcoming *Ulysses: En-gendered Perspectives,* all take this set of questions as their primary focus. More recently, the same general problematic has entered into postcolonial readings of Joyce—*The Irish Ulysses,* my own *James Joyce and the Problem of Justice: Negotiating Sexual and Colonial Difference*—by way of analyses of the long-standing and conflicted feminization of Irishness, which acquired renewed impetus and provoked renewed contestation during the Victorian-Edwardian era. But while issues of gender and sexuality are positively inseparable *from* one another, they are also irreducible *to* one another, so that advances in the one incite but do not necessarily induce advances in the other. By treating sexual desire in general as scripted and circumscribed by a patriarchal and imperialist culture, the feminist and postcolonial turn in Joyce criticism has served to render the heterosexual imperative visible as an arbitrary ideological limit or constraint, *without* expressly addressing it as a problem or overriding the presuppositions that it mandates. Although increasingly denaturalized, sexual desire has continued to be identified, for the most part, with heterosexual desire in Joyce. Although the homoerotics of the novels are no longer disavowed or ignored outright as they were in most of the "first wave" academic treatments of Joyce, the topic has only begun, with the publication of the special issue of the *James Joyce Quarterly*, to receive sustained, systemic analysis or to be integrated into the larger dialogue concerning Joyce's cultural politics.

An informing aim of this collection, accordingly, is to extend and thus to amend the feminist interrogation of Joyce to include an inquiry into the relationship between gender and affective hierarchies in his fictions, between their representation of homosexual difference and their resistance to what Irigaray calls "hommosexual" sameness, the law of the phallus.[3] Three essays in particular ("James Joyce, Tattoo Artist," "In the Original Sinse," and "Père-version and Im-mère-sion") speak directly to Joyce's handling of the manifold complicity of misogyny and homophobia in modern Ireland.

The salient property of Joyce's text that affords us purchase for this labor is, paradoxically, the very property that has long obscured the necessity of performing it. In her essay for this volume, "James Joyce, Tattoo Artist," Jennifer Levine neatly characterizes the property in question as an "easy slide from heterosexual to homosexual possibilities and back again." It is precisely to remark this persistent play or oscillation of erotic directionality in Joyce's work that I have elected to use the Anglo-Irish epithet *quare* in the title as a kind of transnational/transidiomatic pun. *Quare*, meaning odd or strange, as in Brendan Behan's famous play, *The Quare Fellow*, has lately been appropriated as a distinctively Irish variant of *queer*, as in the recent prose collection *Quare Fellas*, whose editor, Brian Finnegan, reinterprets Behan's own usage of the term as having "covertly alluded to his own sexuality."[4] At the purely textual level, however, the word partakes not only of *queer* but also of *square*, a synonym in both the technical and the idiomatic sense for "straight," often understood as the diametric opposite of queer. Unpacked along these lines, the epithet perfectly captures Joyce's inclination and aptitude for queering the dichotomy between the "queer" and the "square/straight," for unsettling the normative and hierarchical distinctions between different modes of sexual expression. This strategy, in turn, can be seen to accord closely with his much-celebrated subversion of the stylistic and generic proprieties of novelistic representation, sexuality constituting, as Jacques Lacan has shown, a primary "cut" in the framing of all meaningful social forms.

Now on the one hand, the heightened lability of erotic valences in Joyce's writing, their relatively liquid passage among culturally reified and polarized positions or profiles, has actually helped to facilitate the heterosexual imperialism of his critical reception. Potential signs and scenarios of homoerotic longing, pleasure, and identification could always be decoded otherwise; and owing to the dominance of the cross-sex grid of intelligibility in Joyce studies, they almost always have been decoded otherwise, generally in terms of some broadly heterosexual deviance from the patriarchal norms of desire. Thus, Bloom's phantasmagoric transsexualism in the "Circe" episode of *Ulysses* has regularly been taken to breach or undermine the law of the father, but rarely the law of the (heterosexual) couple; it has regularly been taken to expose gender as a phantasmatic, culturally scripted performance, but rarely to expose sexual preference as similarly contingent and theatrical. On the other hand, this same heightened lability of erotic valence renders the Joycean text peculiarly responsive to the interpretive paradigm shift effected with the advent of queer theory. Each sign or scenario of desire in, say, *Ulysses* or *A Portrait of the Artist as a Young Man* can be construed to admit, evoke, even signal same-sex as well as cross-sex energies, to bind them in complex economies of phobia and frisson, ambivalence and abandon, recognition and disavowal, displacement and overdetermination. When it comes to the sexual dynamics of Joyce's novels, in other words, this paradigm can never simply replace the cross-gender suppositional framework of traditional, heterosexist criticism with the same-sex suppositional framework of certain gay studies approaches but must rather disrupt this binarism in a variety of historically responsive ways.

That being said, it should come as no surprise that a central, though not uncontested, theoretical resource in the essays to follow is the work of Eve Kosofsky Sedgwick, likely the leading exponent of the transferential relations defining homo- and heteroeroticism *as such*. Of particular moment for a number of the contributors is her conception of male homosocial desire, the structural mediation of male-male relationships by an eroticized competition over and exchange of women, which allows homoerotic charges to be disguised, distorted, supplemented, and vicariously expressed in, among other things, a mix of express homophobia and tacit misogyny.[5] As it happens, the amatory and sexual alliances in Joyce's later and longer works bear an almost exclusively triangular cast: Stephen—E.C.—Cranly, Richard—Bertha—Robert, Bloom—Molly—Boylan, Bloom—Molly—Stephen, Shem—Issy—Shaun, Anna Livia—Humphrey—Issy, and so on. Accordingly, homosociality offers an especially felicitous conceptual instrument for isolating same-sex affects amid that "easy slide" of erotic possibility and then articulating them into a new anatomy of Joycean desire, one that is *(a)* more complex and transgressive than any predicated upon a presumptively universal heterosexuality or, for that matter, a presumptively original homosexuality, and so *(b)* more in keeping with the transgressive complexities of Joyce's signifying practice. By the same token, the other theoretical rubric for which Sedgwick is best known, the "epistemology of the closet," is raised only to be resisted or reformulated by a number of contributors, who find its counterposition of the subject's inner truth to his or her social performance to be historically as well as ontologically untenable.[6]

III

The demonstrated need for a queer theoretical perspective on Joyce's texts is positively overdetermined by the sexual ferment animating their personal and sociohistorical context, conspicuous elements of which will be canvassed in this collection. Certain of the more crucial social developments in this regard unfold in an uncanny parallel with the trajectory of Joyce's own personal and professional life, providing not just "grist for his mill," as Stephen Dedalus finds "all" events were for Shakespeare (*U* 9.748), but a shaping influence on his sensibility and his work too profound to be ignored, either in our research or our teaching.

Joyce was growing up just as a series of explosive events were operating to enforce gender/sexual conventions and to reinforce the public obsession with them, by answering a perceived crisis in British masculinity (a racial corollary to the perceived decline in British geocolonial power) with a legal campaign against that newly constructed social species, the "invert" or "homosexual."[7] The earliest of these events, and the most immediate to the Irish context, was a homosexual scandal involving prominent officials in Dublin Castle, the seat of British governance in Ireland, and thus concentrating sexual and racial and imperial anxiety in an especially potent brew. As Gayle Rubin, among others, has argued, sexual scandals tend to crop up during markedly transitional moments in the social order, and they generally function to consolidate or to reconfigure an array of changing and uncertain social norms confederate with erotic practice or fantasy. As a response to the Dublin Castle affair and other high-profile scandals, the second of these explosive events, the Criminal Law Amendment Act of 1885, would seem to bear out Rubin's thesis, and nowhere more than in section 11 of the bill, which outlaws male-male sexuality as such. Prepared for public consumption by an aggressive newspaper industry, late Victorian scandal seemed to indicate and served to justify a draconian regulation of those sexual activities that were not only seen to deviate from the popular triumphalist vision of British masculinity but were felt to threaten in some way the very class of subject, the English gentleman, who was ultimately responsible for cultivating and contouring that vision.

The third of these explosive events, in which several London notables were convicted of prostituting several West End messenger boys, testified to the precisely exemplary function of the new law—not by discharging that function but in the manner of its failure and the outrage aroused thereby. The first major test of the already controversial section 11, the so-called Cleveland Street trials of 1889–90, were remarkable chiefly for the unusual fret and indignation they incited throughout complacently class-bound Victorian England at the rather unremarkable class inequities in the sentences handed down. The reason such outrage greeted the amnesty predictably awarded the most elite and powerful parties to the scandal was that homosexuality was already being pathologized and policed as a menace to Britain qua elite civilization, qua ruling power, and to the British qua superordinate race. Indeed, the new classification of homosexuality as a *separate* order of being or subjectivity during this period proved systemic with its identification as a *distinct* threat to the racial or national whole and British leadership in the world. If the sexual "degeneracy" of grandees like Lord Arthur Somerset and the Earl of Easton did not confirm popular and press opinion as to the racialized nature of this menace, the judicial indulgence of these grandees, a connivance of the British ruling class at its own decay, served to finish the job. In the end, the resulting backlash found a peculiarly suitable target in Oscar Wilde, whose *figura* as a notorious dandy not only came to signify his "queer" or unconventional sexuality but to resonate of his "queer" or undecidable ethno-class condition: at once Irish arriviste and London gentleman, subaltern bourgeois and faux aristocrat, a fixture in metropolitan society and a colonial hanger-on.

Given this ongoing dialectic of splashy scandal and showy regulation, and the heated public controversy surrounding either polarity, the repression of homosexuality as taboo and its simultaneous return as titillation could not but have a significant effect on the climate of Joyce's sexual acculturation. But given the ethnic and colonial inlay of homosexuality's Victorian construction, this effect could not have been straightforward or univocal, not for someone brought up to identify himself with the role of bourgeois gentleman (however déclassé), respectable Catholic, and irredentist Irish outlaw. On the one hand, as Norris's essay "A Walk on the Wild(e) Side" attests, Joyce did not avoid imbibing the popular prejudice against homosexuality, which tended to accompany the sort of class anxieties he suffered; on the other, partly owing to his highly ambiguous social station, he grew to equate popular prejudices in general, and particularly those of English stamp, with arrant hypocrisy, and his essay on the similarly minded Oscar Wilde shows that Britain's official or legalized homophobia was no exception in this regard (*CW* 201–5). Indeed, as the next segment of life-narrative indicates, it is impossible to disentangle Joyce's attitudes toward homosexuality from his experience of his own hybrid subject position, inasmuch as both are equally if differently delimited by the close reticulation of the Western discourses on sexuality, nationality, and race.

Joyce spent his formative years, the late 1880s, in an Irish Catholic boarding academy, and it was during this period that the sodomitical practices long associated with, and prevalent in, the analogous public schools of England were beginning to cohere as the signs and affects of an innate bodily disposition known as inversion or homosexuality. Both popular commentators like W. F. Stead and "scientific," sexological writers like Ellis, Symonds, and Carpenter portrayed the circumstances of public-school education as tending to solicit the otherwise latent or recessive homoerotic tendencies of young adolescent males.[8] Some of Joyce's letters and essays in subsequent years not only embrace these assumptions about sexual life in the elite boys' schools, they betray an uneasy fascination with the comparative sexual influences of such educational institutions on either side of St. George's Channel. The latter deliberation both presumes and worries a basic interconnection between sexual desire and national identity, while at the same time manifesting Joyce's anxious "enjoyment" in doubting the status of his own sexuality, his "pleasure in [the] displeasure" of sexual incertitude.[9] Moreover, as Joyce's fictional treatment of the same problematic shows: in conjoining the categories of sexual and racial identity, the colonial matrix works to defeat the very sort of essentializing determinations that it almost invariably promotes as instruments of both rule and resistance.

Joyce came to adolescence in the very year that Oscar Wilde thrice came to trial, an event which, by Alan Sinfield's account, fixed "the image of the queer" in the British popular mind,[10] the better to subject him to suspicion, stigma, and surveillance. The widespread interest that the Wilde affair attracted, its sheer magnitude as a public scandal, was doubtless sufficient in itself to fuel Joyce's growing mindfulness of same-sex desire as a potent source of curiosity and contempt, fear and fascination. But there were also corollary factors making this spectacle an important nexus in Joyce's personal and aesthetic development, ancillary reasons why the life, legend, and literary production of Oscar Wilde should have left so deep an impress upon Joyce's career. Joyce drew both his exceptionalist vision of the artist as "genius" and of art as an extended mode of self-creation from the Paterian school of aestheticism, whose coded valorization of Greek love, under the more general rubric of Hellenism, found its liveliest and most overt expression in the work of Oscar Wilde. The most cherished aspect of Joyce's youthful self-image, therefore, did not go untouched by a strengthening cultural association, triggered by Pater and crystallized in Wilde, of the literary artist with queerness. (Tim Dean's essay "Paring His Fingernails" takes up this very connection.)

Furthermore, the fact that Joyce apprehended social persecution as the price of such exceptionalism cannot only be traced, as it most often is, to the childhood trauma wrought by the ruin of his political hero, Charles Stewart Parnell, but also to the commotion created by Wilde's three trials. For this reason, the latter would become a central narrative motif in *Finnegans Wake*, repeatedly melding with the Parnell episode. (Jean-Michel Rabaté moots Joyce's identification of Wilde with Parnell in his contribution, "Of Joycean and Wildean Sodomy.")

To appreciate Joyce's debt to Wilde, however, a debt that fully half of the essays here remark, one must reckon with the discourse of Hellenism that Wilde espoused and even embodied, a discourse whose history was a powerful determinant of the associations that homosexuality bore for Joyce as a young man. Because Hellenism does not provide the explicit focus in any of the essays to follow and yet sets the stage for many of the issues they tackle, I will briefly chronicle this ideological formation here and indicate its impact on Joyce's fictive self-representation.

Wilde's Hellenism had its roots in the efforts of midcentury Oxonian liberals like John Stuart Mill and Matthew Arnold to shift British cultural priorities from a secular and Christian assault on social corruption to a classically minded campaign against social complacency and stagnation. But whereas Arnold's essay "Pagan and Medieval Religious Sentiment" construes the classical ethos as comprising a secular and sacrificial disinterestedness, Mill's signature tract *On Liberty,* which Joyce owned, interprets the same ethos as comprising individual autonomy and intellectual diversity.[11] Whereas Arnold's Hellenism is a discourse of assimilative order, Mill's is a discourse of personal and social innovation, hence one more suited to appeal to the egoistical and anarchistic inclinations of a man like Joyce, whose favorite political philosophers included Max Stirner and Benjamin Tucker. Mill's and Arnold's respective takes on the Hellenic ideal, in turn, consist with their discrepant attitudes toward the Irish question in its cultural aspect. In *On the Celtic Element in Literature,* Arnold celebrates the imaginative emotionalism of the stereotypically feminized Celt, but only to see those qualities colonized by and *integrated* within the rationalistic hegemony of the masculine Anglo-Saxon intellect.[12] In "England and Ireland," by contrast, Mill sufficiently appreciates and respects Ireland's cultural differences with England to foresee, however resistantly, the likely necessity of allowing the colonized island to govern itself, a solution and a rationale that anticipates Parnell's Home Rule agenda.[13] One strand of Victorian Hellenism is thus distinguished by its joint advocacy of personal freedom and national self-determination, principles that Joyce likewise compounded in his two-front attack upon oppressive British rule and repressive Catholic indoctrination.

It was this Millian strain of Hellenism that the Oxford-bred aestheticist lineage of Pater, Swinburne, Symonds, and Wilde extended along aesthetic and sexual lines. Pater's essays "Diaphaneite" and "Winckelmann" directly counter Arnold's domesticated brand of Hellenism with a paganism of self-development and self-cultivation, in which bodily pleasure and intellectual ardor, sensuous experience and spiritual aspiration, achieve a splendid equilibrium.[14] And the sexual overtones of Pater's style, while allusive and often undecidable, unmistakably signaled to his contemporaries that the intellectual "procreancy" of Socratic Eros formed an integral part of his program of cultural regeneration.

In the original version of "Winckelmann," for example, Pater offers a characteristically subtle rejoinder to those who would sanitize Hellenism of its "corrupting" homoerotic valences, or would purify the valences themselves of their bodily aspect. He cites Winckelmann to the effect that "the Hellenic spirit and culture" depend "on certain conditions," which must be "reproduce[d]" if the personal *Bildung* and social renovation promised by "that spirit and culture" is to transpire.[15] The Greek institution of *paiderastia* was at once the most relevant, the most clearly indicated, and the most fraught of these unnamed conditions, particularly for an all-male residential university like Oxford, which already encouraged fairly intense homosocial and homopedagogical bonding. What Pater gently suggests here, in the face of dismay within and beyond the circle of Oxford Hellenists, is that it makes little sense to venerate ancient Greek civilization as a pattern for contemporary renewal while reviling the chief instrument, *paiderastia*, whereby its elites were molded, its values were transmitted, its social order and tradition were reproduced. For Pater, any genuine Grecophilia implied and demanded the moral legitimation of genuine Greek love. But the converse was no less true: the legitimacy with which Pater invested Greek love always assumed a reinvigorating cultural Grecophilia, in which Socratic Eros would serve as a means of individual *Bildung*, what Pater calls "self-culture."[16]

On the one hand, the Hellenism of Oscar Wilde can be seen to synthesize the respective emphases of Mill and Pater's classical programs. As Linda Dowling has argued, Wilde's *The Portrait of Mr. W.H.* delineates the "soul" of neo-Platonism in a distinctively Paterian manner, as a redemptive interfusion of "intellectual enthusiasm and the physical passion of love"; and the same work finds that "soul" to be embodied in distinctively Paterian terms, "homoerotic friendships becoming a vital factor in the new culture and a mode of self-conscious intellectual development."[17] At the same time, Wilde's markedly feminized personal style and flamboyantly antinomian moral attitudes looked to incorporate the erotic dimension within the newly approved latitudes of idiosyncrasy and self-expression which Victorian liberals like Mill had established. *The Picture of Dorian Gray* reflects this design in having Sir Henry Wotton, an "Oxford" exponent of "the Hellenic ideal," enunciate the liberal principle of *Bildung*—"the aim of life is self-development"—as a formula of homoerotic seduction.[18]

On the other hand, Oscar Wilde was instrumental in reducing Hellenism to its most lurid common denominator in the cultural Imaginary. As Linda Dowling has also argued, "after Wilde's trial it would be difficult to pronounce the word 'Hellenism' without an insinuating leer."[19] This debasement of the "Greek" currency, of course, was mainly the result of the same homophobia that motivated the Criminal Law Amendment Act and thus mandated the trial itself. Any phobia, after all, does not just determine a set of reactions to its particular object, but subjects a wide range of association, conscious and unconscious, to the same reaction, producing that flattening effect familiar in stereotype. But Wilde contributed to this reduction as well. As he confesses in *De Profundis*, the relationship with Douglas, which he defended from the witness box in terms of Socratic Eros and spiritual procreancy, had in fact constituted just the opposite: an "unintellectual friendship" and an "intellectually degrading" affair.[20] The friendship had thus betrayed the very Hellenic and aestheticist principles that sanctified it in Wilde's eyes, and betrayed them in a manner that seemed to justify the accusation of bad faith frequently aimed at their adherents.

Mediated by his compatriot Wilde, Oxford Hellenism afforded Joyce a script to be performed or mimicked in his youth and a narrative code to be implemented and manipulated in his fictive representation of that youth. It lent the lived and the written story a shared ideological basis: a discourse of individual freedom and self-development that could address and resist, in concerted fashion, the main intellectual, sexual, and aesthetic constraints of Irish Catholic life and the political inequities of British colonial rule. The combined fact that modern Hellenism was such a pointedly English phenomenon and that the Irish identified their culture as Greece to England's Rome (as in the "Aeolus" episode of *Ulysses*) gave this discourse a certain flexibility and ambivalence for Joyce, properties ideally adapted to his own semicolonial subject position. However, the strong identification of Wildean Hellenism with a mystified homoeroticism—the so-called higher sodomy—not only introduced a new level of ambivalence into the discourse for Joyce, but in the process actually limited its flexibility, threatening to reduce the rich diversity of its intellectual and cultural program to the narrow question of sexual preference. Joyce's deployment of the Hellenic codes finds him navigating carefully between the social leverage they provide and the social liability they admit.

In bestowing a Greek surname upon the thoroughly Irish protagonist of his bildungsroman, Joyce could count on its contemporary audience to interpret Stephen's growth in the light of Hellenic ideals of self-development, particularly when the title of the novel, *A Portrait of the Artist as a Young Man* alludes to Wilde's two exemplary engagements with these ideals, *The Picture of Dorian Gray* and *The Portrait of Mr. W.H.* Moreover, the narrative trajectory of *A Portrait*, in which Stephen struggles uncertainly to assume the role of self-determining artist, reenacts the Dedalus myth precisely in terms of the modern Hellenic imperative to self-cultivation; and the avowed goal of Stephen's aesthetic venture, "to forge in the smithy of my soul the uncreated conscience of my race" (*P* 252), ironically epitomizes the Hellenist dream of a widespread cultural renewal proceeding from the creative *Bildung* of exceptional souls. The homoerotic or paiderastic dimension of "Greek" discourse is by no means elided or suppressed in this narrative of Stephen's manifold *non serviam*, as a number of the essays herein attest (e.g., "Paring His Fingernails," "The Nothing Place," "Thrilled by His Touch"). But the indirect free style of the novel does keep Stephen's repression of his own homoerotic impulses from occupying center stage or magnetizing the reception of Joyce's Hellenic device. Indeed, in a clever twist, Stephen's method of repressing the homoerotic, aestheticizing it out of existence, actually replicates the characteristic defensive gesture of Oxford Hellenism against which Pater and Symonds wrote.

In many respects, the "Telemachus" episode of *Ulysses* is the realistic morning after the romantic night of Stephen's illusions in *A Portrait*. So it should come as no surprise that the Hellenistic philosophy suddenly appears in the raw light of the sexual realism fostered by such medicalizing discourses as psychiatry, psychoanalysis, and sexology. The chief spokesman for Hellenism in the episode is, in fact, the carnally minded medical student, Buck Mulligan: it is he who remarks the absurdity of Stephen's "ancient Greek" name (*U* 1.34); he who claims his own name has "a Hellenic ring" (1.41–42); he who declares "[w]e must go to Athens" (1.43); he who suggests teaching Stephen to read Greek (1.79–80); he who urges Stephen to help him "Hellenize" Ireland (1.158); he who has visited Oxford and saluted the "New Paganism" across its quadrangles, disturbing a gardener with Matthew Arnold's face (1.173–5); he who attributes to Stephen the "real Oxford manner" (1.54); and he who "dress[es] the character" of a Wildean dandy (1.516). For his part, Stephen greets Mulligan's interest in Oxford Hellenism with something akin to Dowling's "insinuating leer"; he translates the invitation to Hellenic Ireland as a homosexual proposition, translates the ragging of Clive Kempthorpe as a homoerotic saturnalia that calls forth the disapproving visage of Matthew Arnold himself, and ultimately translates the phrase "manner of Oxenford" as synonymous with *paiderastia* (*U* 9.1212). Whereas the Hellenism of *A Portrait* remains implicit and Stephen effectively excludes its homoerotic component from consciousness, the Hellenism in *Ulysses* becomes explicit and Stephen views it almost exclusively in a sexual register, adopting a typically jaded post-Wildean attitude toward the discourse. But in either case, Stephen *fails to make the connection* among the diverse aspects of Hellenism, its agenda of self-cultivation, its calls for cultural renewal, its notions of masculine virtue, its legitimation of homosexual love. As a result, Stephen persists in misrecognizing how far his own sensibility, and that of his generation, has been inflected by Hellenism, which simply permeates the "Telemachus" episode in multiple allusions to Arnold, Swinburne, Pater, and, especially Wilde. Stephen's disenchantment on this score amounts to yet another form of enchantment, a dramatic irony summarized in Mulligan's doubly self-canceling claim, "We have grown out of Wilde and paradoxes" (*U* 1.554).

Joyce came to adulthood during what one might call the apex of classical sexology, the statistical midpoint of the staggered careers of Krafft-Ebing, Symonds, Ellis, Carpenter, and Freud, whose concerted attention to the phenomenon of same-sex preference helped to define homosexuality, in professional and lay circles alike, as a distinct ontological condition. Joyce read all of these figures, and exposure was doubtless sufficient in itself both to generate and to evince an abiding intellectual interest in the typologies of sexual difference/dissidence. But once again there were corollary ingredients, bearing upon Joyce's sense of his own identity, that served to season his engagement with these matters, at once sharpening and complicating it. The dominant paradigm of homosexuality to emerge from the sexual sciences of the time was one of gender inversion, a model to which Joyce apparently subscribed in full. In Foucault's words, "homosexuality . . . was transposed from the practice of sodomy onto a kind of interior androgyny, a hermaphroditism of the soul."[21] Whereas the authority of ancient Hellenic culture had been virilizing,[22] male homosexuality was now "scientifically" bound to effeminacy. Male same-sex desire was, in Christopher Craft's words, "assumed to be a feminine desire referable not to the sex of the body but rather to a psychologized sexual center characterized by the 'opposite' gender."[23] On one side, this sexological cross-coding of gender and sexual determination intersected with the imperialist classification of the Celts as a psychologically feminine race, so that perceived Hibernian departures from the Anglo-Saxon ideals of manhood could be at once naturalized and pathologized as some sort of inbred ethnic perversity. The most conspicuous point of this intersection was, of course, the trial of Oscar Wilde, in which, as Alan Sinfield has argued, the identification of the "queer" with effeminacy was consolidated in the figure of an Irish arriviste;[24] this ethnic perversity was subsequently confirmed in what must have seemed a sequel, the likewise spectacular trial of Sir Roger Casement. On the other side, the sexologists' "heterosexual paradigm" of homosexuality prefigures a cardinal project of high-modernist art generally and Joyce's art in particular: the achievement of a cross-gendered voice. In either case, homosexuality acquired a symbolic value for Joyce no less nuanced and conflicted than its experiential value, a symbolic value that *(a)* solicited homophilia and homophobia simultaneously; *(b)* problematized the normative disjunction of same-sex from cross-sex desire. Many of the essays in this volume take up the influence of the *scientia sexualis* upon Joyce's understanding of homoeroticism, and three in particular, "Confessing Oneself," "Thrilled by His Touch," and "Casement, Joyce and Pound," discuss homosexual identity in its relation to colonial subjectivity.

Finally, Joyce arrived at his professional seniority in Paris of the 1920s and 1930s, a fabulous confluence of aesthetic and sexual experimentation, owing in part to the singular tolerance offered homosexuality by the Napoleonic Code. The literary and aesthetic culture of Paris at this time was very much a bookshop and salon culture, and the bookshop and salon culture was in turn fashioned and superintended by a largely lesbian community. As a consequence, the discourses of avant-garde art overlap in an especially intimate way with the discourses of alternative sexual experience and gender performance. Inversion, especially female inversion, acquired a superficially chic and so increasingly familiar aura through a complex intersection of cultural infringements on gender bipolarity

and compulsory heterosexuality: the Sapphic literature and literary salon of
Natalie Barney and her circle; the masquerade, transvestic and homosexual balls,
in both salon and dance halls; the androgynous style of self-presentation in the
dance artistry of Irene Castle and Isadora Duncan; the likewise androgynous
fashion of Chanel's "garconne" line of haute couture; the boyish body styling of
the flapper look; the popularity of cross-dressing among upper-class women.[25]

Joyce's own closest publishing and promotional contacts, the people he
most depended upon professionally, were almost exclusively lesbians. Sylvia
Beach and Adrienne Monnier published the first English and French versions of
Ulysses out of their bookshops, respectively Shakespeare and Company and La
Maison des Amis des Livres, which Joyce regularly visited for literary readings
and society. The couple also labored to secure Joyce's Paris reputation from the
start by arranging a meeting for him with Valery Larbaud, who later translated
Ulysses. In Ellmann's words, both "supported the fragile edifice that was Joyce
in Paris" (*JJII* 651–52). Margaret Anderson and Jane Heap, who visited Joyce occasionally while in Paris, published *Ulysses* in the *Little Review* and were tried,
convicted, and fined for their trouble. Janet Flanner, a friend of Sylvia Beach,
helped to promote the considerable éclat of *Ulysses*, pronouncing its Paris publication in 1922 the literary event of the decade.[26] Djuna Barnes, whom Joyce
originally approached for information about the *Little Review* case, became his
interlocutor, confidante, colleague, and prose portraitist during the period surrounding the release of *Ulysses*. What is more, Joyce attended the famous literary salon of Natalie Barney, who was known as "the pope of Lesbos" for her
apostolic zeal in the propagation of Sapphic love, and Joyce corresponded with
her thereafter concerning the possible production of *Exiles* (*LIII* 18). In Paris,
then, Joyce participated for the first time in a culture, literary or otherwise, in
which lesbianism was *heimliche,* a common part of the universe, so much so that
the city was nicknamed Paris-Lesbos.[27] And as lesbianism became more familiar and so less threatening to him, his writing, which had all but avoided the
question of lesbian sexuality, began to take it up. As demonstrated by two of the
essays in this volume, "In the Original Sinse" and "'A Faint Glimmer of Lesbianism' in Joyce," the end of *Ulysses* and particularly *Finnegans Wake* show a
Joyce divided between received myths and radical ideas in his representation of
female same-sex desire.

I hope that this contextualization of Joyce's writing of the homoerotic points to
one inescapable conclusion. Given the variegated impact and importance that
different cultural and subcultural constructions of homoerotic possibility had
on Joyce's conception of himself and others at each stage of his life, it is far less
surprising that his work repeatedly turns heterosexual attraction inside out
to discover its profound immixture with homosexual desire than that this
methodology has gone largely unnoticed and its political import largely unap-
preciated to this point.

NOTES

1. For an outline of the rhetorical/political import of resignification, see Judith Butler, *Bodies That Matter* (New York: Routledge, 1995), 138–40.

2. Michel Foucault, *The History of Sexuality,* vol. 1, *An Introduction,* trans. Robert Hurley (New York: Pantheon, 1978), 15.

3. Luce Irigaray, *This Sex Which Is Not One,* trans. Gillian C. Gill (Ithaca, N.Y.: Cornell University Press, 1985), 171.

4. Brian Finnegan, introduction to *Quare Fellas,* ed. B. Finnegan (Dublin: Basement, 1994), 6.

5. Eve Kosofsky Sedgwick, *Between Men* (New York: Columbia University Press, 1985), 21–27.

6. Eve Kosofsky Sedgwick, *Epistemology of the Closet* (Berkeley and Los Angeles: University of California Press, 1990), 67–90.

7. My account of this legal campaign is drawn from Ed Cohen, *Talk on the Wilde Side: Toward a Genealogy of a Discourse on Male Sexualities* (New York: Routledge, 1993), 103–25; and Alan Sinfield, *The Wilde Century* (New York: Columbia University Press, 1994), 98, 123.

8. Sinfield, *The Wilde Century,* 65; Havelock Ellis and J. A. Symonds, *Sexual Inversion* (London: Wilson and MacMillan, 1897); Edward Carpenter, *The Intermediate Sex* (1898; New York: Mitchell Kennerley, 1912).

9. For the psychoanalytic concept of enjoyment, see Slavoj Žižek, *Enjoy Your Symptom!* (New York: Routledge, 1992), 48.

10. Sinfield, *The Wilde Century,* 121.

11. Richard Dellamora, *Masculine Desire* (Chapel Hill: University of North Carolina Press, 1990), 61, 102–10; Linda Dowling, *Hellenism and Homosexuality in Victorian Oxford* (Ithaca, N.Y.: Cornell University Press, 1994), 57–66.

12. Matthew Arnold, *Lectures and Essays in Criticism,* ed. R. H. Super (Ann Arbor: University of Michigan Press, 1973), 82.

13. John Stuart Mill, "England and Ireland," in *On Ireland,* ed. R. N. Lebow (Philadelphia: Institute for the Study of Human Issues, 1979), 3–14.

14. My account of Pater's Hellenism is based on Dellamora, *Masculine Desire,* 58–68, 110–16.

15. Dowling, *Hellenism and Homosexuality,* 97.

16. Dellamora, *Masculine Desire,* 60.

17. Dowling, *Hellenism and Homosexuality,* 126.

18. Oscar Wilde, *The Picture of Dorian Gray* (New York: Norton, 1988), 17, 19.

19. Dowling, *Hellenism and Homosexuality,* 35.

20. Ibid., 148.

21. Foucault, *An Introduction,* 43.

22. Sedgwick, *Epistemology of the Closet,* 156–61.

23. Christopher Craft, *Another Kind of Love* (Berkeley and Los Angeles: University of California Press, 1994), 77.

24. Sinfield, *The Wilde Century,* 121.

25. Shari Benstock, *Women of the Left Bank* (Austin: University of Texas Press, 1986), 48, 268–310; Gyula Halasz Brassai, "Sodom and Gomorrah," in *The Secret Paris of the 30's*

(New York: Pantheon, 1976); Elizabeth Ewing, *History of Twentieth Century Fashion* (Lanham: Barnes and Noble, 1992), 78 ff., 92–93, 101; Diana de Marly, *The History of Haute Couture: 1850–1950* (New York: Holmes and Meier, 1980), 147; Valerie Steele, *Paris Fashion: A Cultural History* (New York: Oxford University Press, 1988), 230–31.

26. Benstock, *Women of Left Bank,* 16.

27. Benstock, *Women of Left Bank,* 47.

Intersexualities

A Walk on the Wild(e) Side
The Doubled Reading of "An Encounter"

Margot Norris

Like many of the stories in *Dubliners,* Joyce's "An Encounter" functions as an enigmatic provocation to problematized ethical reading. Consider the shift in ethical assumptions inscribed in the historical arc of the questions that were asked of the story when it was written ("Is this an immoral text?") and those we might ask now ("Is this a homophobic text?"). Yet the puzzling and ambiguous gestures of both the story's writing and its telling—enigmas of both text and narration—further complicate these questions of Joyce's own time and our present moment. Grant Richards first underreacted, then overreacted, to a story whose "enormity" no one in the publishing establishment recognized until Joyce drew their attention to it—"The more subtle inquisitor will denounce *An Encounter,* the enormity of which the printer cannot see because he is, as I said, a plain blunt man" (*SL* 83). What, precisely, is that "enormity," and what is its ethical status if the story's publication depends on, and the author relies on, its expected and desired invisibility? "Many of the passages and phrases over which we are now disputing escaped you: it was I who showed them to you," Joyce wrote Richards. "And do you think that what escaped you (whose business it is to look for such things in the books you consider) will be surely detected by a public which reads the books for quite another reason?" (*SL* 88). Is Joyce positing a double readership—vulgar and cultivated—with different cognitive and moral horizons? If so, how is the text written to conceal itself to one and expose itself to the other? To put it differently, is the text's "enormity" its function as a homosexual text that is both in and out of the closet depending on the gender positioning (what I will later call the *implication*) of the reader. By considering the implications of having readers trope the story as a "homosexual text," one raises questions about the explicitness of its content—which Joyce's friend Thomas Kettle is reported to have considered "beyond anything in its outspokenness he had ever read" (*JJII* 329)—and that content's recognition. I will argue that the text's outspokenness in describing the pervert masks a deeper male reticence about speaking feelings and desires in relation to boys and men.

The best precedent for translating the story's moral perils into political and ideological problems is provided by Joyce himself, in his writings on Oscar Wilde. The case of Wilde prompts a heuristic interrogation of Joyce's intention: why would Joyce—who in his 1909 review of *Salomé* excoriated, with insight and sympathy, the homophobic events of Oscar Wilde's arrest and imprisonment— have written a story in 1905 in which the homosexual is figured as a sinister and sadistic predator of young boys? Joyce's 1909 essay—timely in its insertion between his writing of "An Encounter" in 1905 and its publication controversies in 1912—serves as a useful lens (or cracked looking-glass) for exploring the relationship between homosexuality, homophobia, and textuality in "An Encounter." The essay further serves as constructivist antidote to the essentialized origin that Richard Ellmann imputes to Joyce's grounding of the story in a real boyhood experience—"Joyce pointed out that he had actually taken part in the events described in such a story as 'An Encounter,' and Kettle granted, with reference to the homosexual in that story, 'Yes, we have all met him.'" (*JJII* 329). The collapse of the homosexual and the pervert into a universal immoral type fits neither Joyce's treatment of Wilde nor, as I will point out later, Stanislaus Joyce's account of the original "encounter." In his essay, Joyce explicitly acquits Wilde of being a "perverted monster" (*CW* 204) and constructs etiologies for his homoeroticism that Richard Brown calls "provocatively tolerant," although they include the embarrassing suggestion of hereditary "'epileptiform' madness"[1] and trite blame on the "Anglo-Saxon college and university system with its secrecy and restrictions" (*CW* 204). "An Encounter," I will argue, performs a more sophisticated anatomy and enactment of the textual constructedness of the homophobic object by engaging and arousing what Eve Sedgwick calls "homosexual panic."[2]

Joyce, who chiefly nationalized the sexual scandals that threatened and destroyed Irish writers and politicians,[3] may nonetheless have perceived an attenuated homosexual panic as the parallel condition for the censure of Oscar Wilde and the censorship of "An Encounter." Grant Richards's impulsive and dramatic reversal on the inclusion of the story after Joyce had pointed out its "enormity" has the marks of that aggressive fright of *recognition*—the fear that one's own knowledge of transgressivity exposes itself and therefore requires a powerful disassociative act. George Lidwell, Joyce's solicitor in his publishing disputes, most vividly conveys the rhetorical manifestation of the violently disassociative gestures that characterize homosexual panic when he invokes Gibbon's *The History of the Decline and Fall of the Roman Empire* to characterize his response to "An Encounter."

As to the last paragraphs in the Chapter under the head of "An Encounter," the matter is different. . . . I might quote Gibbon's "Decline and Fall" to show how much the subject is loathed "I touch with reluctance and dispatch with impatience this most odious vice of which modesty rejects the name and nature abominates the idea." (*JJII* 330)

In contrast, Joyce had no trouble recognizing the homosexual theme of Wilde's *The Picture of Dorian Gray* ("It is not very difficult to read between the lines"), and he lauded what he recognized as Wilde's attempt to "come out" ("Wilde seems to have had some good intentions in writing it—some wish to put himself before the world"). He complained only that Wilde failed to be sufficiently explicit ("If he had had the courage to develop the allusions in the book it might have been better") (letter to S. Joyce, 19 August 1906, *SL* 96). Three years later, in his review of *Salomé,* Joyce attributed the "howl of puritanical joy" with which Wilde was persecuted to a hypocrisy with features of clinical homosexual panic, whose mechanism Wilde may himself have predicted—"Oscar Wilde's own defence in the *Scots Observer* should remain valid in the judgment of an objective critic. Everyone, he wrote, sees his own sin in Dorian Gray (Wilde's best known novel). What Dorian Gray's sin was no one says and no one knows. Anyone who recognizes it has committed it" (*CW* 204). In other words, Joyce appeared to recognize that aggressive homophobia might function as a violent disassociation triggered by fears of incrimination and identification implicit in homosexual panic, which as a psychiatric classification "refers to the supposed uncertainty about his own sexual identity of the perpetrator of the antigay violence."[4]

Homophobic anxiety produces culturally regulated protocols of reading with highly disruptive consequences—such as the judicial use of *Dorian Gray* to criminalize Oscar Wilde ("I can imagine the capital which Wilde's prosecuting counsel made out of certain parts of it" [*SL* 96]), or the proposed reduction of "An Encounter" to an indexed gap or blank spot in the published volume of *Dubliners.* (Joyce agreed to accede to George Roberts's demanded omission of the story if "the following note be placed by me before the first story: *This book in this form is incomplete. The scheme of the book as framed by me includes a story entitled An Encounter which stands between the first and second stories in this edition*" [*JJII* 331]). But the implications of these intersections of reading and violence are themselves thematized in "An Encounter" in ways that illuminate the story's own power to arouse homosexual panic. The story's own thematized commentary on canonicity, and on the duplicity of canonical and noncanonical texts, serves the heuristic function of demonstrating under what conditions the homosexual text seduces, incriminates, and invites punishment. I will argue, then, that "An Encounter" is a doubled text that conceals a noncanonical homosocial fantasy whose desirous homosexual undercurrents affright it and oblige it to mask itself as a canonical cautionary tale of imperiled innocence. This doubled text further internally comments on, thematizes, and betrays its own devious duplicity. To pursue this argument I will need to move in and out of the narration, and in and out of the text (the text as the narration modified by its silences and gaps, and supplemented by tacit and implicit information and knowledge). My aim is to show that the narrative is textually constructed (R. B. Kershner writes, "The two boys who skip school are both enacting popular literary plots")[5] and textually operative as "kinetic" rather than "static" writing. The narration of "An Encounter" is not innocent, I will argue, even as it constructs the figure of the sadistic homosexual pervert in order to warrant its innocence, and the innocence of its addressee or reader.

Before turning to the thematized perversion of bibliophilia in the story—the abuse of the library by a "queer old josser" to seduce and incriminate the young boy—consider certain provocative similarities in the rhetorical strategies of the pervert and the narrator. Remember, or imagine, that the initial or "virgin" reader who encounters "An Encounter" for the first time is stimulated, like the boy, to seek adventure "abroad" in a relatively open-ended and generically uncertain narrative that gives little indication of where it is going, what to expect, or what risks it entails. The story's opening is not wholly indeterminate: we might expect a *Bildungsroman,* a romantic quest, a modern fairy tale, a pastoral idyll, modern urban naturalism, escapist nostalgia, an initiation narrative. But there is no preparation for a pornographic outcome to the adventure. Only in retrospect, once the "virgin" reading is irremediably past, do the similarities in the discursive strategies of the narrator and the old pervert become apparent. We realize, then, that we too were bored with banal and benign remarks on the weather, school and books, social differences and cultural regulation, before the complacent lull of the story—delivered with the misleading reassurance of a "good" accent—was jolted by an indecent exposure. This disturbing discursive surprise has a similar effect on the young boy and the reader: a feeling of betrayal, anger, and resentment at having been manipulated into complicity, verbally assaulted, and subjected to a form of sexual aggression. The troublesome ethical locus of the story thereby becomes the shadowy figure of the boy grown up, the "adult" storyteller[6] who knows the adventure's outcome in advance and understands the "enormity" of its possible impact, yet who deliberately defers information that would have protected us against shock and trauma.

This perverse construction of the narrator as the perverse double of the "queer old josser" in the story is meant to serve as a provisional difference intended to dilate the more conventional constructions of the narration's rhetorical and ethical strategies. My speculative demonization of the narrator as a sexual adept is intended to interrogate the story's rhetorical construction of the narratee or "reader" as innocent, as possessing a presexual innocence antecedent to heterosexuality. This innocence threatens to remain a constant outcome of the story's various alternative readings. Whether the story's narrative function is therapeutic (a psychoanalytic remembering of a juvenile trauma for psychic relief) or testimonial (the authority of a victim serving prophylaxis, to protect future children from pederasts), the reader is situated in the ethical space of the unexperienced child. This remains true for the interpretive scenario in which the narrator uses the figure of the pederast to define himself as heterosexual within the overdetermined homosocial milieu of the story's setting. However, the version of this story that unsettles its ethical dynamics most profoundly belongs to the ur-narrative I alluded to earlier—Stanislaus Joyce's version of the brothers' truant encounter with a putative pederast:

> In "An Encounter," my brother describes a day's miching which he and I planned and carried out while we were living in North Richmond Street, and our encounter with an elderly pederast. For us he was just a "juggins." Neither of us could have any notion at the time what kind of "juggins" he was, but something funny in his speech and behaviour put us on our guard at once. We thought he might be an escaped madman.[7]

In this encounter, the old man is a "juggins," a harmless, if peculiar, simpleton whose gestures fail to overly worry, menace, or frighten the young Joyces. The suspicion that the old man was "an escaped madman" appears a romantic elaboration of their initial perception of his mild idiocy. There is no report of an explicit erotic overture, nor of the old man's cunning and elaborate conversation that becomes the climax of the written story. The salient point of the biographical encounter is the boys' ability to read a sexual semiotics inscribed in the man's speech and gestures that "put us on our guard" against a homosexual advance. "An Encounter" thus transformed a defensive presexual experience, in which the boys "knew" something of the old man's sexuality without quite understanding what they "knew," into an offensive assault in which they are refunctioned as innocent asexual victims. Joyce patently seems to have invented the pornographic discourse that criminalizes the "juggins" while at the same time sanitizing the boys' minds to an improbable purity. He thereby supplied his and Stanislaus's mild homosexual panic with the full-blown fantasy of a monstrous sexual bogey.

Joyce's transformation of a boyhood encounter into the fictional "Encounter" could usefully, if paradoxically, exemplify some aspects of the problematical power that the authority of personal experience brings to the workings of "identity politics"—which Diana Fuss sums up as "personal consciousness, individual oppression, lived experience."[8] Personal experience becomes an index of oppression with truth value—a signifier of privileged knowledge—which is exposed in the Joyce anecdote for its counteroppressive potential. The boys (in a logic resembling that of the creation of witches from women) transform a figure of extreme social marginalization into an inchoate sexual predator. A putative *experience* of victimization becomes the authorization for a self-masking *exercise* of victimization. A major philosophical problem with the privileging of experience as the signifier of identity is articulated by Fuss when she glosses Derrida—"while experience may be underwritten by a metaphysics of presence, this does not mean experience is necessarily present to us—in the form of an unmediated real."[9] In Stanislaus Joyce's memory of boyhood experience, the boys "read" an old man according to some tacit prior cultural coding of the homosexual or the pederast that interprets their experience according to preexisting homophobic conventions. In transforming the experience to fiction, Joyce makes the source of the cultural code visible as pornographic discourse, as a literature- and language-generated knowledge of perversity. The old man's ability to deliver a sexually charged narration—"He described to me how he would whip such a boy" (D 27)—as much as the narrator's indirect account of it, partakes of the rhetorical conventions (the program, the demonstration, the speculation) that provoke both Deleuze and Barthes to stress that masochism and sadism should be treated as discourses, as literary or poetic phenomena—perversions with their origins in texts and their names conferred by authors—rather than as forms of behavior. In other words, if the young Joyces, or Joyce's boy narrator, encounter a pederast, their encounter is mediated by the literary discourses and conventions that construct and produce the figure of the pervert and his language. These boys experience not so much an encounter as a construction of an encounter.

The logic of textual mediation is, of course, the foregrounded donnée of the opening of the story. The opening line, "It was Joe Dillon who introduced the Wild West to us," may suppress the mediation of the book rhetorically, but not logically. Clearly it was Joe Dillon's library—"He had a little library made up of old numbers of *The Union Jack, Pluck,* and *The Halfpenny Marvel*"—that introduced the boys not to the Old West, but to literary constructions of the Old West designed to domesticate its exotic peoples and bloody histories into imitable scripts for the "mimic warfare" of juvenile play—"He looked like some kind of an Indian when he capered round the garden, an old tea-cosy on his head, beating a tin with his fist and yelling: 'Ya! yaka, yaka, yaka!'" (D 29). R. B. Kershner's historical elaboration of the substance and significance of the "chronicles of disorder" supplies the extratextual knowledge that the story's contemporary readers had readily available for intertextual interpolation. Kershner's ideological analysis of the unstable moral categorizations of the shifting literary and commercial productions of children's literature and boys' magazines in the late nineteenth century gives us a better estimation of the function and power of their regulation. Such literature's willingness to appeal to youngsters through titillation and sensationalism allowed reading to become contested moral and ideological terrain inviting critical, and often hypocritical, gestures of denunciation. "Ironically for a magazine generally regarded as cheaply sensational," Kershner writes of the *Halfpenny Marvel,* "it claimed the intent of counteracting the influence of unhealthy sensationalism aimed at children. . . . Soon *The Marvel* began printing testimonials such as that of the Reverend C. N. Barham expressing pleasure that the magazine was so 'pure and wholesome in tone.' On the front cover of that issue was a man being tortured."[10]

The sadomasochistic "knowledge" that the boys in "An Encounter" bring to their "encounter" with the queer old josser is presumably already inscribed in their truant reading, but without moral or psychological indexing of its prurience. As Kershner explains, "The sadomasochistic element in boys' periodicals was far less visible to the adults of the late nineteenth century than to ourselves; as will become apparent in the discussion of school stories below, it was an accepted, relatively transparent aspect of the ideology of bourgeois schooling."[11] Yet at stake in the regulation of transgressive reading and transgressive sexuality in the story is not merely the visibility of the perverse, but its *re-cognition*— that is, its repeated and repeatable knowledge—and its *ac-knowledgment*, the publicizing of its knowledge. Regulation itself impedes the ability to "see" and "know" across a generic and institutional divide, as the parable of curricular and extracurricular reading in the story demonstrates. Father Butler fails to see that the *Commentarii de Bello Gallico* and *The Apache Chief* share an imperialistic historical theme with considerable contemporary ideological relevance for the pre-Republican Ireland of his day. Indeed, *The Apache Chief* with its presumable perspective of the embattled and the vanquished, might have served the historical education of Irish boys better than did Caesar's conquest of Gaul. But regulation favors the canon in ways that block the transfer of historical understanding across the generic divide into the popular adventure story. The queer old josser, on the other hand, uses the authority of the canonical to lure the boy into a false *acknowledgment* ("I pretended that I had read every book he mentioned so that in the end he said:—'Ah, I can see you are a bookworm like myself'" [D 25]). He then inserts regulation ("there were some of Lord Lytton's works which boys couldn't read" [D 25]) in order to create a transgressive difference to implicate the boy. Curiously, a common historical theme connects the presumably guilty book—Kershner identifies it as Bulwer-Lytton's *The Last Days of Pompeii*—to the Roman history Father Butler teaches the boys at school. The old man splits the canon in two, into moral and immoral versions across whose divide knowledge may be—culpably—carried.

The bibliophilic seduction of the boy offers an exemplary model for the function of what Eve Sedgwick calls "ignorance effects"[12] in the positioning of the reader of "An Encounter." The boy's investment in cultural literacy shifts with his homosocial context, requiring an ongoing strategic deployment of ignorance and knowledge. The fear of appearing too bookish ("the reluctant Indians who were afraid to seem studious" [D 20])[13] among his peers oscillates with the fear of appearing insufficiently bookish with learned superiors like Father Butler and the seemingly cultivated old man. The possession or dispossession of learning thus becomes a locus of ethical manipulation, including feigning, disguise, and lying. This psychic regulation of degrees of ac-knowledgment signals possible displacements and cathexes between bibliophilic and libidinal desires, in which the reader as much as the narrator may be implicated. In other words, the reader, like the narrator, may be ethically manipulating the degree of literary and sexual knowledge that is brought to (or acknowledged as brought to) the reading of "An Encounter." The challenge is to defend mastery threatened by queer knowledge, on the one hand ("In fact, everyone feels uncomfortable in speaking to others about this subject, afraid that his listener may know more about it than he does," Joyce wrote of the Wilde scandal [CW 204])—and to defend the "privilege of unknowing," as Eve Sedgwick calls it, on the other. When the queer old josser challenges the boys with the canon ("He asked us whether we had read the poetry of Thomas Moore or the works of Sir Walter Scott and Lord Lytton" [D 25]) he manipulates less their ignorance of the library than a desirous and reckless bibliophilia that leads the boy narrator to claim unknown and forbidden knowledge in the seeming interest of cultural mastery.

But the boy's reaction to the old man's interrogation about the library is curious and troubling in its deviousness. Mahony's question in response to the old man's provocative "Of course . . . there were some of Lord Lytton's works which boys couldn't read" (D 25) seems sensible enough to make the narrator's embarrassment and discomfort suspect: "Mahony asked why couldn't boys read them—a question which agitated and pained me because I was afraid the man would think I was as stupid as Mahony" (D 25). The boy's desire to project himself as a bibliophile in identification with the old man overrides the protection of "innocence" that ignorance would confer. Does the boy wish to censor the question because he is agitated and pained for another reason: because he desires a reply whose forbidden content he knows might excite him? The old man appears to interpret his agitation in this way, because he answers Mahony's question with a substitution that doubles his original question about literary experience with a question about sexual experience—"Then he asked us which of us had the most sweethearts" (D 25). If the narrator's remembered embarrassment at Mahony's question is a disguise of snobbery to mask prurience, an alias like the one he assumes with the old man's masturbation ("In case he asks us for our names . . . let you be Murphy and I'll be Smith" [D 16]), then his "ignorance effect" is being produced for the benefit of the reader. Kershner describes a similar doubling as the "radical instability" of the reader of Victorian flagellation pornography—"He is addressed both as one of an elite of sensibility and as a man who shares the unadmitted desires of all men."[14] On the narrational level of "An Encounter," the reader is constructed in a similarly doubled way as a devious and self-disguising figure: like Mahony we too would like to know the censored matter, and like the narrator we too know that it is simultaneously demeaning and dangerous to ask. Like the schoolboys watching Leo Dillon get caught with contraband reading in school—"Everyone's heart palpitated as Leo Dillon handed up the paper and everyone assumed an innocent face" (D 20)—the reader too assumes an innocent face to disguise a palpitating heart when approaching the end of the story.

The beating heart with which the narrative ends—"my heart was beating quickly. . . . How my heart beat" (D 28)—becomes both somatic verbal symptom and betrayal of the ambiguous response to the fantasy of beating. As such, it betrays the narrator's ignorance effects, whose "paltry stratagems" include a variety of ocular maneuvers that together parse a virtual grammar of the gaze: looking *into* eyes, looking *for* eyes, looking *at* eyes, looking *without* eyes. The narrator veils the implication of the eyes in pleasure and desire by indirection and confusion. The two boys' truant communion on the Dublin quays—eating their picnic lunch in silence while "[w]e pleased ourselves with the spectacle of Dublin's commerce" (*D* 23)—culminates in a moment of protoromance on the ferryboat ride that assumes the magic of a homosocial elopement: "We were serious to the point of solemnity, but once during the short voyage our eyes met and we laughed" (*D* 23). This intimate moment of boys looking into each other's eyes is followed by the curious double ocular frustration of the narrator's failure to read a Norwegian ship's name or discover a sailor with green eyes. But the narration makes the green eyes as indecipherable to the reader as the ship's legend—"I came back and examined the foreign sailors to see had any of them green eyes for I had some confused notion . . ." [textual ellipsis] (*D* 23). The narrator's search for male green eyes appears to have been produced so spontaneously under the influence of the shared boyhood idyll that the narration breaks off in confusion and embarrassment before revealing its meaning. Does the *boy* censor his confused notion of the meaning of green eyes, or does the *adult narrator* censor what he knew as a boy? If the ellipsis is the narrator's, and not the boy's, then the meaning of the green eyes is censored for the benefit of the reader—or rather for the benefit of the narrator who needs to avert a self-betrayal that would, simultaneously, damage the reader's innocence. The narrator recovers from the bungled revelation by diluting its narrative consequence ("The only sailor whose eyes could have been called green" [*D* 23]) in the pointless anecdote of the "tall man who amused the crowd on the quay by calling out cheerfully every time the planks fell:—All right! All right!" (*D* 23). The green eyes are, of course, only provisionally all right, for they will return in the story—like the return of the repressed—with hallucinatory force.

The ellipsis has an effect on the reader not unlike that of the unspecified "sin" in *Dorian Gray*: the reader is pressured to supply a meaning at the risk of self-incrimination. Critics of the story have traditionally acted out a tenacious refusal to surrender the "privilege of unknowing" in their confrontation with this narrative trap. The likeliest possibility—that the boy believes sailors with green eyes are homosexual—tends to be suppressed and displaced onto a contiguous substitute, legitimated by the inevitable overdetermination of censored blanks. Tindall writes that "the boy centers his notions of escape and adventure in 'green eyes,' a private symbol of his romantic ideal."[15] Kershner seconds this general interpretation of "a realization best left unconscious, because to put it in words would be to denude it of the mystery upon which the image feeds," and goes on to supply it with a specific literary figure—"specifically, he is looking for the young, red-haired, green-eyed sailor who is the hero of picaresque adventures in the diluted tradition of Marryat."[16] Both Tindall and Kershner attribute the ellipsis to the boy, rather than to the retrospective adult narration. This fore-closes the layered possibility that the boy's "innocent" romantic symbol has, by the time of the retrospective telling, become infected with the adult narrator's awareness of, and discomfort with, the homosexual significance of green. Both in the aesthetics of Oscar Wilde, and the sexology of Havelock Ellis ("inverts ex-hibit a preference for green garments"),[17] the color was associated with homo-sexuality. If the narrator censors the meaning of "green eyes" to avert a betrayal of either juvenile homosexual desire or adult homosexual panic, the censoring maneuver nonetheless alerts us to a more pointed peculiarity of the narration. Why does the highly literate adult narrator, whose reading references specifi-cally situate his boyhood adventure in the 1890s, make no retrospective com-ment on Oscar Wilde's trial and imprisonment in 1895–97, a topic surely of rel-evance to his memory of a juvenile encounter with a pederast at about the same time?

If the boy's encounter with the foreign sailors is marked by expectant at-traction, his encounter with the old man is marked by expectant repulsion. He therefore initially conspicuously avoids looking at the eyes that he had "exam-ined" so pointedly as a symptom in the sailors. Nonetheless, his attention to the old man's body—if less focused—is keen, and his procedure is as clinical, if less shrewd, in detecting and reading bodily symptoms. In avoiding the old man's eyes, he concentrates his ocular focus on the mouth, which he reads for signs of decay and decadence: the ashen-gray moustache ("He seemed to be fairly old" [D 24]), the missing and stained teeth ("I saw that he had great gaps in his mouth between his yellow teeth" [25]), and the unpalatable content of the oral interior behind the gaping apertures ("I disliked the words in his mouth" [25]). The boy's reading of the old man's physiognomy is constructed of expectations learned from paranoid literary encounters with foreigners and strangers—Little Red Riding Hood's dim penetration of the wolf's disguise ("Grandma, what large teeth you have") or the maw of the one-eyed Cyclops. The boy likewise registers symptoms of somatic agitation, which he interprets naively ("I wondered why he shivered once or twice as if he feared something or felt a sudden chill" [D 25])—more naively than little Stephen Dedalus, who precisely maps the asso-ciative etiology of the shiver in his meditation on caning: "A long thin cane would have a high whistling sound and he wondered what was that pain like. It made him shivery to think of it and cold. . . . It made him shivery: but that was because you always felt like a shiver when you let down your trousers" (P 45).

The scrupulous anatomy of juvenile homosexual panic that Joseph Valente traces in Stephen's schoolboy experiences of real and fantasized punishment in Portrait is suppressed and displaced in "An Encounter."[18] Like the boy, the reader is obliged to read symptomatically a set of inconsistent responses in the boy that curiously mirror the old man's own inconsistent and illogical sentiments toward sexuality. The boy is as surprised by the old man's liberality as by his illiberality—a set of surprises interrupted and punctuated by a surprising failure to be surprised. When the old man excuses himself ("saying that he had to leave us for a minute or so, a few minutes" [*D* 26]), the boy, apparently shaken by his fetishistic fascination with girls' hands and hair, appears unsurprised that the man elaborates the quotidian urination with a further sexual display:

> —I say! Look what he's doing!
> As I neither answered nor raised my eyes Mahony exclaimed again:
> —I say . . . He's a queer old josser!
> —In case he asks us our names, I said, let you be Murphy and I'll be Smith. (*D* 26)

The boy's averted eyes and lack of surprise symptomatize a knowledge that the narrative elsewhere shields, and the quickly contrived disguise signals the boy's understanding that the old man's irregular and provocative behavior—presumably masturbation—is intended for his and Mahony's benefit.

The inconsistency in the boy's shrewdness and naïveté is striking and, I believe, intended to be suspect. After carefully mounting his guard after the masturbation, his literal response to the provocative question about whipping ("I was going to reply indignantly that we were not National School boys to be *whipped*, as he called it" [*D* 27]) seems as studiously ignorant as his surprise at the old man's insistence on the subject. Indeed, it is a peculiar slippage of an idiom, wrapped in a slippage of a figure, that snaps the boy's rigorous ocular control. Having identified Mahony with the generic victim of punishment in his sadistic fantasy, the old man's locution—"what he wanted was to get a nice warm whipping" (*D* 27)—uncomfortably collapses (through the double meaning of "wanted") sadistic and masochistic desire into a single, overdetermined, sentiment. Could it be recognition and identification evoked by this charged sentiment that prompts the boy to perform the deferred gesture of looking up to seek the green eyes?

> I was surprised at this sentiment and involuntarily glanced up at his face. As I did so I met the gaze of a pair of bottle-green eyes peering at me from under a twitching forehead. I turned my eyes away again. (*D* 27)

The most dramatic change Joyce makes in revising his holograph version of "An Encounter" for the 1910 edition of the story is the color of the old man's eyes: the "sage-green" eyes of the handwritten manuscript become the "bottle green" of the 1910 proofs, and the "bottle-green" of the 1914 proofs.[19] The change from a natural to a manufactured analogue for the color produces some specific and significant effects. Not only do the "bottle-green" eyes convey greater hardness and translucence than the "sage-green" eyes, but they conjure up a pair of internalized spectacles (thick and green like the bottoms of bottle glass) that intensify the old man's vision, on the one hand, but make his eyes armored and impenetrable, on the other. For the boy, the impact of encountering the man's gaze as "bottle-green" would be to encounter a set of doubled, or fortified, eyes that see and glare without being themselves perfectly visible, and whose thickness and dark tint project an alien and unreciprocable desire.

The boy's search for green eyes leads to a nightmare version of green eyes; his quest for adventure leads to misadventure, but also of a peculiarly parallel, if twisted, relation to his desire. One could dilate the ellipsis of the boy's unnamed quest as the pastoral, asexual version of homosexuality that the British public, according to Joyce, construed as Wilde's aestheticism—"a vague idea of delicate pastels, of life beautified with flowers" (*CW* 202)—before Wilde's love letters were read in court and their veiled homoeroticism made visible ("I love to see you wandering through violet-filled valleys, with your honey-coloured hair gleaming" (*CW* 204). The boy's miching with his friend on the Dublin waterfront may be more robust and quotidian, but it conjures an urban homosocial idyll that lacks only a dreamy male figure, a sailor with green eyes, to create a romantic plenum. The boy's walk on the wild side may have followed an unconscious historical plot, a walk on the Wilde side that at a moment of recognition, like that of the Victorian public during Wilde's trial, affrighted itself sufficiently to twist desire into a sinister distortion—"their author was denounced as a degenerate obsessed by exotic perversions" (*CW* 204). Wilde's "famous white ivory walking stick glittering with turquoise stones" (*CW* 202) becomes transformed in "An Encounter" into the tapping stick of an old man ("always tapping the ground with his stick, so slowly that I thought he was looking for something" [24]) whose discourse turns it into a vicious cane for lasciviously whipping young boys. The moral of the social cautionary tale of "An Encounter"—that truant boys may meet sinister sexual predators abroad—has a psychological double: that the vague homosexual desires of young boys may be twisted, by fear of censure and punishment, into self-punishing phantoms of terror and panic.

The operation of homosexual panic in the narrator and in the narration becomes more readily visible when "An Encounter" is juxtaposed with its thematic counterpart: the story "Counterparts" in *Dubliners*. Both stories end with the image of a boy being beaten, a parallel that produces the contrapuntal sociological moral that child abuse—the beating of innocent boys—need not be sought abroad and need not be eroticized or attributed to demonized strangers. Children, both boys and girls, are in greater danger of violence and injury from their fathers at home ("The boy uttered a squeal of pain as the stick cut his thigh. He clasped his hands together in the air and his voice shook with fright.—O pa! he cried. Don't beat me, pa!" [*D* 98]) than from pederasts abroad, both in fiction and in the life of Joyce's day. Joyce's source for the end of "Counterparts" was Stanislaus's diary entry reporting their Uncle William terrorizing the six- or seven-year-old Bertie.[20] Nor was familial violence warranted as free of sexual coloration or motivation. Nora Barnacle's brutal beating from her uncle Tom Healy ("Tom beat Nora with his thorn stick until she fell to the floor, clutching his knees and begging him to stop") may have been provoked by Nora's sexual maturation ("She may also have sensed an incestuous longing behind Tom Healy's rage").[21] But if Joyce's *Dubliners* stories "An Encounter" and "Counterparts" are semantically echoic, their hermeneutical echo resonates with a striking difference, a psychic disturbance that readings tend to repress by coding it as ethical. By sociologically imbricating or overlapping the theme of abused childhood, the doubled stories suppress or obscure the exaggerated affective power—the hysteria of outrage, anxiety, disgust, excitement, the "beating heart" of the ending—that the insertion of sexual fantasy, the transgressivity of tabooed erotic elements, the homosexuality, the pederasty, the sadomasochism, produces in "An Encounter." By letting the stories echo against each other, the irony of this affective and ethical discrepancy—that a speculative erotic discourse has a profoundly more disturbing effect than the representation of an actual violence and cruelty—subjects the reader response to ethical scrutiny. The reader is thus positioned or "gendered" (in Teresa de Lauretis's sense)[22] by a response whose disassociative reflexes align it with the symbolic power and coercive force of patriarchy.

It is important to remember that, as Kershner reminds us, the old man's pornographic discourse is translated through a double prism of perception— "it emerges as an amalgam of the boy's and the old man's language—or, more precisely, of the old man's language and the two languages of experience and retrospection embodied in the boy's narration."[23] The obsessional, mesmerizing quality of the old man's speech has, therefore, an uncertain locus. Is its hypnotic effect a property of the old man's speaking or of the young boy's hearing? The possibility that the boy internalizes the magnet that attaches to the old man's erotic field may account for the markedly different responses that the boy narrator and Mahony have to the old josser. Both hear the same monotonous voice unveiling its erotic mysteries, but they respond differently to this Siren's song. The narrator's rigid ocular control contrasts with Mahony, "who was regarding us with open eyes" (*D* 25), and who openly looks at what the old man is doing while the narrator refuses to change his gaze or raise his eyes. While the narrator is therefore "still considering whether I would go away or not" (*D* 26), Mahony escapes from the hypnotic orbit, first by using the pretext of the cat, and when that pretext is lost, by simply staying away—"he began to wander about the far end of the field, aimlessly" (*D* 27). Mahony's greater innocence may translate, in the presence of knowledge, into freedom from implication that allows him to escape not only the old man's physical clutches ("my heart was beating quickly with fear that he would seize me by the ankles" [*D* 28]), but also his psychological clutches. He escapes implication, too, in the romantic role into which the narrator has cast him—of the dashing boy with the dark complexion and the jaunty cricket club badge on his cap—who comes to the rescue of an innocent in distress. At the end of their adventure, the boys at last have the three players you must have to arrange a siege, but the plot has changed from cowboys and Indians into villain, damsel, and hero. "How my heart beat as he came running across the field to me! He ran as if to bring me aid" (*D* 28). The famous last line of the story—"And I was penitent; for in my heart I had always despised him a little" (*D* 28)—confesses a change of heart and ends the boy's adventure with a confessed blossoming of refigured homosocial affection that has survived its brutal disruption by homosexual panic.

My opening suggestion, that "An Encounter" may have been written to function as a homosexual text simultaneously in and out of the closet, may account for the widely divergent readings the story produces. The narrator's shrewd feints of innocence, ignorance, and unease with sexual feeling and arousal in the story provoke a variety of guarded, disavowing, disassociative responses from the reader or critic. William York Tindall's is illustrative of the most effective form of this evasion, the informed sidestep of the issue of perversity ("The news that perverts are around is no news at all") followed by its sublation into the theme of paralyzed idealism ("Case history is there to reveal something else, something at once theological, ecclesiastical, and moral").[24] In reading the story as an elaborate allegory of coded religious questing, the story's sexual agitations are focalized in the old man and firmly set aside as an irrelevancy. Thirty years later, Kershner's brilliant ideological elucidation of the story's popular intertexts shapes much of the key to the closet without fully acknowledging the narratorial attempts to secure its door. Kershner's key resides in his unraveling of the doubled and deceptively ambiguous nature of the popular texts the story's boys read, which shape them into readers uncertain and anxious about managing their response. The narration of "An Encounter," I would suggest, becomes such a doubled text, generically ambiguous enough to have its pornographic climax subordinated to theological parable, rhetorically provocative enough to lull, worry, subdue, excite the reader into responding, like the boys, with palpitating hearts and assumed innocent faces. No reading can truly domesticate this cunning and troubled textual performance. But in the light of queer theory it becomes possible, at least, to go beyond the wordplays, symbols, and paradoxes with which we evade the homosexuality of Wilde— "Tame essence of Wilde," as Stephen puts it (*U* 9.532)—and recognize in the boys' walk on the wild side, their walk on the Wilde side.

NOTES

1. Richard Brown, *James Joyce and Sexuality* (New York: Cambridge University Press, 1985), 80.

2. Eve Kosofsky Sedgwick, *Epistemology of the Closet* (Berkeley and Los Angeles: University of California Press, 1990), 19.

3. Richard Brown argues that "Joyce evidently identified with Wilde in the same kind of way that he identified with Parnell: both, for him, were Irishmen condemned for sexual crimes by an unjust, hypocritical morality" (*James Joyce and Sexuality*, 81).

4. Sedgwick, *Epistemology of the Closet*, 20.

5. R. B. Kershner, *Joyce, Bakhtin, and Popular Literature: Chronicles of Disorder* (Chapel Hill: University of North Carolina Press, 1989), 36.

6. The narrator tends to be figured as the "boy" of the story retrospectively, but still in boyhood, telling his experience. But the narrator's "good" accent—as he himself would call it—betrays a sophisticated vocabulary and diction quite beyond even the brightest and most studious of preadolescent boys—"a spirit of unruliness diffused itself among us," "those chronicles of disorder," "we ate sedulously," "brandishing his unloaded catapult," "escalated," "our jaded thoughts," "mimic warfare," "Lest I should betray my agitation," etc.

7. Stanislaus Joyce, *My Brother's Keeper: James Joyce's Early Years*, ed. Richard Ellmann (New York: Viking Press, 1958), 62.

8. Diana Fuss, *Essentially Speaking: Feminism, Nature, and Difference* (New York: Routledge, 1989), 113.

9. Ibid, 114.

10. Kershner, *Joyce, Bakhtin*, 33.

11. Ibid.

12. Eve Kosofsky Sedgwick, *Tendencies* (Durham, N.C.: Duke University Press, 1993), 23.

13. Kershner writes, "The boy's fear of appearing overly studious to his classmates is of central significance in the ideological framework of the story. Both of the adults in the story—Father Butler and the 'old josser'—immediately invoke a culturally reified distinction between boys who are active, unthinking, and lower-class and those who are studious, responsible, and upper-middle class." *Joyce, Bakhtin*, 35.

14. Ibid., 45.

15. William York Tindall, *A Reader's Guide to James Joyce* (New York: Noonday Press, 1959), 9.

16. Kershner, *Joyce, Bakhtin*, 37.

17. Gregory W. Bredbeck, "Narcissus in the Wilde," in *The Politics and Poetics of Camp*, ed. by Moe Myer (New York: Routledge, 1994), 57. I am indebted to Brian Loftus for directing me to this information in Bredbeck's essay.

18. See Valente's "Thrilled by His Touch: The Aestheticizing of Homosexual Panic in *A Portrait of the Artist as a Young Man*" in this volume.

19. *The James Joyce Archive*, ed. Michael Groden, et al. *Dubliners: A Facsimile of Drafts and Manuscripts*, arranged by Hans Walter Gabler (New York: Garland Publishing, 1978), 4, 5, 6.

20. Stanislaus Joyce, *The Complete Dublin Diary of Stanislaus Joyce*, ed. George H. Healey (Ithaca, N.Y.: Cornell University Press, 1962), 37.

21. Brenda Maddox, *Nora* (Boston: Houghton Mifflin Company, 1988), 22.

22. Teresa de Lauretis, "The Technology of Gender," in *Technologies of Gender: Essays on Theory, Film, and Fiction* (Bloomington: Indiana University Press, 1987).

23. Kershner, *Joyce, Bakhtin*, 44.

24. Tindall, *Reader's Guide*, 19.

On Joycean and Wildean Sodomy

Jean-Michel Rabaté

I have always felt that the best approach to the sexual thematics underlying *Ulysses* is to link the strong undercurrent of homosexual images to the issue of paternity: if all the tantalizing hints of "Wilde's love that dare not speak its name" do in fact allude to Bloom or Mulligan, then the question of "homosexuality" (a term that is inadequate for many reasons, and that I prefer to replace with *sodomy*) cannot be dissociated from a more general discussion of incest.[1] Joyce's ambivalent stance on the issue of homoeroticism—which makes it difficult to pinpoint a tentative ideology of resistance or deviance in his works— always tends to reinscribe itself in the question of triangular desire originating in the family romance. Desire thus understood invokes the cultural dimension of paternity and maternity, but without the ideological anchor of a Nature taken as the norm of sexual propriety.[2]

Thus, whereas Aquinas's theory of incest defined as "avarice" is instrumental in helping Stephen qualify what could be broadly called a Freudian thesis, Joyce does not use Aquinas's scale of values (in which sodomy is not too harshly viewed)[3] when he lets Stephen oppose all perversions to the almost unthinkable transgression constituted by male homosexual incest, an incest linking father and son in a "love" taken so literally as to prove the lack of a divine love from the Father to all His metaphorical sons. Such an unthinkable impossibility in nature allows Joyce to define, as it were *a contrario,* the absolute Law regulating proper and improper sexual exchanges:

> They [fathers and sons] are sundered by a bodily shame so steadfast that the criminal annals of the world, stained with all other incests and bestialities hardly record its breach. Sons with mothers, sires with daughters, lesbic sisters, loves that dare not speak their name, nephews with grandmothers, jailbirds with keyholes, queens with prize bulls.[4]

Typically, Stephen prefers to quote from classical myth than to allude directly to the "new Viennese school," and in such a way that the centrality of a "love that dare not speak its name" remains ambivalent, since, in the context, nothing testifies to the exclusion of the father-and-son relationship. Yet the rest of the paragraph posits such a paradigmatic impossibility of male homosexual incest. Stephen, being cruelly aware of his mythical ancestor's invention, which enabled Queen Pasiphaë to enjoy intercourse with a bull, cannot but accept a difficult heritage; Daedalus used all his genius in the deployment of *ignotas artes* that smack of perversity. This is also why Simon Dedalus's first name scrambles up the name of the king who built a labyrinth in order to hide the fruit of such an unnatural coupling, the Minotaur. If we are ready to take the figure of the labyrinth as an allegory of critical interpretation, then we can never forget the obscure nexus around which it revolves.

When the "Circe" episode returns to this locus classicus, it is once more through Stephen's voice in what appears to be merely a drunken extemporization but could also come from the deeper layers of his unconscious. Stephen says:

> *Ex exaltabuntur cornua iusti.* Queens lay with prize bulls. Remember Pasiphaë whose lust my grandoldgrossfather made the first confessionbox. Forget not Madam Grisel Steevens nor the suine scions of the house of Lambert. And Noah was drunk with wine. And his ark was open. (*U-JJ* 530)

Stephen manages to shock even Bella, who replies with "None of that here. Come to the wrong shop," as if the type of perversion Stephen alludes to was to remain beyond the limits of an "honest" brothel. Stephen's "perverted transcendentalism" implies a complex interaction between Greek myths and Christian rites; their conjunction does not fail to take Irish history in a vice, as it were, since the old and proud families of the Ascendency can claim to descend from some animal in Noah's ark, as befits an episode prone to evoke bestialization in all its aspects, with the difference that here this ark sounds suspiciously like an arse. Joyce will ultimately follow Stephen's suggestion in *Finnegans Wake* when he shows how the two brothers unite as Buckley in order to shoot and/or sodomize the Russian general. *Ulysses* always provides the possibility of a mocking variation on its own central myths, as if the voice of the Nameless One who narrates the Cyclops episode was one of the masks left ready for the reader. If, indeed, "jewgreek is greekjew" in *Ulysses,* then the perversion of the two positions culminates in snide suggestions of homosexuality and incest, suggestions that spare absolutely no one in the novel.

The main filter through which homosexuality is thus less designated than suggested is Douglas's phrase "love that dare not speak its name." One could notice that in *Ulysses,* it is love in general that dare not speak its name—as the recent controversy about Gabler's reintroduction of the "word known to all men" has shown. The name of love is never easy to utter, let alone define. And when Aquinas defines love, in a famous passage of his *Summa*, as "to wish someone's good" (*Quia amare est velle alicui bonum*),[5] he also takes pain to show that one can wish one's own good as well as someone else's and lists among the causes of love "similarity": *similitudo* can cause love to be born out of a pleasure in closeness and near identity such as the species can provide; however, as Aquinas notes shrewdly, too much similitude can also provoke to another extreme, namely hatred. Thus one should resist the temptation to name too crudely the "sin" (that can be partially translated as "homosexuality" for want of a better term). In this respect, one can take as a model Joyce's main authority, Wilde. One of the few texts of his that are directly quoted in *Ulysses* is the famous "platonic dialogue" on Shakespeare, *The Portrait of Mr. W.H.*—after all, another "Portrait of the Artist" as a young homosexual. This, at least, is the interpretation that was most commonly given to Wilde's essay, an interpretation that reappears in Mr. Best's rather jumbled version: Shakespeare would have written his sonnets for a young man he was in love with (in Wilde's own terms):

> He felt, as indeed I think we all must feel, that the Sonnets are addressed to an individual—to a particular young man whose personality for some reason seems to have filled the soul of Shakespeare with terrible joy and no less terrible despair.[6]

We can note that, during the discussion in the library, Stephen rather mocks Mr. Best's dilution of Wildean paradoxes and sneers at his "tame essence of Wilde" (*U-JJ* 190). The real essence of Wilde is indeed wilder, less tractable, less amenable to genteel banalities.

Space would not suffice to present a systematic study of Wilde's essay, but following Lawrence Danson's lead, I wish to focus on the curious strategy his narrative unfolds. As Danson writes, "Wilde creates a daisy chain of converts and skeptics to tell his story, and the resulting self-subverting narrative enlists a tale of scholarly detection in the service of the indeterminate."[7] The narrator hears from his friend Erskine how Cyril Graham, a beautiful friend fond of acting and cross-dressing, has identified the W.H. of Shakespeare's dedication as a certain Willie Hughes. When Erskine remains unconvinced by the theory, Cyril adduces a portrait of Willie Hughes. Erskine quickly finds out that this is a cheap forgery. Hearing that Cyril Graham has subsequently committed suicide, the narrator (but not Erskine) is ready to believe in a theory that is powerful enough to force someone to die for it. He writes a letter to Erskine stating his own belief, but he curiously loses his belief in the very act of writing the letter, which however convinces Erskine once more of the truth of the Willie Hughes theory. Erskine then announces that he, too, is ready to commit suicide if this can prove the theory valid. When the narrator rushes to him, Erskine is already dead; but it turns out that this was the result not of suicide but of consumption. The vertiginous series of assertions and negations whirling in a breathtaking succession aims at problematizing the very notion of belief in any given theory. It seems therefore that the last person to have been converted to this theory (or perverted by it) is Stephen—when he confirms Eglinton's suspicion that he does not believe his own theory about Shakespeare. Stephen's refusal to assume the full paternity or responsibility for a theory we have witnessed him rehearse at length is homologous to the Wildean caveat. As Danson writes: "Any attempt to stop the play of Wilde's narrative and say what it is *really* about will either demonize or neuter it."[8] Like Wilde, Joyce knows that imputations of sexual perversion often reveal more about those who proffer them—much as the marquis of Queensbury's allegation that Oscar Wilde was "posing as a so*m*domite" produces a slip of the pen that probably betrays the presence of his own son behind the scandal.

Before drawing the full consequences of such a hermeneutic principle, let us return to one of the most crucial introductions to Joyce's fiction, the beginning of "The Sisters" in *Dubliners*. This story has received all the attention it deserves, yet something remains unsaid in the famous "sin" linking the young narrator and the old paralytic priest. An exchange takes place during the boy's dream: the boy sees himself partaking of a smile that suggests a perverse communion. "I too was smiling feebly, as if to absolve the simoniac of his sin." The anaphoric /s/ sounds stress the contagion of a sin which also suggests "sodomy" (it could almost be rephrased as: "as if to absolve the sodomic of his son")—at least in the Dantean mode of canto 15, when Dante and Virgil meet Brunetto Latini. Brunetto's true role and place have still to be ascertained: he was not generally taken as a homosexual yet appears among the Sodomites and calls Dante "my son" twice in the canto (15.31 and 37), whereas Dante confirms the paternal function he has played for him, stressing the "dear, good paternal image" he has kept of Brunetto (15.83–84).[9]

It would be tempting to see in the repressed term of "sodomy" the fourth or missing corner of the "gnomon" evoked by the boy in the first paragraph of the story. Even at the risk of appearing somewhat Manichean, I would like to stress a dichotomy that has often been overlooked: if the notion of epiphany calls up a "shining forth," a luminous revelation, the gnomon contains an anaphanic counterprinciple and hints of a dark and incomplete disclosure. It is fitting that Sodomy should be seen as "visible darkness" and never fully emerges out of its dim casket or closet. Sodomy would thus appear as the arch-sin, precisely because in its inception it just describes a city in which human relations are perverted, without bringing a clear accusation against male homoeroticism. Chapter 19 of Genesis stresses that the particular sin committed by the inhabitants of Sodom is a transgression against the sacred law of hospitality. The Sodomites are the Bible's Lestrygonians, as it were, who sexually cannibalize any stranger coming their way. And, indeed, Lot is ready to offer his two virgin daughters to protect the angels from the mob's lust. The irony is obviously that the daughters he was ready to sacrifice in a rare instance of charity will later, after the destruction of Sodom and their flight into the mountain, take advantage of his sleep and have him conceive two sons, thus starting the lines of the Moabites and of the Ammonites. Again, "sodomy" generates an incest apparently condoned by the Bible and by history.

In the context of *Dubliners*, "sodomy" seems fitting to provide a name for Dublin's illness; it gives a pattern from which one might derive a similar "Dubliny." The rain of fire that destroys Sodom and Gomorrah also provides the Sodomites of *Inferno* with a punishment neatly designed by the *contrapasso*. Bloom rightly situates these cities next to the Dead Sea and connects them not with male homoeroticism but with an exhausted female organ:

> Brimstone they called it raining down: the cities of the plain: Sodom, Gomorrah, Edom. All dead names. A dead sea in a dead land, grey and old. Old now. It bore the oldest, the first race. . . . Dead: an old woman's: the grey sunken cunt of the world. (*U-JJ* 59)

Female sterility is their sin, not male homoeroticism, according to Bloom at least. In that sense, one could read *Ulysses* as a novel describing the necessity and the impossibility of hospitality: if Stephen had accepted Bloom's offer of a shelter during the first hours of June 17, 1904, he would not only have accepted him as a surrogate (or "symbolic") "father," but would have had to conform to one of the many developments foreseen by his host—of which marrying Milly or becoming Molly's new lover would only be two (and heterosexual at that) of all the other possible outcomes. Stephen cannot accept any more than he can return to the tower; both male tempters, Buck Mulligan and Leopold Bloom, perform a sodomite variation on simony in offering him a substitute family (necessarily perverse in some way) and a last attempt to accept life in Dublin. A more radical exile than a stay in a nearby mountain (accompanied or not by tempting young females) is required of him. In *Ulysses* as in "The Sisters," the only solution is the abrupt discontinuity of leave-taking, which triggers the work of mourning of the young boy, or accounts for the "inexplicable" way Stephen refuses Bloom's hospitality. This is how Joyce manages to posit a paternity that is neither "real" (since Simon Dedalus is still present) nor "symbolic" (or Homeric, Bloom forcefully fitted in Odysseus's shoes), but that plays with distance, absence, and alterity in order to avoid the trap of perversion.

What is the core of this curious relation that borders on lack of relation? The problem is to avoid any "love" that would testify to some corruption, and to replace it by a mutual "shame." This seems to define the nexus of what Stephen calls "original sin" in connection with his discussion of Shakespeare. Shakespeare is driven by an urge to create, possibly in order to blind himself to truth, since he is always already dispossessed of whatever he may produce. This derives from his first defeat, his having been seduced by his future wife.

> No later undoing will undo the first undoing. The tusk of the boar has wounded him there where love lies ableeding. If the shrew is worsted yet there remains to her woman's invisible weapon. There is, I feel in the words, some goad of the flesh driving him to a new passion, a darker shadow of the first, darkening even his own understanding of himself. (*U*-JJ 188)

Stephen's demonstration is quite cunning in that it links the role of femininity in Shakespeare's "undoing" to an original reformulation of the definition of "original sin" in the Maynooth Catechism. Such an "undoing" is literally another form of paralysis (etymologically, "untying"), while Shakespeare could appear here superimposed on James Flynn. Original sin entails the male sharing of a knowledge akin to a contagious disease, yet which paradoxically weakens the understanding of the disease. This opens onto the specifically Joycean notion of a "gnomon" linking simony and sodomy. Something resists comprehension in the transmission of an unnameable sin chaining father and son together but in an absolute void. The central element to be stressed here is obscurity, not the precisely homoerotic factor (which is always to be avoided at any cost) in and of the structure.

It took many years before Joyce could simply face the fact that what he was exploring was precisely the obscurity that surrounds sin and paternity alike. He had also meanwhile to resist an impulse to name it all too clearly. This can be seen in the shifting evaluation of Oscar Wilde's transgression. In a letter from August 1906, Joyce writes about Wilde's *Picture of Dorian Gray:*

> It is not very difficult to read between the lines. Wilde seems to have had some good intention in writing it—some wish to put himself before the world—but the book is rather crowded with lies and epigrams. If he had had the courage to develop the allusions in the book, it might have been better. (*LII* 105)

In 1906, Joyce still clings to a romantic notion of an author faulted for "not daring" to speak the name of the perversion he describes, still hesitant to "come out," as it were. His wit and epigrams are mere disguises for a truth that ought to be exposed fully. Only three years later, in the paper written in Italian for the *Piccolo della Sera,* Joyce has become more sophisticated, more wary of naming this "truth." He quotes the famous statement Wilde gave as a defense of his only novel to the *Scots Observer* and then generalizes boldly:

> Everyone, he wrote, sees his own sin in Dorian Gray (Wilde's best known novel). What Dorian Gray's sin was no one says and no one knows. Anyone who recognizes it has committed it.

Here we touch the pulse of Wilde's art—sin. He deceived himself into believing that he was the bearer of good news of neo-paganism to an enslaved people. . . . But if some truth adheres to his subjective interpretations of Aristotle, to his restless thought that proceeds by sophisms rather than syllogisms, to his assimilations of natures as foreign to his as the delinquent is to the humble, at its very base is the truth inherent in the soul of Catholicism: that man cannot reach the divine heart except through that sense of separation and loss called sin. (*CW* 204–5)

The Italian context cannot suffice to explain this extraordinary reversal of Wilde's explicit values; while treating him as a crypto-Catholic, Joyce seems indeed to be speaking about himself. What Wilde has spent all his life denying any validity, namely the sense of religious transgression, returns as the full repressed it was. In fact, by naming his "sin" just "Sin" (and not "Sodomy" for instance), Joyce suggests that the Sin, if it is to keep its full value, cannot be reduced to a sexual content. The sin's meaning is produced by an interpretation that performs what it identifies. The "picture" is thus indeed a mirror for the reader who projects his or her fantasies. And the entire piece on Wilde moves tellingly from a meditation on Wilde's proud "titles" (Oscar Fingal O'Flahertie Wills Wilde; see *FW* 46.20) by which he was addressed during the trial, to an acceptance of the final role selected for himself by the Irish dramatist: that of a fallen Christ. He also represents the "dishonoured exile" whose death in Paris in 1900 not only marks the end of the fin de siècle era, but also heralds a new period—in which young Irish aesthetes attempt to "grow out of Wilde and paradoxes" and yet remain, as Mulligan's phraseology suggests, bound up in Wilde's sophistic and enthymemic network, more nourished by Wilde's thought than they fancy.

Wilde thus looms large in *Finnegans Wake,* in which he seems to have replaced another victim of Irish and English hypocrisy, Parnell. Both Parnell and Wilde used self-defeating tactics and exemplify the central predicament of the great man turned into scapegoat, be it in the field of politics or aesthetics. Indeed, Wilde almost perversely attracted doom by interfering in a bitter struggle between a father and a son (the marquis of Queensbury and Lord Alfred Douglas). The lopped-off corner of a symbolic gnomon would be an adequate figure limning their post-oedipal rivalry. Like Meredith's *The Ordeal of Richard Feverel*—with its opposition between a "System" of education and misguided spontaneity—it is clearly "a history of Father and Son." I have already alluded to Queensbury's misspelling of *sodomite* as "somdomite." This misspelling led Wilde to take the fateful decision of suing for libel. In his "To Oscar Wilde posing somdomite," it seems that Queensbury expressed anger at the fact that Wilde was a mere "poser,"[10] while betraying his rage in front of his own son. During the trial, Wilde's first mistake was to lie about his age, declaring he was thirty-nine when he in fact was forty-one; he thus was forced to appear in doubt about his own age and to expose his own denegation: "I have no wish to pose as being young. I am thirty-nine or forty."[11] In *Finnegans Wake,* where Wilde becomes one of the central characters, Joyce stresses the general intermeshing of culpability in order to universalize sodomy:

> We've heard it aye since songdom was gemurrmal. As he was queering his schoolthers. So was I. And as I was cleansing my fausties. So was he. And as way ware puffing our blowbags. Souwouyou. (*FW* 251.36–252.03)

This relatively transparent sentence affirms the catholicity of reciprocal sinning. Sodom still defines the Wildean sin, but the fall of this particular city becomes part of the universal comedy whose Viconian coordinates make it inseparable from the way civilization needs the social construction of family and the Law to survive.

Such an assertion of communal transgression nevertheless seems deprived of any tragic character, as when Shaun accuses Shem of all possible sins and states that he will finally tackle directly "the malice of your transgression" (*FW* 189.03) by diving with his brother and their female audience into a universal fountain of life and sin, "while we all swin together in the pool of Sodom?" (*FW* 188.23–24) This "swin" is ineluctably linked to the difficulty met by all the jurymen in the *Wake* when they try to dissociate the accusations of sodomy from the pandemic incest in the Earwicker family. Sam Slote has recently shown that an entry in VI.B.2 refers to the strange case when Wilde's father, the renowned otologist, was accused of having chloroformed and raped a patient: "HCE names/—chloroformed/incest."[12] This reappears as another accusation against HCE when he is thought to have drugged and abused Issy. The irony is that both in Doctor Wilde's case and in Earwicker's, it is their wives who come up to offer the strongest defense of their husbands' morality.

Wilde is thus an arch-sodomite for Joyce not only, not even mainly, because of the homosexuality that emerged with many lurid details during his trial. He is heir to a suspicious doctor who founded the Royal Victoria Eye and Ear Hospital in Dublin, and whose name had already been translated once: as Oscar Wilde's son narrates it, the origin of the name was Dutch and was translated as "builder":

> A certain Ralph Wilde from Durham was supposed to have crossed over to Ireland and have settled as a builder in Dublin. This is apocryphal. My ancestor's name was unquestionably de Wilde, and its Dutch pronunciation puzzled the simple Irish folk, with the result that "de Vilde" very soon became "the builder."[13]

Whether Joyce knew of this story or not is not clear, yet a passage in the *Wake* could allude to it, when mentioning the "charnelcysts of a weedwastewoldwevild when Ralph the Retriever ranges to jawrode his knuts knuckles" (613.19–22). It is relatively easy to admit that Wilde also falls into the great category of doomed "masterbuilders," precisely because his name—and his works—confirm the link between sin and son, and also between the building of Dublin and biblical sodomy.

To conclude, I would like to say that despite Joyce's adherence to the anti-homoerotic prejudice of his time, he does not actually condemn (or endorse) a "sodomy" that becomes tantamount to the arch-sin, precisely because it is never reducible to transgressions such as those a tribunal might define. Joyce's purgatorial and comic sense of sodomy locates it primarily in language, sees it indissociable from the web of slander and gossip that always needs fresh butts to feed its endless discourse. All this noise barely hides a fundamental unspeakability. *Finnegans Wake* is built on this paradox and constructs the only adequate linguistic equivalent for such a collective obsession. Its material is offered by obscene jokes, tall tales such as those of the Norwegian captain or the Russian general, family narratives such as the Father's encounter with a young man in Phoenix Park where privates are wont to masturbate and sexy girls to urinate—all of which remains hinged around the omnipresence of guilt. A guilt that never denies sexual division, since it relies upon it, but transgresses infinitely all other boundaries so as to force all readers to admit a common legacy of sin which makes us all "sons of the sod":

> To say too us to be every tim, nick and larry of us, sons of the sod, sons, littlesons, yea and lealittlesons, when usses not to be, every su, siss and sally of us, dugters of Nan! Accusative ahnsire! Damadam to infinities! (*FW* 19.21–30)

NOTES

1. I have developed this point in "A Clown's Inquest into Paternity," in *The Fictional Father,* ed. Robert Con Davis (Amherst: University of Massachusetts Press, 1981), 73–114; this article is taken up, with a few modifications, in *James Joyce, Authorized Reader* (Baltimore: Johns Hopkins University Press, 1991).

2. In that sense, Joyce would be at the opposite of a Pound who still castigates Usura as Sodomy in his *Cantos,* both being "Contra Naturam" as Aquinas and most of the medieval theologians had it.

3. I owe a lot to Joseph Peguigney's excellent article, "Sodomy in Dante's *Inferno* and *Purgatorio,*" *Representations* 36 (fall 1991): 22–42. As he notes on p. 23, sodomy was indeed one of the "sins against nature" for most medieval theologians, but for Aquinas it was only halfway between bestiality and masturbation.

4. I cite Jeri Johnson's annotated edition of the original 1922 *Ulysses* (Oxford: Oxford University Press, 1993), 199. Among other qualities that distinguish it from current editions, it has an excellent (original) typography. Subsequent references are given in the text, abbreviated *U-JJ*.

5. Aquinas, *Summa Theologica* I, art. 2, par. 1, in *Summa Sancti Thomae,* ed. F. C.-R. Billuart (Paris and Rome, 1872), 2:397.

6. "The Portrait of Mr. W.H.," in *The Works of Oscar Wilde* (London: Spring Books, 1963), 941.

7. Lawrence Danson, "Oscar Wilde, W.H., and the Unspoken Name of Love," *ELH* 58, no. 4 (1991): 980.

8. Ibid., 981.

9. One will have recognized André Pézard's controversial thesis in *Dante sous la pluie de feu* (Paris: Vrin, 1950). See Peguigney's "Sodomy," 26–29, for an intelligent contextualization of this interpretation. For Dante's *Inferno,* see *The Divine Comedy of Dante Alighieri,* trans. Allen Mandelbaum (New York: Bantam, 1982), 135–37.

10. Marquess Queensbury took pains to focus on Wilde's appearance only. The following exchange is typical: "Then I asked: 'Lord Queensbury, do you seriously accuse your son and me of improper conduct?' He said, 'I do not say you are it, but you look it.' (Laughter)" (H. Montgomery Hyde, ed., *The Three Trials of Oscar Wilde* [London: William Hodge, 1948], 119). Wilde's appeal for "seriousness" is debarred by the upsurge of laughter triggered by Queensbury's reply. After an admonition by the judge, Queensbury reasserts: "But you look it, and you pose as it, which is just as bad." Joyce took the hint: what matters is not the "matter" or substance of the indicted perversion but its appearance. The crux of such alleged "perversion" is that no one can possibly distinguish between seriousness and laughter, "posing" and sexual "facts," transgressing and pretending to transgress. This is an insight that has been later developed by Jean Genet, as I have tried to show in "Jean Genet: La position du Franc-Tireur," *L'Esprit Createur* 35, no. 1 (spring 1995): 30–39.

11. Hyde, *Trials of Oscar Wilde,* 120.

12. Sam Slote, "Wilde Thing," paper read at the 1992 Dublin Joyce Symposium. See also David Hayman, *The Wake in Transit* (Ithaca, N.Y.: Cornell University Press, 1990), 130–38, for links between the Tristan-Isolde-Mark configuration, incest, and Wilde's "sin."

13. Vyvyan Holland, *Son of Oscar Wilde* (London: Rupert Hart-Davis, 1954), 14.

Rethinking the Closet

Thrilled by His Touch

The Aestheticizing of Homosexual Panic in *A Portrait of the Artist as a Young Man*

Joseph Valente

In his letters and essays, Joyce alludes repeatedly to the homoerotic activities supposedly rife in English or Anglo-Saxon boarding schools and implicit in their representative social and athletic customs (see especially *SL* 74, 136; *CW* 201–2).[1] In the process, he not only displays a familiarity with the burgeoning *scientia sexualis* of his day, he flaunts a facility with the subcultural argot, dropping arcane phrases like "captain of fifty's regime" in the manner of a *cognoscente* (*SL* 136). Yet he does so by way of disclaiming any and all knowledge or awareness with such things. The dynamic that Freud called disavowal, admitting to consciousness by way of a qualifying refusal, is instinct in virtually every one of these references.[2] At the same time, Joyce seems to have scrupulously avoided the use of terms that name same sex desires and relations directly, preferring the sort of euphemisms that punctuate Stephen's discussion of Shakespeare in "Scylla and Charybdis": "brothers in love" (*U* 9.1046), "Tame essence of Wilde" (*U* 532), "play the giddy ox" (*U* 1.171), "cities of the plain" (*SL* 86), "captain of fifty" (*SL* 136), "lady highkickers" (*SL* 74), and so forth. To paraphrase yet another of these prevalent euphemisms, Joyce does not speak the name of homosexuality so much as he names the absence of such speech. Nowhere is this lack of plain speaking any plainer than in Joyce's essay "Oscar Wilde: The Poet of *Salomé*, in which he refuses to give Wilde's "strange problem" or "crime" a name, even as he judges it "the logical and inescapable product of the Anglo-Saxon college and university system, with its *secrecy* and restrictions" (*CW* 204; emphasis added).[3] What could account for this unwonted circumspection from a man long since resigned to offending hypocritical sensibilities with his writing (*SL* 83)?

When one considers Joyce's own educational career at an elite, all-male

47

boarding school, Clongowes Wood College, it becomes apparent that he has constructed homoeroticism along the lines of what Jonathan Dollimore has called "the proximate."[4] Being socially adjacent to the self, the proximate is that which can be most effectively dissociated from the self. Because it is right *here*, I can see or grasp it, and so it cannot be *right* here; the near-me can only be the not-me. And yet owing to this adjacency, the essential reality of the proximate, the full extent of its relations to the self, always remains to be discovered; it can always be turned back upon the self, *a vous*, or even accommodated by the self in other guises and contexts. Like the colonial forms of ethnoracial affiliation (English vs. Irish), like the socially marked idioms of a given language (slang vs. "standard"), homo- and heterosexual affect are at once constituted symbiotically and defined disjunctively, the perfect ideological condition for the concept of "proximate-ness" to emerge. In Joyce's case, his critical and epistolary allusions to homosexuality insist upon a disjunctive definition, asserting his heterosexual identity through a professed ignorance of its designated other; yet their enunciative context and performance repeatedly belie his intent, pointing to the fundamental imbrication of these erotic tendencies.

What makes the proximate at once ineluctable and dangerous, of course, is also what gives it a specific shape, valence, and site of operations—the existence of normative power relations. In the modern world of male entitlement, the proximate-ness of homo- and heterosexuality has taken on a particularly explosive form to which Eve Sedgwick has given the name "homosexual panic."[5] Sedgwick summarizes patriarchy itself as a "set of relations between men which have a material base and which, though hierarchical, establish or create interdependence and solidarity among men that enable them to dominate women."[6] Patriarchal institutions, accordingly, like the elite male boarding school, be it Anglo-Saxon or Irish Catholic, serve to promote what Sedgwick calls male homosocial desires: a chain of fellowship, affection, boosterism, and engagement, competitive and otherwise, of which the conventional misogynistic *heterosexual* relationship can be seen as a defining articulation. Appropriated by, circulated among, and situated between men as objects of contest, rivalry, and reconciliation, women have traditionally been conscripted as the vehicles of a homosocial desire that excludes and devalues them. That is, the "intense and potent bonds" that women share with men work to enforce the deep-structural complicity of men in preserving their own privilege.[7] The heterosexual imperative functions as the handmaiden of the law of the father.

But precisely because homosocial desire is consolidated by the putative "otherness" of heterosexuality, which opens the space of gender inequity, homosocial desire finds itself rent by the putative "sameness" of homosexuality, which, by short-circuiting the approved wiring of desire, threatens to upset the homosocial flows of power. And yet, Sedgwick notes, male homosexuality emerges from these same patriarchal institutions as a *particular form* of male homosociality:

the continuum of male homosocial bonds has been brutally structured by a secularized psychologized homophobia, which has excluded certain shiftingly and *arbitrarily* defined segments of the [same] continuum from participating in the overarching male entitlement, in the complex web of male power over the production, reproduction and exchange of goods, persons and means.[8]

Richard Dellamora seconds this point, mapping its precise social and historical coordinates:

Late in the century, masculine privilege was sustained by male friendships within institutions like the public schools, the older universities, the clubs, and the professions. Because, however, the continuing dominance of bourgeois males also required that they marry and produce offspring, the intensity and sufficiency of male bonding needed to be strictly controlled by homophobic mechanisms.[9]

And yet, no bright line can be drawn separating homosocial affects and intimacies and homosexual ones. Quoting Sedgwick once more:

the paths of male entitlement required certain intense male bonds that were not readily distinguishable from the most reprobated bonds, an endemic and ineradicable state of . . . male homosexual panic [anxiety over what is, what is not, who is, who is not] became the normal condition of male heterosexual entitlement.[10]

The modern educational system in general and the elite boarding school in particular, where boys learned the ways of male entitlement under the pressure of powerful and labile erotic pulsions, have afforded a prototypical arena for the experience of homosexual panic.

Joyce not only betrays just this sort of sexual unease in his private correspondence, but, I will be arguing, he transfers these attitudes to his fictive alter ego, Stephen Dedalus, in a more extreme, explicitly "panicky" mode, which systematically shapes the most crucial decisions that Stephen enacts: his appeal to Conmee, his refusal of the priesthood, his assumption of an aesthetic vocation, his self-exile. A number of critics have, over the years, pointed to the operation of homoerotic energies in *A Portrait*—for example, in the smuggling episode or in Stephen's final interview with Cranly—and a couple have even asserted the importance of these same energies as a component of Stephen's psychology.[11] I would like both to extend and to challenge this scholarship by demonstrating that these homosexual energies are indissociable from Stephen's phobic denial of them; that this denial constitutes a *fundamental determinant* of the novel's basic narrative structure and hence of Stephen's destiny; and that in his elaboration of Stephen's denial, Joyce *stages and thereby transvalues* his own disavowal of the homoerotic.

By taking this approach, of course, I do not mean to imply any simple autobiographical identification of the figure of Dedalus with that of Joyce; the panic and denial that Stephen displays are not synonymous with Joyce's unease and disavowal, but heuristic parodies or exaggerations thereof, in keeping with what Hugh Kenner has called Joyce's cubist method of self-portraiture. I do mean to propose, however, that the combination of projection, misrecognition, and self-awareness connecting author and alter ego comprises a certain homoerotic ambivalence, whose operation in the text helps to demystify Stephen's strongest claim to being Joyce's surrogate, his will to artistry.

II

The very title of the novel invokes fin de siècle homoeroticism and does so in a characteristically Joycean fashion, by establishing, at the outset, the text as intertext. As Vicki Mahaffey suggested to me, the phrase "a portrait of the artist" is a quite peculiar locution, which makes its derivation from one work in particular, Oscar Wilde's *The Picture of Dorian Gray,* that much more assured, especially since Dorian's portrait *keeps* him a young man. During the opening scene of Wilde's famous novel, Basil tells Henry:

> every portrait that is painted with feeling is a portrait of the artist, not the sitter. The sitter is merely the accident, the occasion. It is not he who is revealed by the painter; it is rather the painter . . . who reveals himself.[12]

In this light, Stephen can be taken either as a self-portrait in the ordinary sense or as a self-portrait strictly by virtue of being "a portrait painted with feeling," a condition likely to disfigure the ordinary self-portrait with a certain self-indulgence. Stephen must, therefore, not only be seen as both Joyce and not Joyce; he must also be seen as revealing Joyce precisely to the extent that he is *not* a self-depiction (being instead merely a portrait painted with feeling) and disfiguring Joyce to the extent that he *is* a self-depiction, altered by that feeling.

But Joyce's interest in the intercourse between revelation and representation in Wilde exceeded questions of the pragmatics of self-portraiture. It had a nakedly ethicopolitical edge as well. Joyce's primary response to *The Picture of Dorian Gray* was disappointment that Wilde had dissembled in presenting the homosexual charge binding Dorian, Basil, and Henry, that Wilde's own complex self-representation had not been more of a (sexual) revelation.

> I can imagine the capital which Wilde's prosecuting counsel made out of certain parts of it. It is not very difficult to read between the lines. Wilde seems to have had some good intentions in writing it—some wish to put

himself before the world—but the book is rather crowded with lies and epigrams. If he had had the courage to develop the allusions in the book it might have been better. I suspect he has done this in some privately printed books. (*SL* 96)

Like this letter, however, which conspicuously declines to develop "the allusions in the book" any more than Wilde does, leaving the homosexuality therein an "open secret,"[13] Joyce's title repeats the gesture of circumspection, leaving the *homotextual* relations between his novel and Wilde's at the level of "epigram." Or perhaps it would be truer to say, Joyce's title answers Wilde's deliberate circumspection with an unconscious disavowal; it simultaneously reveals and conceals the intense homotextual relation between his bildungsroman and his precursor, revealing the "textual" affinity, in its most Derridean sense, while concealing or eliding the "homo." Whereas the "feeling" that makes Dorian's portrait a "portrait of the artist" involves Basil's homoerotic attraction to his "sitter," as Joyce recognizes, Joyce's "feeling" for his "sitter" could only be construed as narcissistic, a modality of desire properly understood as the precondition for any object relation, homo- or hetero-. By remaining at the level of epigram, the title, *A Portrait of the Artist,* translates the open secret of *Dorian Gray's* sexual economy into an open option or open possibility. That is to say, whereas *Dorian Gray* veils its specific erotic "truth" in order to betray it selectively, enacting a classic economy of repression and desire, *A Portrait* announces but does not specify its erotic truth, entertaining a *jouissance* of suspension and volatility—a point to which I will return in my conclusion.

By the same token, the improbable Greek surname of Joyce's alter ego, the marker of his prospective artistic identity, would inevitably be construed, in the aftermath of the entire Wilde controversy, as invoking the Hellenistic cultural movement that the name Dorian Gray had served to sensationalize. But here again, the name Dorian alludes *specifically* to the homoerotic component of that late Victorian cult of aestheticist self-development, the Dorians being regarded as the prototypical exponents of "Greek love." The name Dedalus, by contrast, carries far less determinate sexual connotations: the "old artificer" (*P* 253) not only fathered Icarus on a slave girl, he mentored and then murdered Perdix, and he pandered to the unnatural lusts of Pasiphaë, the queen of the Cretans, who were themselves generally reputed to have introduced the institution of *paiderastia* into Greece (a belief built into the etymology of the word itself).[14]

A similarly displaced homotextual relation presents itself in the symbol of Stephen's Irish art (no, not the cracked mirror [*U* 1.143–44], though it is telling that Wilde presides there as well), the impossible green rose. Stephen's aesthetic career begins on a significant pun, significantly repeated.

> O, the *wild* rose blossoms
> On the little green place.
> He sang that song. That was his song. (*P* 7; emphasis added)

And again,

> Perhaps a *wild* rose might be like those colors. And he remembered the song about the *wild* rose blossoms on the little green place. (*P* 12; emphasis added)

Joyce underlines and clarifies the pun in *Finnegans Wake,* where it serves to stake the process of history itself on the wages of illicit sexuality:

> has not the levy of black mail from the times the finish were in it, and fain for wild*e* erthe blossoms followed an impressive private reputation for whispered sins? (*FW* 69.2–4; emphasis added)

With this in mind, Stephen's subsequent musing—"But you could not have a green rose. But perhaps somewhere in the world you could" (*P* 12)—unmistakably recalls Wilde's famous "green carnation," which was an aestheticist emblem of imaginative artifice, the conventional reading of Stephen's rose, and, correlatively, a badge of the homosexual subculture of fin de siècle England,[15] a sense that Stephen's flower intimates sotto voce. By deploying this symbolic nexus in this fashion, Joyce puts Stephen in the position of registering, "owning" in some sense, the emergent cultural identification of artistry and homoeroticism that the aestheticist movement had adumbrated, but he simultaneously avoids any suggestion that Stephen could himself be aware of, or even subliminally invested in, such an identification. Joyce thereby sets up a recursive dynamic wherein Stephen's preordained vocation *will have been grounded* in an inarticulate homoeroticism once, and only once, his exposure to the taboos informing compulsory heterosexuality have catalyzed same-sex desire *as* a dread of the unspeakable, something to be expressed only in the negative form of a denial. So even before Stephen's homosexual panic begins to condition the contents of his life narrative, its genesis works a significant complication in the form of that narrative. Instead of unfolding on the latency model, which neatly conforms with the linear, quasi-organic development typical of the *Künstlerroman,* Stephen's homosexual affects irrupt in an ana-chronistic knot or fold known, in Freudian terminology, as a "deferred action," in this case the retroactive generation of a subsequently phobic desire. To speak of Stephen's homoerotic investments, accordingly, is always to speak of his simultaneous experience, denial, and diversion of them, galvanized in his Clongowes education.

Stephen's speculation on the green rose immediately follows his reflections on the widely suspect Simon Moonan. The homoerotic overtones of this interlude nicely encapsulate the temporal knot of deferred action, for they reveal *both* a naïveté too complete to be inhibited and a knowingness too acute to be innocent.

We all know why you speak. You are McGlade's *suck. Suck was a queer word.* The fellow called Simon Moonan that name because Simon Moonan used to tie the prefect's false sleeves behind his back and the prefect used to let on to be angry. But the sound was ugly. Once he had washed his hands in the lavatory of the Wicklow Hotel and his father pulled the stopper up by the chain after and the dirty water went down through the hole in the basin. And when it had all gone down slowly . . . made a sound like that: *suck.* Only louder. . . . There were *two cocks that you turned and water came out:* cold and hot . . . and he could see the names printed on the cocks. That was *a very queer thing.* (*P* 11)

I have quoted this passage at length because

1. through the repeated use of terms like *suck, queer, cocks, and so forth,*[16] it lays down psychosymbolic associations among Stephen's developing fever, his ongoing fascination with, and aversion to, standing water and waste, and a retroactive homosexual panic;

2. as a link in the reversible chain of Stephen's psychic development, it puts an erotic spin on the sort of homosocial roughhousing that lands him in the square ditch and causes his fever. Stephen, remember, a designated mama's boy, will not trade his dandyish "little snuffbox" for Wells's macho "hacking chestnut, the conqueror of forty" (*P* 10); the box and the nut function as genital symbols for the respectively feminized and masculinized positions of Stephen and Wells. Since the incident exemplifies the sexualized aggression that Joyce attributed to English boarding-school activities, and since Joyce was likewise shouldered into the ditch, with similarly febrile consequences (*JJII* 28), it is worth noting that the square ditch runs along the perimeter of Clongowes and forms its boundary with the old English pale.[17] It is, in other words, a border zone where the masculinized Anglo-Saxon "conqueror" and the feminized Irish conquered meet and, partly as an effect of the conquest itself, where their ethnoracial differences are both marked, even exaggerated, and overridden, even erased. With respect to Joyce's cherished distinction between the rampant homoeroticism of English public-school life and the comparative innocence of its Irish counterpart, the square ditch constitutes an objectified instance of "the proximate" itself, that is, a thin margin of dissociation into which the subject might always land or be pushed, and his kinship with the other be uncomfortably reaffirmed;[18]

3. in light of points one and two, it establishes a basis on which to overcome an inveterate critical assumption, that because Stephen does not fully grasp the implications of the "smugging" scandal until later on, he is not really party to the homosexual energies circulating among the Clongowes students as they remember or recount the "crime" and anticipate

the similarly titillating punishment. The mode of Stephen's knowledge is unconscious, which is to say it unfolds in the *futur anterieur*.

As it turns out, these three narrative functions are strictly correlative. For what most powerfully eroticizes the Clongowes scene for Stephen is not the prosaic specification of Moonan and Boyle's offense ("smugging"), nor even the poetic rehearsal of their punishment ("It can't be helped / It must be done / So down with your breeches / And out with your bum" [*P* 44]). It is rather the way the taboo on their activity (i.e., a prohibition enforcing secrecy and enforced by shame) molds Stephen's private elaboration of these accounts and the way his elaboration, in turn, interacts with other environmental cues like the sound of the cricket bats.

As Stephen speculates on the offense, his effort to exculpate Moonan in his own mind lends a distinctly libidinal complexion to his memories of the boy, as if the sense of transgression itself, any transgression, carries its own highly labile erotic current.

> What did that mean about the smugging in the square. . . . It was a joke, he thought. Simon Moonan had nice clothes and one night he had *shown him a ball of creamy* sweets that the fellows of the football fifteen had rolled down to him along the carpet. . . . It was the night of the *match against the Bective Rangers* and the ball was made just like a red and green apple only it opened and it was *full of the creamy sweets.* (*P* 42; emphases added)

Stephen's earlier fantasy about leaving on vacation already incorporated his experience with Moonan in a plainly, if unconsciously, homoerotic fashion: "The train was full of fellows: a *long, long chocolate train* with *cream facings*" (*P* 20; emphases added). This is a classic instance in which commonplace homosocial reinforcement, highlighted by the affiliation with team sports, merges almost seamlessly with the "most reprobated" sexual imagery and investments. Once again, Stephen undergoes the panic this double bind arouses as an "agony in the watercloset" (*U* 15.2643), a dread associated with waste and standing urine:

> But why in the square? You went there when you wanted to do something. It was all thick slabs of slate and water trickled all day out of tiny pinholes and there was a queer smell of stale water there. (*P* 43)

Being the site of a certain mutual genital exposure, the male lavatory space always carries some homoerotic potential; as a result, the introduction of a more *explicitly* sexual element, tapping as it does Stephen's existing fear and confusion, renders the excremental function itself "queer" and therefore unspeakable for him. You went to the lavatory to "do something" that apparently dare not be named.

As Stephen speculates on the punishment, his dread and his desire come simultaneously into view.[19] He imagines the prospect of being caned less in terms of pain than in terms of "chill": "It made him shivery to think of it and cold . . . it made him shivery" (*P* 45). That this chill bespeaks a sexualized frisson becomes immediately evident in Stephen's focus on the ceremonial unveiling of the "vital spot" (*P* 44): "He wondered who had to let them [the trousers] down, the master or the boy himself" (*P* 45). Stephen's consideration of the protocol involved suggests a mutuality of participation in the act of undressing that bares the sexual energy animating the exemplary discipline. His subsequent vision of the caning itself implies a literalized dialectic or reciprocity between beater and beaten that issues in a sense of positive and implicitly homoerotic pleasure.

> Athy . . . had rolled up his sleeves to show how Mr. Gleeson would roll up his sleeves. But Mr. Gleeson had round shiny cuffs and clean white wrists and fattish white hands and the nails of them were long and pointed. Perhaps he pared them too like Lady Boyle. . . . And though he trembled with . . . fright to think of the cruel long nails . . . and of the chill you felt at the end of your shirt when you undressed yourself yet he felt a feeling of queer quiet pleasure inside him to think of the white fattish hands, clean and strong and gentle. (*P* 45)

As the passage mushrooms into a full-blown if displaced sexual fantasy, Stephen takes center stage as the subject of warring sensations, an outer chill and an inner glow, an anticipated pain and an experienced pleasure, an involuntary engagement but a voluntary imagining, a sexual affect at once savored and denied. Indeed, Joyce exploits the equivocality of the word "queer" in this passage in order to mark not only the homoerotic nature of Stephen's ambivalence, but also to mark the ambivalent, uncanny impact of the homoerotic upon Stephen, his mixture of fear and fascination, attraction and repulsion, which is the recipe for a "panic" born of "proximate-ness."

This proximate-ness, in turn, with its ambivalent affect, gives a sharply ironic twist to Stephen's subsequent pandying. It is not just that Stephen receives punishment for something he never did, scheme to break his glasses, nor even that he is made the scapegoat for a sexual scandal he imperfectly comprehends, which is how he comes to interpret the matter (*P* 54); no, what is ironic is that in the unconscious, where the thought or wish can stand for the deed and carry the same transgressive force,[20] there is indeed a recursive symmetry, if not equity, to Stephen's punishment. If, as Stephen and the other boys suspect, the pandyings actually respond to the homoerotic indulgences of the smuggling "ring," then Stephen can be seen as an accomplice after the fact, participating vicariously in these indulgences through his fantasy construction of Mr. Gleeson's discipline. In fact, the imagined caning and the real pandying communicate with one another precisely through Stephen's erotic preoccupation with his masters' hands. Having taken a "queer quiet pleasure" from the contemplation of Mr. Gleeson's "white fattish hands, clean strong and gentle," Stephen seems to expect something of the same gratification from the prefect's fingers, in which he initially discerns a like quality, and Stephen finds Father Dolan's betrayal of this sensual promise to be, in some respects, the most galling aspect of the whole episode. His mind returns to it obsessively in the aftermath.

[H]e thought of the hands which he had held out in the air with the palms up and of the firm touch of the prefect of studies when he had steadied the shaking fingers. (*P* 51)

He felt the touch of the prefect's fingers as they had steadied his hand and at first he had thought he was going to shake hands with him because the fingers were soft and firm: but then in an instant he had heard the swish of the soutane sleeve and the crash. (*P* 52)

And his whitegrey face and the nocoloured eyes behind the steelrimmed spectacles were cruel looking *because* he had steadied the hand first with his firm soft fingers and that was to hit it better and louder. (*P* 52; emphasis added)

Since we are dealing with Stephen's *perception* of the scene, the insistent, fetishistic repetition of "soft," "firm," "fingers," "touch," and "steadied," along with the bizarre causal priority accorded Dolan's duplicitous touch, must be seen as recalling some sort of baffled desire as well as trauma, or rather an overlapping of the two psychic movements. Stephen's trauma at the pandying fixates upon the master's touch because that is where Stephen's unconscious wishes insert themselves into both the smugging scandal and the larger homosocial-sexual economy of Clongowes. It is the point at which he has eroticized, and so from a certain point of view merited, the priests' brutal sanctions on such eroticism.

Stephen's subsequent protest at the injustice of his thrashing likewise belies his fascination with the male body, which is, of course, the impulse being disciplined.

[A]nd the fifth was big Corrigan who was going to be flogged by Mr. Gleeson. That was why the prefect of studies had called him a schemer and pandied him for nothing. . . . But he [Corrigan] had done something and besides Mr. Gleeson would not flog him hard: and he [Stephen] remembered how big Corrigan looked in the bath. He had skin the same colour as the turfcoloured bogwater in the shallow end of the bath and when he walked along the side his feet slapped loudly on the wet tiles and at every step his thighs shook a little because he was fat. (*P* 54)

Stephen wants to assert a distinction between guilty, robust Corrigan and poor, little innocent Dedalus. But in doing so, he discloses a familiarity with Corrigan's physique apparently gleaned from watching his "every step" "in the bath," and the desire such familiarity would suggest seems further corroborated by the way Corrigan's bodily image simply takes over Stephen's juridical meditation. At the same time, his comparison of Corrigan's pigmentation to the dirty water in the bath recalls his own immersion in the square ditch and so indicates how profoundly this desire interfuses with dread.

Far from resolving this double bind, Conmee's vindication of Stephen and his schoolmates' ensuing homage only cements it. After his interview with the rector, Stephen is "hoisted" and "carried . . . along" (*P* 58) in a homosocial bonding ritual that obviously makes him quite uncomfortable, for he immediately struggles to extricate his body from their grasp. And it is only once "[h]e was alone" that "[h]e was happy and free" (*P* 59). He then proceeds to dissociate himself in a categorical fashion from any sense of triumph over the prefect and so, by extension, from the celebratory fellowship of his peers. The reason is not far to seek. The very image in which his sense of gratification crystallizes, a sound "like drops of water in a fountain falling softly in a brimming bowl" (*P* 59), is but the inverse of his image of the dreaded "smugging" square, "all thick slabs of slate and water trickled all day out of tiny pinholes." The aestheticized emblem of personal fulfillment thus encodes and carries forward the cloacal image of taboo sexual longing. Just as the prospect of painful social humiliation—being singled out for a caning—triggers in Stephen a "queer quiet pleasure" amid anxiety, owing to its homoerotic undercurrents, so the fruits of Stephen's social victory trigger an unconscious anxiety amid validation, an anxiety registered along the associative chains of Stephen's mental imagery.

In this regard, the fact that this ambivalent water rhapsody actually emanates from a game of cricket, a sport exported from the elite playing fields of England to those of Ireland, implicates the author's unconscious as well in the structure of homoerotic disavowal. As Trevor Williams has argued, Joyce frames Stephen's success with a motif of colonial-cultural hegemony as a way of qualifying or undercutting its ultimate meaningfulness, in keeping with the alternating elevation/deflation mechanism of the narrative as a whole.[21] But in the process, Joyce necessarily undermines his own cherished distinction between the athletic customs of English and Irish boarding schools at precisely the moment when the sexual anxiety that distinction was designed to forestall infiltrates the crowning symbol of Stephen's young life—the brimming bowl.

The resurgence of Stephen's "homosexual panic" in spite, and even because, of his social triumph presages Joyce's treatment of the issue throughout the remainder of the novel, beginning with Stephen's entry into officially heterosexual activity, from courtship rituals to whoring excursions. Joyce consistently surrounds Stephen's participation in these practices with conspicuous forms and indices of sexual/gender inversion, which, by the end of the century, was the dominant model of homosexuality in both the popular imagination and in the burgeoning discourse of sexology.[22] Foucault even goes so far as to claim,

> the psychological, psychiatric, medical category of homosexuality was constituted from the moment it was characterized . . . [as] a certain way of inverting the masculine and the feminine in oneself. Homosexuality appeared as one of the forms of sexuality when it was transposed from the practice of sodomy onto a kind of interior androgyny, a hermaphrodism of the soul. The sodomite had been a temporary aberration; the homosexual was now a species.[23]

That is to say, homosexuality was paradoxically conceived in and as resistance to the very possibility of same-sex desire, reassimilated in its very emergence to the heterosexuality from which it was seen to deviate. As Christopher Craft observes, "sexual inversion explains homosexual desire as a physiologically misplaced heterosexuality . . . referable not to the sex of the body . . . but rather to a psychologized sexual center characterized as the 'opposite gender.' "[24]

Uranian activist Karl Heinrich Ulrichs gave the earliest and most enduring public expression to the idea of sexual inversion when he described male homosexuals as having "a feminine soul enclosed in a male body."[25] In 1870, Carl Westphal transposed this formulation into a medical/psychiatric register. His paradigm of a "contrary sexual instinct," where a person was physically of one gender and psychically of another, was embraced in turn by such prominent psychosexologists as Ellis, Symonds, Carpenter, Freud, Krafft-Ebing, and Burton, (all of whom Joyce read and, on this score, credited).[26] Krafft-Ebing located various gradations of sex/gender inversion in a "neuro-(psycho)pathic state" in his clinical tome, *Psychopathia Sexualis,* which was of course Joyce's primary resource for his representation of Bloom's encyclopedic perversions in "Circe"; and Burton traced a liability to sex/gender inversion to certain geoclimactic zones in *The Thousand Nights and a Night,* which played a no less decisive role in Joyce's conception of *Finnegans Wake.*[27] In addition to being pervasive in Joyce's intellectual milieu, the inversion formula proved amazingly tenacious, so much so that Ellis and Freud continued to espouse or assume the model even after they had controverted or repudiated it, and Symonds and Carpenter felt compelled to assent to the model despite fairly deep misgivings.[28] This tenacity, I would suggest, proceeded directly from the hegemonic force of the heterosexual norm, which inversion preserved, as Eve Sedgwick has noted, within homosexual desire itself.[29]

Joyce's deployment of this received idea, however, as with so many others, works to reverse or disrupt its received social force. Interwoven as they are with distinctively masculine, heterosexual rites of passage, the inversion motifs in *A Portrait* situate homoeroticism neither as a simple alternative to, nor an anomalous deviation from, some naturalized heteroerotic incitement, but as an element uncannily symbiotic with that incitement and menacing to its normalization. Firstly, just *before* the Harold's Cross children's party—Stephen's "coming out" as a heterosexual male—an old woman mistakes him for a female, repeating the phrase "I thought you were Josephine" several times (*P* 68). Often treated as an isolated epiphany, this incident has little if any pertinence to the rest of the narrative, other than being the first of several instances in which gender inversion attaches specifically to Stephen. As such, it can be read as one of those incompletely processed "lumps" in which the subterranean concerns of a text concentrate themselves in a nearly illegible form. In support of this thesis, I would note that just *after* the party, Stephen actually bears out this gender (mis)identification in terms of the standard Victorian sexual typology. On the tram ride home with E.C., he assumes what was thought to be the essentially, even *definitively* feminine role of sexual passivity and withdrawal, receiving without responding to her perceived sexual advances.[30]

Once again, just before her attendance at Stephen's Whitsuntide performance, their first encounter since the party, a significant instance of gender misidentification supervenes. There appears backstage "a pinkdressed figure, wearing a curly golden wig and an oldfashioned straw sunbonnet, with black pencilled eyebrows and cheeks delicately rouged and powdered." The presiding prefect asks facetiously, "Is this a beautiful young lady or a doll that you have here, Mrs. Tallon?" It turns out, of course, to be the "girlish figure" of a boy, "little Bertie Tallon," a circumstance that provokes "a murmur of curiosity" and then "a murmur of admiration" from the other boys. In Stephen, however, this transvestite spectacle precipitates a telling "movement of impatience. . . . He let the edge of the blind fall . . . and walked out of the chapel" (*P* 74). Why would Stephen react or overreact in this fashion? Perhaps because the superimposition of the signifiers of feminine desirability upon a schoolboy's already "girlish figure," the accompanying expression of the other schoolboys' admiration, and the disingenuous participation of the prefect combine to tap the ambivalence at the heart of Stephen's sexual desire, by recalling the roots of that ambivalence in his own school experience as the "little" boy, the mama's boy, the feminized boy. A subsequent passage, however, indicates that still more is at stake.

> All day he had thought of nothing but their leavetaking on the steps of the tram at Harold's Cross. . . . All day he had imagined a new meeting with her for he knew that she was to come to the play. The old restless moodiness had again filled his breast as it had done on the night of the party but had not found an outlet in verse. The growth and knowledge of two years of boyhood stood between then and now, forbidding such an outlet: and all day the stream of gloomy tenderness within him had started forth and returned upon itself in dark courses and eddies, wearying him in the end until the pleasantry of the prefect and the painted little boy had drawn from him a movement of impatience. (*P* 77)

And why does the moodiness attached to Stephen's sexual "growth and knowledge," not to mention the restlessness accumulated over his day of brooding on Harold's Cross, vent themselves *specifically* in response to a schoolboy's drag performance? Perhaps because Stephen's sexual ambivalence, tapped by this transvestic scenario, persists in such a way as to disturb the ease of his enlistment in the rolls of compulsory heterosexuality, his dalliance with E.C. being a critical step in this process. Notice, in this respect, that Stephen figures his feelings for E.C. as a "stream of gloomy tenderness" moving "in dark courses and eddies," a metaphor that unmistakably keys into and recirculates the homoerotic valences and associations of Stephen's past experience with dark or eddying courses of water: the square ditch, the sink at the Wicklow Hotel, the shallow end of the bath at Clongowes. Given this commingling of the "streams" of heterosexual affect with the "courses" of (water)closeted homosexual desire, Stephen's prescription for calming his heart after he misses E.C., the "odour" of "horse piss and rotted straw" (*P* 86), seems a recognizable-enough displacement.

Finally, Stephen's venture into the brothel area is characterized by a literal and symbolic inversion of the phallic mode of heterosexual activity. He serves as the object or locus rather than the agent of penetration. First, "subtle streams" of sound "penetrated his being" (*P* 100). Then, "His hands clenched convulsively and his teeth set together as he suffered the agony of . . . penetration" (*P* 100). Upon entering the prostitute's room, it is Stephen who becomes "hysterical," Stephen who is "surrendering himself," and Stephen who is passively penetrated by "the dark pressure of her softly parting lips" (*P* 101). Moreover, Joyce frames Stephen's long-anticipated (hetero)sexual transfiguration with lavatory motifs familiar from Clongowes. He depicts Stephen prowling "dark, slimy streets," penetrated by "subtle streams" of sound, and issuing "a cry which was but the echo of an obscene scrawl which he had read on the oozing wall of a urinal" (*P* 99–100). In this way, Joyce unsettles the popular, *bildungsmythos* of a young man's self-conscious graduation from homosexual play to heterosexual maturity and (re)productivity, and he replaces it with an ambivalent complication, a progressive overlapping and interfolding of sexual preferences that is registered at one level of self-narration only to be denied or externalized at another. Such interfolding even extends to Stephen's repentance for these sexual excesses at the religious retreat. For his nominally *heterosexual* sins, he imagines an eternal punishment expressive of his profound dread at his unacknowledged *homosexual* desires: a weedy field of "solid excrement" populated by bestial creatures with long phallic tails and faces whose similarity to and contact with the weedy field give them an anal cast (*P* 137).

Keeping this sexual ambivalence at bay (what we might call the normative working through of homosexual panic) exerts a subtle yet potent pressure on the subsequent course of Stephen's development. On the one hand, his unconscious anxiety about the homoerotic component of his sexual drives can be seen as fueling his repentance and renunciation of their illicit enactment. On the other hand, and more importantly, a gradual accretion of images and associations of sexual inversion and memories of the homosocial interplay at Clongowes work to hold Stephen back from the logical terminus of his recovered piety, turning his consideration of the religious life toward a relieved demurral.

The latter point becomes evident over the course of his vocational interview with the director of Belvedere. The director opens the interview with a comment on "the friendship between saint Thomas and saint Bonaventure" and goes on to criticize the feminine design of "the capuchin dress" known as *les jupes* (P 154–55).[31] Stephen's silent, embarrassed response is a meditation upon the "soft and delicate stuffs" of women's clothing followed by a meditation on the Jesuit body, in both senses of the term.

> His masters, even when they had not attracted him, had seemed to him always intelligent and serious priests, athletic and highspirited prefects. He thought of them as men who washed their bodies briskly with cold water and wore clean cold linen. (P 155–56)

In a context thus informed by questions of homosocial affection and institutionalized cross-dressing, the director's ensuing gesture of releasing the blind's cord suddenly cannot but trigger, in both Stephen and the reader, the unconscious memory of Bertie Tallon in drag and Stephen's own impatient response: letting the edge of the blind fall.

As Stephen leaves the director, he begins to envisage his daily life as a priest in more concrete detail, and the (homo)eroticized traces of the past gather more thickly and affect Stephen more intensely.

> The troubling odour of the long corridor of Clongowes came back to him. . . . At once from every part of his being and unrest began to irradiate. A feverish quickening of his pulses followed. (P 160)

An olfactory cue, always the strongest for Stephen, puts him in the grip of an excitement that can be explained neither on a purely nonsexual basis nor in terms of simple attraction or repulsion, but only by way of the annihilating proximate-ness of a taboo desire, its alien and (self-)alienating intimacy. The memory of the bathhouse atmosphere at Clongowes returns to Stephen with precisely this quality, being *in* and yet not *of* him.

> His lungs dilated and sank as if he were inhaling a warm moist unsustaining air which hung in the bath in Clongowes above the sluggish turf-coloured water. (P 161)

The last phrase, it should be noted, substantially repeats Stephen's mesmerized description of big Corrigan's naked body. So when Stephen goes on to ground his refusal of the clerical life on "the pride of his spirit which had always made him conceive himself as a being apart in every order" (*P* 161), he represses one of his libidinal aims in the service of the larger economy of desire that feeds his "panic." Stephen does not, as he later thinks, refuse the priesthood simply by obedience to a "wayward instinct" (*P* 165), but also out of fear of yet another "wayward instinct" implicated in his possible acceptance. This misprision resonates specifically in the odd, ambiguous phrase "apart in [not from] every order." To be "apart in" an order, after all, is also to be "a part in" that order; it is to find oneself in a situation of belonging and estrangement simultaneously, the condition of the proximate.

That Stephen's professedly homosocial discomfort cannot be dissociated from homosexual anxiety grows even clearer during the climactic scene on the strand, where Stephen receives his "true" calling. His fetishistic (which is to say implicitly misogynistic) overvaluation of the bird girl's physical presence follows a correspondingly aversive overreaction to the physical presence of his unclothed schoolmates.

> It was a pain to see them and a swordlike pain to see the signs of adolescence that made repellent their pitiable nakedness. Perhaps they had taken refuge in number and noise from the secret dread of their souls. But he, apart from them and in silence, remembered in what dread he stood of the mystery of his own body. (*P* 168)

The phallic ("swordlike") nature of Stephen's pain, his confounding of his dread of others with a dread of self and, finally, the now familiar solace he takes in a fantasy of dignified solitude, all indicate a recurrence of Stephen's homosexual panic. The representation of his state of being upon removing himself from the spectacle of his naked classmates even recalls the description of his state of mind upon extricating himself from his classmates' celebratory embrace at Clongowes.

> He was alone. He was unheeded, happy and near to the wild heart of life. (*P* 168)

> He was alone. He was happy and free. (*P* 59)

The crucial development on this occasion is that Stephen is able to legitimate his resource of splendid isolation through the romantic myth of the artist.

The bird girl can serve as Stephen's muse only insofar as she confirms this phantasmatic self-conception and thus delivers him from the embarrassments of censored and ambivalent sexual impulses. This function would go some way toward accounting for the extraordinary rapture she incites in him.[32] Stephen might be seen as placing her in a transferential position between himself and his naked peers, in much the same way that individual women, according to

Sedgwick, are consistently being enlisted as eroticized points of mediation "between men" in order to forestall the "panic" that arises with the arbitrary, institutionalized disjunction between homosocial and homosexual practice.[33] At the same time, in order to perform this function, the bird girl must appeal to the braided homo- and hetero-cathexes motivating Stephen's gaze, and on apparently straightforward heterosexual grounds. That is, she must enable a simplification and sublimation of Stephen's perverse desire, which is where the aesthetic framework becomes crucial. In this regard, it is important that she is not a bird woman, but a bird girl, poised in her incipient physical maturity between complete and incomplete gender differentiation. The repeated description of her look as "girlish" stresses as much by connecting her with that other "girlish figure," little Bertie Tallon. In fact, Joyce sets up a sort of textual ratio between the performances of Bertie and the bird girl, each of which constitutes a species of "drag" in that *(a)* each induces in its respective audience an admiration entirely bound up with some kind of aestheticized semblance: Bertie's garish overlay of feminine cues, the bird girl's concealed displacement of masculine ones; and *(b)* each induces in its respective audience an admiration that is itself in disguise, its homoerotic component hidden from consciousness.

Understood in these terms, the bird girl fits into Stephen's psychic economy in much the same way that Sybil Vane fits into Dorian's, as an objective correlative of a straightforward heterosexual investment that only exists "on stage," through aesthetic misrecognition. That is to say, in keeping with his reading of *Dorian Gray,* Joyce associates Wilde's brand of aestheticism not with his sodomite inclinations but with his dissimulation of them. For this reason, Joyce has Stephen's soaring inspiration express itself in what amounts to a broad stylistic parody of Wilde and Walter Pater, and he thereby establishes a subtle link between the sublimity of Stephen's aesthetic delirium and the repression and displaced release of the homosocial affect aroused by the swimmers (a dramatic irony perfectly in keeping with the cultural identification of art and same-sex desire fostered by Pater and consolidated by Wilde). It is remarkable, in fact, the extent to which the entire episode unfolds under (a pun on) the name of Wilde. Stephen's "ecstasy of flight made . . . wild his breath and . . . wild and radiant his windswept limbs," and "an instant of wild flight had delivered him" (*P* 169). "A new wild life was singing in his veins" (*P* 170). "He was . . . near to the wild heart of life . . . willful and wildhearted, alone amid a waste of wild air" (*P* 171). "He strode . . . singing wildly to the sea" (*P* 172). Once "her image had passed into his soul," the bird girl is figured as a "wild angel" (*P* 172). Just as the first signature song of baby Stephen touches punningly and significantly on Wilde, focusing upon a "wild rose" (*P* 7), later to transmogrify into the impossible "green rose" (*P* 12), so Stephen's first moments as a self-proclaimed artist have Wilde written all over them—over his flight, his song, his aesthetic object. From its flowering back to its roots, the narrative of Stephen's aesthetic destiny is staked upon his obsessive en-crypting of homoerotic desire, that is, his encoding of this desire and his laying it to rest. And the name of Wilde, always there and not quite there, re-marks this mechanism of denial.

Much the same structure characterizes Stephen's theoretical colloquium with Lynch. Sexualized byplay, such as Lynch's rubbing of his groin, is mediated by reference to an aesthetic ideal of female beauty, the Venus of Praxiteles, and routed through her mutual appropriation by the interlocutors. When Stephen introduces the question of body with the exhortation, "Let us take woman," and Lynch fervently responds, "Let us take her!" (*P* 208), they align themselves in an aestheticized version of the erotic triangle that Sedgwick takes to be the para-digmatic figure of homosociality/homophobia. It is important to recognize in this regard that notions of triangulated same-sex desire much like Sedgwick's were already abroad in the late nineteenth century and were readily available to Joyce. In *The Renaissance,* for example, Walter Pater, whose prose we saw paro-died in the decidedly homosocial "beach" episode, advanced an equally ho-mosocial interpretation of Chaucer's *The Knight's Tale,* opining that "one knows not whether the love of both Palimon and Arcite for Emelya, or of those two for each other, is the chiefer subject"—a reading that seeks to place an ideal of male love at the heart of the aesthetic experience.[34] For Stephen, of course, the aes-thetic is the discursive mode that raises the mind "above desire and loathing" (*P* 205), and yet it is precisely this nominal status that makes art the perfect cover for the taboo, which is itself defined by the cooperation of what "the flesh shrinks from" and "what it desires" (*P* 206). Stephen's sense of the aesthetic as being properly sequestered "in a mental world" (*P* 206) is what allows it to fa-cilitate covertly the discharge of homosexual libido. Witness, for example, the sublime culmination of his theoretical communiqué. The vision of the arche-typal artist, God, "paring his fingernails" (*P* 215) harnesses and transforms the desire attached to Stephen's memories of the sexually ambivalent hands of Tusker (Lady) Boyle and the punishing yet pleasure-giving hands of Mr. Gleeson.

Here we have then the erotic hinge on which the *Künstlerroman* aspect of the narrative can be said to turn. Whereas the religious life figures for Stephen the perilous slide of homosocial relations toward homosexual exposure, prompting his flight, the aesthetic vocation figures the sublimation of homoso-cial ties through the elaboration of a heteroerotic ideal. It thus serves him as a kind of supplement to the heterosexual imperative, a subsidiary distancing or mediating agency of homosocial bonds. That the heterosexual imperative should need the supplement of aesthetic transformation, however, is a sign of its ultimate vulnerability.

Such vulnerability is borne out in Stephen's friendship with Cranly, which features the closest thing *A Portrait* has to a French triangle: Stephen projects upon Cranly a mutual competitive interest in E.C. This triangle is modeled in turn onto an oedipal triangle, in which the paternalistic Cranly remonstrates with Stephen over the proper devotion to be paid his mother. We seem, in other words, to be moving toward what Sedgwick would see as a normative hetero-sexual/homophobic resolution. But it does not work. For if Stephen requires a heteroerotic ideal to sublimate his stubborn homoerotic ambivalence, his rare-faction of E.C. paradoxically renders her too shadowy and insubstantial a figure to mediate his powerful homosocial relationship with Cranly. Stephen's fleeting sense of romantic rivalry notwithstanding, Cranly increasingly comes to *take over* the place of E.C. as Stephen's object of affection. True to the terms of the novel outlined thus far, this transfer of erotic intensity and intimacy to a male figure passes through the register of religious intercourse.

Shortly before Stephen's initial thoughts of Cranly, there occurs a moment of gender misidentification of the sort that occurs prior to Stephen's first date with E.C. Stephen's father adverts to him as a "lazy bitch" (*P* 175). Joyce hereby intimates a structural parallel between Stephen's relations with E.C. and Cranly, a sort of dueling courtship. Stephen's thoughts themselves are fairly bursting with a barely repressed homoeroticism. He begins by wondering

> Why . . . when he thought of Cranly he could never raise before his mind the entire image of his body but only the image of his head and face. (*P* 178)

The habit of mind Stephen observes would seem to locate Cranly, like the aes-theticized image of Venus, exclusively "in a mental world," in this case by sub-stantially blotting out his bodily existence. But the "mental world" in which Stephen would cloister his friend is sacerdotal rather than aesthetic, and as the following passage indicates, Stephen's identification of the clerical orders with marked homosocial-sexual bonding has survived his rejection of them.

> The forms of the community emerged from the gustblown vestments. . . . They came ambling and stumbling, tumbling and capering, kilting their gowns for leap frog, holding one another back . . . smacking one another behind . . . calling to one another by familiar nicknames . . . whispering two and two behind their hands. (*P* 192)

The largely confessional nature of Stephen's mental intercourse with Cranly, in which he recounts "all the tumults and unrest and longings of his soul" (*P* 178), plugs directly into this homoerotic fantasy of church life, too directly in fact to escape Stephen's notice altogether. Even as he contemplates Cranly's "priestlike face," Stephen is brought up short remembering "the gaze of its dark womanish eyes," and "through this image" of gender inversion "he had a glimpse of a strange dark cavern of speculation" (*P* 178)—the very cavern, I would submit, that the present essay has traversed.

Stephen does not really explore this "cavern" until his last interview with Cranly, when he announces his imminent departure from Ireland. Most read-ers of this scene have followed Richard Ellmann in taking the homosexual implications to emanate largely, if not entirely, from Cranly—"Stephen's friend is as interested in Stephen as in Stephen's girl" (*JJII* 117).[35] But Stephen is the one taken with Cranly's "large dark eyes" (*P* 245), which he earlier finds "woman-ish"; Stephen is the one who inquires, with significant double entendre, "Are you trying to make a convert of me or a pervert of yourself?" (*P* 242); and Stephen is the one whose sexual interests are left most ambiguous.

> Yes. His face was handsome: and his body was strong and hard. . . . He felt then the sufferings of women, the weaknesses of their bodies and souls: and would shield them with a strong and resolute arm and bow his mind to them.
> Away then: it is time to go. A voice spoke softly . . . bidding him go and telling him that his friendship was coming to an end. (*P* 245)

Stephen here follows the cultural script of placing the figure of woman between himself and his homosocial counterpart, just as he did with the swimmers and with Lynch, but beside Cranly she disappears into a vapid generality. By the end of the passage, in fact, it is hard not to see Cranly as Stephen's *real* object of sexual rivalry rather than a rival for the favor of another. As if to emphasize this reversal, when an actual woman appears further on, mediating "the strife of their minds," Stephen perceives her in transgendered terms; he sees her "small and slender as a boy" and hears her voice "frail and high as a boy's" (*P* 244). That the transferential woman now figures in Stephen's mind as boyish, a Bertie Tallon in reverse, reflects the preeminence of Cranly in his affections.

Finally, if Cranly initiates the physical contact in this encounter, Stephen is the one who responds positively to it. Moreover, having eroticized the priestly office since his time at Clongowes, Stephen insistently positions Cranly as a cleric manqué, a priest without portfolio or "the power to absolve" (*P* 178). In this way, Stephen can himself experience sexual frisson without institutional subordination. This may in fact be the key to Stephen's relationship with Cranly. In order that Stephen may resolve the trauma of the doubtful or duplicitous "touch" of his masters, such as Father Dolan, he enlists Cranly to extend to him the "touch" of a doubtful mastery, a touch that elicits a less immediate sense of dread. But precisely because Stephen can be so "thrilled by his touch" (*P* 247), Cranly embodies the most profound danger yet to Stephen's heterosexual self-conception. He not only represents the persistence of Stephen's religious sensibility in, and despite, his apostasy ("Your mind," he says, "is supersaturated with the religion in which you say you disbelieve" [*P* 240]); he also represents the persistence of its homoerotic attractions in and despite Stephen's aesthetics of Woman.

As the vessel of this persistence, I would suggest, Cranly plays *the* decisive role in motivating Stephen's self-exile. For at this point Stephen can only reconstruct the aesthetic mission as a safely heterosexual adventure by making its

completion somehow contingent upon separating himself from the "one person ... who would be more than a friend" (*P* 247), however much Stephen
would like to project that sentiment onto Cranly alone. Surely it is no coincidence that this pivotal conversation with Cranly breaks off, assuring Stephen's
departure, just when the possibility of homosexual attraction and involvement,
which has been diverted, displaced, and misrecognized throughout the novel, is
finally, if inconclusively, broached. Stephen's last unanswered question, "Of
whom are you speaking" (*P* 247), virtually epitomizes homosexual panic as a
neurotic obsession with the identity, status, and location of homo-hetero difference and virtually defines Stephen as its captive.

III

Can we extend this diagnosis to Joyce and to his leave-taking? This question cannot but return us to the pragmatic riddles concerning self-revelation and fictional representation introduced at the outset of this essay. The unstable differential equation between Stephen and Joyce, wherein the portrait necessarily
distorts or disguises the author in the process of portraying him, means that fictional self-exposure is by its nature a refuge as well, a way of confessing, as
Stanislaus Joyce said, "in a foreign language" (quoted in *JJII*). Such self-portraiture requires no deliberate forms of secrecy, none of the "lies" or evasions with
which Joyce charged Wilde, for it disrupts the logic of the closet itself, insofar as
any space or practice of concealment is predicated on some theoretically decidable onto-epistemological difference between the referencing subject *(sujet
d'enunciation)* and the subject of reference *(sujet d'enonce)*.[36] Not only does the
generic hybridity of *A Portrait* (fictive autobiography/"factive" bildungsroman)
work to inmix these textual positions, but so too does the novel's peculiarly
claustrophobic *style indirect libre,* which persistently confounds, without wholly
conflating the perspectives of narrator and protagonist.

The effect of these overlaid strategies of rhetorical foreshortening is to disable the boundaries between autobiographical expression and elision, display
and dissimulation. First of all, any disclosure Joyce might have packed or wished
to pack into his depiction of Stephen, including the stirrings of homoerotic desire and discomfort, ultimately prove indistinguishable from the exercise of poetic license as a mode of denial—which is not to say that denial is necessarily all,
or even a part, of what such disclosures in fact amount to. By the same logic,
Joyce's anatomy of Stephen's defensive or self-closeting strategies, particularly
those involving homosexual panic and artistry, remains indeterminably an act
of self-exposure, based on the implied correlation between author and alter ego,
and an act of self-mystification, based on the generic incertitude surrounding
the nature, degree, currency, and reliability of that correlation. In either case, the
(epistemological) indeterminacies of Joyce's sexual self-representation encode
a certain (ontological) instability of authorial selfhood as their originating con-

dition, an irreducible slippage between the ego and alter ego that implies the alterity of the ego itself.

From an epistemological standpoint, the distinctive generic modality of Joyce's novel—detailed, accurate, yet decisively fictional self-portraiture—makes the sexual candor that Joyce demanded of other writers easier, less risky, because it makes the credulity of the reader impossible. *A portrait of the artist is an open closet.* But from an ontological standpoint, the generic modality of *A Portrait* shows the sexual candor that Joyce recommended to be harder, more problematic, because it altogether subverts the Imaginary author, the illusion of a unitary identity, whose authentic, interior core can be alternately expressed or occulted. *An open closet betokens a liminal subject-construction, one that lives both within and beyond psychic enclosure.*

The last thesis is perhaps best illustrated by drawing the contrast between my concept of the open closet and D. A. Miller's famous construct of the open secret. Defining the open secret, Miller writes that "in a mechanism reminiscent of Freudian disavowal, we know perfectly well that the secret is known, but we nevertheless must persist, however ineptly, in guarding it."[37] We do not simply hide a given piece of intelligence, in other words, we conceal our collective knowledge of that intelligence, allowing the secret to pass in a paradoxically un-secreted state. Our motives for doing so would seem to go to the very structure of subjectivity in liberal bourgeois society. Only the withholding of secrets en-ables each of us to build and consolidate a privatized interior space that counts as our "real" estate, that is, our proper self and our property. The openness of these secrets, in turn, enables us to signal the existence of this still-inviolate space to others, thereby securing the social value without which our (self-)pos-session would have no reality. As Miller puts it, the open secret, far from col-lapsing the binarisms established by the dynamics of secrecy—"private/public, inside/outside, subject/object"—instead "attests to their phantasmatic recov-ery."[38] It performs this function by sustaining within its discursive form that ap-parently decidable difference between the inner substance of personal identity *(sujet d'enunciation)* and the dissembling manifest practices that guarantee it *(sujet d'enonce).* The pretense of ignorance at work in the open secret offers phantasmatic confirmation that there is indeed something to be known about the subject, the importance of which is proportionate to the energy expended in hiding it. Since the Victorian era, the epicenter of this "secret subject" has typ-ically been the complex itinerary of his or her sexual desire.[39]

In "Oscar Wilde: The Poet of *Salomé*," Joyce briefly anticipates Miller's analysis, arguing that the Wilde affair pivoted less on the commission of sexual misdemeanors than on the violation of the (homo)sexual as open secret.

> Whether he was innocent or guilty of the charges brought against him, he undoubtedly was a scapegoat. His greater crime was that he had caused a scandal in England, and it is well known that the English authorities did

everything possible to persuade him to flee before they issued an order for his arrest. An employee of the Ministry of Internal Affairs stated during the trial that, in London alone, there are more than 20,000 persons under police surveillance, but they remain footloose until they provoke a scandal. (*CW* 203–4)

And yet as we have seen, and as the wording of this passage bears out, Joyce participates in the dynamic of open secrecy through his reliance on strategies of euphemism and "Freudian disavowal," which lay a discreet silence over the erotic practices he addresses even *as* he addresses them, and even as he denounces the "secrecy and restrictions" surrounding them (*CW* 204). As such, Joyce's essay would seem to exemplify the power of the open secret to extend indefinitely the regime of the closet by circulating speech itself as a form of censorship.

In *A Portrait of the Artist,* Joyce reverses the terms of this discursive economy. Instead of a rhetorical form, the open secret, which establishes the subject's essential truths in the act of pretending to disguise them, Joyce fashions a rhetorical form, the open closet, which suspends or undermines such truths in the act of pretending to divulge them. Whereas the former mode centers the subject in terms of its unspoken desire, the immanent signified of its sexuality, the latter decenters the subject across a chain of signifying positions in which its desire is articulated. In the first case, the subject harbors a profound mystery to be exposed; in the second, the subject instances a radical uncertainty that remains flush with the text of its exposition—hidden, if you will, in plain sight. To illustrate the open secret in literary practice, Miller observes that Dickens, having "abandoned autobiography for the Novel," "encrypts" his secrets in the figure of David Copperfield.[40] Joyce, by contrast, having reclaimed autobiography for the novel, uses Dedalus to "screen," in both contradictory senses of the word, his own sexual desire and anxiety. *Dedalus's sexual ambivalences veil Joyce's while putting them on display and display them while putting them under a veil of doubt.* The open closet consists precisely in this practice of double inscription, and, as such, it orchestrates what, in Lacanian parlance, might be called a sexuality of the "not all,"[41] that is, a sexuality that defeats the categories of identity on which it continues to depend or, to turn things around, a sexuality that is framed by categories that cannot finally contain it.

On the one hand, this "not all" is the enabling condition of *jouissance,* the extreme verge of erotic intensity which, far from consolidating subjectivity, effracts it.[42] On the other hand, it is structurally homologous with the proximate, the rigid enabling condition of Joyce's sexual unease and Stephen's homosexual panic. Both the proximate and the "not all" figure border zones where the fundamental psychosymbolic difference, the difference between sameness and otherness, collapses. *Jouissance* registers this interval as a site of ecstasy; the proximate registers it as a site of anxiety. The distinction between them, in other words, is purely evaluative, and it hinges on the relative affective priority ac-

corded the jointly compelling aims of finding oneself and losing oneself, of so-
lidifying one's social identity and of escaping that identity to engage some form
of alterity.

A Portrait of the Artist does not so much reflect as enact an ideological slide
along this continuum. At the narrative level, Joyce caricatures his already exaggerated concerns about his own status (sexual, artistic, class, etc.) in a figure
undecidably "identified" with himself. At the narrational level, through his
distinctive use of the free indirect style, he continues to participate in the perspective being caricatured. To use the familiar terms of Joyce criticism, by maintaining a certain stylistic "sympathy" with his self-portrait, Joyce becomes subject to the very "irony" he directs at Dedalus. He thereby challenges, while
continuing to acknowledge, his egoistic obsession, and in this very process, he
shifts from the more defensive address of his letters and essays to a more ex-
pansive one. For the subject of self-portraiture that he winds up projecting is
not at all a closed, coherent identity but an ongoing transference between
painter and sitter, authorial and alter ego, voice and image—a subject in whom
there is perpetually something of the "not all." In a very real sense, then, Joyce is
"thrilled"—his subjectivity made to quiver or tremble—by the "touch" of his
own self-portrait. Stephen's narcissistic anxiety proves essential to Joyce's narcissistic *jouissance,* Stephen's homosexual panic indispensable to Joyce's open
closet. Joyce's strategy of disavowal, with which this essay began, is not so much
dissolved or transcended in *A Portrait* as it is internalized and sublated. Instead
of disavowing the homoerotic as an intimate threat or disturbance to his identity, Joyce disavows the identity so disturbed and threatened, owning and disowning Stephen Dedalus in the same literary motion.

NOTES

1. Richard Ellmann notes Joyce's association of homosexuality with public-school
education (*SL* 74, 96). Joyce's opinion that English public schools were an incubator of
homoerotic passion and practice conformed both with the popular sense of things—as
described by Ed Cohen in *Talk on the Wilde Side: Toward a Genealogy of a Discourse on
Male Sexualities* (New York: Routledge, 1993), 38—and with the writings of prominent
contemporary sexologists and commentators, including Ellis, Symonds, Carpenter,
Stead, Benson, and Jerome. See Havelock Ellis and J. A. Symonds, *Sexual Inversion* (London: Wilson and MacMillan, 1897), 37, 138, 141, and 267 (where they cite Ulrichs, the father of the inversion model, to the same effect); J. A. Symonds, "A Problem in Modern
Ethics," in *Studies in Sexual Inversion* (privately printed, 1931), 112; Edward Carpenter, *The
Intermediate Sex* (1896; London: Mitchell Kennedy, 1912), 85. Joyce apparently read all of
these books. See Richard Brown, *James Joyce and Sexuality* (Cambridge: Cambridge University Press, 1985), 78–107. For Stead, Benson, and Jerome, see Alan Sinfield, *The Wilde
Century* (New York: Columbia University Press, 1994), 65.
2. "Negation," in *The Standard Edition of the Complete Psychological Works of Sig-*

mund Freud, ed. and trans. James Strachey, 24 vols. (London: Hogarth Press and the Institute of Psycho-Analysis, 1953–74), 19:235–39.

3. Here again, Joyce's attitude consists with contemporary sexual studies, echoing in particular Edward Carpenter in *The Intermediate Sex,* 90–91. See also Richard Dellamora, *Masculine Desire* (Chapel Hill: University of North Carolina Press, 1990), 208: "As male homosexuality became visible in public and in texts during the 1890's 'the emphasis on gender construction of the British male' that characterized the schools began to be perceived as problematic."

4. Jonathan Dollimore, *Sexual Dissidence* (New York: Oxford University Press, 1991), 14–17.

5. Eve Kosofsky Sedgwick, *Epistemology of the Closet* (Berkeley and Los Angeles: University of California Press, 1990), 182–212, and *Between Men* (New York: Columbia University Press, 1985), 83–96. On page 195 of *Epistemology,* Sedgwick doubts whether the "arguably homosexual" objects of her own analysis properly bear out or embody the experience of homosexual panic, which "is proportioned to the non-homosexual identified elements of . . . men's character." Accordingly, she continues, "if Barrie and James are obvious authors with whom to begin an analysis of male homosexual panic, the analysis I am offering here must be inadequate to the degree that it does not eventually work just as well—even better—for Joyce, Faulkner, Lawrence, Yeats, etc." In this respect, my essay can be seen as a continuation of Sedgwick's project, an attempt not only to explore Joyce's writing by way of her conception but also to demonstrate the adequacy of her conception by way of Joyce's writing.

6. Sedgwick, *Epistemology of the Closet,* 184.

7. Sedgwick, *Between Men,* 25–26.

8. Sedgwick, *Epistemology of the Closet,* 185.

9. Dellamora, *Masculine Desire,* 195.

10. Sedgwick, *Epistemology of the Closet,* 185.

11. These critics include James F. Carens, "A Portrait of the Artist as a Young Man," in *A Companion to Joyce Studies,* ed. Zack Bowen and James F. Carens (Westport, Conn.: Greenwood Press, 1984), 255–359; Jean Kimble, "Freud, Leonardo, and Joyce," in *The Seventh of Joyce,* ed. Bernard Benstock (Bloomington: Indiana University Press, 1982), 57–73; Chester Anderson, "Baby Tuckoo: Joyce's Features of Infancy," in *Approaches to Joyce's Portrait: Ten Essays,* ed. Thomas Staley (Pittsburgh: University of Pittsburgh Press, 1970), 136–42; and Sheldon Brivic, *Joyce between Freud and Jung* (Port Washington, Wash.: Kennikat, 1980), 28–29, 47.

12. Oscar Wilde, *The Picture of Dorian Gray,* in *The First Collected Edition of the Works of Oscar Wilde,* ed. Robert Ross, vol. 12 (1908; London: Dawsons, 1969), 8.

13. I will be treating D. A. Miller's concept of the open secret at length later in the essay. See *The Novel and the Police* (Berkeley and Los Angeles: University of California Press, 1988), 192–220.

14. For the Dorians and Greek love, see J. A. Symonds, "A Problem in Greek Ethics," in Ellis and Symonds, *Sexual Inversion,* 179–86. For a history for the Cretans and *paiderastia,* see 183. For a history and anatomy of the Hellenistic movement in its divers phases—sociopolitical, aesthetic, and erotic—see Linda Dowling, *Hellenism and Homosexuality* (Ithaca, N.Y.: Cornell University Press, 1994). For Daedalus's checkered career, see Mark Morford, *Classical Mythology,* 2d ed. (New York: McKay, 1977), 394–96.

15. In his own words, Wilde "invented that magnificent flower," the green carnation,

as a "work of art." Richard Ellmann, *Oscar Wilde* (New York: Vintage, 1987), 424–25. The green carnation became a symbol of aestheticism memorialized in Robert Hichens, *The Green Carnation* (New York: Dover, 1970). According to Alan Sinfield, with *The Green Carnation*, "The consolidation of queer identity began to take shape around Wilde" (*The Wilde Century*, 118).

16. Elaine Showalter correctly contends that the term *queer* had homosexual connotations before the yellow nineties (*Sexual Anarchy* [New York: Viking, 1990], 112). All subsequent references to and uses of the term will assume a distinct homosexual valence. For the homoerotic resonances of the above passage, see also Leonard Albert, "Gnomonology: Joyce's 'The Sisters,'" *James Joyce Quarterly* 27 (winter 1990): 360–61; Brivic, *Between Freud and Jung*, 24; Kimball, "Freud, Leonardo, and Joyce," 66.

17. For this information, I am grateful to Vicki Mahaffey, who gathered it on a visit to Clongowes in 1992.

18. This dynamic of proximate-ness played itself out quite humorously in Joyce's indirect dialogue with H. G. Wells. Wells objected to the "cloacal obsession" of *A Portrait*. Joyce's reply to Frank Budgen reveals the kind of ethnoracial dichotomy that we have been adducing: "Why it's Wells' countrymen who build waterclosets wherever they go." But in a private comment to another friend, Joyce acknowledged "How right Wells was" (*JJII* 414).

19. James F. Carens speaks of the Clongowes episode as denoting an element of sexual ambivalence in Stephen. "A Portrait of the Artist as a Young Man," 319.

20. This is what Freud means by the omnipotence of the unconscious wish, a crucial motif everywhere in his work. See, in particular, *Totem and Taboo*, in *Standard Edition*, 13:94–124.

21. Trevor L. Williams, "Dominant Ideologies: The Production of Stephen Dedalus," in *The Augmented Ninth*, ed. Bernard Benstock (Syracuse: Syracuse University Press, 1988), 316.

22. See Richard Dellamora, *Masculine Desire*, 199; and Sinfield, *The Wilde Century*, 110. I use the hybrid term sexual/gender inversion here advisedly. Although George Chauncey Jr. has argued that some distinction between sexual and gender inversion had evolved by the late nineteenth century (see "From Sexual Inversion to Homosexuality," *Salmagundi* 58–59 [1982–83]: 114–46), all of the contemporaneous studies that I will be citing exhibit a hopeless entangling or conflation of the two categories. One outstanding example of this tendency can be found in the influential nineteenth-century study, Albert Moll, *Perversions of the Sex Instinct* (Newark: Julian, 1931), 63–77. Moll was even known to quote a male homosexual as declaring, "We are all women." See Ellis and Symonds, *Sexual Inversion*, 119. Another outstanding example can be found in the work of Ellis and Symonds themselves, who proclaim, "There is a distinctly general, though not universal, tendency for sexual inverts to approach the feminine type, either in psychic disposition or physical constitution, or both." *Sexual Inversion*, 119.

23. Michel Foucault, *The History of Sexuality*, vol. 1, *An Introduction*, trans. Robert Hurley (New York: Pantheon, 1978), 43.

24. Christopher Craft, *Another Kind of Love* (Berkeley and Los Angeles: University of California Press, 1994), 77.

25. Quoted in Sinfield, *The Wilde Century*, 110.

26. Carl Westphal is quoted in Craft, *Another Kind of Love*, 35. See Ellis and

Symonds, *Sexual Inversion*; Carpenter, *The Intermediate Sex*; Sigmund Freud, *Three Essays on Sexuality*, in *Standard Edition*, 7:136–48; Richard von Krafft-Ebing, *Psychopathia Sexualis* (1892; New York: Stern and Day, 1965), 186–294. The sex/gender inversion model is also espoused by somewhat lesser known sexologists such as Tarnowsky, who differentiated inborn from acquired inversion; Gley, who "suggested that a female brain was combined with masculine glands"; and Magnan, who "hypothesized a woman's brain in a man's body." See Symonds, *Studies in Sexual Inversion*, 126, 135–36. For Joyce's reading in this area, see R. Brown, *James Joyce and Sexuality*, 78–107. Brown claims that Joyce's sexological views most closely approximated those of Havelock Ellis, perhaps the most comprehensive exponent of sex/gender inversion. One notorious incident in particular confirms Joyce's subscription to the gender inversion model. According to Ellmann, he "scandalized a homosexual poet," Siegfried Lang, "by placing two fingers in [a pair of miniature ladies'] drawers and walking them towards the unhappy poet" (*JJII* 438), a taunt that recalls the phrase "lady highkickers" (*SL* 74).

27. Krafft-Ebing, *Psychopathia Sexualis*, 223; Richard Burton, *The Book of the Thousand Nights and a Night* (1884; New York: Limited Editions, 1934), 6:3771–73.

28. Christopher Craft remarks that despite Freud's "deconstruction" of any "natural object of desire" in *Three Essays*, the "inversion metaphor . . . nonetheless continued to operate with impressive immunity throughout Freud's subsequent writings on homosexuality" (*Another Kind of Love*, 37–38). In 1913, Ellis gave a major address that aimed to dissever "inverted" behavior, sexual and otherwise, from same-sex desire, but he went on to reassert the connection two years later in the third edition of *Sexual Inversion*. See Chauncey, "Sexual Inversion to Homosexuality," 122–25.

Symonds saw Ulrichs's inversion theory as based on a "somewhat grotesque and metaphysical conception of nature," but he embraced it as an antidote to the alternative degeneration model (*Studies in Sexual Inversion*, 140). Carpenter likewise both downgrades Ulrichs's ideas and the inversion metaphor they popularized and yet entertains it and finally celebrates the "normal type of the Urian man," who fits Ulrichs's conception perfectly, "possessing thoroughly masculine powers of mind and body [and] combin[ing] them with the tenderer and more emotional soul nature of a woman—and sometimes to a remarkable degree" (*The Intermediate Sex*, 27 and 31). On this point, I dissent from Tim Dean's reading of Carpenter in "Paring His Fingernails: Homosexuality and Joyce's Impersonalist Aesthetic," later in this volume.

29. Sedgwick, *Epistemology of the Closet*, 87. Her argument is borne out in the words of Ellis and Symonds themselves: "Even in inversion, the imperative need for a certain sexual opposition still rules in full force" (*Sexual Inversion*, 130).

30. For Ellis and Symonds, to feel as a man toward an object of affection means taking the active role in sexual relations; to feel as a woman means taking the passive role (*Sexual Inversion*, 63). Freud identifies male inversion with sexual passivity in "Leonardo Da Vinci and a Memory of His Childhood" (1910), *Standard Edition*, 11:86–87. Later, Freud actually declared of the Wolf Man, "He understood now that active was the same as masculine, while passive was the same as feminine." *The History of an Infantile Neurosis, Standard Edition*, 17:47.

31. Kimberly Devlin reads the director's elliptical swipe at the Capuchin dress as a "test" intended to ascertain whether Stephen's interest in holy orders might be motivated by homosexual or transvestite impulses, a gambit that is "scandalously reinterpreted" in

the Butt and Taff episode of the *Wake* dream as a sexual overture on the part of the father. "In the *Wake*," she concludes, "the patriarch's flaws are located not in any mere intellectual limitations, as they are in *A Portrait* (see *P* 156), but rather in . . . his repressed and unacknowledged interest in the sexually taboo." But the director is, in fact, uncertain as to whether Stephen has any interest in the clerical life at all, so that as a test his unspoken stricture on *les jupes* seems premature. Moreover, as I will presently demonstrate, the patriarch's flaws are only restricted to "mere intellectual limitations" in *A Portrait* so far as Stephen's *conscious* mind is concerned; unconsciously, Stephen registers and reacts to intimations of homoeroticism in the priest's words. The interview, in other words, is not just "scandalously reinterpreted" as a sexual overture in the *Wake*, it is scandalously interpreted as such all along. See Kimberly Devlin, *Wandering and Return in "Finnegans Wake"* (Princeton: Princeton University Press, 1991), 23.

32. Speaking more generally, Sheldon Brivic contends that "it is because heterosexuality is a reaction against homosexuality in our artist that it is held so intensely" (*Between Freud and Jung*, 47).

33. Sedgwick, *Epistemology of the Closet*, 184–85.

34. Elsewhere in *The Renaissance*, Pater treats Abelard's nominally heterosexual desire for Eloise as a cover for same-sex desire, prompting Wilde to comment, in "The Critic as Artist," "We have whispered the secret of our love beneath the cowl of Abelard." The "cowl" that E.C. is wearing during the previously discussed tram episode (*P* 70, 222) may well owe something to the "cowl of Abelard," especially since Stephen makes a cowl of his blanket during the composition of his "villanelle" to E.C., which confesses "the secret of [his] love," under the cover(s) of a feminine identification (*P* 221–22). See Dellamora, *Masculine Desire*, 152–53 for all relevant quotations.

Another crucial articulation of triangulated same-sex desire that Joyce certainly read is Stoker's *Dracula*. This Irish novel is organized from start to finish around the homosocial/homophobic relations between the count and his adversaries (Jonathan Harker, Seward, Van Helsing, etc.) as mediated by the novel's two women, Mina Harker and Lucy Westenra. Bram Stoker, *Dracula*, in *The Essential Dracula*, ed. Leonard Wolf (New York: Plume, 1993).

35. An outstanding exception is James Carens, who takes specific issue with Ellmann, arguing that Stephen is "drawn" to Cranly and partakes of "the current of latent homosexuality in the scene" ("Portrait of the Artist," 304, 323).

36. Reading this essay in its earlier, shorter version, Tim Dean construed my formulation of the open closet as "a form of evasion or hypocrisy," a not unreasonable interpretation that I try to correct herein. See his essay "Paring His Fingernails: Homosexuality and Joyce's Impersonal Aesthetic" in this volume. I am, accordingly, obligated to him for pressing me to clarify my argument and thus helping to instigate a rather extensive revision/expansion of the essay's concluding movement. For the *sujet d'enunciation-sujet d'énonce* distinction, see Jacques Lacan, *Ecrits* (Paris: Editions de Seuil, 1966), 800–801.

37. Miller, *Novel and Police*, 207.

38. Ibid.

39. Miller explicitly equates the "open secret" with the "secret subject" and follows Foucault in centering that subject in terms of sexuality. See *Novel and Police*, 205; and Foucault, *An Introduction*, 69–70.

40. Miller, *Novel and Police,* 199.

41. For Jacques Lacan's concept of the "not all," see his essay "God and the Jouis-sance of the Woman," in *Feminine Sexuality,* ed. Juliet Mitchell and Jacqueline Rose (New York: Norton, 1982), 134–48.

42. I am indebted for this thread of the argument to Tim Dean, "Hart Crane's Poetics of Privacy," *American Literary History* 8 (spring 1996): 83–109.

"The Nothing Place"
Secrets and Sexual Orientation in Joyce

Garry Leonard

What was after the universe? Nothing. But was there anything around the universe to show where it stopped before the nothing place began? (*P* 16)

A secrecy that must always be rigorously maintained in the face of a secret that everybody already knows . . . is the very condition that entitles me to my subjectivity in the first place.[1]

Secrets, silent, stony, sit in the dark palaces of both our hearts: secrets weary of their tyranny: Tyrants, willing to be dethroned. (*U* 2.170–72)

I

In Joyce, it is right there in the beginning with Father Flynn: what's Flynn's secret? What are the sisters hiding? What's Old Cotter not saying? It is against all this secrecy that the narrator has a sense of him-"self." Because he does not know it, it does not know him, and so "it" is one thing, and "he" another. And as fascinated as he is to experience his own interiority in this way, he is equally fascinated with the liminal area between the "me" and the "not me" it seems to demarcate: "It filled me with fear, and yet I longed to be nearer to it and to look upon its deadly work" (*D* 9). The "it," in this case, is said to be the sound of the word *paralysis,* but it is the barrier between the word and the world, the self and the other, that the boy both wishes to shore up and, *at the same time,* feels imprisoned by. This same curiosity about the liminal—about where one thing begins and another ends—will exist in him as inarticulate affect when he is falling asleep (another, literal, liminal state) and he feels him-"self" recede to the nodal point where the disorganized state of the Imaginary order blurs into the supposed certitude of the Symbolic order: "I felt my soul receding into some pleasant and vicious region; and there again I found it waiting for me" (*D* 11). The "it," experienced as a borderline between self and other, then becomes a secret: "It began to confess to me in a murmuring voice" (*D* 11). The boy's sense of his own interiority is indistinguishable from his sense of secrecy. The difference between who he is and who he is not is the difference between what is known of him and what he alone knows.

Lacan's notion of the ego as intrinsically paranoid is nicely realized in the tone of this story because the secret is the "thing" around the universe to show where it stops, and "the nothing place"—or what I would call the fantasy of subjectivity—begins. The boy fears, on a constant basis, that what he knows in secret will become known to others, and such a discovery will dissolve, or at least distort, his sense of what demarcates the "me" from the "not me." It is how secrets function in the fantasy of subjectivity, not what they "mean" that Joyce always features. During intersubjective exchanges, such as the one between Gretta and Gabriel, secrets appear, retroactively, to grant positionality to subjects such that they either experience their "selves" as beings who signify (conscious creatures), if they are in control of the secret, or as ones who are signified (creatures of the unconscious), if they are not. It is Gretta's unexpectedly grounded presence as something with integrity that baffles Gabriel—"he longed to be master of her strange mood"—and it is a dissolution of his own subjectivity that follows upon learning what he takes to be her secret: "His own identity was fading out into a grey impalpable world" (D 217, 223). In what I will argue is a direct parallel, Freud, like Joyce, will draw attention away from the presumed "content" of the dream (its secret) to the form the dream takes (which makes it seem there is a secret, when, in fact, there is not).

To accumulate secrets is to feel an increase in interiority, which is also to feel like a subject capable of producing meaning and constructing interpretations. To have secrets discovered, or to feel pressured to confess them, is to feel increasingly subject to the Symbolic order in general, and the law in particular, and thus to collapse into a posture of feeling judged rather than able to judge others. As Foucault has argued, sexuality itself, in the twentieth century, also became aligned with secrecy, not because there *was* any secret about it, but because positing sexuality *as* secret gave license for various "official" discourses to implant it, under the pretence of seeking it out. And then, suddenly, science and pedagogy are there to help, and a goal is established toward which the subject must steer, and now sexuality has an "orientation," and soon after that taxonomies of perversion and normalcy are established to help us first declare, and then maintain, our "sexual orientation." What I will be suggesting is that "sexual orientation" is much more about positionality and secrecy than it is about desire.

Indeed, as Žižek has pointed out, "Sexuality is the only drive that is in itself hindered, perverted. . . . sexuality strives outwards and overflows the adjoining domains precisely because it cannot find satisfaction in itself, because it never attains its goal."[2] And so the question might be asked this way: how can something with no attainable goal have an intrinsic "orientation"? How can we orient something that never arrives anywhere? We can't, and so the next question is why do we try, and this is a bit more easily answered; "sexuality," according to Foucault, is "an especially dense transfer point for relations of power."[3] Mapping sexuality is a way for knowledge and power to become mutually and interpenetratively supportive and to mask *the production* of sexuality as a "discovery." "When you entrust someone with a mission," Lacan suggests, "the aim is not what he brings back, but the itinerary he must take."[4] Sexual "orientation" is the way to assign the drive an itinerary, and then to chart its progress, on a "normal"/"perverse" axis, and thus create an excuse, and suggest a method, for accessing the subject's presumably sacrosanct "interiority" under the guise of merely accessing it in order to correct it.

The exercise of power made possible by the establishment of "sexual orientation" also makes secrecy into a sort of currency: some secrets are worth more than others, and, most specific to my purpose in this essay, an attraction to someone of the same sex becomes a secret if one does not disclose it, and a perversion if one does. In the historical period of the twentieth century, whether one is attracted to a member of the same sex, and to what extent, is very much "knowledge," and, because it is not a part of legally recognized rituals of (heterosexual) courtship, knowledge that it is felt needful to cover in "secrecy." But, as Sedgwick's notion of the "homosocial" makes clear, same-sex desire *is a continuum* with no real markers other than what is imposed by a given "science" in order to adhere to, and help constitute, the rules of intelligibility operating in a given culture.[5]

Sedgwick's idea of the homosocial makes it clear there is nothing absolute about any of these positions, and yet we still tend to label the apparent discomfort of a presumably "heterosexual" man in the presence of "homosexuality" as evidence of "latent" homosexuality. But does it continue to make sense to look for "latent" homosexuality if we shift our attention to a paradigm that suggests sexuality itself is produced, and "sexual orientation" is merely a construct that obscures this? Does a secret between a "heterosexual" man and a "heterosexual" woman function the same as a secret between two "homosexual" men, or a "homosexual" man and a "heterosexual" man? Or, in Joycean terms, is Stephen's evident uneasiness around Cranly and Mulligan nothing but evidence of "latent" homosexuality, or can it be looked at from the more nuanced perspective of him constantly shoring up the fantasy of his subjectivity by trying to hide what he knows from Cranly and Mulligan, even as he tries to know what they hide? Discovering another man's secret(s), while keeping one's own hidden, is a way of shoring up one's perceived interiority as a "masculine" subject by coolly decoding everything one's "friend" says with reference to the secret one has taken from him unawares.

This is precisely the situation Richard Rowan brings about when Bertha reports to him the progress of Robert's secret wooing of her. Richard's own sense of self is strengthened by knowing what Robert knows, only because he also knows Robert does not know that he knows. Richard becomes a sort of moral voyeur, watching Robert dissemble in a manner Robert presumes is successful, but which Richard sees, in fact, as completely transparent. Certainly a case can be made that Richard and Robert are physically attracted to each other. Irigaray's insights would suggest they each sublimate their desire for each other into their desire for the same woman. Their sexual relationship with her becomes, by proxy, a sexual relationship with each other, but the intervention of her body between them obscures this. And yet we are not solely dependent on the theories of Irigaray to argue this; it is pointed out by Joyce himself in the notes: "The bodily possession of Bertha by Robert, repeated often, would certainly bring into almost carnal contact the two men. Do they desire this? To be united, that is carnally through the person and body of Bertha as they cannot, without dissatisfaction and degradation—be united carnally man to man as man to woman?" (E 157). Added to Irigaray's insights, of course, this would be an argument positing latent homosexuality between Robert and Richard, and I don't want so much to refute this point of view as to draw some attention away from merely attempting to fix their "sexual orientation" somewhere on the continuum of the homosocial, and, instead, draw attention to how they are both trying to shore up a sense of their own interiority by trying to keep secrets from one another about the "true nature" of their relationship to Bertha and each other.

What is "true," in each instance—that is, true in the sense of confirming an inviolable sense of interiority, and thus of a subjectivity capable of producing meaning—is whatever secret yet remains after "all" has been divulged. Both Richard and Robert want to be in a position relative to Bertha about which the other man knows nothing. What Bertha knows is unimportant except to the extent that it relates to what she chooses to keep secret, and what she wishes to divulge, and to whom. While, for the moment, she has chosen to tell Richard "all," and not tell Robert she has done so, she might reverse that procedure and leave Richard in the dark. This, too, results in a "homosexual" attraction between Richard and Robert, almost by default, in the sense that neither desires Bertha so much for her erotic potentiality as they do for her capacity to secure the interiority of one man by helping him breach the interiority of another. For this reason, both the men admonish Bertha not on the subject of whom she might choose to have sexual intercourse with, but to which man will she offer herself as a place where he can deposit his secrets safely.

When Lacan suggests "the woman" can serve only as a catalyst for the fantasy of the masculine subject, this is not sexual fantasy as rehearsed in so-called pornography, but the fantasy of subjectivity itself. "The Woman" secures a man's interiority, but only in such a way as to appear to breach it again at some later point. The treacherous women in Western culture, from Lilith through Delilah and Duessa to the femmes fatales of film noir, chronicle the fatal moment when a woman who has helped a man produce a secret destroys his strength by exposing that secret to others. For Richard and Robert, what is really at stake is not their relationship to Bertha, but each of their relationships to their own ideal ego. This is most evident, perhaps, when Richard admits he both wanted Robert "not to do anything . . . secret against me" and, at the same time, "longed to be betrayed by you and by her . . . secretly" (*E* 88). When Robert admits he "acted in the dark, secretly" and asks, "[H]ave you the courage to allow me to act freely?" (*E* 89), Richard makes it clear between whom the fight really lies: "A duel—between us?" (*E* 89). And the duel would not center around who Bertha gave her body to, but which man's secrets she consents to protect at the expense of the other man's sense of his own interiority (and, by extension, his relative position in the Symbolic order, and his "reality"). Vying for position over who is to have secrets and who is to be divested of them is the whole point. The content of the secret is as irrelevant as the manifest content in a dream.

The point, in either case, is to determine how the structure of the secret permits a given conscious position, just as the point of dream interpretation is to determine how the structure of the dream denotes an unconscious position. In this context, secrets can be seen as *points de capitons*—the buttons that fix upholstery to the frame of furniture, giving it a "shape"—and "sexual orientation" is the label given to this shape. "Heterosecrecy" often appears to involve a masculine subject producing a secret with a feminine subject in a manner that promotes a feeling of autonomy and self-origination—but only as long as the secret is kept "in confidence" by the feminine subject. "Homosecrecy" involves the competitive trafficking of secrets between and among men for fiscal and psychological gain at the other's expense, using the feminine subject as the repository of secrets, where men seek to make confidential deposits and illegal withdrawals.

So there may be an attraction between Robert and Richard that fits the so-called orientation of homosexuality, but, at the same time, and separate from this, it is a superior sense of consciousness that they both are vying for. When Richard confronts Robert at the hour Robert had appointed to secretly meet Bertha, Robert offers to tell him all: "Let me speak frankly with you; let me tell you everything" (*E* 74). But Richard's trump card is to deny Robert even the appearance of having anything to say that Richard does not already know: "I know everything. I have known for some time" (*E* 74). As Joyce remarked in the notes, the only way for Robert to regain the upper hand is to "suggest that he knew from the first that Richard was aware of his conduct and that he himself was being watched and that he persisted because he had to and because he wished to see to what length Richard's silent forbearance would go" (*E* 157). In Lacanian terms, the modern subject is reacting against the increasing sense of having been produced by the Symbolic order and is struggling to recapture the Cartesian position of one who produces. If the modern subject cannot produce his own reality reliably, then, at least by knowing something someone else does not, he can participate in the production of their reality and gain some measure of relief against the twentieth-century inversion of Cartesian consciousness, exhaustively cataloged, in different ways, first by Nietzsche, Freud, and Marx, and more recently by Derrida, Lacan, and Foucault, where consciousness becomes an effect, rather than a cause, and both desire and psychic interiority become retroactive constructs rather than a priori phenomena. On an existential level, it is the Hollywood equivalent of actors who hope one day to direct.

In Lacan's essay on Poe's "The Purloined Letter," Lacan reads the movement of the letter from one person to another as an allegory for the way a signifier moves from subject to subject, always determining that subject's "reality" for the length of time the subject possesses it. The subject may experience acquiring the signifier as the fortuitous possession of a secret others do not know, but, inevitably, there is a more comprehensive secret, unknown to this subject, at which point the very signifier that guaranteed "reality" serves to systematically distort it. The precise content of the letter is irrelevant; it is its function as that which creates positionality for those who take it, those who lose it, and those who know nothing of it, that we are invited to watch, and to watch shift, every time the letter changes hands. Thus, it is not the content of the letter that persuades the minister that the queen wishes to keep it secret from the king, but merely her furtive attempt to hide it.

The letter in Poe's story, as it moves from person to person, also moves from the register of heterosecrecy to homosecrecy, in the following manner: If the queen had shown no desire to hide the letter, the minister might have read it and still had no idea that it might profit him to steal it. But his observant habit of noticing what people seem anxious to hide (a good psychoanalyst, indeed!) allows him to stumble on a point of secrecy in a marriage and steal the queen's ability to choose to withhold it from the attention of the king. It is precisely this situation Richard Rowan is anxious to prevent by making it clear he is prepared to hear anything Bertha has done, and the only wrong act she can permit is not to tell him what that is. The queen's secret and the minister's theft are not about passion but about power, and this may be a way to historicize homosecrecy in the twentieth century, where one man's loss (the king's) is another man's gain (the minister's).

But we need to be more precise about what this power is: it is the power to constitute knowledge, to formulate discourse, and thus make things happen in one way rather than another (that is to say, a Foucauldian notion of power). In heterosecrecy, what is at stake is the right to produce meaning *from a specific position,* a political position invested with power, such as a king, a judge, a priest. What is at stake in homosecrecy, however, is the protection of the right to produce meaning *at all,* from any subject position. The disclosure of a heterosecret might serve to demote one from an official capacity to a less powerful, unofficial capacity (the denouement of your everyday political scandal), but the disclosure of a homosecret demotes one from normal to abnormal, from a constituter of knowledge to an object of knowledge, from biological to pathological. If a heterosecret diminishes an individual, a homosecret silences them. As Showalter notes, the word *blackmail* at the turn of the century implied homosecrecy, because this kind of disclosure was so potentially devastating from a specifically financial point of view, apart from personal anguish, and so the willingness to pay to keep it secret, and the amount one might be willing to pay, was higher than any other sort of secret.[6] Indeed, blackmail is the nexus point where the role of the secret in the psychic economy and the role of the secret in the financial economy converge. Some secrets are worth more than others because the disclosure of them will cost the subject more.

In economic terms, heterosecrecy and the "style" it permits might lead to various forms of success, and the disclosure of the secret might cause some degree of forfeit, *but the legitimacy of heterosexuality as an authorized subject position is never challenged.* In homosecrecy, disclosure means a loss of signifying capacity *as a subject,* and the censure is not limited to a particular circumstance. At issue is one's legitimacy as a signifying subject. Significantly, in sensation novels, the terrible secret is often just that—illegitimacy—and, in the case of Sir Percival in Wilkie Collins's *The Woman in White,* disclosure of the secret would render all that "Sir" Percival has forfeit. The disclosure of homosecrecy, like the disclosure of illegitimacy, renders all contracts null and void, both at the moment and retroactively. Labeling the homosexual "orientation" as a perversion, rather than legislating the act of sodomy as illegal, is also a way of excluding the homosexual subject from a position as a meaning-producing subject within the Symbolic order.

The secret that discloses "illegitimacy"—whether in terms of biological heritage or sexual orientation—strips one of all that past contracts have secured and forbids the formation of contracts in the future, and there is no more poignant depiction of it than the fate of Oscar Wilde after his conviction. *All* human subjects must create the illusion of a foundation, origin, and naturalized legitimacy to become a "personality" with agency and the capacity to signify, but the exposure of homosecrecy makes all agency fraudulent, null and void, while the exposure of heterosecrecy casts certain acts of signification into doubt (including contracts) but does not extend so far as to deny the subject the ability to signify at all. For this reason it is much more effective, in terms of social control, to make people *feel* like perverts, rather than telling them that they are. The former strategy turns the mind against itself, while the latter tends to offer the mind, through the process by which it feels called upon to resist the label, an opportunity to know itself better than before, and be even less subject to social control in the future. In the case of Oscar Wilde, the attempt to make him feel perverse and thus flee to France (the British legal system seemed to assume one must follow the other) fails, and so, reluctantly, Wilde is held up to the public eye as a spectacular pervert and thrown in jail. Significantly, Joyce did not think for a moment Wilde was on trial for anything he was or anything he did; he was arrested because he refused to arrest himself: "His greater crime was that he had caused a scandal in England, and it is well known that the English authorities did everything possible to persuade him to flee before they issued an order for his arrest" (*CW* 204). In a rather impressive forecasting of Foucault, Joyce goes on to note there are, at any one time, thousands of people being watched by the law, and the point of the peculiarly modern gaze of the police is not to apprehend perversion, but to ascertain whether or not the individual is being sufficiently secretive regarding something the police already know about him (the current "don't ask / don't tell" policy in place in the American military is a similarly paradoxical gaze): "An employee of the Ministry of Internal Affairs stated during the trial that, in London alone, there are more than 20,000 persons under police surveillance, but they remain footloose until they provoke a scandal" (*CW* 204). Creating a scandal appears to mean becoming visible to an inconveniently large segment of society.

The movement from performing an act, to being seen as "oriented" by that act—that is to say, the movement from outlawing sodomy to making homosexuality "perverse," and, equally, the movement from permitting sexual intercourse between a man and woman to designating the heterosexual as normal—simultaneously inaugurates the binary perverse/normal that constitutes the notion of sexual orientation, and gives birth to "secrets," in a demonstrably *modern* sense, as that which creates the retroactive effect of "interiority," which can then be misrecognized as the illusory foundation of subjectivity. Subjectivity is an effect of relationship, not an essence, but producing a secret of one's own or stealing (disclosing) someone else's, permits the Enlightenment stance that consciousness is a central given from which all meaning is generated (i.e., "I think therefore I am"). If, as Foucault claims, the turn of the century invented the homosexual as a subject (where formerly there was only a description of an act: sodomy), then, at the same time, a modern form of secrecy came into being: I am/am not a homosexual/heterosexual. This sense of secrecy, in turn, constitutes the crucial component of *modern* subjectivity, because it is a nodal point around which a sense of interiority (inside/outside differentiation) congregates.

The subject in psychoanalysis, according to Lacan, tries to shore up the ego by uncovering and deciphering the secret that invests it with authority, in an attempt to unknot the symptom, but discovers instead the secret that there is no secret, and that the ego itself *is* a knot, *is* a symptom. Indeed, Lacan characterizes the ego as a virtual paradigm of mental illness. The point, when one submits to the edicts of ego psychology, is to develop a "personality" that functions better within the power regime of capitalism, and this is why Lacan dismisses so-called ego psychology as "the psychology of free enterprise."[7]

The patient is given instructions on how to appear more "normal" (i.e., salable), in a manner that does not draw attention to the fact of normality as a constructed category. When Basil Hallward does not want to tell Dorian's name to Lord Henry, he defends his decision thus: "I have grown to love secrecy. It seems to be the one thing that can make *modern* life mysterious or marvelous to us."[8] And so, Dorian Gray himself, the quintessential modern subject, keeps his secret portrait in the attic, and this secret permits him to appear charming and desirable to all who don't know what he knows. Later, it will turn out, there is nothing in the attic after all; he produced the secret and his personality simultaneously. Personality is the art of producing a secret in such a way as to make "the commonest thing delightful."

The modern "personality" can appear to be more valuable than it is, and this appearance, eventually, becomes the new value. As Lady Bracknell says of Algernon, he "is an extremely, I may almost say an ostentatiously, eligible young man. He has nothing but he looks everything." Formerly, in order to qualify as "someone," one needed to own property and come from a suitably impressive bloodline, which is to say the labor that produced one was evident. But with the rise of the mercantile class, a class able to make vast fortunes by advertising and marketing such packaged items as spurious health pills, one could also achieve upward social mobility by repackaging what used to be known as "character" (i.e., good breeding) into personality (i.e., style). Naturally, the art of posturing, because it was so effective at transcending social boundaries, came under attack as insincere by the very people whose boundaries were being transcended.

Wilde demonstrated that sincerity is the luxury of the inclusive—the self-affirming principle of people of wealth and property who control access to their own society. Sincerity, one might say, is in the eye of the key-holder. "The true mystery of the world is the visible, not the invisible," Lord Henry intones, and this is so because the secret is invisible and, like the unconscious itself, can be discerned only by way of its effect; it is not there, and that doesn't matter because it's point is to function as a placeholder for a presumed interiority, and not to "mean" anything. It is Dorian Gray (who really ought to know) who sounds a surprisingly Lacanian note; we are told he "used to wonder at the shallow psychology of those who conceive the ego in man as a thing simple, permanent, reliable, *and of one essence*. To him, man was a being with myriad lives and myriad sensations" (emphasis added). Which is to say his subjectivity is an effect of relationship.

With fascinating ambivalence, Joyce first gestures toward the "freak of nature" explanation for the recently constituted homosexual, of which Wilde is presumed to be an unfortunate specimen: "This is not the place to examine the strange problem of the life of Oscar Wilde, nor to determine to what extent heredity and the epileptic tendency of his nervous system can excuse that which has been imputed to him" (*CW* 203). Having declined to examine the issue from this clinical point of view, Joyce proceeds to offer a culturally contextualized explanation for Wilde that, while it still pathologizes, also manages to suggest a formulation not so far removed from Sedgwick's idea of the homosocial: "But the truth is that Wilde, far from being a perverted monster who sprang in some inexplicable way from the civilization of modern England, is the logical and inescapable product of the Anglo-Saxon college and university system, *with its secrecy and restrictions*" (*CW* 204; emphasis added).

As Joyce's structuralist analysis of Wilde's trial suggests, and as his fiction frequently affirms, it is not necessary that secrets be interesting, or that they "be" at all, only that the fact of them be declared, for them to underwrite the mystery of interiority both intrasubjectively and intersubjectively (that is to say, both for one's "self" and others). Declaring a secret, and/or protecting one from disclosure, creates the inside/outside binary and creates a fiction of inaccessibility that can be misrecognized as psychological integrity. Stephen's enduring fascination with Cranly's arm on his arm might reasonably be typed as "latent homosexuality," but might be more subtly analyzed as a fascination with the dominant modern strategy for the creation of subjectivity: formulating identity by implying to someone you have a secret and then experiencing their wanting to know as proof of interiority—they are one thing, and you are another, and you must therefore have a boundary, however nebulous it sometimes seems. Even when Stephen debates this interior/exterior as a child, he cannot see how containment is possible: "What was after the universe? Nothing. But was there anything round the universe to show where it stopped before the nothing place began? It could not be a wall but there could be a thin thin line there all round everything" (*P* 16). "The nothing place" would appear to be the "pleasant and vicious region" the narrator of "The Sisters" also recedes. Identity is the "thin, thin," and oh-so-breachable line between interiority ("the universe") and what we might align with Lacan's idea of the Real: "the nothing place."

Lacan speaks of "the decisive *orientation* which the subject receives from the itinerary of a signifier."[9] Controlling the itinerary of the secret, in the conscious realm (Symbolic order), compensates for the feeling of being controlled by the itinerary of the signifier in the unconscious realm (Imaginary order). When Sedgwick outlines a "theory" of the closet, then, she focuses too exclusively on "sexual orientation" as a phenomenon that produces the closet for the self-identified homosexual. Her characterization of the closet as "the regime of the open secret" has implications for all intersubjectivity, all intrasubjectivity, and all epistemology, above and beyond the last century's fixation on "sexual orientation." It is not so much that heterosexuals can show signs of "latent" homosexuality, or that homosexuals can show signs of "latent" heterosexuality. Rather, *the fantasy of subjectivity itself,* for which sexual "orientation" is a major organizing principle, *needs secrets:* secrets that are shared (confession/disclosure); secrets that are discovered (detection, surveillance); secrets that are buried even from one's self, although they may be known to others (repression, trauma); secrets we agree to keep secret solely by agreeing never to discuss them with any of the other people who know them (open secrets).

The point is not mystery but appearing mysterious, and the real secret becomes that there isn't one, and *this* is the retroactive "essence" of both person-ality and the aura of the commodity: how does Plumtree's potted meat make home an abode of bliss? The absurdity of the claim presumes a secret; like Wilde's Algernon, the package has nothing, but looks everything. As D.A. Miller asserts, "[A] secrecy that must always be rigorously maintained in the face of a secret that everybody already knows . . . is the very condition that entitles me to my subjectivity in the first place." The secret is to knowledge production what the phallus is to meaning production: it can perform its function only when veiled. By "inventing" homosexuality and designating it a perversion (quickly followed by hundreds of other perversions in the catalogs of Krafft-Ebing and Ellis), the utilization of secrecy in the formulation of subjectivity becomes in-stitutionalized, regardless of "orientation." Being normal requires that one keep secret evidence of abnormality, which means normality becomes a strategy for hiding evidence of abnormality. Confession becomes the dominant discourse of modern subjectivity because it purges the individual of a secret that has be-come conscious by making it also public, and resets what remains unconfessed as the secret normalcy hides. Historically inflected taxonomies, organized along the axis perverse/normal, discursively constitute various positions of desire ("orientation"), in ways that legitimate or delegitimate knowledge and thus con-trol access to power.

The obsession with confession in modernity (Foucault's observation, of course) becomes an insatiable need to feel the truth effect of what is always al-ready a fiction: identity. In this context, it is worth mentioning Padraic Colum's remark that "in its structure, *Exiles* is a series of confessions."[10] As in so much of Joyce's fiction, characters confess in order to feel alive. "I think I ought to go now," Bertha says to Robert, a phrase we know to associate with a woman try-ing to flee a compromising situation. "Not yet," Robert says, but it is not for a physical act he wishes to detain her: "There is one confession more," he says (*E* 107). In a similar manner, the "climax" of "Two Gallants" is not a man se-ducing a woman, but Corley holding out as a secret, as long as possible, whether or not he got a gold coin from the slavey.

The narrator of "An Encounter" witnesses the way Father Butler must sup-press popular culture in order to clear the way for Roman history ("Is this what you read instead of your Roman History?" [*D* 20]). And the narrator, with con-siderable prescience, understands that the confiscated material is not "rubbish," but part of the secret economy he already accepts as part of his grounding as a signifying subject: "Though there was nothing wrong in these stories and though their intention was sometimes literary they were *circulated secretly at school*" (*D* 20; emphasis added). What both Father Butler and the old man en-countered later have in common, despite apparently different attitudes about "sexual orientation," is that both want to invade the narrator's secret "nature." Father Butler wants to grab *The Apache Chief* out of secret circulation, and the old man first asks the narrator if he has a sweetheart and then responds to the narrator's response by insisting "everyone" does, and one shouldn't lie about it. Any emphasis on this encounter as merely sexual obscures the extent to which the old man is someone who wants to extract a secret from the boy. The old man's fantasy is one where his own subjectivity seems to grow in certitude as another subject gives up a secret. In this sense, the old man is much like Father Butler, and much like Father Flynn (also probing what the boy knows on a daily basis). In fact, he's like any priest in a confessional who keeps his own counsel while persuading others to expose the "silent, stony secrets" that serve as a foundational basis for the fantasy of subjectivity.

"An Encounter" is neatly divided, literally, between the educational discourse of Father Butler dispersed in the classroom and the polymorphously perverse discourse of the old man delivered in an open meadow. This rhetorical and geographical split shows up again at the very base of the narrator's consciousness, a split that is painfully experienced when *The Apache Chief* is confiscated by Father Butler and the students reading it are humiliated by him: "*This rebuke* during the sober hours of school . . . *awakened one of my consciences*" (*D* 20; emphasis added). Both consciences are produced, but one is secret and private (Dorian's picture in the attic; the narrator's secret delight in pulp fiction) and the other public, *made possible* by the secret (Dorian's "personality" and "charm"; the narrator's studious exterior). Because the second conscience is built on the interiority produced by the first, it is susceptible to collapse if the closet where the secret conscience is kept is forced open by another. The point is that the secret conscience empowers and destabilizes. The secret pleasure of Dorian's double life is also the horror that kills him when he is no longer able to keep them separate in his own mind. Because of his secret cave, Edmund Dantes becomes the count of Monte Cristo, and, because of a strong identification with this model, Baby Tuckoo becomes Stephen Dedalus, whose watchwords become "silence, exile and cunning." What he fears, quite rightly as a twentieth-century subject, is that his secret "nature" will be extracted from him and then returned to him after it has been duly cataloged, in order to generate the modern discourses that will be "taught" to him so he might discipline himself according to a process of self-surveillance. As Lois McNay has put it in her explication of Foucault's analysis of confession: "Through various techniques—interrogation, hypnosis, the questionnaire—individuals are induced to reveal the most intimate and precise details about the nature of their desires. . . . The knowledge acquired from the confessional is then recodified into the discourse of medicine, psychiatry, education, which establish a normalizing field—a regime of truth—in which individuals are categorized as deviant, normal, etc."[11] The process of producing a confession in order to misrecognize its secretiveness as interiority is also the process scientific discourse uses in order to distinguish what is "perverse" from what is "natural"; as a result, the secret that is interrogated does not disappear.

Two consciences remain, but, for the masculine subject in the twentieth century, there is an economic pressure to keep the secret conscience hidden because if someone discovers it, and "robs" it, the "personality" will be bankrupt and the right to whatever one owns suspect. Stevenson's Dr. Jekyll tried to alternate personalities, assuming no one would suspect he was also Mr. Hyde; Dorian Gray took extraordinary precautions to make sure no one would stumble upon his portrait; later popular culture incarnations such as Batman and Superman will likewise have a way of keeping both "consciences" alive in a manner based on secrecy. But an early example of this psychological feature—one directly relevant to Joyce—is present in Dumas's split "masculine" hero. Anyone discovering the cave could rob it of its treasure and destroy "the count of Monte Cristo" as a produced subjectivity and a "personality" made possible only by wealth. While Foucault is clear that secrets are not the point and discovering them is not the answer, I would only qualify this, with reference to Freud, Marx, and Lacan, and agree *the content* of the secret is not the point, but *the function* of *secrecy* is crucial to the production of modern subjectivity; different sexual "orientations" have different matters at stake in terms of disclosure, but all modern subjects have a "closet." Foucault is quite right to say secrets are not "the truth," but secrecy, because of the way it functions, permits one to produce a subjectivity judged capable of producing a truth effect, often in the form of confessing.

The whole issue of "sexual orientation" implicit in the binary homo/hetero, was made necessary by an historically specific sense of sexual *disorientation*. Here, for example, is Stephen Dedalus listening to Cranly, after Cranly has been arguing that a mother's love could be assumed to be real: "Stephen, who had been listening to the unspoken speech behind the words, said with assumed carelessness:—Pascal, if I remember rightly, would not suffer his mother to kiss him." Stephen, like Dupin, is wearing his green spectacles, scanning the room for signs of Cranly's secret(s), while maintaining a tone of "assumed carelessness." His remarks are apt, however, and more manipulative than he lets on, because they goad Cranly into more and more rash statements, beginning with "Pascal was a pig" all the way up to the angry suggestion Christ might have been a hypocrite and "a blackguard." At which point, Stephen is able to masterfully inquire "are you trying to make a convert of me or a pervert of yourself?" (*P* 242). Cranly is twisted into knots, and this seems to tighten the "knot" of Stephen's subjectivity. Stephen's suggestion that Cranly has turned himself into a "pervert" seems to duplicate the much more general pathologizing of the perversion of "homosexuality" in order to constitute the normative state of heterosexuality, except it is Cranly's fantasy of subjectivity that becomes dis-oriented in order to orient Stephen's.

Having a secret orients the subject because it disorients the "other" and thus can be imagined to disorient the "Other," as well, and thereby leave the "self" standing as the originator and generator of meaning. Dupin with his green glasses, Stephen with his "assumed carelessness," even Bloom observing with "his backward eye" feel themselves in a position of being grounded as the unobserved observer (the phallus) independent of the "content" of the letter (i.e., whether their partner is physically intimate with another, or not). The normal paradox of desire is that a man strives to have his autonomous self-sufficiency authenticated by a woman, but his necessity that she do this for him negates any positive effect of what it is he would have her do. Much of heterosecrecy, then protects the "masculine" subject from knowing the woman masquerades as that which confirms what in fact he's not: the phallus. In homosecrecy, where one man learns the secret of another, the position is much more like an unobserved observer whose self-sufficiency appears to be confirmed in contrast to the man who prattles on unaware that his listener is in the position described by Stephen: "listening to the unspoken speech behind the words." When Stephen is asked if he has a vocation, what appeals to him is the idea of being made privy to a private discourse that, like *The Apache Chief*, " circulates secretly" among priests, giving them the knowledge and the power to wrest secrets from others, send them away to repair their breached subjectivity with penance and remorse, all the while feeling omniscient and grounded: "He listened in reverent silence now to the priest's appeal and through the words he heard even more distinctly a voice bidding him approach, offering him secret knowledge and secret power. . . . He would know obscure things, hidden from others. . . . He would hold his secret knowledge and secret power, being as sinless as the innocent" (*P* 159). It is a habit with Stephen not to listen to what is being said, but to hear "a voice" of speaking what is unsaid.

It is also instructive to compare Bloom's heterosecrecy with Stephen's homosecrecy. Bloom strives to keep the letter in circulation between himself and Molly. If he reads it when her back is turned, or she hides it completely and makes no mention of it, it will become an inaccessible secret rather than an "open" secret. Heterosecrecy seems designed to permit a continuation of intimacy, even when the fact of the secret implies the relationship is less intimate than each partner publicly pretends. To take another famous example of heterosecrecy in Joyce, why has Gretta never told Gabriel of Michael Furey? Certainly he regards it, once she has disclosed it, as a secret she has kept for years, and may be keeping still ("perhaps she had not told him the whole story" [*D* 222]), but it seems equally possible that her disclosure is a bid for greater intimacy with him, a request for understanding. One reason the disclosure is so devastating to Gabriel, however, is that he has been fantasizing about the intimacy of their relationship with specific reference to the way the relationship produced secrets he now takes to be constitutional of his own subjectivity.

During the trip back to the Gresham Hotel, he has been reviewing in his own mind "like the tender fire of stars moments of their life together, that no one knew of or would ever know of." His desire for an erotic encounter with her is matched by his desire to share these secrets anew: "He longed to recall to her those moments" (*D* 213). Not only does the chance to do this never arrive, but the discovery that she was reviewing a secret unknown to him *while* he was carefully reviewing the secrets known to both of them creates nothing less than a crisis in consciousness: "While he had been full of memories of their secret life together . . . *she had been comparing him in her mind* with another. A shameful consciousness of his own person assailed him" (*D* 219–20). There is a striking lack of evidence that Gretta is doing any "comparing." Certainly she is preoccupied, but her remark that he is a "generous person," while not what Gabriel was in the mood to hear, at least suggests she is not sorry he's there, and her ability to cry herself to sleep in front of him shows a basic trust in him, but this is as nothing, from Gabriel's perspective, set against her sharing a secret with another man, superior to any secret she has ever shared with him. This secret has crowded out any "secret life" he suddenly fears he only imagined they had.

It is this that makes him feel as if "they had never lived together as man and wife." The masculine subject, as Judith Butler puts it, "only appears to originate meanings and thereby to signify. His seemingly self-grounded autonomy attempts to conceal the repression which is both its ground and the perpetual possibility of its own ungrounding."[12] The heterosecrecy seems necessary for the conjugal peace of the "masculine" subject, who must imagine all the secrets of his wife are secrets he shares. Molly's adultery is secondary to Bloom as long as he knows of it, and Molly, for her part, suspects that he knows, and so it is an "open secret" between them, if not exactly a shared one. So even when two "masculine" subjects are not vying one on one to shore up their subjectivity at the other subject's expense, men are also examining their relationships with women to shore up a sense of heterosecrecy for fear that some other man has deposited a secret in their wife of which they are unaware (a different way to view the position of the cuckold).

Richard Rowan makes clear that, like Bloom, what he fears is not that Bertha will have an affair, but that she will do so without telling him and that, still worse, this will prevent him from telling Robert that he knows, has known, and will always know what Bertha and he do or refuse to do together. In other words, content is incidental to form. What Richard is fighting for is not to prevent or provoke *but to occupy a position* as "the one with the letter"—the one who has it in his power to disclose what others might otherwise choose to keep secret. Initially, Richard is winning the battle of homosecrecy when Robert propositions Bertha, unaware that Richard and Bertha have already discussed this probability and Richard has, essentially, given his permission for it to take place. Curiously, Richard's question to Robert is not "why do you wish to make love to my wife," but why he wishes "*to keep secret* your wooing" (*E* 75; emphasis added). It's a bizarre question because wooing that is not secret is not wooing at all, and Robert makes this point, in a time-honored manner, when he tells Bertha that "secrets can be very sweet" (*E* 103). The battle is over positionality, not over who has or does not have sex with whom.[13]

In Lacan's allegorical terms, Richard wants to master his unconscious signifier once and for all—to produce and thus control the secret that underwrites his consciousness, however painful that might be to his sense of Bertha's "faithfulness." Indeed, in his own mind at least, he gets his wish at the end of the play; when Bertha assures him nothing happened and he insists he will never know, he asserts mastery over the secret that masters him. He is so terrified of being subject to the secret Robert and Bertha might have shared that he appropriates it as his "wound." Making it clear that he knows he can never know, he tries to make it his secret that there is no secret, which is a curious way of becoming the phallus, a symbol of completeness that—because it does not exist—cannot perform its function unless veiled. He manages to convert "not knowing" into his secret, or, to put it another way, he manages to orient himself by disorienting Robert and Bertha. Suddenly, neither what Robert did nor what they might do can shift him from the position, not of "the subject who knows," but of the foreclosed position of "the subject who will never know" and who, thus, can never, or so it seems, be in the position where Robert or Bertha can keep a secret from him.

The struggle between men as to who is to keep a secret inviolate and who is to wrest it from the other without the other knowing this has been done has an economic base. In the case of heterosecrecy, where there is no general pathologizing taking place in the larger culture, the trafficking in secrets seems to have a primarily existential basis—whose authority is most legitimated?—which, in turn, decides whose reality poses as what is Real. In homosecrecy, however, there is a materialist rivalry. This is perhaps most potently contained in the practice of "blackmail," which Showalter tells us was understood, especially after the Labouchere Amendment to the Criminal Law Amendment Act of 1885, as mostly referring to threats to expose the "secret" of homosexuality.

Certainly *The Picture of Dorian Gray* depicts an atmosphere where people generate anonymity and false identity to avoid blackmail. About *Dr. Jekyll and Mr. Hyde,* another masterpiece of masculine "doubling," Stephen Heath makes the point that "the organising image for this narrative is the breaking down of doors, learning the secret behind them."[14] Showalter, commenting on this, notes, "the narrator of Jekyll's secret attempts to open up the mystery of another man, not by understanding or secret sharing, but by force . . . breaking down the door to Jekyll's private close with an axe . . . into what Jekyll calls 'the very fortress of identity.' "[15] "Personality" is the ability to generate meaning in such a way as to generate profit—money—or, in the case of a salable personality or "celebrity," what Bourdieu call "cultural capital": an "aura" credited to an individual that can be used to attract money. But Showalter is wrong to equate the moment of knocking down the door with the moment of disclosure. By then the location of the secret is already known, and it has become known through the process of detection, that is, ignoring content and "listening" for what is unsaid but nonetheless signified, in the form that projects a promise of hidden meaning ("content" that is not there). Žižek describes "classical political economy," in a similar manner, as "interested only in contents concealed behind the commodity-form, which is why it cannot explain the true secret, not the secret behind the form but 'the secret of this form itself.'"[16] To push this analogy further, the ego is the factory that produces evidence of subjectivity (product) that through discourse (advertising) is turned into a commodity, one with apparent content, but in fact a retroactive formation whose only secret is that there is no secret. Thus we have the profile of the Lacanian subject: posing as a producer of knowledge—indeed, as the foundation and source of knowledge—but based on a permanent lack that constitutes a subject incapable of knowing itself. As Freud liked to say, in reference to his "discovery" of the unconscious, the ego is no longer mistaken for the center of the universe.[17]

From a Marxist point of view, it is much more the disclosure of the homosexual secret that might lead to the loss of property, money, and/or employment. But I propose a deeper infrastructure still: any disclosure of a secret such that it can no longer serve to hide the fact that there is no secret will destroy the individual both as a subject and a property owner. The discovery that Dorian Gray is not the portrait—that it is not a secret, after all—causes him to be found, dead and loathsome, next to the attractive, unaltered portrait. Because "legitimate" discourse permits a subject to act in a manner designed to accrue profit, disclosure of something that "shows" that discourse was "illegitimate" the whole time renders forfeit all that one has amassed. This is as true for emotional transactions as it is for financial transactions.

We need to understand that Marx's description of commodity fetishism as the production of a secret is parallel to Freud's and Lacan's presentation of the ego, or what we might call the fetish of "personality," as equally the production of a secret. In both cases, the secret is that there is no secret, and to move from a futile analysis of "hidden content" to questions of why the production is formed this way requires we put on the green spectacles of historicization and scan the room for the trivial detail that is the empty organizing principle of all that we see. Like the unconscious itself, the (empty) secret can be viewed only in terms of its effect, and then only when it is being withdrawn or reintroduced into circulation. In this sense, the effect a secret can produce is like the dream or the symptom in that it will nowhere appear as the hidden cause of what in fact it alone constitutes. This is that moment, so frequent in fiction and life, where we say of someone, "They were acting strange; I don't know why." So the Freudian high priest of our time is the psychoanalyst, and the Marxian high priest—his brother under the skin—is the detective. Significantly, the boy of "An Encounter" characterizes the "literature of the Wild West" as "remote from my nature" and confesses, "I liked better some American detective stories which were traversed from time to time by unkempt fierce and beautiful girls" (*D* 20). And this puts him directly in parallel with Stephen Dedalus, who, likewise, quickly learns that prospering in boyhood means learning how to traffic in secrets. The terrifying moment of the opening of *Portrait,* when he hides under the table, is brought about because he has said something upsetting to others and experiences himself as apparently full of a secret meaning he himself cannot fathom.

This moment is relived when an older boy asks him whether or not he kisses his mother, and his two answers—yes and no—equally call forth ridicule: "He felt his whole body hot and confused in a moment. What was the right answer to the question? . . . Wells must know the right answer for he was in third of grammar" (*P* 26). But looking for the right answer is as ineffective as the police searching the minister's flat day after day. There is no "right answer"; the point is *positionality,* and Stephen is objectified ("his whole body hot and confused in a moment"), so that Wells experiences himself as the subject who knows. And what Wells knows, of course, is that there is no answer, that the secret is there is no secret. A similar moment occurs in the much-discussed passage where the boys learn of an incident of "smugging" having taken place. Here, whoever has the more primal secret becomes the subject presumed to know: "Athy, who had been silent, said quietly:—You are all wrong. All turned towards him eagerly." Note how carefully Athy divulges the secret so as to center himself: "I will tell you but you must not let on you know. He paused for a moment and then said mysteriously . . ." (*P* 242). Never mind what he said; note how he reinserts a letter/secret into the intersubjective economy in such a way as to pose as the subject who knows.

Much earlier, he does the same thing to Stephen, in an exchange with no sexual overtones. "I say! . . . You know, he said, you can ask that riddle another way? . . . The same riddle, he said. Do you know the other way to ask it? . . . There is another way but I won't tell you what it is" (*P* 25–26). The young Stephen is as confused as when hiding under the table or answering about the kissing of his mother: "why did he not tell it?" And yet it is at least one sign of Stephen's emergence as a "detective" when he baffles his class with a riddle in the "Nestor" chapter of *Ulysses.* It is not enough to be a detective and search out other people's secrets, either to blackmail them into submission to your will (objectify) or cause them to feel intense gratitude for your returning a "stolen" secret to them. One must also take constant inventory of one's own interiority to make sure no one has, or is about to filch, something.

Stephen's evident delight in being taken hold of by Cranly, plus his breathless confirmation of a real bond between them ("you made me confess to you"), also results in Cranly's intimating that yet more intimacy might be possible, but not if Stephen leaves Ireland: "And not to have any one person . . . who would be more than a friend, more even than the noblest and truest friend a man ever had" (*P* 247). There is homoeroticism here, but, in my reading, Cranly is asking if they can both reveal to each other the secret of subjectivity: the secret that there is no secret, and that everyone is afraid and lonely to a greater extent than they feel free to admit. Dupin-like, Stephen turns over Cranly's words again, listening for the unspoken, which is so inarticulate as to be imagined as music rather than thought: "His words seemed to have struck some deep chord in his own nature" (P 247). Yes, and in Stephen's "nature," too, but here Stephen is willing to go no farther: "Had Cranly spoken of himself, or himself as he was or wished to be?" Stephen then answers his own question in a manner intended to distance himself from Cranly, but to do so more on existential grounds than grounds of sexual attraction or repulsion: "He had spoke of himself, or his own loneliness which he feared." And then finally Stephen responds, but in a manner that suggests Cranly's purloined letter is in full view: "Of whom are you speaking?" (P 247). And Cranly, his secret in plain view, but no longer undetectable (the position in which Dupin puts the minister in "The Purloined Letter"), finds himself reduced to a silent backdrop that allows Stephen's question to resonate: "Cranly did not answer." This is the last word, or rather the last silence, of the novel proper, and we end with Stephen's muscular attempt to shore up interiority represented by his entirely self-centered and "secret" journal entries.

The portrait of an artist is also the securing of subjecthood; the journal entries seem to take place in the private cave he once imagined himself as having when pretending to be the count of Monte Cristo. For the time being, Stephen feels empowered, in possession of the letter that signifies him; the nonexistent phallus is functioning because, also for the moment, it is veiled and thus allows him to signify for others ("create in the smithy of [his] soul the uncreated conscience of [his] race" [P 253]). Even the choice of a smithy as metaphor is significant: a workplace where enough heat is generated in an enclosed space to alter the shape of apparently impervious objects. Of course this cannot last because sooner or later he will realize the letter is missing; either because he rechecks it in a moment of doubt, or in a scene of public humiliation because he has presumed to use it when it is, in fact, no longer in his possession. We can see this rhythm throughout Portrait, most notably in the triumph of sensation that closes each chapter and the sense of diminished hopes and prospects that opens the next.

What I have tried to highlight in this essay, primarily by challenging "sexual orientation" as an essential mode of being, is that for Joyce's early narrators, as well as for Richard and Stephen, any sense of self as "masculine" is directly related to their confidence in themselves as subjects capable of signification, and that this confidence, by and large, comes from secrets kept in Stephen's secret cave. Steal from the cave and he becomes "feminine," not in terms of sexual orientation, but strictly in perceived phallic potential, which is an effect of relationship, not an essence, and its ability to pose as essence relates to a retroactive sense of one's own interiority brought on by producing a secret and/or stealing someone else's. Heterosecrecy, with its assured claim to a normative status, tends to support the intersubjective economy of the ego's fantasy of coherence, whereas homosecrecy, because of its constituted status as "perversion," always seems to involve the "holy of holies" secret—the secret that there is no secret (it is perhaps not surprising that Stephen has trouble understanding the difference—in terms of his identical vague feeling of horror—among the various crimes of smugging, sneaking into the sacristy and stealing the holy wine, and committing a sin for which there can be no forgiveness).

Indeed, one of the secrets he longs to know, should he take the priesthood as vocation, is "the sin for which there is no forgiveness" (*P* 76). Note the presymbolic dimension of this sin, in line with the "perversion" of homosexuality that Wilde's lover famously classified as something the essence of which is secretive when he allowed the voice of homosexual love to say: "I am the love that dare not speak its name."[18] But what is erotic here is not simply the homoerotic, but the erotic power that threatens and fascinates by revealing and reveiling the secret of there being no secret; it is a secret which permits the knot of subjectivity to form around the very void that both makes it necessary and renders it fantastic. In other words, the "masculine" subject produces a secret neither he nor anyone else can "know" (Richard Rowan) and shows us, in the process (as does Athy, as does Dorian Gray), that the production of a secret and the production of the self *are the same thing.* Heterosecrecy, in a "normative mode," *succeeds in obscuring this relationship,* just as homosecrecy, in a "perverse" mode, *threatens to highlight it.*

NOTES

1. D. A. Miller, *The Novel and the Police* (Berkeley and Los Angeles: University of California Press, 1988), 195.

2. Slavoj Žižek, *The Metastases of Enjoyment: Six Essays on Woman and Causality* (New York: Verso, 1994), 126.

3. Michel Foucault, *The History of Sexuality,* vol. 1, *An Introduction,* trans. Robert Hurley (New York: Vintage, 1980), 103.

4. Jacques Lacan, *The Four Fundamental Concepts of Psycho-Analysis,* trans. Alan Sheridan (London: Hogarth Press, 1977), 179.

5. Eve Kosofsky Sedgwick, *Epistemology of the Closet* (Berkeley and Los Angeles: University of California Press, 1990), passim.

6. Elaine Showalter, *Sexual Anarchy: Gender and Culture at the Fin de Siecle* (New York: Penguin Books, 1990), passim.

7. Jacques Lacan, *Ecrits: A Selection,* trans. Alan Sheridan (London: Tavistock, 1977), 38.

8. Oscar Wilde, *The Complete Plays, Poems, Novels and Stories of Oscar Wilde* (Bristol, England: Parragon, 1995), 20.

9. Jacques Lacan, "The Seminar on 'The Purloined Letter,'" trans. Jeffrey Mehlman, in *The Purloined Poe,* ed. Shoshana Felman (Baltimore: Johns Hopkins University Press, 1985), 29.

10. Padraic Colum in James Joyce, *Exiles* (London: Triad Grafton, 1979), 10.

11. Lois McNay, *Foucault: A Critical Introduction* (New York: Continuum, 1994), 122.

12. Judith Butler, *Gender Trouble* (New York: Routledge, 1993), 47.

13. Joseph Valente, *James Joyce and the Problem of Justice: Negotiating Sexual and Colonial Difference* (Cambridge: Cambridge University Press, 1995), 153. Valente also notes, with reference to this exchange about secrets, Richard's "intrusion to inform Robert of his knowledge," and characterizes him as both "the apostle of erotic appropriation" and "a devotee of stealth, secrecy, and darkness."

14. Stephen Heath, quoted in Showalter, *Sexual Anarchy,* 110.

15. Showalter, *Sexual Anarchy,* 110.

16. Slavoj Žižek, *The Sublime Object of Ideology* (New York: Verso, 15).

17. Sigmund Freud, "A Difficulty in the Path of Psychoanalysis," in *The Standard Edition of the Complete Psychological Works of Sigmund Freud,* ed. and trans. James Strachey, vol. 17 (London: Hogarth Press, 1955), 138–40.

18. Alfred Douglas, "Two Loves," quoted in Richard Ellmann, *Oscar Wilde* (New York: Alfred Knopf, 1988), 326.

Homophobia and Misogyny

James Joyce, Tattoo Artist
Tracing the Outlines of Homosocial Desire

Jennifer Levine

I have been trying to understand why it is that as *Ulysses* begins its third and final section a new character, D. B. Murphy, makes his appearance—and why it should be that character in particular, and in that chapter, "Eumaeus."[1] In doing so, I am surprised to find myself playing Sherlock Holmes: consulting dictionaries of slang, encyclopedias of sexual practice, gazetteers of Ireland. Why should "Eumaeus" invite such hermeneutical anxiety? After the verbal pyrotechnics of "Oxen of the Sun" and the dizzying transformations of "Circe" it seems almost disappointingly intelligible. Its prose has been called lazy, exhausted, slipping out of control. Or is it a way of arranging words alert to the comic, and more insidious, meanings of repetition? "Eumaeus" is, arguably, the most Wakean chapter of them all, and not just because it is caught up in a peculiarly sleepy moment. There is a sly humor at work in every sentence: a rhetoric of innuendo that makes connections furtively, but with a knowing wink.

This essay records my attempts to track the oblique gestures of the episode, circling in particular around Murphy's tattoo and his South American postcard, and making a brief excursion along the way to *The Merchant of Venice*. I will argue that a significant subtext for "Eumaeus" (and perhaps the reason for its indirection) turns on homosexuality. Ultimately however, my focus is on the wider terrain of homosocial desire that Eve Kosofsky Sedgwick has mapped out in *Between Men*. She calls the term *homosocial* "a kind of oxymoron . . . . [that] describes social bonds between persons of the same sex; it is a neologism, obviously formed by analogy with 'homosexual,' and just as obviously meant to be distinguished from 'homosexual.' In fact, it is applied to such activities . . . as 'male bonding,' which may, in our society, be characterized by intense homophobia, fear and hatred of homosexuality." Her project is to draw the homosocial "back into the orbit of 'desire,' of the potentially erotic . . . [in order] to hy-pothesize the potential unbrokenness of a continuum between homosocial and homosexual—a continuum whose visibility, for men, in our society, has been radically disrupted."[2] Sedgwick's point is not that all men are repressed homo-sexuals, nor will it be my claim that the "secret" of *Ulysses* is this or that charac-ter's, or the author's, hidden homosexuality, but rather that it makes sense to reinsert homosexual desire into the historically changeable structure of men's relationships with men. I use the word *desire* as Sedgwick does, to name a struc-ture of relationship rather than a particular emotion. Analogous to the psycho-analytic concept of libido, it is "the affective or social force, the glue, even when its manifestation is hostility or hatred or something less emotively charged that shapes an important relationship."[3]

Is Bloom and Stephen's world held together in this way? The question may be posed again by asking: what happens in *Ulysses*? My immediate answer is that men—many men—talk. Two men in particular walk through the city, crossing paths in a variety of ways, eventually meeting. And then? They stand outside in a garden, in the dark, taking a companionable but not uncompetitive pee. (As René Girard has taught us to see, rivalry may be the strongest form of inti-macy.)[4] The one woman with a significant role in this scenario is largely framed as a character by what men say about her. When she finally has her own say, she has no audience except herself. Molly Bloom is cut off from the swirl of talk and letters that constitutes Dublin as a social space. Unlike Penelope, she presides over a house at which hardly anyone, not even the postman, calls.[5] To summa-rize the narrative in this way is not to accuse Joyce: he is not "guilty" of margin-alizing women. It is rather to acknowledge that what he offers in *Ulysses* is an astute analysis of relations between men. More particularly, in "Eumaeus," he opens a window onto the nexus of homophobia, anti-Semitism, and misogyny. He does so at least in part through D. B. Murphy, whose appearance in the cab-man's shelter sets Bloom, and the Eumaean narrative that represents him, ner-vously on edge.

"Eumaeus" begins by insisting on what happens before one can begin. "Prepara-tory to anything else Mr. Bloom brushed off the greater bulk of the shavings and handed Stephen the hat and ashplant and bucked him up generally in orthodox Samaritan fashion" (*U* 16.01–03). The sentence looks backward in another sense too, echoing and displacing the opening lines of the book, with its *shaving*s, its *brush*ing, and its general *buck*ing up. D. B. Murphy provokes a similar retro-spective arrangement. Like Mulligan (and more recently like Bloom) he is "game for . . . shaving and brushup" (16.656). Like Simon Dedalus he is a disappointed father. Like Richie Goulding, for whom Simon Dedalus has such contempt, he speaks with an occasional stutter. Like Stephen he wears borrowed trousers and appears to be "bad in the eyes" (16.1674). Like Deasy, Polonius-like and garru-lous, he "boards" Stephen. Like Bloom, he is a wanderer on his way home, a father, a husband, and possibly a cuckold, a man who may receive mail under a false name, who is accused by a bogus nationalist of not being a true Irishman, and who, as Bloom will do in this chapter, shows off his photo of a woman, breasts on view. Placed near the end of *Ulysses,* Murphy produces a kaleidoscopic set of echo effects that multiply and disperse him back across the text.

Because of this centrifugal movement, he seems to illustrate the more general semiotic point about character: that a Murphy (like a Stephen or a Bloom) has no essential identity and is most properly understood as a set of attributes temporarily clustered around a proper name.[6] When Stephen asks, "What's in a name?" (16.364), his question resonates in similar ways. No inherent truth, is his implicit answer—just a process of imposture, of standing in for the thing itself, as signifiers stand in for and inevitably betray what they might wish to signify. "Sounds are impostures, Stephen said . . . like names" (16.362–63). Interestingly, it is right after this, with the claim that "Shakespeares were as common as Murphies," that Murphy himself comes to life. He springs out of a discussion of language and in the end comes to rest in language, in a slip of the tongue, with Gumley fast asleep, "to all intents and purposes [still] wrapped in the arms of Murphy, as the adage has it, dreaming of fresh fields and pastures new" (16.1726–28). Of D. B. Murphy we will hear no more. Nevertheless, bracketed though he is in the apparently phantasmagoric effects of language, he is real enough to Bloom to make him, and the narrative of "Eumaeus," very nervous. This, rather than Murphy's unreality, is my point of departure.

Of all the characters that he replicates, Murphy has his most complex relationship with Bloom—not only because of the various ways in which he is like him but also because of the intensity of Bloom's reaction to him. From the very beginning, it seems, he sets off some internal alarm. Why else would Bloom want to warn Stephen not to answer Murphy's question ("And what might your name be?") by touching his boot? The narrative marks the odd intimacy of the gesture as "warm pressure from an unexpected quarter." In the three-way dialogue that follows, with Bloom initially "all at sea," it is interesting to watch him, terrier-like, worrying at Murphy. (And to note as well Stephen's relative willingness to engage with Murphy—quite unlike his pose with everyone else. Indeed, Stephen will be the only one to respond to Murphy's question about his home town, Carrigaloe, because it is in the neighborhood of Cork, his father's birthplace.)[7] Bloom "pursues" Murphy "without flinching a hairsbreadth" (16.409), then "unobtrusively" (16.414). As soon as the sailor's postcard reaches him, "without evincing surprise, unostentatiously" (as if playing Sherlock Holmes, whose characteristic "Curious coincidence" he has just invoked [16.414]) he turns it over "to peruse the partially obliterated address and postmark" and (unsuccessfully, because there is none) to read the message (16.487–88). Soon after, when the conversation turns to world travels, he cannot resist enquiring about Gibraltar. In part of course he is fascinated by anything that touches on Molly. But another part of him is determined to catch Murphy out in a lie.

—Have you seen the rock of Gibraltar? Mr Bloom inquired.

The sailor grimaced, chewing, in a way that might be read as yes, ay or no.

—Ah, you've touched there too, Mr Bloom said, Europa point, thinking he had, in the hope that the rover might possibly by some reminiscences but he failed to do so, simply letting spirt a jet of spew into the sawdust, and shook his head with a sort of lazy scorn.

—What year would that be about? Mr B interrogated. Can you recall the boats?

Our *soi-disant* sailor munched heavily awhile hungrily before answering:

—I'm tired of all them rocks in the sea, he said, and boats and ships. Salt junk all the time. (16.611–23)

If the answer is inconclusive, Bloom insists on giving it a meaning. The narrative itself marks his response by calling it interrogation, and (as if sharing Bloom's doubts), having named Murphy "our *soi-disant* sailor" and "such a wily old customer" (16.625), it skeptically describes the resistant interviewee as "tired *seemingly*" (16.624; emphasis added). Much later, as Bloom steers Stephen out of the shelter, it is clear that he still has his eye on Murphy, almost as if his own leaving depended on Murphy's staying. "A move had to be made because that merry old soul . . . who appeared to be glued to the spot, didn't appear in any particular hurry to wend his way home" (16.1625–27).

Murphy is presented as a teller of tales, a trickster: another Odysseus on his way home. But unlike Homer's character, he is anxious to be known—or so it seems. The sign he bears on his chest, unlike the scar on Odysseus's knee, is not palpably significant. (You will recall that Odysseus is recognized by his old nurse when, bathing his legs, she touches the old scar. Murphy, in contrast, must palpate the tattooed profile himself in order to make it yield its meaning. "—See here, he said, showing Antonio. There he is cursing the mate. And there he is now, he added, the same fellow, pulling the skin with his fingers, some special knack evidently, and he laughing at a yarn" [16.683–85].) This is a nice irony in an episode as attached to the word "palpably" as "Eumaeus," where it is used five times (though nowhere else in *Ulysses*), yet where the act of touching is nervously kept to a minimum. Bloom's reaction to the streetwalker who is "palpably reconnoitring" (16.705) is very pointed: the last thing he would want to do is touch her. Even with Stephen Bloom is careful. He does not hand him the bun and the coffee: he pushes them across the table toward him (16.360, 366). Molly's picture too—though clearly used as a point of contact—is carefully placed on the table for Stephen to look at. Stephen does not pick it up. The episode that finally brings Bloom and Stephen together puts the very notion of being "in touch" into palpably ironic focus.

In "Eumaeus" mistaken and false identities crop up repeatedly. In "Eumaeus," too, there is hesitation about the most elementary acts of naming. Part of it may derive from Bloom's situation. It is very late, and he is in one of the roughest parts of Dublin, near the railroad tracks. The potential for violence comes close to the surface near the men's public urinal as he and Stephen walk past "a group of presumably Italians in heated altercation" (16.310). Untranslated, unexplained, threat and counterthreat erupt in a foreign language. The argument is still audible as they enter the cabman's shelter, a place whose sheltering safety is compromised by a keeper who looks uncannily like Fitzharris, one of the Dublin Invincibles. Ill at ease in low surroundings, Bloom is the respectable man anxious to assert (if only to himself) that things are not as they should be. Thus: "The keeper of the shelter . . . put a boiling swimming cup of a choice concoction labelled coffee on the table and a . . . bun, or so it seemed" (16.354–56). Bloom then pushes "the cup of what was temporarily supposed to be called coffee" (16.360) and later "the socalled roll" (16.366) toward Stephen. But not everything is attributable to Bloom's ironic gaze. As Derek Attridge has suggested, the narrative is constantly "looking over its shoulder."[8] The description of Murphy's tattoo, "an image . . . in blue Chinese ink intended to represent an anchor" (16.668–69), might be sarcastically Bloomian, but it is also part of *Ulysses'* wider meditation on the (im)possibility of knowledge and the problematic nature of identity.

Even in the early chapters, and increasingly so in the later ones, one of the characteristic strategies of the novel has been to withhold names and thus allow all the possibilities of identification and misidentification to accumulate. In this larger rhetorical context, Murphy is peculiar. I am struck first of all by the narrative's anxiety to name him (as if positing a never-ending supply of epithets might hold him more securely in place), and second by Murphy's own anxiety to name and identify himself. "Murphy's my name" he asserts (perhaps defensively, after claiming friendship with a certain Simon Dedalus, last seen in Stockholm touring with Hengler's Royal Circus). "D.B. Murphy of Carrigaloe. Know where that is?" Stephen does: Queenstown Harbour—not far from Cork. "That's right, the sailor said. Fort Camden and Fort Carlisle. That's where I hails from. I belongs there. That's where I hails from. My little woman's down there. She's waiting for me, I know. . . . She's my own true wife" (16.415–21). A little later, he will push his discharge papers on the group. The narrating language is equally insistent: it names him explicitly as "the sailor" twenty-two times, thirteen of them within a particularly concentrated five pages, and at least sixty times in all his variants. He is described, for example, in the following ways in episode 16: "one redbearded bibulous individual . . . a sailor probably" (337–38); one of the "Murphies" (364); the "redbearded sailor" (367); "the seaman bold" (382); "Murphy's my name" (415); "your brokenhearted husband D B Murphy" (439–40); "the communicative tarpaulin" (479); "the doughty narrator" (570); "the globetrotter" (574–75); "the rover" (615); "Our *soi-disant* sailor" (620); "such a wily old customer" (625); "the old seadog, himself a rover" (653–54); the

"Skibereen father" (666); "the exhibitor" (677); "That worthy" (681); "the latter personage" (697); "skipper Murphy" (726); "our mutual friend" (821); "the individual in front of him" (830); "a wellpreserved man of no little stamina" (832); a "weirdlooking specimen" (835); "friend Sinbad" (858); "Shipahoy" (901); "the old stager" (930); "skipper" (969); "That worthy" (971); "the redoubtable specimen" (983); the "impervious navigator" (1011); "that rough diamond" (1012); "the old tarpaulin" (1021); "the other, obviously bogus" (1045); "Jack Tar" (1456); "that merry old soul, the grasswidower in question" (1625–26); "that equivocal character" (1630); "for as to who he in reality was let x equal my right name and address" (1635–36); "the ancient mariner" (1669); "the seafarer with the tartan beard" (1676); "oilskin" (1704); "the arms of Murphy" (1727). The exuberance of the naming reminds me of an earlier nautical account in "Oxen of the Sun," where the insistence on describing the scene—again, and again, and yet again—highlights the textual basis of identity and threatens to torpedo whatever "reality-effect" the writing might lay claim to.[9]

The words strain to make Murphy known, yet render him increasingly suspect. The postcard he passes around, addressed to "Señor A. Boudin, Galeria Becche, Santiago, Chile" (16.489), does not help. For a writer as attuned to other languages as Joyce was, it cannot be insignificant that this name and address are so linguistically improbable. The sequence begins and ends by flagging "Spanishness." Yet the name "Boudin" is not just typically French: it is impossible in Spanish. (The diphthong would have been streamlined long ago into a single *o* or *u*.) Similarly "Becche," its double *cc* followed by *h*, disallows it as Spanish but marks it as Italian. (Since each of these languages treats the *ch* combination in precisely opposite ways, one has to decide which language it is "in" before attempting to pronounce it.) The clash of exclusively Spanish, French, and Italian phonemes recalls other improbabilities: that a Greek would be named Antonio (as Murphy insists he is), or that the Peruvian man-eaters Murphy claims to have seen in his travels would appear on a postcard from landlocked Bolivia. Or, to take Murphy's phrase literally, that the native women whose "diddies" he remarks on could also be "ballocknaked." As if to underline all the other incongruities, problems of concord—"I seen," "I hails," "I belongs" (16.389, 419, for instance)—trouble Murphy's speech.

Against this background of unlikelihood and contradiction, Murphy's own anxiety to prove himself, to establish his identity and to have it recognized, sets off alarm bells. Besides, he avoids answering certain questions—most curiously the ones about his tattoo.

There are, more precisely, three tattoos on Murphy's chest. There is the standard seaman's anchor and, above it, "the figure 16 and a young man's sideface looking frowningly rather" (16. 675–76). It is these two images that I want to read here, by suggesting that a modest little Italian word, *la smorfia*, might provide us with their syntax.[10] Its reverberations in "Eumaeus" are uncanny. In the first place, the word is derived from the Italian name of the god of dreams, Morfeo, whose English name, Morpheus, is punningly confused with Murphy's at various points in the episode. And Morpheus is the son of Sleep, under whose spell Joyce's Eumaean Dubliners are beginning to fall. His name, which is derived from the Greek word for "form," indicates his function: to take the shape of human beings and to show himself to people in their dreams.[11] But the primary meaning of *smorfia*, linked to its Greek root, has to do with facial expressions. A *smorfia* is a grimace, an affected pulling of the face, specially the mouth, into a smile or a smirk. *Fare una smorfia*, to pull a face, pretty much describes what Murphy does to the face on his chest, manipulating its grimace into a smile. "—See here, he said, showing Antonio. There he is cursing the mate. And there he is now, he added, the same fellow, pulling the skin with his fingers, some special knack evidently, and he laughing at a yarn" (16.683–85)]. The word's secondary reference, originally local to the area around Naples though by 1900 common throughout Italy (and, I am suggesting here, known and exploited by Joyce) is to "the book of dreams." More precisely, it designates a folk numerology that identifies dreams with the corresponding numbers in lotto, a game of chance played with ninety numbered cards. (see fig. 1)[12] Number sixteen shows the figure of the artist *(pittore che dipinge):* perhaps the Eumaean tattoo artist at work? As Murphy tells us, "Fellow, the name of Antonio, done that. There he is himself, a Greek" (16.678–79). I derive three things from this conjunction of texts to serve as an opening framework: the identification of Murphy (like Antonio, whose self-portrait he bears on his chest) with the figure of the artist; a more specific identification of Murphy with Morpheus (another Greek), skilled in assuming the form of human beings, whose disguised performances reveal the dreamer to himself; and more generally a figuring of the artist as essentially an actor, a trickster, a dream-worker. When Stephen and Bloom look into the mirror together at Bella Cohen's, they see reflected back at them the face of Shakespeare, as if identifying them to each other in the same antlered and ridiculous image (15.3821–24). Now, in "Eumaeus," their meeting is refracted back to them by D. B. Murphy, "artist." And he in turn bears on his own chest a second, miniature, portrait of the artist—Antonio, the "fellow who done that"—figuring a potential *mise-en-abime* that is implied by the tattooed sixteen as well, for it neatly conflates the world represented and the act of representation. It is all happening on the sixteenth day of June, 1904, and in *Ulysses* it is happening in the sixteenth episode. By the same token, it is tempting to read the tattooed but mobile profile as a Janus face, like the mask of theatrical representation: frowning on one side, laughing on the other. Among the adjectives that best describe Murphy, "self-dramatizing" certainly comes to mind. He does not simply tell his stories; he seems to perform them. Arriving into Dublin on a "homing" ship, Murphy is a kind of Homer—and not unlike the other makers of fictions (Shakespeare, Wilde, and Joyce himself)—written into *Ulysses*. He is "a bit of a literary cove in his own small way" (16.1676–77). Like Joyce he wears

10. Un Cannone
e Palle.

11. Trappola
da Topi.

12. Cappellaio.

13. Candeliere
acceso.

14. Bottigliere.

15. Molino
a vento.

16. Pittore
che dipinge.

17. La pace.

18. Poeta
e Suonatore.

Fig. 1

thick "goggles" and appears to be "bad in the eyes"(16.1672, 1674). He is like Shakespeare, too, particularly the Shakespeare that earlier episodes have projected. He may well be a cuckold. And his identity, like "Rutlandbaconsouthamptonshakespeare['s]" (9. 866), is decidedly slippery. There is definitely something "queer" about him.

But what is it that Murphy's performance reveals? And to whom?

I have not forgotten that Murphy has presumably been "outed" with the claim that the number sixteen itself, tattooed onto his chest, was commonly known on the Continent to signal homosexuality.[13] But quite apart from that, the interchange *about* the tattoo sticks in the mind, in particular Murphy's equivocal response to the question, "And what's the number for?" (16.695), the ambiguous "sort of a half smile" (16.698) that accompanies his response, and his repeated insistence that Antonio was a Greek—a claim that provokes memories of Mulligan on Bloom: "O, I fear me, he is Greeker than the Greeks" (9.614–15). The other Greek mentioned on more than one occasion in the chapter is Achilles, whose tenderness for Patroclus, as much as his Achilles tendon, was his "most vulnerable point" (16.1640). "Eumaeus" seems determined to exploit the innuendoes released by two of its most memorable puns: its reference to "tender Achilles" (16.1640 and 1716), and "the arms of Murphy" into which the sleepy Gumley is finally "wrapped" (16.1727, echoing 16.947–48).

If Murphy himself refuses to say what the number on his chest "is for," does *Ulysses* itself suggest an answer? By the time we encounter it tattooed on the sailor's body, *sixteen* is already overdetermined. It marks Bloom's entanglement with both Molly and Stephen. He has been married to her for sixteen years. He is sixteen years older than Stephen. More significantly, Bloom and Stephen's awareness of each other is expressed in precisely numerical terms. At Bella Cohen's, for example, when Stephen remembers that he broke his glasses "yesterday," he adds "Sixteen years ago" (15.3629), recalling his humiliation by Father Dolan at Clongowes. Soon after, Bloom points to a weal on his hand—reminder of a fall twenty two years ago: "I was sixteen" (15.3714). Stephen notices the pattern right away. (It might be the only thing he does notice about Bloom.) "See? Moves to one great goal. I am twentytwo. Sixteen years ago he was twentytwo too. Sixteen years ago I twentytwo tumbled. Twentytwo years ago he fell off his hobby horse" (15.3718–20). "Ithaca" insists on this pattern, cranking it up to absurd proportions: "16 years before in 1888 when Bloom was of Stephen's present age Stephen was 6. 16 years after in 1920 when Stephen would be Bloom's present age Bloom would be 54. In 1936 . . . their ages initially in the ratio of 16 to 0 would be as 17½ to 13½" (17.447–50). These ruminations, like others in *Ulysses,* bring to the fore an insistent relationship between the numbers six, sixteen, and twenty-two, a combination that crops up again in the sixteenth episode. I am thinking of the moment when, in a typically Eumaean attempt "to change the subject" (16.1172), Bloom meditates on "cultured fellows [like Stephen] that promised so brilliantly nipped in the bud of premature decay and nobody to blame but themselves" (16.1183–5). There then follows an oblique and innuendo-laden run through some of the scandals of late Victorian Britain, at the center of which we find "briefly, putting two and two together, six sixteen which he pointedly turned a deaf ear to" (16.1195–96). The passage is worth a closer look for a number of reasons. First, because of its pretence at skirting embarrassing topics while at the same time luring its audience on with a coy wink and a nudge, and then because of the way Murphy makes his way into thoughts about Stephen and the temptations in his path. Note the close juxtaposition of "sixteen . . . Antonio . . . and the tattoo" in the tangle of "others" compromised by this account. And note, finally, the easy slide from heterosexual to homosexual possibilities and back again:

> And then the usual *denouement* after the fun had gone on fast and furious he [O'Callaghan of the "mad vagaries" and "other gay doings"—16. 1187] got landed into hot water and had to be spirited away by a few friends, after a strong hint to a blind horse from John Mallon of Lower Castle Yard, so as not to be made amenable under section two of the criminal law amendment act, certain names of those subpoenaed being handed in but not divulged for reasons which will occur to anyone with a pick of brains. Briefly, putting two and two together, six sixteen which he pointedly turned a deaf ear to, Antonio and so forth, jockeys and esthetes and the tattoo which was all the go in the seventies or thereabouts even in the house of lords because early in life the occupant of the throne, then heir apparent, the other members of the upper ten and other high personages simply following in the footsteps of the head of the state, he reflected about the errors of notorieties and crowned heads running counter to morality such as the Cornwall case a number of years before under their veneer in a way scarcely intended by nature, a thing good Mrs Grundy, as the law stands, was terribly down on though not for the reason they thought they were probably whatever it was except women chiefly who were always fiddling more or less at one another it being largely a matter of dress and all the rest of it. Ladies who like distinctive underclothing should, and every welltailored man must, trying to make the gap wider between them by innuendo and give more of a genuine filip to acts of impropriety between the two, she unbuttoned his and then he untied her, mind the pin, whereas savages in the cannibal islands, say, at ninety degrees in the shade not caring a continental. (16.1189–1212)

We note, of course, the unnamed actions "running counter to morality . . . in a way scarcely intended by nature," the "women . . . who were always fiddling . . . at one another," the "acts of impropriety." But it is difficult to read this passage without pausing at "section two of the criminal law amendment act" and at "the Cornwall case." Might the references disentangle the whole web of innuendo?

In both cases the allusion is ambiguous, possibly indicating heterosexual or homosexual improprieties—or both. Weldon Thornton's note is instructive:

> W. Y. Tindall's statement . . . that this is the act and section under which Oscar Wilde was convicted is mistaken, but understandably so, and it points up the potential confusion here. Wilde was actually convicted under section eleven, not section two, of the Criminal Law Amendment Act, 1885, but some type fonts, more common in British typography, make it impossible to distinguish between the numerals for roman numeral two and arabic numeral eleven. See, for example, *Finnegans Wake*, p. 61.9, where this same Act is mentioned, but the numeral that is used makes it impossible to tell whether section two (roman) or section eleven (arabic) is referred to. The possibilities are complicated by several factors: If Oscar Wilde is being alluded to, then section eleven is the one intended, but if not, section two might be appropriate, for, while section eleven deals with homosexuality, section two deals with attempts to draw any woman or girl into unlawful carnal connection, or attempts to procure women for sexual purposes. In the Act itself, the sections are designated by arabic numerals, but Joyce may not have known this. And there is the possibility that Joyce himself saw the sections of the act referred to in numerals and mistook an arabic eleven for a roman two.[14]

The "Cornwall case" leaves things equally unresolved, for it could refer either to the 1870 divorce suit at which Edward VII, then duke of Cornwall, was called to the witness stand because two of his friends were named as correspondents, or to a later case in 1884 when "two officials of Dublin Castle, named Cornwall and French were publically involved in an extensive homosexual circle."[15] I am not surprised that of all the numbers he might have tattooed on Murphy's chest, Joyce chose the one that implicated his main character both with a woman and with another man.

Karen Lawrence has noted that, throughout "Eumaeus," the 'bottom' of the social body returns in a number of guises, despite bourgeois attempts at upward mobility and the sanitation of waste."[16] She cites the horse's bottom and the "three smoking globes of turds" (16.1876–77) it leaves on the road, "the lives of the submerged tenth, viz. coalminers, divers, scavengers etc" (16.1225–26) that populate Bloom's thoughts, and the often punning references to anality. The salty "Lot's wife's arse" (16.980) in the song of the sailor is only one of a number of references to the bottom—like the reference to "buggers" (16.672), to "the cabman's shelter, Butt Bridge" (17.2057), to the knife in the "butt" (16.582), to the "end of the tether" (16.952, 16.1874)—and, after the horse's deposits, a potential double entendre in Bloom's thought that Stephen will have "*heaps* of time to practice literature" (16.1860–61; emphasis added).[17] "Eumaeus" is interesting for Lawrence because, unlike "Circe," "the bottom returns" in the arena of public life rather than in an intensely private psychological realm. As such, its drama is not merely accessible to historical and ideological analysis. It demands it. She cites the work of social and cultural historians on the construction of bourgeois cultural identity. In that process the state was "divided into the purified, legitimate body of people and the underworld of loafers, drunks, prostitutes" that, like the body's bottom, was to be kept hidden.[18]

I want to argue that the anal fixations of "Eumaeus" can be read not only as an allegory of socioeconomic relations but also, more literally, within a (homo)sexual context. The end that returns in chapter 16 is eroticized. Perhaps because of that it is the most nervous of all the episodes in *Ulysses*, but (in spite of the schema published by Stuart Gilbert) it is the anus—not the nerves—that functions as its "organ." Murphy's account of a killing in Trieste, in which the knife "went into his back up to the butt" (16.582), sets the scene specifically in "a knockingshop" (16.580) and makes a point of saying that the murder weapon was just like his own "claspknife" (16.578). Bloom reformulates the account with ethnocentric abandon, sliding from "those italianos" and their "stab in the back touch" (16.865) to "those poignards they [Spaniards] carry in the abdomen" (16.875–76).[19] Should the oddness of these two phrases, and their proximity to each other, not recall Molly's "Give us a touch, Poldy. God, I'm dying for it" (6.80–81)? Later, dreaming up a glamorous and successful future for Stephen, the episode speaks of "a capital opening . . . a stiff figure . . . a backerup" (16.1853–56). It chooses "*tête à tête*" (16.1889) to describe what goes on at the end between Stephen and Bloom, "boarded" (16.368) to indicate just how Murphy approaches Stephen, and "diddled" (16.423) to name what a sailor does to Davy Jones.[20] By sheer accumulation, the sexual innuendoes begin to take on a life of their own.

At a subliminal level that, once noticed, calls for interpretation, "Eumaeus" is underscored by a web of homoerotic allusions. Murphy is the spider at the center. He has three texts attached to him, all of which he shows off in the cabman's shelter: his rather suggestively named "seaman's discharge," his tattoo (with its equivocal self-advertising), and the postcard addressed to a Señor A. Boudin, whose name, like so many other details in this episode, invites further speculation. If I consult a French dictionary, I am struck first of all by the culinary blurring of anal and phallic thresholds: *boudin*, or blood sausage, is made by stuffing bowel casings. A secondary meaning applies *boudin*, by analogy, to any part of the body or indeed to any object that has a spherical or sausagelike shape. The entries show how the sausage has been invested with sexual anxieties—as much for women, who might with *boudin* be named ugly, frumpish, an easy lay, a pushover, a prostitute (no more than identical to her sexual value: a *boudin* is a prostitute's earnings), as for men, whose sexual potency the word puts in question. *Boudin blanc* is as much a penis as it is a sausage, and the phrases *tourner en os de boudin* (a play on *avoir l'os*, which means to have an erection) and *finir*

en eau de boudin (derived from the process of sausage making in which the water the guts are washed in is of no further use, mere garbage) both mean to fail,
fall through, fizzle out, come to nothing.[21] The play on sexual collapse is obvious. Beyond the dictionary, cultural history yields its own suggestive clues. "Le
Boudin" is the marching song of the French Foreign Legion, an icon of rampant
masculinity within an exclusively homosocial culture.[22] Murphy's pseudonym
might also owe something to a real Boudin (first initial M.), whose work on sexual and nervous degeneracy forms part of the nineteenth-century pseudo-
science of race and sexuality—a discourse with which Joyce was familiar
through Krafft-Ebing and Weininger.[23] Boudin's analysis of German census sta-
tistics claimed that there were higher rates of psychopathology among Jews than
among either Catholics or Protestants. His explanation, inbreeding, was picked
up by Jean-Martin Charcot and by Krafft-Ebing and then given a particular
twist by Weininger, for whom Jewishness was identified with effeminacy and, by
implication, with homosexuality. In the wake of "Circe," "Eumaeus" hovers
around questions of sexual "abnormality" and gender confusion. More particularly, the self-designation "Boudin" brings together the "problems" of homosexuality and Jewishness and reminds me of Bloom's exaggerated femininity at
the very point when he turns to Stephen as Jew and as victim: "He turned a long
you are wrong gaze on Stephen of timorous dark pride with a glance also of en-
treaty at the soft impeachment for he seemed to glean in a kind of a way that it
wasn't all exactly" (16.1088–90). It also makes me want to look more carefully at
a Jewish character's obsession with a merchant seaman from Carrigaloe.

At this point *The Merchant of Venice* provides a gloss (even if a highly speculative one), by implying in its own way an identification between homosexual
and Jew. The play is alluded to at various points in *Ulysses* but most significantly
and most often in "Eumaeus."[24] I want to use it here as a way of understanding
Joyce's homosexual subtext. (My reading is heavily indebted to Seymour Kleinberg, who sees the erotic triangle of Shakespeare's sonnets refracted and complicated by the mercantile context of the play, and argues that from the very
first scene it elaborates "the web of money and love, homoeroticism and anti-
Semitism.")[25] In *The Merchant of Venice* the connections between homophobia
and anti-Semitism are more fully drawn, but they are not foreign to "Eumaeus,"
where an allusive homophobic panic plays itself out, and where (as indeed
throughout *Ulysses*) Bloom's status as Jew—though "in reality," he says, he is
not—continues to haunt him. The triangular relationship between Antonio,
Bassanio, and Shylock provides an interesting analogue to the ways in which
Murphy, Stephen, and Bloom are implicated with each other. It may help to explain why—though the question "is Murphy a homosexual?" seems both unanswerable and somewhat beside the point—he is undeniably the focus for
Bloom's anxieties. For, in a similar way, "It is irrelevant what Bassanio and Antonio have actually done under the guise of their publicly admired courtly
friendship. It is entirely relevant that Antonio thinks himself disgusting."[26]

There are two merchants in Shakespeare's play: Shylock the Jew of course, but also Antonio the "lover" of Bassanio; he is marked by melancholia, self-disgust, and a hatred of Jews remarkable even in anti-Semitic Venice. Kleinberg argues:

> Antonio hates Shylock not because he is a more fervent Christian than others, but because he recognizes his own alter ego in this despised Jew who, because he is a heretic, can never belong to the state. He hates Shylock, rather than himself, in a classic pattern of psychological scapegoating. What Antonio hates in Shylock is not Jewishness, which like all Venetians he merely holds in contempt. He hates himself in Shylock: the homosexual self that Antonio has come to identify symbolically as the Jew. It is the earliest portrait of the homophobic homosexual.[27]

Antonio's hatred binds him, inevitably, to his enemy. Or rather, the law binds him, for as Jew and as homosexual they are both, equally, heretics and aliens. Under Elizabethan law sodomy and heresy were read interchangeably as capital offenses.[28] (Indeed, even etymologically the sexual crime has its roots in heresy: *buggery* is a corruption of *bougrerie,* a reference to eleventh-century Bulgarian heresies, subsequently applied to the Albigensians in the Languedoc, who were suspected, among other heretical transgressions, of favoring homosexuality.) The more substantial missing term in this equation is money, for the crime of usury (with which the Jews were identified and to which they were confined), like nonheterosexual eroticism, was seen as inherently sterile: sodomy, like usury, was false coining. (Closer to our own time it is interesting that *queer* in its present usage as "homosexual" is not noted by the *OED* until the early 1930s. But *queer* as counterfeit, false coining, has been current since the mid-eighteenth century. By the same token, the original meaning of *bougre* was not "bugger" but "usurer" and perhaps more generally "heretic.")[29] This history is worth recalling when we come to *Ulysses,* where Bloom, who points out that it was all a question of the money question, is marked by the stigmata of the Jew moneylender, and where Murphy is marked—quite literally, if we accept Gifford's decoding of the number sixteen—by the stigmata of homosexual desire. Reading Murphy-Boudin's entrance into the novel through Shakespeare's plot makes Bloom's amorphous anxiety more intelligible. Murphy becomes a focus and a mirror for Bloom's sense of himself, at this moment, as an outsider and a failure. As Antonio is to Shylock, so too, I would argue, is Bloom to Murphy— but with a twist. In the play the homosexual hates the Jew who mirrors him. In *Ulysses* the Jew hates the (projected) homosexual who mirrors him.

Implicitly the translation of "natural" sexuality into "honest" financial practice defines women as well. They are the medium of exchange, the blank coins to be imprinted and authorized by a patriarchal economy. This is a familiar trope for readers of Shakespeare and of Joyce—not surprisingly, since the yoking of money and love is everywhere in our culture.

Of all the Dubliners Bloom and Stephen could run into in "Eumaeus," how fitting that he should be Corley, whose contemptuous use of a woman's fondness Joyce had exposed earlier in "Two Gallants." The gold coin she offers him in that story will probably subsidize drinks with Lenehan (*D* 60). It is clear, in that story at least, which relationship takes precedence. In the exclusively male society of the cabman's shelter, the marginalization of women shades into misogyny. Murphy circulates his South American postcard with the claim that it shows "maneaters." In fact it shows "a group of savage women in striped loincloths, squatted, blinking, suckling, frowning, sleeping amid a swarm of infants" (16.475–77). The contradiction is eloquent. Here the gaze of misogyny, overlapped on the gaze of racism, translates a woman feeding her young into the spectacle of a woman savagely feeding *on* her young. Woman's murderous sexuality is implied later on as well, when the conversation turns to Kitty O'Shea with a mixture of contempt, fear, and desire. She is "[t]hat bitch, that English whore . . . [who] put the first nail in his coffin," even though a "[f]ine lump of a woman all the same" who "loosened many a man's thighs" (16.1352–55)—displacing the Homeric death that loosens many a man's knees. Bloom's well-meaning horror of the prostitute in the lane is another version of the same fear.

Like Murphy, Bloom too will circulate the image of a woman, though more selectively and only to Stephen. It may seem wrongheaded to set his proud, even touching, display of Molly's charms in the context of misogyny, but this moment in "Eumaeus" highlights the possibility suggested in "Circe" (15.3790–93), and then again in "Penelope" (18.81–83 and 1004–9) that Bloom is more than acquiescing to his wife's adultery; he is colluding in it. Molly lubricates Bloom's relationships with other men. She might well transpose Bloom's question about M'Coy to herself and ask, "Wonder is he pimping after me?" (5.191). That question provokes another. Why would a husband do that? One answer of course would note Bloom's particular, and possibly perverse, psychosexual formation. Another would have to consider how, in a patriarchal society like Joyce's Dublin, in spite of the fact that homosexual relations are utterly proscribed and heterosexual desire is the norm, it is the bonds between men (what Sedgwick calls homosocial relations) that "normally" take precedence. Indeed, it has been argued that this apparent contradiction is a defining feature of patriarchal society. Feminist anthropology makes the point "that patriarchal heterosexuality can best be discussed in terms of one or another form of the traffic in women: it is the use of women as exchangeable, perhaps symbolic, property for the primary purpose of cementing the bonds of men with men."[30]

By showing Molly's picture (in marked contrast to his polite reticence about "Madame"—6.693—with anyone else in Dublin) Bloom underlines the special intimacy of his link to Stephen. The brief "Bandez! Figne toi trop"

(16.1454) that breaks into the narrative just at this point is strange, but rich with implication. Most likely but not necessarily mumbled by Stephen, the phrases can be loosely rendered as some variant on "Get stuffed." More literally the words mean "get it up" (as if these things could be commanded), followed by "arsehole," and then the reflexive "[to] yourself too much."[31] The juxtaposition of the phallic and the anal is the fulcrum joining two currents of Bloom's thought: his visit earlier in the day to the National Museum to gaze on the back-sides of "those Grecian statues" (16.1450), delectably ample, like Molly's, and, as recorded in the paragraph that follows, an increasing consciousness of his own backside. In his reading of this second part of the passage, Derek Attridge picks up on the way "'moving a motion' and 'sat tight' hover on the edge of anal sig-nification," blurring the line between the sexual and the excretory. Between the two functions, he notes—in Joyce as in Freud—there is easy passage.[32] "What the style of Eumaeus achieves, for all its attempts at propriety, is a vivid demon-stration of the impossibility of fixed boundaries and significations when the structures of language are permeated by the dissolving energies of erotic de-sire."[33] It is a desire, I would add, that similarly blurs the line between hetero-and homoerotic pleasure. That Bloom is in some way luring Stephen with Molly's picture does not necessarily mean that he "wants" Stephen sexually, but the Wakean network of innuendo and the nervousness that surrounds it sug-gest that the homosocial and the homosexual are not as distinct as our culture tells us they must be, and that in this scenario women are assigned a mediating role. These, I think, are the wider issues being explored by Joyce.

One of the things we can say about homosexuality is that, like misogyny, its cultural meaning is not fixed. Abhorred in one time and place, it may be ac-knowledged and respected in another; degenerate effeminacy here, it can be an expression of full masculinity there. But as Eve Sedgwick has argued, whenever there is homophobia, there is also always misogyny. This is the situation of Bloom's Dublin. In the angry altercation between the street vendors that Bloom and Stephen come across (right by the men's public urinal, near the train sta-tion: sites notorious for homosexual encounter), the opening gambit is reveal-ing: "Puttana madonna, che ci dia i quattrini! Ho ragione? Culo rotto!" (16.314). "Puttana Madonna," the whore-virgin: limit terms of womanhood, but now, be-tween men, transformed into enraged expletive. The final "Culo rotto" (literally: broken arse) is equally ambiguous. It is as likely to mean "you lucky bastard" as to imply more literally, with homophobic venom, that "you" have a torn (feminized) body. Embedded in the fight over money, and bracketed between misogyny and homophobia, the contradictions of patriarchy are laid bare.

Like all of *Ulysses*, "Eumaeus" offers an account of homosocial relations. More particularly, it encodes issues of homoeroticism, male bonding, anti-Semitism, and women's place in patriarchal relations. Compulsively repeating the phrase "the other" like a nervous tick,[34] the episode takes as a subtext the role of the homosexual Other and makes D. B. Murphy the locus of Bloom's anxiety. As Morpheus, inhabiter of dreams and shape-changer,[35] he re-presents Bloom back to himself in an unnerving form that Bloom may not see entirely clearly but that the Wakean logic of innuendo makes apparent to the reader. Murphy triangulates the meeting between Bloom and Stephen as a cuckolded and possibly homosexual Shakespeare does in "Circe."

That the narrative should run along a trail of covert allusions and verbal slippages seems entirely appropriate, for "Eumaeus," somnolent and weary, is already alert to the logic of dreams. Joyce places himself in the tradition of the other great interpreters of dreams: Freud most immediately and, two thousand years before him, Artemidorus, both of whom rely on slips of the tongue to reveal meaning.[36]

But then, who is the dreamer? I have undertaken to read "Eumaeus" suspiciously, and against the grain, in order to pick up the homoerotic nap in the homosocial weave. To what extent must such a reading identify the writer's entanglement in his fictional scenario? Is it only Bloom's anxieties that are at stake, or am I inevitably suggesting that they are also Joyce's? (I am not convinced, as Hugh Kenner is, that all the rhetorical quirks in the episode can be laid at Bloom's doorstep.[37]) And if the panic is Joyce's, why might that be so? I leave the question open, largely because I do not feel qualified to answer it.[38] It is important, however, to reflect on the ways in which the issues identified here speak to a more general ideological formation that we still share with Joyce and his contemporaries, but that is beginning to shift and even to come undone. In that unraveling perhaps we can see more clearly what has been unspoken, and therefore invisible, in men's relationships with men.

NOTES

This essay is dedicated to John Hulcoop, who has been my teacher and friend for thirty years, and who has so generously shared his reading of "Eumaeus" with me.

1. In "uncorrected" editions Murphy's initials are W. B.—presumably the typist's misreading, which Joyce, according to Gabler, "inadvertently reinforced." I like to think of this uncertainty, as does Gabler, as adding "an ironic touch to the motif of dubious identity in the chapter." *Ulysses: A Critical and Synoptic Edition* (New York: Garland Publishing, 1984), 3.1750.

2. Eve Kosofsky Sedgwick, *Between Men: English Literature and Male Homosocial Desire* (New York: Columbia University Press, 1985), 1–2.

3. Sedgwick, *Between Men*, 2.

4. See René Girard, *Deceit, Desire, and the Novel: Self and Other in Literary Structure*, trans. Yvonne Freccero (Baltimore: Johns Hopkins University Press, 1976), chap. 1.

5. Not much has changed for Molly since Gibraltar, where she remembers "waiting, always waiting . . . not a letter from a living soul except the odd few I posted to myself with bits of paper in them so bored sometimes . . . as bad as now with the hands

hanging off me looking out of the window . . . and no visitors or post ever except his cheques or some advertisement like that wonderworker they sent him addressed dear Madam" (18.678, 698–99, 702–3, 715–16).

6. See, for instance, Roland Barthes, "The Proper Name," in *S/Z*, trans. Richard Miller (New York: Hill and Wang, 1974), 94–95.

7. Carrigaloe is one of Ireland's more obscure little places. It is hardly surprising that no one else responds to Murphy's question. In keeping with the Eumaean invitation to go "sherlockholmesing" (16.831), I was amused to find that the only map on which I could locate it was a CIA gazetteer originally stamped "classified information" (*Preliminary N.I.S. Gazetteer: Ireland* [Washington, D.C.: Central Intelligence Agency, 1950]).

8. Derek Attridge, *Peculiar Language: Literature as Difference from the Renaissance to James Joyce* (Ithaca, N.Y.: Cornell University Press, 1988), 175.

9. For a discussion of "Oxen of the Sun," ll. 639–46, see Jennifer Levine, "*Ulysses*," in *The Cambridge Companion to James Joyce*, ed. Derek Attridge, (Cambridge: Cambridge University Press, 1990), 156.

10. See *I Grandi Dizionari Sansoni* (Firenze Roma: Sansoni Editore, 1970); *Dizionario Etimologico Italiano* (Firenze: G. Barbera Editore, 1975); *Dizionario Italiano Ragionato* (Firenze: G D'Anna-Sintezi, 1988); *Grande Dizionario Della Lingua Italiana* (Torino, Unione Tipografico-Editrice Torinese, 1961).

11. See, for instance, Ovid's story of Ceyx and Alcyone, in which Morpheus appears to Alcyone (in a dream) in the form of her drowned husband, forcing her to see his fate and to acknowledge her own, as widow. Morpheus may also be read as the projection of Alcyone's (the dreamer's) desire.

12. "Un cabalista pratico," *Antica Smorfia Napoletana: Il gioco piu antico della tradizione popolare napoletana per immagini e voci* (Romê: Prisma Libri, 1988). This fairly recent compendium of *la smorfia* opens with a series of ninety numbered woodcuts called *sogni figurati*, illustrated dreams.

13. Don Gifford with Robert J. Seidman, *"Ulysses" Annotated,* rev. ed. (Berkeley and Los Angeles: University of California Press, 1989), 544. Gifford's claim that in European slang and numerology the number meant homosexuality has been remarkably difficult to confirm. I, therefore, would hesitate to highlight it, particularly when there are so many other elements in "Eumaeus" that point in a similar direction. By implication, however, Stuart Gilbert's footnote in *James Joyce's "Ulysses,"* 2d ed. (New York: Alfred A. Knopf, 1930), 310 about *Les Tatouages* in the Collection de Psychologie Populaire de Dr Jaf, may be relevant. Commenting on Murphy's description of Antonio—"a Greek he was"—and the number tattooed on his chest, Gilbert claims that *six* and *sixteen* were Neapolitan slang for certain sexual practices or positions. More significantly, though, the particular tattoo cited as evidence by Dr. Jaf includes the signature of the tattoo artist, who is also the lover of the woman who bears it. The thought of Antonio as "lover," I will argue, is not entirely foreign to "Eumaeus."

14. Weldon Thornton, *Allusions in "Ulysses"* (Chapel Hill: University of North Carolina Press, 1968), 447–48. Thornton refers to W. Y. Tindall's *A Reader's Guide to James Joyce* (New York: Noonday Press, 1959), 219.

15. Gifford, *"Ulysses" Annotated,* 551, quoting H. Montgomery Hyde, ed., *The Three Trials of Oscar Wilde* (London: William Hodge, 1948), 382.

16. Karen Lawrence, "'Beggaring Description': Economies of Language and the Language of Economy in 'Eumaeus,'" typescript of the keynote address at the James

Joyce Symposium, Monte Carlo, June 1990, 28. I am grateful to Lawrence for making her text available.

17. Lawrence, "Beggaring Description," 28.

18. Lawrence, "Beggaring Description," 29, cites Peter Stallybrass and Allon White, *The Politics and the Poetics of Transgression* (Ithaca, N.Y.: Cornell University Press, 1986), passim, and Allon White, "Hysteria and the End of Carnival: Festivity and Bourgeois Neurosis," in *The Violence of Representation: Literature and the History of Violence,* ed. Nancy Armstrong and Leonard Tennenhouse (London: Routledge, 1989), 157–70.

19. Interestingly, Bloom's well-intentioned theory as to the why and the wherefore of national character and, in particular, of Mediterranean violence, partakes of the same racist logic as nineteenth-century accounts and explanations for homosexuality: it was all due to the heat. See Sedgwick, *Between Men,* 182–84.

20. The *OED* explicates *to board* as to approach, make up to, accost, assail, address, make advances to. The sexual implications of *diddle* are given by Eric Partridge, *Dictionary of Slang and Unconventional English,* 8th ed. (London: Routledge and Kegan Paul, 1984). Its meanings shade from swindling and trifling through shaking to copulating. It is also, since the 1870s, schoolboy slang for "penis."

21. See Émile Littré, *Dictionnaire de la Langue Francaise* (Gallimard: Hachette, 1968); *Tresor de la Langue Francaise: Dictionnaire de la Langue du XIXe et du XXe Siecle (1789–1960)* (Paris: Edition du Centre National de la Recherche Scientifique, 1971); and *Harrap's Slang Dictionary: English-French, French-English* (London: Harrap, 1984).

22. I owe this reference to John Gordon's *James Joyce's Metamorphoses* (Totowa, N.J.: Barnes and Noble, 1981), 137. The allusion, like so many other details in "Eumaeus," is read by Gordon as evidence that Murphy is a projection of Mulvey: a rival to Bloom more profound than Boylan can ever be and, therefore, the source of his agitation. Gordon's argument about "Eumaeus" is extensive and forceful but not, finally, persuasive. It ascribes the narrative's anxiety too simply to Bloom, and to a single emotion—jealousy.

23. On M. Boudin, see Robert Byrnes, "Bloom's Sexual Tropes: Stigmata of the 'Degenerate' Jew," *James Joyce Quarterly* 27 (winter 1990): 309. For Joyce's interest in Richard Krafft-Ebing and Otto Weininger see, more generally, Byrnes, 303–23, citing Marilyn Reizbaum: "The Jewish Connection, Cont'd," in *The Seventh of Joyce,* ed. Bernard Benstock (Bloomington: Indiana University Press, 1982). Also see Richard Brown, *Joyce and Sexuality* (Cambridge: Cambridge University Press, 1985); and Ira B. Nadel, *Joyce and the Jews* (Iowa City: University of Iowa Press, 1989).

24. Consider, first of all, the teasing reference to Antonio: "the Antonio personage (no relation to the dramatic personage of identical name who sprang from the pen of our national poet)" (16.839–40) and also the more direct quotations: "O tell me where is fancy bread" (16.58–59) and "the harmless necessary animal of the feline persuasion" (16.870).

25. Seymour Kleinberg, "The Merchant of Venice: The Homosexual as Anti-Semite in Nascent Capitalism," *Journal of Homosexuality* 8 (spring–summer 1983): 117.

26. Kleinberg, "The Merchant of Venice," 120.

27. Kleinberg, "The Merchant of Venice," 120.

28. Kleinberg, "The Merchant of Venice," 120. See also John Boswell, *Christianity, Social Tolerance, and Homosexuality* (Chicago: University of Chicago Press, 1980), 283–86, for the more general European context.

29. Boswell, *Christianity, Social Tolerance,* 284, 290.

30. Sedgwick, *Between Men,* 25–26, here refers to Gayle Rubin's "The Traffic in Women: Notes on the Political Economy of Sex," in *Toward an Anthropology of Women,* ed. Rayna R. Reiter (New York: Monthly Review Press, 1975), 157–210.

31. In a note on this phrase, which in the Rosenbach Manuscript is almost illegible, Gabler notes that the French translation of *Ulysses'* "S.O.D.," from Cyclops's barrage of honorary titles (12.1894), is rendered as "Chevalier du Figne"—Knight of the Arsehole; sodomist; pederast. See *Ulysses: A Critical and Synoptic Edition,* 3:1751.

32. Attridge, *Peculiar Language,* 180.

33. Attridge, *Peculiar Language,* 182.

34. See, for instance, 16.1172–1215 (much of which is quoted above) for six instances of "other" and "another" within a single paragraph. I offer the following note from Partridge as well: By 1925 *the other* had come to imply homosexuality as a criminal offense, and not just heterosexual copulation, as in "a bit of the other." In this particular paragraph, Joyce seems to be hinting at both possibilities.

35. I am reminded that Morpheus's transformations link him to Proteus, the shape changer, and that structurally the relationship between the chapters "Eumaeus" and "Proteus" (the third of part 1 and the first of part 3) is chiastically symmetrical. It is precisely at the end of "Proteus" that Stephen turns his face and, without knowing he is doing so, sees the ship that will bring Murphy to Dublin: "Moving through the air high spars of a threemaster, her sails brailed up on the crosstrees, homing, upstream, silently moving, a silent ship" (3.503–5).

36. Artemidorus Daldianus, *Dell'interpretazione dei sogni,* trans. Pietro Lauro Modonese (Rome: dell'Elefante, 1970). See in particular George Seferis's introduction to the volume, noting Freud's acknowledgment of his links to Artemidorus.

37. See Hugh Kenner, *Ulysses,* rev. ed. (Baltimore: Johns Hopkins University Press, 1987), 130.

38. See, for a rather more confident assertion, Ruth Von Phul, "Gorgios," *A Wake Newslitter* 2 (June 1965): 20–21:

> The fact that Joyce, who seems to have been really bisexual, suffered all the rest of his life from recurring homosexual temptation explains Joyce's implacability toward Gogarty, Gogarty's fear of what Joyce might write about him, and after *Ulysses,* Gogarty's defensive gambits of alternately branding Joyce as a hoaxer or mad.

No evidence is presented, but I gather from Fritz Senn that Von Phul claimed there had originally been a letter (since lost or destroyed) indicating that Joyce had been seduced by Gogarty in Dublin, and then by a sailor in Trieste. The circularity of the argument is hardly reassuring: that the evidence is missing implies that it had been suppressed and thereby confirms that it really existed. I pass the story on here—with reservations—in case any reader may be able to confirm it. In doing so, I realize that I am also illustrating the potential minefields in the biographical approach. A more fruitful line of argument might instead follow up a repeated motif in Joyce's fictions and in the letters to Nora: the (possibly) deceived lover's obsession with his male rival, and the implication that that relationship is at least as compelling as the heterosexual one.

Père-version and Im-mère-sion

Idealized Corruption in *A Portrait of the Artist as a Young Man* and *The Picture of Dorian Gray*

Vicki Mahaffey

Coupled together, Joyce's *A Portrait of the Artist as a Young Man* and Wilde's *The Picture of Dorian Gray* (from which Joyce drew the first part of his title)[1] expose the complementary parental mechanisms by which children are corrupted, offering critiques that are precise enough to distinguish between specific, harmful exercises of authority and authority in general (which need not be synonymous with corruption). Revealingly, in both cases the child is corrupted not by homosexuality, but by homophobia; not by openness, but by secrecy; not by the real, but by the objectifying force of the ideal.

In *A Portrait of the Artist as a Young Man,* it is the father whose voice coaches Stephen's education/corruption, instructing him in homophobia and in misogyny, thereby producing in him the socially acceptable norm of perverse masculine desire (what Jacques Lacan calls *père*-version: "Perversion [*père-version*] being the sole guarantee of [a man's] function as father").[2] *Portrait* shows how a male child is inducted into patriarchy: schooled in homosocial bonding, chastised for expressing such bonds sexually (thereby learning homophobia), and displacing his ideal onto women, seen not as subjects but as displaced objects of desire (what Lacan refers to as "La femme," the universalized woman who does not exist).[3] Joyce identifies the heterosexual father as the driving force behind Stephen's initiation into "normal" heterosexual perverse desire; like Daedalus, the father thinks he is giving his son wings to escape the labyrinth of sexual despair, but for Stephen, as for Icarus, these wings of "escape" are instead the agents of a disastrous fall: he learns that the pursuit of an ideal precludes interpersonal relationship, that paternal authority is isolated and strangely disembodied.[4] *Portrait* shows Stephen turning from his biological father to the celibate fathers of the Church, to God the Father, and finally to the idea of a disembodied author, without ever being able to experience relation; although he grandly says no to God in the tradition of Lucifer, he has not learned to say no to the phallic function, to experience and accept his own insufficiency and self-division. Only in Leopold Bloom does Joyce develop the model of a father who lacks the self-protective and disabling delusions of omnipotence.

In *The Picture of Dorian Gray*, Wilde explored another model for the operation of perverse desire, one I have labeled *im-mère-sion* because it is presided over by the mother and because it affects the child in an opposite and yet comparable way: instead of raising the child above the real, it uses repression to situate him below it, to lock him in the cordoned-off room of the mother's unconscious. *Immersion* comes from the Latin *immergere,* "to dip, plunge, sink (into)"; in astronomy, it refers to "the disappearance of a celestial body behind another or in its shadow"; with reference to a title or an estate, to immerge is "to become merged or absorbed in that of a superior, so as no longer to have separate existence" *(OED).* If the father's exercise of desire isolates the child, directing him to transcend the real, the mother's exercise of "immersed" desire denies the child a separate existence, condemning it to live in the shadow cast by her own repression.[5] If the father unconsciously subordinates social intercourse to the principles of magnetism, teaching the child to polarize the sexes in a literal sense, so that unlike poles attract and like poles repel (thereby constructing heterosexuality as compulsory), the mother who idealizes her child and sacrifices her own pleasure in the process subordinates *herself* in a way that ties the child helplessly to her. Like Yeats in "Among School Children," Wilde's target is the "nuns and mothers" who "worship images," and Wilde's reply to those mothers is an uncompromising critique of their unnatural constraint and self-denial, a self-stifling that resembles the unnatural closeting of homosexual desire. Wilde conflates the amorous and maternal tendencies to construct the lover/child as an impossible ideal (or, in Lacanian terms, as the "phallus" that everyone wants but no one can have), showing that the fruit of im-mère-sion is not sterile detachment, but corrupt enslavement. Furthermore, by conflating closeted homosexual love with idealizing maternal love, Wilde suggests that such enslavement—im-mère-sion—is the danger that haunts homosexual love, in sharp contrast to heterosexual love, which is haunted by the opposite and identical intimation that "there is no sexual relation."

The Interdependence of Homophobia and Misogyny in *A Portrait of the Artist as a Young Man*

When, in "A Love Letter," Lacan asserts, "The soul is conjured out of what is *hommosexual,* as is perfectly legible from history,"[6] he seems to be using his neologism "hommosexual" not to mean homosexual in the usual sense, because he has just said that this conjuring of the soul by men is a sexless process. Instead, the emphasis is on the intertwining of *homme* and *homo* in "hommosex-ual"; the "normal" attitude of men *(hommes)* toward desire precludes the sex-ual, and at the same time it is a love of men for men—it is the reflection of a so-cial structure that Eve Sedgwick more clearly identifies as "homosocial."

In *Between Men: English Literature and Male Homosocial Desire,* Eve Sedgwick isolates and questions the asymmetry between what she calls the ho-mosocial-homosexual continuums for men and women. She argues that for women, we see the relationship between female bonding on the one hand, and lesbianism, on the other, as a more or less seamless progression, whereas for men, homophobia produces a radical discontinuity between male homosocial bonds and homosexual intimacy.[7] Homosocial bonding is the basis of patri-archy (as Gayle Rubin and Luce Irigaray have influentially argued), but that bonding is upheld, not by an understanding of its continuity with male homo-sexuality, but by a violent denial of such kinship, a denial that takes the form of homophobia.[8]

It is well understood among theorists who work on sexual politics that misogyny and homophobia are the twin children of patriarchy, that both women and male homosexuals must be recreated as objects of desire and loathing, respectively, for patriarchy to work. In fact, it is the necessary con-struction of women as desirable objects and men as forbidden objects that de-fines the "compulsory heterosexuality" prescribed by patriarchy. The problem, of course, is that under such a system only heterosexual men are granted the status of subjects; moreover, this privileging of male subjectivity ensures a stul-tifying sameness in sexual and social politics.

I am fully in sympathy with Sedgwick's antihomophobic and feminist in-quiry. On the structural level, it is absolutely clear that women and male ho-mosexuals have been (differently) commodified; you could almost say that they have been cast as the fuel and waste products, respectively, of the patriarchal sys-tem of social production. But I'd also like to call attention to the ways in which certain practices of women and male homosexuals either effectively resist or else unconsciously replicate the objectifications to which they themselves have been subject. Effective resistance to objectification involves a huge burden of con-sciousness, a constant vigilance over the behavior of oneself as well as that of others toward the self, a refusal to succumb, in theory or in practice, to the se-duction of stereotypes. Unconscious replication of oppression, however, tends to be enacted upon the least empowered members of a patriarchal system—children. Joyce's famous illustration of the ease with which disempowerment in adults can be translated into tyranny over children is "Counterparts," but he also exposes the ways in which both mothers and gay men may objectify children. Mothers may objectify their children in one of two ways, by capitalizing on their use value (turning them into mere instruments of the mother's own will), or by turning them into ideal love objects. Joyce dramatizes the maternal tendency to turn children into passive instruments of maternal will in "Eveline," "A Board-ing House," and "A Mother." Moreover, he explores the tendency of adult men to treat children (both male and female) as sexual objects in "An Encounter." It is interesting, parenthetically, that Joyce has the man in the field respond erotically to *both* the softness of young girls *and* the disobedience of young boys, a disobedience that seems to justify the pleasure of whipping them. The story is carefully constructed around the man's *two* monologues—on girls and boys, respectively—which has the effect of discouraging or complicating any knee-jerk homophobic response. By constructing the story this way, Joyce makes it clear that the focus of his implied critique here is *not* a critique of sexual orientation, but the sexual abuse of children, which includes incest as well as other forms of pedophilia.

Joyce demonstrates that *all* love relationships, gay and straight, are haunted by a tendency toward perversion, defined by Jacques Lacan in the first seminar as desire that "finds its support in the ideal of an inanimate object."[9] Interestingly, although Lacan notes in passing that "the intersubjective relation which subtends perverse desire is only sustained by the annihilation either of the desire of the other, or of the desire of the subject," he is less concerned in this seminar with the deleterious effect of perverse desire on the object of desire than he is with exploring its effect on the *subject*. He argues that the *value* of perversion is that *because* "it can find no way of becoming grounded in any satisfying action" it allows one to experience human passion more profoundly. The perverse lover is in search of *himself*; therefore his experience of desire opens up a gap within himself within which "all manner of nuances are called forth, rising up in tiers from shame to prestige, from buffoonery to heroism, whereby human desire in its entirety is exposed, in the deepest sense of the term, to the desire of the other."[10]

Lacan makes it clear that perverse desire ensures "a reciprocal relation of annihilation" because such desire cannot be satisfied by possession of the object—the object is lost through its realization. Moreover, Lacan argues, such a relation also dissolves the being of the *subject*—subject as well as object are eroded by perverse desire.

In perverse desire, then, the object is also an ideal, which is why no lasting satisfaction can be obtained simply by possessing the object. Possession of the object simply displaces the ideal onto some other object. This is important because it helps to explain Stephen's failure to achieve maturity—defined as the ability to achieve intersubjective relation—in *Portrait*. Stephen, as a young man, learns the rules of perverse desire, but never experiences or learns to appreciate his own fractured subjectivity, a subjectivity that may not even be compatible with rigidly defined gender categories at all.[11]

The first two chapters of *Portrait* show Stephen undergoing a socialization process with boys and then girls which initiates him into the world of perverse (insatiable) desire by way of the attitudes that are imposed upon him: the necessity of homosocial bonding, homophobia, and misogyny. Homophobic and misogynistic attitudes are frequently intertwined in *Portrait*; moreover, it is the voice of Stephen's father that is the most authoritative proponent of these attitudes—he is infecting Stephen with his *père*-version. The law of the Father is here, quite literally, to bond with men without sexual intimacy and to objectify women through the desire for sexual intimacy.

The first voice in the novel is the voice of the father, telling the child a "fairy tale" story of his origins. The father is the author and narrator of the story; he is not represented within it, which along with his position as first speaker gives him his authority. Those represented within the story, as characters rather than narrators, are Stephen, played by Baby Tuckoo, and his mother, who appears as the moocow.

> Once upon a time and a very good time it was there was a moocow com-
> ing down along the road and this moocow that was coming down along
> the road met a nicens little boy named baby tuckoo.

To cast the mother as a moocow—even before she meets baby tuckoo—ranges from the humorous to the appalling, but the child accepts it, charmed perhaps by the rhyming link between the names for mother and child ("moo" and "koo"), and apparently oblivious of the devolution of the mother to a milk-giving animal (a devolution familiar in children's stories).

When Stephen goes to Clongowes, he overhears many sexual innuendoes that he records but fails to understand, many of which are associated not with food (as in the case of the moocow) but with bathrooms or lavatories, which trigger homosexual associations. First, Stephen recalls the fellow who tells Simon Moonan that he is McGlade's suck, which makes Stephen recoil at the ugliness of the sound (*P* 11) and remember the draining of the sink water when his father pulled up the chain in the lavatory of the Wicklow Hotel. There is of course "smugging" in the square, where the boys' waterclosets are located, as well as the square ditch into which Wells has pushed Stephen. Stephen draws attention to the place where the smugging took place by asking,

> But why in the square? You went there when you wanted to do something.
> It was all thick slabs of slate and water trickled all day out of tiny pinholes
> and there was a queer smell of stale water there. (43)

Stephen's fear of the "warm turfcoloured bogwater" at Clongowes represents a fear of sexuality partly through the association of male homosexuality with lavatories, but in *Ulysses* Stephen also explicitly associates the water he fears with women. Again, the threat of sexuality from men and women is presented as equivalent.

Even Eileen puzzles Stephen with sexual metaphors when she puts her hand into his pocket where his hand was, says that "pockets [are] funny things to have" (43), and runs away laughing. It is clear from *Stephen Hero*, where Stephen refers to women as "marsupials," that Joyce associated pockets with female genitalia, as would Flann O'Brien after him in *At Swim-Two-Birds*. The sexual threats from men and women are experienced as commensurate, although at Clongowes the threat from Eileen is remembered (when Stephen is puzzling over the smugging) rather than immediate.

In the midst of the vague sexual threats represented by the older boys in the square, Stephen is buoyed up by his father's warning: whatever he did, never to peach on a fellow (*P* 21). As his father primed him for misogyny by introducing his mother as a moocow, he here uses slang to send Stephen a double message about boys. He legitimates homosocial bonding through the dominant meaning of the phrase—never betray or inform on a fellow. But a now obsolete meaning of *to peach* is also to breathe hard from exertion, to pant; deeply encoded in his father's language is the injunction not to pant on a fellow, not to express his friendship sexually.[12]

Interestingly, the word "smugging" also carries a meaningful constellation of associations. *Smug* is a form of *snug*, which is associated with privacy and snuggling. A snug is also a hard knob, and *snugging* is a nautical term for the operation of rubbing down a rope to give it a smooth finish *(OED)*. It is apparent how the word came to be associated with male arousal, but the meanings of the word *smug* are also relevant to an understanding of the sexual politics at work here. *Smuggy* also means "grimy," "smutty" (it is related to *smoggy*), an association reinforced by the fact that the smugging takes place in the oozing square (which in turn encourages Stephen to consider the *activity* "dirty"). But the primary meaning of *smugging* is to steal, and in fact this is what the boys think at first that Simon Moonan and Tusker Boyle's gang have done—stolen cash from the rectory or wine from the sacristy (*P* 40). The connection between homosexuality and stealing serves to point up the commodification of sexual exchange. If homosexual activity is "stealing," then it is logical that Stephen decides in the next chapter to *pay* to gratify his sexual desires, which he does in his encounter with the female prostitute. What he has been taught is that sexuality, whether homo- or heterosexual, circulates via an economic exchange; the difference is that patriarchal law designates one as unlawful—stealing—and the other as compulsory, which is why Stephen must always be in pursuit of a prostitute or Mercedes, a temptress or a bird girl. Joyce, however, goes on to associate female sexuality with orality and male homosexuality with elimination, thereby positioning them as opposite but equal extremes in a bodily (oral/anal, or pre-reproductive) system of production. Chapter 2 ends with the pressure of the prostitute's tongue between Stephen's lips, an emphasis that puts *him* in the female position. Gender identity, then, like sexual orientation, is fluid. Furthermore, the similarity between heterosexual and homosexual desire, as both have been socially constructed, is underlined by the image of the doll in the prostitute's room, sitting on the easy chair with her legs apart (101). This doll recalls Bertie Tallon, dressed as a girl for the Whitsuntide play, of whom a prefect asks, "Is this a beautiful young lady or a doll that you have here, Mrs Tallon?" (74) It turns out to be neither a lady nor a doll, but a painted boy. Once again the expected gender categories have been subverted, and at the same time the undressing of the prostitute has been imagistically linked with the cross-dressing of boys. Both in this context represent an imitation of sexuality, an appearance of sexuality that bears the same relation to lived sexuality that a doll bears to a person.

Stephen, however, doesn't really take the imprint of perverse desire in a way that is satisfactory to his father: his ultimate acceptance by his schoolfellows at Clongowes is too mythic, and his pursuit of female sexuality too literal and fetishized. Both of these relatively exaggerated expressions of homosocial bonding and compulsory heterosexuality threaten by their very excess to expose the principle of objectifying and thereby distancing the sexuality of the other— both male and female—on which they are built.

Stephen learns his lesson somewhat superficially because all his actions and discoveries are overcoded by the voice and fortunes of his father, who serves as a disembodied guide in a way that is later taken over by priests, only to take its most congenial form in the ideal of the triumphantly transcendent author (a view of authorship that differs significantly from Joyce's). It is his father's voice, directing Stephen to be a gentleman in all things and never to peach on a fellow, that inspires Stephen's victory at Clongowes, and it is his father's misfortunes that prompt him both to begin writing (he tries to write a poem to Parnell on the back of one of his father's second moiety notices [*P* 70]) and to pursue women. As Stephen begins to brood upon Mercedes at the beginning of chapter 2, his meditations are repeatedly interrupted by realizations that his father is in trouble (64): "he became slowly aware that his father had enemies and that some fight was going to take place. He felt too that he was being enlisted for the fight" (66). Later, Stephen is haunted by the hollowsounding voices of his father and masters urging him to be a gentleman and a good catholic above all things (83), and he perceives a likeness between his father's mind and that of a smiling, well-dressed priest that seems to desecrate the priest's office (84).

The problem with his father's voice, like the desires it authorizes, is that it is disembodied. Stephen's mother, who is not yet disembodied, becomes audible to him only after her death. What this disembodiment seems to mean to Stephen is a lack of full commitment, an incipient if unintentional hypocrisy in which precepts aren't backed up by physical enactments. It is easy to see why Stephen's second father, Bloom, had to be so very physical—to the point that Mulligan sees him as a sexual threat to Stephen: "He is Greeker than the Greeks! Get thee a breechpad!" One implication is that the relationship between men— including that between fathers and sons—isn't physical enough.

Wilde Im-mère-sions of Desire

Initiated into the transcendent sterility of perverse desire by his father in *A Portrait of the Artist as a Young Man,* alienated from the fuel and waste of bodily production, as represented by women and homosexual men, respectively, Stephen only becomes subject to the dangers of im-mère-sion (or "in *mère* son," the son locked in the mother/horse, like Ulysses in Troy) in *Ulysses*, after his mother has died. Perversion unnaturally ages a child; in *Portrait*, Stephen, watching his father and his cronies, thinks, "His mind seemed older than theirs: it shone coldly on their strifes and happiness and regrets like a moon upon a younger earth" (*P* 95). Im-mère-sion, in contrast, makes a child younger than he is: in *Ulysses* Stephen is associated with an embryo (an association made explicit in the schema of "The Oxen of the Sun"), and in *The Picture of Dorian Gray* Dorian keeps an appearance of unnatural youthfulness. Perverse desire, authorized by the father, designates the woman as the male fetish; immersion, authorized by the mother, fetishizes the child itself, who in turn looks for his own image as love object (these are two different forms of narcissism). What is corrosive about immersion comes not only from the mother's limiting idealization of the child, but also from the mother's idealization of her own desire, her denial of the sexual overtones of that desire and of the fact that she idealizes the child in order to buttress her own repression, a process that keeps the child tied to her.[13]

In *The Picture of Dorian Gray*, Basil is depicted not only as a man who secretly desires Dorian, but also as his "mother," the creator of his physical image: the portrait that Basil has painted and labeled his masterpiece. Basil's fear of exhibiting the finished portrait betrays the extent to which he has identified it both with himself and with the secret of his desire. When he tells Harry that "every portrait that is painted with feeling is a portrait of the artist, not of the sitter," that "[i]t is not he [the sitter] who is revealed by the painter; it is rather the painter who, on the colored canvas, reveals himself," he betrays the extent to which he has appropriated Dorian, thereby revealing "the secret of [his] soul."[14]

Basil's picture represents the merging of the beautiful self-image Basil desires and Dorian's (real) body; by painting it, he has, at one stroke, repainted himself as he would like to be and frozen Dorian as that which—at a distance—mirrors and supports his own desire.[15] What Basil doesn't know is that only at the level of appearances can Dorian mirror Basil's ideal; by annexing Dorian to his own needs, Basil ensures that Dorian will reflect *all* of him, which means that Dorian must also secretly act out the desires Basil has repudiated and denied. The portrait is what integrates Basil's noble intentions and his subterranean desires, made corrupt through secrecy; just as Basil fears that it will betray the secret of Basil's soul, it will later reveal the secrets of Dorian's. Basil's "secret" is his love for Dorian, a love that dare not speak its name; Dorian's secret is that he is Basil's counterpart and his progeny—Basil and Dorian not only mirror each other's submerged desire, but Basil has also, like Frankenstein, *produced* Dorian, who, like Frankenstein's creature, is maddened at the monstrosity of his creation out of repressed desire. Basil *refuses* to express his socially unacceptable love for Dorian; Dorian, whose image Basil has literally created, is doomed, in sharp contrast, to realize every impulse that Basil would deny, thereby revealing the corruption implicit in beauty.

What Basil failed to do—what he never even attempted to do—is to try Lord Henry's prescription for living. While Basil is painting Dorian's image, Lord Henry's musical voice advises,

> I believe that if one man were to live his life out fully and completely, were to give form to every feeling, expression to every thought, reality to every dream,—I believe that the world would gain such a fresh impulse of joy that we would forget all the maladies of medievalism, and return to the Hellenic ideal,—to something finer, richer, than the Hellenic ideal, it may be. But the bravest man among us is afraid of himself. The mutilation of the savage has its tragic survival in the self-denial that mars our lives. We are punished for our refusals. Every impulse that we strive to strangle broods in the mind, and poisons us. (*DG* 185–86)

Dorian tries to do what Henry has suggested, but with disastrous results, since his impulses are not his own. Dorian's libertinism, his sensual self-indulgence, are the *products* of Basil's repression, his obedient goodness, his commitment to sublimation, and his love of secrecy. There is no physical contact between Dorian and Basil; their common—and interdependent—secrets meet only through the mediation of the portrait, hidden away in the room of Dorian's childhood.

What is fascinating about the helpless complicity of Basil and Dorian is that it conflates the sublimation, the idealized closeting of homosexual desire and the grotesquely repulsive product of such denial with another highly idealized, sublimated relationship ringed round with taboo: the relationship of mother to child. Here, the prohibition against incest serves the same function as the ban on homosexual intercourse—it prompts the mother to idealize and thereby hide or deny the highly erotic and ambivalent nature of the relationship, a repression that sentences the child to take up psychic residence in the cordoned-off room of the mother's unconscious desires, as well as awakening in the child a forbidden desire for the mother, who through repression has made herself unavailable, a mere *representation* or portrait of femaleness. (Incidentally, the overlap between injunctions against homosexuality and those prohibiting incest helps to explain the humorous appropriateness of Joyce's conflation of the two in *Finnegans Wake*, where he describes buggery as "insectuous.")

Dorian Gray, then, is a powerful indictment against the corrupting piousness of compulsory heterosexuality *and* virtuous motherhood. Basil is at once Dorian's would-be lover and his mother, as is even clearer in the 1890 edition of *Dorian Gray* published in *Lippincott's* (which Wilde revised—toned down—in response to the furor over its publication in England, where the publishers had to withdraw it from the newsstands). In the *Lippincott's* version, Wilde clearly implies that Basil and Lord Henry are lovers. In the garden scene, immediately before the two men together produce Dorian's consciousness of himself (Basil producing consciousness of the body through his mirror-portrait, Henry producing consciousness of the mind—generating thought—through words), Wilde relates that "the two young men went out into the garden together, and for a time they did not speak" (*DG* 176). Wilde suggests that they not only produce Dorian's self-image, but they also jointly "parent" him in this encounter in the garden before Dorian appears. Wilde again reinforces the identification of Basil with motherhood in another deleted passage, in which the narrator explains that "there was something in Basil's nature that was purely feminine in its tenderness" (*DG* 230).

The ostensible villain of *Dorian Gray* is Lord Henry; it is he, with his musical voice and magical words, who kindles in Dorian a wild curiosity, who plays the role of the devil in this modern morality tale. He is the snake in the garden, explicitly associated with evil, who inspires Dorian to yearn for immortality, for eternal youth. His temptation, like that of Satan to Eve, is for man to be as God, to eat the forbidden fruit of the knowledge of good and evil, which Dorian accordingly does. Henry *is* irresponsible in his friendship with Dorian; he toys with him, views him with the fascinated detachment of a scientist toward a specimen. But nothing happens to Henry; it is Basil—the "good" mother, the champion of conventional morality propped up by Victorian repression—whom Dorian brutally murders in a fit of uncontrollable loathing. Dorian is seized with an irresistible need to *show* Basil the rotten fruit of his idealism; Basil is the only one to whom Dorian ever shows the portrait of himself once it has begun to express the corruption of his soul, and as he invites Basil into the locked room to see the painting of his corrupt soul, Dorian taunts, "Come: it is your own handiwork" (*DG* 259). When the picture is revealed, Dorian asks bitterly, "Can't you see your ideal in it?" (122) Dorian's one despairing attempt to make Basil understand his mistake of denying the chiaroscuro of the soul is his insistence, "Each of us has both heaven and hell in him, Basil" (122).[16] Basil doesn't get it; all he sees is that once Dorian was good and now he's bad—he begs Dorian to repent. It is for this Dorian kills him.

Later, Dorian struggles to explain his action by saying to Alan Campbell, "You don't know what he had made me suffer. Whatever my life is, he had more to do with the making or marring of it than poor Harry has had. He may not have intended it, [but] the result was the same" (*DG* 270). Wilde's account of the moral of *Dorian Gray* reinforces the implication that the original sin was *Basil's*, and that it inhered in Basil's poisonous combination of excessive love combined with renunciation (this is what idolatry *is*). The moral, according to Wilde: "All excess, as well as all renunciation, brings its own punishment."[17]

One way of articulating the problem of Basil's relationship to Dorian that also defines both the institution of motherhood as it is traditionally defined and repressed homosexual desire is suggested by some lines that Wilde deleted in the manuscript of *Dorian Gray*. Originally, when Basil confesses his idolatry to Lord Henry, Lord Henry protests against the wickedness—and even worse the silliness—of "making yourself the slave of your slave" (*DG* 180 n.7). What makes motherhood potentially more invidious than even fatherhood, Wilde suggests, is that it is a slave-slave relationship, a state of being dependent on one's dependent. Wilde is one of the few writers I know of to explore the destructiveness, not of master-slave relationships, but of slave-slave relationships. The problem crops up again in *Teleny*, the anonymous erotic novel from 1893 (two years after the book publication of *Dorian Gray*) sometimes attributed to Wilde and others.[18] It tells the story of an all-encompassing, passionate love between a man with Dorian Gray's initials, Des Grieux, and an Hungarian pianist (not a painter) named Teleny. Initially, Des Grieux resists his attraction to Teleny with all his power, and interestingly his resistance is both expressed and unconsciously resolved in a nightmare in which Teleny is not a man but a woman, and the prohibition he breaks is not concerned with sodomy but with incest. Des Grieux dreams that Teleny is his sister and that he is discovered having intercourse with this "sister" by his mother. Des Grieux is completely unaware of his anger toward his mother (whose promiscuity he blames not on her but on his father, who had gone mad). Promiscuity, like motherhood, can also be described as an addiction to slave-slave relationships, and Des Grieux defends them to the end. What makes his relationship with Teleny so wonderful, however, once he can allow himself to yield to it, is that theirs is a *reciprocal* master-slave relationship, in which each takes turns being master and slave, which is presented as unbelievably fulfilling. Unfortunately, what interrupts the bliss of Des Grieux's relationship with Teleny is, as in his dream, his mother. He surprises Teleny having intercourse with a woman for money to pay his debts, and when the woman turns around, Des Grieux recognizes her as his own mother. Because he is so deeply identified with Teleny, Des Grieux experiences this as both betrayal *and* incest, which has the effect of interrupting pleasure with death: Des Grieux tries, unsuccessfully, to drown himself, and Teleny succeeds in stabbing *himself*. The mother, here, is both Des Grieux's conscience, which will not let him have his illicit love, and the personification of that illicit desire, which breaks all taboos and, in the process, destroys the self. She is a version of Bella Cohen in *Ulysses*: the mother who is also a whore, who generates an unbearable ambivalence in her son by combining, like Basil, excess love and renunciation. She is the whore who becomes impossibly conflated with the virginal ghost of May Dedalus, whose bridal veil disguises rotting flesh, and who simultaneously asks her son to yield to the sins of the flesh and to repent them.

When read as background to *Portrait* and *Ulysses*, Wilde's novels help to expose Stephen's helpless, angry dependence on the woman who depends on him. He both absorbs a vision of woman as virginal whore and loathes her for accepting that role by agreeing to be pure in a way that casts a shadow of corruption that will haunt her child. Stephen's self-contradiction, his bondage to a disintegrated soul and body that produces "a realism that is bestial, and an ideality that is void" (*DG* 180), is his mother's legacy. Moreover, one reason Stephen can't stand Mulligan is that Mulligan threatens the structure of Stephen's own repression. Not only does he quote Wilde frequently and twit Stephen about the homosexual overtones of Bloom's concern for him, but the intimacy between them also triggers Stephen's own defenses against homosexual desires, which makes Stephen repeat his mother's sin of repression in a different key. Finally, Mulligan's callous indifference to Stephen's mother's death threatens to bring Stephen's own anger at her to consciousness, which would confirm his fear that he has killed her by acting out her unconscious desires as well as her conscious ones.

One sobering fact about both Wilde and Joyce is that the artistic framing of their bondage to their mothers failed to contain the problem. Wilde, who indicted mothers for putting their sons on pedestals in *Dorian Gray,* and who again cried out against women's idealizations of men through the character of Sir Robert Chiltern in *An Ideal Husband,* asking, "Why can't you women love us, faults and all? Why do you place us on monstrous pedestals?" (*Artist as Critic* 521), replicated the exact same pattern in his relationship with Lord Alfred Douglas, who told him devastatingly, "When you are not on your pedestal you are not interesting" (*De Profundis, Artist as Critic* 887). Similarly, Joyce, who represented Stephen's anguished resistance to his mother's ghoulish purity, establishes a relationship in which once again he fans the flame of his lover's innocence with his guilt.

Joyce seems to have seen *Dorian Gray* as Wilde's *Hamlet;* both ghost stories have to do with the way that parental ignorance and denial overdetermine the lives and loves of their children.[19] This is illustrated most economically by exploring the previous life of something John Eglinton says about Stephen in "Scylla and Charybdis": "He will have it that *Hamlet* is a ghoststory. . . . Like the fat boy in Pickwick he wants to make our flesh creep" (*U* 9.141–43). When the *Lippincott's* edition of *Dorian Gray* appeared in July 1890, *Punch* published a cartoon caricaturing the event (see fig. 1). Oscar is represented not as the *fat* boy but as the "Fad" boy, holding out a copy of *Dorian Gray* to Mrs. Grundy, arbiter of middle-class values. The caption reads, "Oscar Wilde's Wildest and Oscariest work . . . a weird sensational romance." What the Fad boy says as he hands his dangerous book to the middle class is what Stephen is imputedly saying as he proffers his Hamlet theory to Lyster, Russell, Best, and Eglinton, "I want to make your flesh creep!"[20] Such an aim is, in one respect, a valuable antidote to the operations of père-version and im-mère-sion, both of which authorize flows of desire that attempt to transcend or deny the painful and complex orientations of the flesh.

PARALLEL.

Joe, the **Fat Boy** in Pickwick, startles the Old Lady ; Oscar, the **Fad Boy** in
Lippincott's, startles Mrs. Grundy.

Oscar, the Fad Boy. " I want to make your flesh creep ! "

Fig. 1. (From *The Annotated Oscar Wilde: Poems, Fiction, Plays, Lectures, Essays, and
Letters*, ed. H. Montgomery Hyde [New York: Clarkson N. Potter, 1982], 208.)

NOTES

1. Stanislaus claims that he suggested the title and that it was inspired by his read-ing of Henry James's *The Portrait of a Lady,* but the odd disposition of articles in Joyce's phrase—*a* portrait of *the* artist—suggests that although Stanislaus may have suggested the metaphor of portraiture, the actual title subtly recalls another portrait—this one by a fellow Irishman—the picture of Dorian Gray. In *The Picture of Dorian Gray,* Wilde uses the same locution that Joyce would later adopt, although here the disposition of the articles reads more naturally. The painter Basil Hallward, explaining to Lord Henry Wotton why he is reluctant to exhibit his picture of Dorian Gray publicly, avers that "every portrait that is painted with feeling is a portrait of the artist, not of the sitter. The sitter is merely the accident, the occasion. It is not he who is revealed by the painter; it is rather the painter who, on the colored canvas, reveals himself." In the preface to *Dorian Gray,* however, Wilde offers a view of art that trumps Basil's; he proclaims, "It is the spec-tator, and not life, that art really mirrors." By alluding to *Dorian Gray* in his title, Joyce suggests both that his novel is autobiographical (a portrait of the artist) and that it isn't; that it is, on the surface, a self-portrait, but that below the surface it is a mirror (which is also what Dorian's portrait is for Basil). And as Wilde warns in his preface, "Those who go beneath the surface do so at their peril."

2. Seminar of 21 January 1975, from the third issue of *Ornicar? Feminine Sexual-ity: Jacques Lacan and the École Freudienne,* ed. Juliet Mitchell and Jacqueline Rose, trans. Jacqueline Rose (New York: Norton, 1982), 167. My understanding of Lacan has been im-measurably enriched by lively and contentious discussions with the members of our Lacan study group: Deborah Luepnitz, Patricia Gherovici, Nick Miller, and Jean-Michel Rabaté, as well as by more spontaneous discussions with Joseph Valente. Of course, re-sponsibility for my errors and idiosyncrasies is mine alone.

3. See "God and the *Jouissance* of the Woman," chapter 6 of seminar 20, *Encore* (1972–73), in Mitchell and Rose, *Feminine Sexuality,* 138–48, in which Lacan argues that to make up for the fact that there is no sexual relation, we introduce a third party into the love affair, an ideal woman who does not exist, whose function as an ideal, an all, makes her a vicereine for God.

4. Lacan makes a similar point more obliquely when he writes the French equiv-alent of "one loves" *(on aime)* as "on âme" (one souls). He insists that "there is no sex in the affair. Sex does not count." This primarily male ethic is "outsidesex" *(hors-sexe).* See "A Love Letter *(Une Lettre d'Âmour),*" in Mitchell and Rose, *Feminine Sexuality,* 155.

5. I do not mean to suggest either that *women* inevitably suffocate their children or that *men* abandon them. There is no necessary relation between women, mothers, and immersion, on the one hand, and men, fathers, and perversion on the other; what I am describing is not a natural or biological tendency, but one that is rooted in society's polarization of the social roles of father and mother.

6. Lacan, "A Love Letter," 155.

7. Eve Kosofsky Sedgwick, *Between Men: English Literature and Male Homosocial Desire* (New York: Columbia University Press, 1985), p. 5.

8. Sedgwick's analysis is supported, from another angle, by Suzanne Pharr's em-phasis on the "interconnectedness of all oppressions": "It is virtually impossible to view one oppression, such as sexism or homophobia, in isolation because they are all con-nected: sexism, racism, homophobia, classism, ableism, anti-Semitism, ageism. They are

linked by a common origin—economic power and control—and by common methods of limiting, controlling and destroying lives." One of the elements common to all oppressions is "a *defined norm*, a standard of rightness and often righteousness wherein all others are judged in relation to it. This norm must be backed up with institutional power, economic power, and both institutional and individual violence." See *Homophobia: A Weapon of Sexism* (Inverness, Calif.: Chardon Press, 1988), xii, 53.

9. *The Seminar of Jacques Lacan, Book 1: Freud's Papers on Technique, 1953–1954,* ed. Jacques-Alain Miller, trans. John Forrester (French version 1975; New York: Norton, 1988), 222.

10. Lacan, *Seminar 1,* 221.

11. See Suzanne Pharr's contention that "in a world without homophobia, there will be no gender roles" (*Homophobia,* 7).

12. The sexual overtones of the verb *to peach* are apparent again in *Finnegans Wake,* where the two sexually enticing "jinnies" are also referred to as "peaches"; see *FW* 57.4, 65.26. 113.17, 251.24.

13. The implications of this argument should not be read as an endorsement of sexual conduct between mothers and children (or between fathers and children). Wilde is careful to say, in a letter to the editor of the *St James Gazette* in defense of *Dorian Gray,* that "limitations should be placed on action," but limitations should not be placed on thought or on art. *The Artist as Critic: Critical Writings of Oscar Wilde,* ed. Richard Ellmann (Chicago: University of Chicago Press, 1968), 243. Wilde's position is curiously close to that of St. Stephen, the first Christian martyr, after whom Joyce named Stephen Dedalus. St. Stephen was stoned to death for accusing his hearers of being "uncircumcised in heart and mind, like your fathers before you." Both Wilde and Joyce write in the tradition of St. Stephen, urging their readers to circumcise their hearts and minds, but not to do away with appropriate restraints on action. To understand this distinction is "to recognize the essential difference between art and life," about which, Wilde points out, many readers are "in a perfectly hopeless confusion" (*The Artist as Critic,* 243).

14. *The Picture of Dorian Gray: Authoritative Texts, Backgrounds, Reviews and Reactions, Criticism,* ed. Donald L. Lawler (New York: Norton, 1988), 176. Hereafter cited parenthetically in the text as *DG.*

15. On another level, Wilde suggests that as Dorian—translated into art—has the capacity to mirror Basil, exposing the corruption that shadows his desire for perfection, so Wilde's book (another artistic mediation) has the capacity to mirror the reader. In a famous letter to the editor of the *Scots Observer* (9 July 1890), Wilde asserts, "Each man sees his own sin in Dorian Gray. What Dorian Gray's sins are no one knows. He who finds them has brought them" (*The Artist as Critic: Critical Writings of Oscar Wilde,* ed. Richard Ellmann [Chicago: University of Chicago Press, 1968], 248). Wilde's claim supports his assertion in the preface: "It is the spectator, not life, that art really mirrors."

16. What Dorian says to Basil anticipates what Wilde's blackmailer, a man named Clyburn who worked with Allen, will later say to him after Clyburn has given him back the compromising letter that he had written to Lord Alfred Douglas. Wilde gave Clyburn half-a-sovereign and Wilde said, "I am afraid you are leading a wonderfully wicked life." Clyburn replied, "There is good and bad in every one of us." Wilde told him he was a born philosopher. From newspaper account of the first trial, *Times,* 5 April, quoted in Ed Cohen, *Talk on the Wilde Side: Toward a Genealogy of a Discourse on Male Sexualities* (New York: Routledge, 1993), 157.

17. Wilde, *Artist as Critic*, 240.

18. Oscar Wilde et al., *Teleny*, ed. John McRae (London: GMP Publishers, 1986).

19. For a related argument on Joyce's reading of *Hamlet*, see my "'Minxing Marrage and Making Loof": Anti-Oedipal Reading," *James Joyce Quarterly* 30 (winter 1993): 219–37.

20. *The Annotated Oscar Wilde: Poems, Fiction, Plays, Lectures, Essays, and Letters*, ed. H. Montgomery Hyde (New York: Clarkson N. Potter, Inc., 1982), 208.

Homocolonial Relations

Casement, Joyce, and Pound
Some New Meanings of Treason

Robert L. Caserio

in memoriam Larry Levis

A reader of Roger Casement's diaries might imagine that Casement was an early fan of Joyce—a fan who so identified with Joyce's work that in his intimate musings he dressed himself up in a version (albeit punctuated) of Molly's monologue: "Saw fair hair force and all July 1906 . . . at Carlyle Circus. Met him at corner Donegall St. waiting for me and got on it and up. I longed. Long limbs as of old. Touched. Joe McCullagh. Splendid. Millar came to tea but altho' clean and strong nothing did not go room." But Casement wrote these words in 1911. So why in Joyce's name invoke an excerpt from Casement's diary?[1] Because, uncanny stylistic similarities aside, Roger Casement and James Joyce are as intertwined as Shem and Shaun. Casement has a claim on Joyceans that still needs adequate acknowledgment.

Sir Roger Casement, an Irish employee of the British Foreign Office, distinguished himself by reporting to the ministry, in 1903 and 1912, imperialistic abuse of native populations by international industrial groups, in the Belgian Congo and in the Brazilian Putomayo region. Conrad's *Heart of Darkness* is pale in comparison. Casement, who loved Ireland, did not miss the irony in coming to be knighted by the rulers of his own native populations. When the outbreak of World War I again postponed British promises of Home Rule for Ireland, Casement rebelled. In 1916 he traveled on a secret mission to recruit Irish POWs in Germany and to bring Irish men and German arms back to Ireland in support of an Easter uprising of neutral Ireland against England. Casement's mission failed. He no sooner landed in Ireland from a German submarine than he was arrested and sent to London. He pled that as an Irish neutral he was immune to the charge of treason, but he was tried and found guilty. The verdict seemed assured by a fact apparently more sensational than treason: Casement's homosexuality, discovered by the Crown in the defendant's diaries, which an-

notate gay encounters across three continents. Circulating photographic repro-
ductions of these "black diaries" during the trial, the prosecution was able to im-
mobilize even Casement's committed supporters. It was able, above all, to quash
Casement's appeal for clemency.[2]

Casement's book on Irish independence, which meditates on the Irish as a
lost tribe of Israel, was in James Joyce's library in Trieste.[3] Yet Casement's *story*—
the story of a subaltern who prophesies postcolonialism—has barely turned up
in the library of Joycean commentary. "Casement, Sir Roger (1864–1916)—Irish
rebel. I worry," writes Glasheen in 1977, "about not finding more of him in
FW. Joyce must have been interested in his 'Black Book' [and in] his [Adler]
Christansen [*sic*],"[4] a Norwegian sailor, Casement's last lover, who accompanied
Casement to Germany. Although Enda Duffy's *The Subaltern Ulysses* at last re-
stores Casement to *Ulysses,* Glasheen's shrewd worry is still not attended to for
the *Wake.*

I propose that we can find more of Casement in *FW*: I mix gratitude to
Duffy with the claim that even his restoration of Casement to Joyce is not strong
enough. First we need to consider the appeal of the Casement story to Joyce during his obsession with Shem and Shaun. We have become, thanks to studies like
Manganiello's, conscious of the political character of the twins—of the way they
figure the divided Ireland that in the 1920s emerged out of the Home Rule
promises. Fraternal division projects a conflict about national identity, loyalty,
and treachery that is the conflict embodied in Casement. Was his collaboration
with Germany in 1916 treachery to the English king? He was hanged for treachery, but what country was it that he belonged to: the United Kingdom, belliger-
ent England, or neutral Ireland? the Ireland represented by Ulstermen in the
north, or the Ireland represented by Catholics in the south? Loyalty and treachery in the man who was knighted for distinguished foreign service, and for un-
masking imperialist inhumaneness in the Congo and in Brazil, fraternize in the
same soul. Was he right to oppose imperialism abroad, but wrong to oppose it
at home? Which soul is the noble and just one; which soul the debased and traitorous one? Just as Casement prefigures the *Wake*'s contradictious twins, his
contradictious loyalties and politics equally figure HCE. During Casement's
trial in June 1916, his proponents and opponents sound like the patrons of the
pub in the *Wake*'s crucial, central part II, chapter 3. Through a murky medium
of debate, the pub crawlers one moment envision the integral man on trial as
disintegrated and degenerate, the next moment envision him as single and up-
right. The observers become the twins, divisively characterizing the father: at
once everyone's heroic paterfamilias and "chastemate" (*FW* 548.07)—and everyone's familial and national tyrant and betrayer.

Casement's cloudy fidelity on trial might seem overly specific to tie to
Joyce's work, which insistently links particular cases to things in general, to
mythic universals. And since in the *Wake* the drama is always about the unreli-
ability of evidence in all investigations, can one specify Casement's presence

there in a way that gets beyond momentary significance? Perhaps it is through Casement's implication in a web, or a litter, of forgeries, and of claims or counterclaims about the forged status of his crime, that a stronger tie to the *Wake* might be determined. Casement's diaries are a palimpsest, the data of ordinary life written over by a catalog of homosexual promiscuity. In the newspapers published the morning after Casement's sentencing the already-open secret of the diaries became officially public. With this public notice—in headlines such as "Paltry Traitor Meets His Just Deserts . . . The Diaries of a Degenerate," which sound like the moral vulgate that Joyce loves to mimic—a drama begins about the authenticity of Casement's crime.[5] The friend-defenders of Casement start to claim that the diaries of a degenerate are the forgeries of imperial power; that the empire has taken to framing a true patriot by making him appear a homosexual cad. The claim forecasts one of the *Wake*'s narratives. ALP defends her husband from alleged crimes, including sins of homosexual conduct, along lines that claim the evidence against him is forged.

The drama about Casement and counterfeiters has continued. As if the *Wake* had written the scenario, there is a version of ALP's famous letter defending her husband's virtue in Alfred Noyes's insistence in 1957, and again in Richard Mackey's insistence in 1956 and 1966, that the sexual entries in the Casement diaries—including the data of Casement's dalliance with soldiers and with every sort of "cad," in public parks—were forgeries inserted by Scotland Yard, or by a Home Office employee who was himself to be arrested in the 1930s in a Hyde Park lavatory on a lewdness charge (his defense was that he was doing research), and who was presumed to know intimately the vice that Casement, in contrast, was innocent of. A variant of this defense—which protects Casement against the charge of treason by protecting him against the charge of homosexuality—is the idea that the Scotland Yard forger took the homoerotica he penned into Casement's notebooks from another diary, not by Casement, which Casement had acquired to witness sexual evils committed by rubber company officials against Putomayan natives.[6] I do not mean of course that these post-*Wake* litterings should be read into the *Wake*'s genesis. But Joyce seems prescient about the shape of Casement's posthumous history.

I take it that the prescience results from a deep imaginative attention to the "paltry traitor." Although at the time of Casement's trial Joyce was in Zurich waiting out attempts to censor erotic aspects of the story of *A Portrait*'s hero-forger, Joyce can not but have been stirred, even at long distance, by the new Irish martyrdom; and when in 1925 the journalist Peter Singleton-Gates announced (erroneously) that he would soon publish the Casement diaries, Joyce had not long begun the *Wake* and must have been reminded of the 1916 trial. There is an important link too from Joyce to Casement through Joyce's (and Pound's) patron, John Quinn, whom Casement visited in America in 1914 to raise funds for a free Ireland; it was on the visit to Quinn that Casement picked up, while cruising, the Norwegian sailor Christensen, Casement's collaborator in the tailoring of his treacherous outfit. It was to Quinn, among other prominent Americans, that Scotland Yard in 1916 showed the photographs of the Casement diaries to discredit Casement among sympathizers with Irish Home Rule in the United States.[7] Ellmann's biography does not mention Casement; but that Quinn and Joyce never discussed and debated the queer Casement intrigue is unlikely.

Above all, for the creator of Shem and Shaun, a simple but uncanny symmetry invokes Roger Casement's presence in *Finnegans Wake*. Casement, a man who instances anti-imperialist patriotism and treachery and illicit sexual passion, and who is implicated in a controversy connecting forgery and crimes in many a public park, models Earwicker; and doubles anti-imperialist Parnell, who (before the revelation of his erotic sin) was also implicated by forgery in crimes in Phoenix Park. But whereas Parnell is Joyce's betrayed patriot, Casement is Joyce's patriot traitor. And whereas Parnell adulterously desires woman, Casement promiscuously desires man. I propose that the *Wake*, framed in terms of Casement's impact on Joyce, permits the artist to rectify an imbalance: until and through the writing of *Ulysses*, Joyce's erotic and political center, however qualified by homosexuality at the margins, is heterosexual; but in the *Wake*, the heterosexual center of interest in Joyce's earlier work gains a homosexual twin. Even the *Wake*'s twins, the one relatively straight, the other relatively queer, might indicate the contrastive sexual orientations in the twin works, *Ulysses* and the *Wake*. One twin is queer for the other. And this is a family matter. It is strongly arguable that in the *Wake* marriage and family are represented as an ever-anxious defense against primary homosexual impulse, whether the impulse be male or, as the *Wake* would say, "lispian." Why should we longer feel "hesitency" about giving a full weight to the attraction of HCE toward the three soldiers and toward the young buck soliciting him at the *Wake*'s infamous crime scene in the park, in chapter 2? From William York Tindall in 1959, who both addresses, but also plays down, the way HCE desires males, as just "another story" about the guy, to Patrick McCarthy in 1984, who speaks of "the homosexual subplot of the park episode,"[8] there is a critical tendency to subordinate and just plain sink the queerer aspects of the *Wake*, to make them lesser rumors among the *Wake*'s sounds.

Creditable enlistments of Freud by Joyceans have served this subordination. The case is different with Lacanian uses of Freud, insofar as they have stimulated feminist and lesbian-feminist rereadings of Joyce. But I look forward to the day when the implication of the *Wake* and the homosexual aspects of Freud's Wolf Man and Rat Man cases is taken for granted. Most of the enlistments of Freud so far make male homosexual thematics in the *Wake* serve the retelling of a heterosexual primal scene.[9] Gordon's useful book illuminates the role of privies and their association with "musey-rooms" in the *Wake*. But Gordon gets finicky when Joyce's privy material appears to undergo same-sex eroticization. He speaks, holding his nose, of "the notoriously anal Oscar Wilde"; he asserts

Freud's derivation of homosexuality *from* "the primal scene"; and it is with surprising single-mindedness that he repeats the *Wake*'s story of HCE's boy twins peering through a keyhole at their parents' intercourse. Such spying *is* a *Wake* component; but it is reduced to absurdity when the prominence of male buttocks in the *Wake* is interpreted, as Gordon interprets it, not as the result of a homoerotic turn but as the result of a narrative donnée whereby HCE must have been, naturally, during heterosexual intercourse, thrusting his naked behind back toward the watchers on the other side of the keyhole opposite his bed.[10] But Gordon is to be respected for involving Freud in a pursuit of an exactly determinate plot for the *Wake*. Joyce's art of indeterminacies—although influenced by Freudian ambivalences, and protodeconstructive—demands the pursuit. For the *Wake* incites us to have things both ways. We must do without a plot, but we must have one.

The problem of how much more determinate the plot of the *Wake* can be remains, like lispian matters, to be addressed. But that the plot must thicken in a queer direction seems needful in response to Duffy's account of Casement in *Ulysses*. Duffy shows that a deficiency of Freudian inquiry into male homosexuality's place in Joyce can be repaired by postcolonial studies, which merge considerations of subordinated sexuality with subaltern politics. For Duffy, Casement's illicit characteristics, homosexual and anti-imperialist, could not but be a magnet for Joyce's attention. In the "Cyclops" episode of *Ulysses*, Duffy argues, Joyce uses Casement to meditate on the way colonialist power enmeshes in disabling stereotypes those who resist it. The anticolonialist rebel is made over by colonialism into a martyr or a hero or a barbarian—and all three roles remove the rebel "from the arena of moral or political choice." The British exploitation of Casement's diaries worked this way: Casement's political agency was metamorphosed into that of a demonic terrorist, and hence into that of a moral degenerate. With Casement's "choice of political action . . . pictured [by the imperialist state] as the merely predictable expression of an inner secret," the political repression of the subaltern could be perpetuated. His fellow subalterns must either expel him as a dubious demon, or sublate their doubt by picturing him as a martyr. In either case, the rebel is removed from the realm of practicable politics; locked in stereotype, he cannot figure among imaginations of "a subject worthy of an independent post-colonial community." Duffy's Casement-derived thoughts are all said to be impacted by Joyce in Bloom's audition in "Cyclops" of Casement's name. Duffy concludes that, because Bloom in the episode can see what stereotyping has made of Casement, Bloom is able to imagine, even to stand for, the "worthy" future "counterhegemonic subject" of a realistically considered postcolonial community.[11]

Thus Duffy's account designates Casement as the origin of an elaborate political meditation in Joyce. But how much does Casement's erotic life enter into Duffy's accounting? Within ten pages, as it is, Casement undergoes a submersion. And the critic's abstract themes become indifferent to Casement's eros.

"The diaries' contents are trite and mundane,"[12] Duffy remarks, in a way that is apparently realistic about sex, rather than repressive. But in this argument it is hard to tell the difference. When Bloom is announced as the seer of a worthy postcolonial community, an all-too-conventional substitution has taken place: Duffy has dislodged Casement, an actual gay male, and put in his place Bloom, an imaginary man who desires woman. This imaginary being is dubbed the one "worthy" to imagine, in all complexity, a postcolonial state.

This first literary-critical resurrection of Casement does not turn up the queer sound of the *Wake.* But to hear a loud and queer narrative in the *Wake* is important not only because it gives more voice to more than heterosexual eros. After all, I like Duffy's political gist. It is important to audit the *Wake*'s homosexuality because, in the light of Casement's variant doubling of Parnell, the specific political and historical transmissions encoded in the *Wake* will become more audible and legible. For example, how might Casement affect one's reading of the character Joyce names Kersse in the pub scene? We learn (at *FW* 311.5) that an avatar of HCE is a Norwegian sailor who decides to give up cruising and settle into marriage and engages a tailor, Kersse, to make him a wedding garment. The tailor provides the clothes, and the tale, to cover the sailor's metamorphosis from seaman into mate. But why is the tailor named Kersse, especially given an alternative pronunciation: "Carse"? Ellmann's relation of Kersse to a Dublin tailor is perhaps more diverting than useful—especially since McHugh's attention to Ellman permits McHugh to ignore a clue from Glasheen. Glasheen tells us that Joyce intends Kersse to name Sir Edward Carson, the barrister who sent Oscar Wilde to Reading Gaol; and that *Kersse* and *Carse* also mean "curse." We need to develop Glasheen's notes, for Wilde's prosecutor had Joyce's attention but has not had the attention of Joyceans, and Carson's relation to Casement has gone unremarked. Cursed Kersse, an Irish censor of Ireland, is straight-jacketing the sailor and suggesting that HCE's homoerotic impulses are ill-suited for marriage. The sailor and the tailor have a falling-out, which suggests a dream-thought: marriage curses homosexuality and jails it. Roger Casement is a second Wilde: Did Joyce know that the Norwegian ship on which Casement and Christensen sailed to Germany was named *Oskar II*? Casement is Oscar II, but with a difference: Wilde does not quite double Parnell, because Wilde's trial was not politically centered on a patently Irish cause. Casement is Parnell II. But Casement is geminated: Parnell II and Oscar II. What has Carson to do with Oscar II? Carson created in 1913 the Ulster militias who vowed that they would secede from, and bear arms against, a free Ireland should Irish Home Rule be granted. It was the Ulster threats that decided Casement to go to Germany. But there was no getting around Carson's influence. Carson's bosom associate in the formation of the Ulster Volunteers was F. E. Smith. Smith turns out to be the judge at Casement's trial. He permitted the circulation of Casement's diaries. Through Smith, Carson was able to condemn—and this time to kill—his second Wilde. It was Carson, moreover, who in 1904 argued a treason case that set a precedent *against* actions like Casement's neutrality-inspired appeal to Germany.[13]

The conflict between sailor and Kersse, understood in terms of the history I have sketched, prefaces the *Wake*'s literal center: a homosexual primal scene, a vision of the Irish in general, who are given dream logic names: "Russian general," and "General Buckley," which means bucklike, boylike, cadet or cadlike in general. Buckley stands for "the general" populace and for the *Wake*'s vexed protagonist, a Roger Wilde or Oscar Casement on trial for the betrayal of social authority and political order that is still identified with homosexuality. In the Phoenix Park sin, Earwicker's relation to three buggering, or smugging, soldiers is at issue.[14] Now, introduced with Buckley are Butt and Taff, soldiers on the side opposing the general. Butt and Taff are outraged by what the general stands for, albeit it is his squatting down that arouses them. They see him at stool, and they take the general's natural urges as an obscene proposition. In revenge for the supposed proposal, Butt and Taff shoot Buckley in his exposed rear.

This story about shooting is one of the accepted narratives recovered by scholars from the *Wake,* so as to throw defining light on a text that always betrays story lines. In spite of the treacherous possibilities, it seems certain that the general does get shot in the rear. Something else straightforwardly narratological goes on. Joyce changes the focal distance governing the presentation of the two soldiers. In the *Wake*'s early chapters the soldiers in the park are given from an outside view. Now the reader sees as they see. They see censoriously and desirously; the exhibition of the general's privates and buttocks makes it possible for them to indulge a frenzy of aroused attention. The soldiers and the general (is he the third soldier in the park?) are arousing and playing with each other, and readers can gather that this is both what Earwicker saw in the crime scene in book 1, and what he has participated in. At the same time Butt and Taff are Earwicker's sons; Earwicker, like drunken Noah in Genesis's scene of temptation to homosexual incest, is being looked at, scorned, and yearningly made sexual love to by his cadets, who are themselves homoerotically bonded. The endless possibilities of interpretation begin and end, it seems, in homosexual eros—and in a sodomized male end. And if, when Butt and Taff see Buckley, they are seeing the Irussian or Irishian general, they or he configure a very queer nation. Contemplating the queer nation, the *Wake* text is incited to transgress every limit or taboo on homosexuality.

After the first twenty pages of *Wake* II.iii detail the fortunes of the sailor's homosexual desire being "cawcaught[,] Coocaged" in heterosexual tradition, heterosexuality exalts itself on what Joyce calls "this mounden of Delude," in the service of "Delude of Isreal" (*FW* 331.18–19). But there is a falling-off. Then the *Wake* narrative remounts the scene of homosexual desire, with the next twenty-page stretch, the Butt-Taff-Buckley episode. Butt is introduced in response to a desirous cry: "We want Bud. We want Bud Budderly. We want Bud Budderly bodily" (*FW* 337.32–33). From this invocation of butts, butt-buds, and brother bodies, Butt receives a bodily message, described thus: "the hissindensity buck far of his melovelance tells how when he was fast marking his first lord for cremation the whyfe of his bothem was the very lad's thing to elter his mehind" (*FW* 350.14–17). Taff joins Butt in "homosodalism" here. Both fire off at the general, mixing love and aggressive "waste" in one detonating "creamation." And perhaps Buckley is also a Carson figure, whose mind the boys are altering by involving it in what he represses. The heroes Casement and Wilde turn the tables on Carson and on Ulster: these pages forge new entries for blacker diaries. Yet phantasmagoric as the *Wake*'s turning of the tables is, the history woven into it mitigates the fantasy, which burgeons *under the rule of* a concrete Anglo-Irish political episode. If the *Wake* departs from history by virtue of its homosodalism, its departure enables a powerful return.

When Joyce's Butt explodes at Buckley, "the abnihilisation of the etym" takes place (*FW* 353.22). This famous phrase, always torn out of narrative context, describes the art of *Finnegans Wake,* in which atoms of ideas and words, their etymological bases, or bottoms, are trashed and re-created by nuclear fissions and fusions. Joyce's art uses a Freudian etym, the Oedipal primal scene, not to endorse the etym's domination, but to abnihilise it. The *Wake*'s use of Freud also is subordinated to the use of homosexuality in specific relation to Irish politics. Abnihilisation in Joyce indicates homosexual desire, and its anal erotism especially, as what resists the Irish primal scene: a home rule (with its nuclear family etym) that seeks empire over Home Rule. Joyce seems to think that home rules are not unruly enough, however, especially if they lack the abnihilising force of Homo Rule. But is Homo Rule a worthy or an unworthy imagination for any community? We can tolerate Joyce's dream of a new political rule by same-sex "creamation," if we are in queer studies. But for all studies, Casement-inspired Homo Unruliness in Joyce leaves disturbing abnihilisations in its wake. Less frequently subverted nuclei or etyms are, I propose, also under attack by homo-force: the pure self-determination of nations, pure anti-imperialism, or pure politics; ideas of the eventual purity of sex and sexual liberty, straight or gay; purification etyms of all kinds. In grasping anew the homosexuality that governs the *Wake,* and in taking Casement as a figurehead for revisionary reading, I note that the single-minded purity of Casement's intentions to serve Ireland as if Ireland were an etym could not help but be muddied by treacheries within himself as well as without. In Germany, Christensen was flamboyant and promiscuous; and thus unintentionally he helped British intelligence keep an eye on Casement's moves. Yet Casement's embrace of his indiscrete companion was stubborn, in spite of its potential for damaging his political project. Casement's erotic impulsions perhaps helped to betray Ireland rather than save it.

To live out (as well as to read in) the abnihilisation of etyms is no easy, ideal form of either side-taking or pragmatic trimming. The *Wake* impels one to read, think, and feel one's committed meanings or emphases along divergent, self-contradictory lines of meaning and emphasis. This is not having things both ways *comfortably*. Under the determining effects of a committed division, one is bound to feel abnihilised too. At any moment the expression of thought and belief, or the pursuit of practice along one line of meaning or of structure, will betray another, alternative line. Casement-inspired homosexual eros in the *Wake* pictures a Joycean politics in which treachery is an inescapable impurity of personal, erotic, and political practice.[15] In saying this, I touch the center of what I propose is a queer *Wake*'s relevance to literary history and criticism and to real, political history.

Treason plays a principal role in the various modernisms that produced Joyce, that inhabit him from without and from within. Joyce's fascination with Casement's treason and erotic practice is, arguably, a fascination with himself as traitor, in political and sexual terms. This thematics of treachery occasions a modernist siblings' civil war when Pound in the 1930s defects from support of the *Wake*. "I think the whole of egoistic psychological nuvveling is gone plop," Pound writes Robert McAlmon; "the whole damn lot of 'em *won't* look at the reality." He complains about the *Wake*, paradoxically in *Wake*-ese (and conscious of Joyce's moving his focus from heterosexual Bloom to the *Wake*'s general buggery): "have we had enough of the pseuderasts and the Bloomsbuggers? Enough, enough, we have had quite enough." The attack on Joyce—expressed to gay McAlmon!—"confirmed the lines of [Pound's] own development. Literature should pay attention," so Forrest Read formulates the project, "to what is going on at the present moment; preserving public morality is more important than exploring psychological hinterlands."[16] The hinterlands of Bloomsbuggery, to judge from Pound's tale of a sodomite sailor, in Canto 12, is usura, unnatural increase. Pound judges Joyce as if Joyce were Casement, a traitor to art by virtue of buggering (or earwigging) history and politics.

The *Wake*-like irony is that Pound becomes the traitor. While the treachery—as in *Wake* II.3, via radio transmissions—occurs after Joyce's death, Joyce again seems prescient of real future history. The *Wake*'s duplicit, displaced meanings suggest a structurally dynamic, compulsory need—semiotic, psychic, erotic, and historical—for treachery in the modernist world. If desire's psychic roots are repressed, available only as a form of displacement, then dominant desires—heterosexual ones, for example—are always keeping somewhere a black diary. Dominant desires, no less than subordinate ones, belong to another locus, are in the pay of a secret foreign agent. One's country, whether sexual or native, is another country; one's citizenship depends on a betrayal of allegiance. The Casement figure specifies the historical gist of a treacherous human condition. Given modern democracy's self-contradictory nonegalitarian exclusions (Casement is excluded, patriotically and erotically, from citizenship); given modern democracy's history of self-contradictory injustice (no one brought Carson or Smith to trial for preparing armed sedition in Ulster), modern democracy is legible as the practice of an ideological self-betrayal, a historical treason.[17] It is the perfect political form of a social psyche whose diverse but equal components mean different, and contradictory, things at once; of a social psyche that betrays its contradictory impulses in "slips"; and that sets itself conscious purposes at the cost of treacherous returns of the purposes it has repressed. Idealizing this treachery, we call it complexity or contradiction. But, in the wars of modern history, partisans, opponents and neutrals, whether democrats or totalitarians, perhaps have betrayal most in common.

Some such idea would "cover," would make intelligible, both Pound's wartime treason and his rescue from a Casement-like fate. Again ironically, Pound's demand that historical treachery should come to an end impels the poet's traitorous last phase. I think it worth suggesting that the same impatient demand impels one strong arm of our literary-critical community. When one has read the books by E. Fuller Torrey and by Robert Casillo that retry Pound and render, even if forty years late, an implacable judgment of treason against him, how can one not believe it wrong—wrong in the light of morality and democracy—that Pound was not executed? During his broadcast years, Pound became a correspondent with another Irish Joyce—one William Joyce, aka Lord Haw-Haw, a broadcaster to the English from Germany on behalf of Hitler's rule. Thanks to a precedent instituted by Carson, the traitor Joyce was unable to escape the same end as Casement's.[18] In contrast, thanks to what Casillo and Torrey document as the betrayal of egalitarianism by a cabal of American psychiatrists and poets, the traitor Pound escaped his just desert of hanging. These fierce critics remind me of what Casement's defense counsel said about the discovery of the black diaries and the defense's decision not to bring them into court: "I finally decided that [for Casement] death was better than besmirching and dishonor."[19]

I decided, at least while I read Casillo and Torrey, that for Pound and for us his death would have been better than a life of continued besmirching; that his death would have been better than *The Confucian Odes, The Women of Trachis,* and the last *Cantos.* This decision shared, I think, in the moral temper of American literary criticism of the last decade, in its politically, ethically, and intellectually purifying aims, uncompromising—hence Pound-like—even as it condemns Pound. But I confess that to speak about the purity of the critics is to speak with Joycean duplicity, a turncoat toward my own severity. It is wrong to betray justice; yet one's sense of justice curdles, no less than does one's sense of injustice. Justice and injustice are Butt and Taff, Shem and Shaun, one seeking to betray the other. And the complexity of cultural life, especially of a multicultural life, makes the betrayal of one complex of cultural allegiances by another an inevitable occasion.

We are wary of the potential for treachery in literary studies. A measure of how wary we are—so wary that intellectual lives are perhaps moved most by fear of the mud of treachery, even if we don't discuss the subject—is Edward Said's radio broadcasts, *Representations of the Intellectual.* As one scans the transmissions, one notes the critic's desire to purify the intellectual of complicity with betrayal, even as he calls the intellectual to speak distasteful truths to power. There is aversion to treachery in Said's criticism of Stephen Dedalus's impurities as an intellectual: he is only "an obstinate and contrary young man," Said says. Said's picture of the intellectual who is no alienated Dedalian exile is comforting: speaking truth to power is tough, but possible; and since Said says intellectual analysis "forbids calling one side innocent, the other evil,"[20] being drawn in two attractive contradictory directions at once, and the agony of betraying one attraction or allegiance by another, is avoided. In Said's book there is no allusion to the *Wake*'s suggestion that betrayals are inescapable for us, no matter what responsibilities to truth or power we undertake, and no matter what side of eros we are on.

I must return these remarks to the Casement-inspired homosexuality in the *Wake*. What can new attention to Casement do to Joyce's book, and to a critical domain that is prepared for this attention, but that is worried about the ways erotic, intellectual, or political commitments can be, will be, treacherous? The worry about betrayal has been intensified by another one of the strong arms of our cultural formation: poststructuralism, which, as Derrida has told us, makes a match with the *Wake*'s pandemic undecidability; with the way the *Wake* shows indeterminacy and determination to be twins. Derrida never intended deconstruction to be a cult of intellectual purification—indeed, quite the reverse; but at the level of practice, a poststructuralist can emphasize the lustrating rather than contaminating effects of his discourse. With characteristic brilliance, Jean-Michel Rabaté's "On Joycean and Wildean Sodomy" moves the term *homosexuality* to the side of its thesis, because Rabaté sees that the term is implicated in prior concepts: sodomy, triangular desire, even simony. "Joyce suggests," Rabaté writes, "that the Sin [of sodomy], if it is to keep its full value, cannot be reduced to a sexual content."[21] Instead, sodomy in the *Wake* becomes general transgressiveness, an ebb and flow of "endless discourse" and "fundamental unspeakability." This argument, exuberantly ascetic, purifies the critic's impulse to determine a limited stand for the critic or the critic's object. The limited stand will be shown to betray the limitlessness that makes limits possible. Purified thus, the critic or the writer can stand everywhere, as well as on a particular site, but cannot, wherever he or she is, betray a position. The position has already been betrayed. The critic or the writer, foreknowing the treachery, cannot do him- or herself wrong because the treachery has been made nominal. The *Wake* offers itself as a superb instance of the foreknowledge that purifies error by comprehending error universally, ahead of time. In the process, homosexuality can be one of the things purified, by being, at once, present and absent, itself and not itself: Joyce "does not actually condemn (or endorse) a 'sodomy' that becomes tantamount to the arch-sin."[22] The purifying tendency I speak of (Said's broadcasts are an example) comprehends treachery by antisepticizing it.

But some criticism has now undertaken a move against this purity, whether poststructuralist or postcolonial or traditional-Joycean. If to determine the *Wake* is to betray it without antisepsis, for some critics the treachery must be engaged. The *Wake* accepts the treacherous move, I think. Casement can be a model for the critic, just because he is stubbornly determined, by politics and sex. To see Carson and Casement figure in the Joycelitter, against the grain of the litter's indeterminacy, is to understand the work's indeterminacies as the products, the reflections, of historical determinants. It is to see the indeterminacies, as well, as strategies for making determinations—albeit treacherous ones.[23] Coming from a different intellectual quarter than my own, a strong revisionary reading by Emer Nolan of the attack on Buckley's rear also illustrates the *Wake*'s openness to determinations of sense. But Nolan's reading still needs to betray its homesite. Arguing that "we have overlooked the determinate nature of Joyce's 'ambivalence' towards Ireland," Nolan approaches the episode by noting Shem-Butt's decisive intervention in the scene. Usually Shem hangs back from practical efforts; here Joyce assigns him the executive power that is customarily Shaun-Taff's. Nolan writes:

> We witness the point at which the modernist writer—the Viconian interpreter of history . . . —is transformed into a Viconian participant. . . . Butt is impelled towards action by his reluctance to become a keening Celtic artist or a passive bystander. . . . It is this *intervention* which produces the "abnihilisation" . . . during which everything is, as the stage-directions inform us: "ideally reconstituted."[24]

Right as this is, Nolan's analysis leaves out the scene's buccal-anal male-to-man sex. The omission suggests that a purifying impulse drives the analyst, that the homosexual material is worrying: will it betray the critic's political point? How *could* "queer" be an *ideal* reconstitution? But, then, why should it be? One might hope, if only for vitality's sake, that a queer initiative would betray ideality. But I agree with Nolan about the determinate upshot of the scene. The treacherous erotic pollutant makes the reconstitutive ordering all the more definite. Joyce does not see that the cross-currents of eros impede or suspend a new determination of political practice.

As criticism moves toward further determination of the *Wake*'s meaning; and as criticism involves the movement with judging the *Wake*'s men to be guilty as charged of homosexuality—and the book too!—other sources of determination can be recruited. One underattended source is literary history; another, already productive, is feminist reading of the work's lesbian aspects. I was pointed toward Casement's and Carson's impact on Joyce by Djuna Barnes and Iris Murdoch. It seems unlikely that Joyce's fondness for Barnes—to whom he gave the manuscript of *Ulysses* in 1923, and to whom he read *Work in Progress*—made him unresponsive to the fact of her lesbian passion and *her* interest in homosexuality. Perhaps *Nightwood* (1936) is offered by Barnes to Joyce as a homage, and yet as a criticism of what she took to be squeamishness about homosexuality in *Ulysses*. *Nightwood* revises "Nighttown," by translating Bloom's transvestite fantasies into the character of gay Dr. O'Connor, who is transvestite in fact. The translation can be read as notice of the way Joyce had seemed to entertain homosexuality only in his head, as fantasy undetermined by reality. Barnes pictures the real sexual life of O'Connor and *Nightwood*'s heroines as difficult and intractable, treacherous in practice, and likely to be betrayed by derealizing imaginations. Was *Ulysses* or the *Wake* an evasive derealizing of eros, puritan after all? This implicit question in Barnes's work might have made Joyce rethink homosexuality's role in his career—in a way predictive of how Joseph Valente shows that Joyce forged his vocation as a flight (foredoomed) from buggers. Did Joyce respond to Barnes by intensifying the homosexual determinations of the *Wake*?

There is less speculative risk with regard to Iris Murdoch's relation to Joyce. *The Red and the Green* (1965) rewrites *Ulysses* and the *Wake*, re-creating Dublin in a light that starkly pictures the neurotic edges of the Easter 1916 uprising. How to evaluate Murdoch's bleak presentation of Irish politics and sex is a problem that I set aside: I only need to point out the homosexuality Murdoch emphasizes in the narrative. The British and the IRA are represented by two protagonists, one of whom, the British soldier, is undoubtedly in love with the Irish rebel. The Irish rebel is in love with his own brother. Repressed homosexuality and incestuous homoeroticism leaks throughout the novel's world; and Murdoch suggests a match between Casement, no sooner arrived than arrested, and the arrested erotic love of both soldier-opponents and twinlike brother insurgents.

The cost of the arrested sexuality is not paid only by the males in *The Red and the Green*. Irish women, bearing the brunt of homosocial substitutes for sexuality, are imprisoned in a queer male imaginary. The women are constrained to play the role of Ireland "herself," a fetish produced by a deeply unhappy heterosexuality. Via her retelling of the *Wake*'s crimes, Murdoch determines (like Glasheen) that Irish women—the maids in Joyce's park—are spectators of what goes on among the men. Not just imperialism's patriarchal business goes on. The source of the women's betrayal is the unaccountable nature of erotic desire, especially evident in homosexuality's surprising prominence. At the novel's end, in 1938, Eros's treacheries make the women, who summon up remembrance of loves past, see in 1916 an equivalent of the scorched cities of the plain. Their lot resembles Lot's wife's. In a recent paper on *Finnegans Wake*, Robert Polhemus discovers how ALP is associated by Joyce with the same Sodomite wife.[25] ALP too, in the *Wake*'s finale, looks back on the desire that is her lot, on the desire that she is losing and coming to loathe. The Joycean puns fuse Lot and loathing, perhaps because, in the light of HCE's attachment to bucks, cads, and cads' butts, ALP is looking back on the sodomy, the sin against heterosexuality, that has chilled and betrayed her marriage.

What, finally, in terms of queer criticism, can be made of HCE's and ALP's alienation, the fruit of queer treachery? ALP's attempt to protect the patriarch from the public disclosure and confirmation of his homosexuality fails. The pathos of the failure (another instance of abnihilisation) does not occasion a celebratory tone. In contrast, the failure of Kersse's threats appears just, and to be rejoiced at; his failure means the revocation of curses that scourge human sexuality. But it appears to be unjust that Anna Livia should, thanks to the lifting of curses, be deprived of her man, be left in isolation—"penisolate" (FW 3.6). Presumably, Joyce resists celebration at the Wake's final turn in order to resist a desire to purify life of conflict and wrong. He avoids making the reader feel that reconstituted etyms, even if they spell the victory of Casement's homosodality over culture's cursing, would expel treachery forever. Still, is this resistance to purity not at the woman's expense? ALP's female being is more scourged than the male's. If the male form of life in Joyce's story resolves into a desire for sexual sameness, for Homo Rule, at the same time as the female maintains the pluralisms of differentiated existence, is she not left uncompensated and without a home?

Feminist criticism has begun to answer. It makes a case lately for an Anna who is unredeemed by a homesite, who no longer matches the Wake's world with a feminized poststructuralist purification of all the limitations upon meaning. The Wake divides and divorces the opposite-sex pairings, breaking up the solidarity of male and female, resolving each into a poignant self-sufficiency and self-pleasuring. This resolution, rather than reach at infinities, reaches at limits for desire. Patriarchy crumbles, but polymorphous perversity—of eros and of meaning—contracts. The field of perversity takes up, for male and female both, homosexuality as the new but limited etym of life. The infinity of heterosexual desire and coupling is betrayed.

The possibility for such an interpretation is traced in Sheldon Brivic's Joyce's Waking Women as an outcome of feminist criticism. Starting with the intuition that "Joyce can free his women only by having them reject [betray?] him, or his [male and patriarchal] side," Brivic sees narrative determinations in the Wake whereby ALP divorces herself from male-female marriage, to return to the heaven of her separate gender. The result is "interfeminine eroticism." Although the Wake evokes the intermingling of genders, of androgyny, nevertheless, a determinate victory (like Butt-Shem's), a sexual singleness or sameness, conquers bisexual duplicity. When ALP "realizes that she did not lead her own life: it was lived for her by others who partook of the system that made her a woman," Brivic writes, "her assertion of her independence leads to a lesbian vision." Judging from recent meditations by Lesley McDowell, ALP's daughter follows in her mother's wake—insofar, that is, as her mother separates from life in a heterosexual imaginary. Although Issy is often, as befits a queer book, merely a sissy, a female impersonation worked up from camp impulse in the twins, she grows into her own. Her own means separation from the lisping boys, from marriage and maternity too. She happily takes a place among "the doaters of inversion" (*FW* 526).[26]

But, as I have remarked, we must guard against making idealized abstractions out of the *Wake*'s lesbianism or its male homosexuality, as another way of purifying them. Joyce's narrative embeds homosexuality in the story of treachery. There, doting on inversion, men and women are set free from each other; but patriarchy and matriarchy, fatherland and motherland, are thereby betrayed. This story of treasons, determined internally by the text, determined externally by the history that includes Casement's war against Carson and his kind, is the *Wake*'s major pre-text, and a plot we can trust.

I end with a minor pre-text, however, a sly treachery of Joyce's, characteristic of the betrayals to be found in literary territory. Looking back, lispian Livia solicits "mememormee," her remembrance of things past. The sly treachery turns out to be Joyce's receiving foreign aid from France to abet the *Wake*'s Irish rebellion against the English—and against the English language's normative use. Turning up the sound of homosexuality in the *Wake* brings into hearing the *Wake*'s affinity with Proust's *Sodom and Gomorrah,* where Proust asserts that sodomites never remain faithful to fatherland or motherland. Earwicker's trial for treachery also varies Proust's Dreyfus case. Joyce has hidden Proust in his work, just as he's hidden Casement, in plain sight. Critics have tended to see the relation of Joyce and Proust as Joyce wanted it to be seen: as a nonrelation. At the time of the *Wake*'s conception Joyce said to Ford Madox Ford in contemptuous tones that he had not read Proust, but that "he had been told that a single sentence of Proust would fill a whole magazine."[27] The single sentence of Joyce that fills a whole *Finnegans Wake* betrays Joyce's claims of disaffiliation. Of course, there is a precedent for the use of secret French aid on behalf of Irish rebellion against the English. An eighteenth-century ballad tells the tale of French aid for the Shan Van Vocht, the Poor Old Woman Ireland. Roger Casement's pen name in the *Irish Review* was Shan Van Vocht.[28] Owning or disowning Proust or Casement or Carson or Pound is Joyce's queer Irish literary business—and betrayal—as usual.[29]

NOTES

I thank Marcel Cornis-Pope, Kristoffer O. Jacobson, Karen Lawrence, Michael Levenson, Joseph Valente, and John M. Warner for their encouragement. The original version of this essay was presented in a session arranged by the International James Joyce Foundation at the Modern Language Association convention in San Diego, December 28, 1994.

1. Peter Singleton-Gates and Maurice Girodias, *The Black Diaries: An Account of Roger Casement's Life and Times with a Collection of His Diaries and Public Writings* (Paris: Olympia Press, 1959), 574 (May 9, 1911).

2. See René MacColl, *Roger Casement: A New Judgment* (London: Hamish Hamilton, 1956); and B. L. Reid, *The Lives of Roger Casement* (New Haven, Conn.: Yale University Press, 1976).

3. Vincent J. Cheng, *Joyce, Race, and Empire* (Cambridge: Cambridge University Press, 1995), 130, 305 n. 10.

4. Adaline Glasheen, *Third Census of Finnegans Wake: An Index of the Characters and Their Roles* (Berkeley and Los Angeles: University of California Press, 1977), 52.

5. MacColl, *Roger Casement*, 268.

6. H. O. Mackey, *The Life and Times of Roger Casement* (Dublin: C. J. Fallon, 1954), 108–14; Alfred Noyes, *The Accusing Ghost; or, Justice for Casement* (London: Victor Gallancz, 1957), 105 and passim; H. O. Mackey, *Roger Casement: The Truth about the Forged Diaries* (Dublin: C. J. Fallon, 1966), passim; MacColl, *Roger Casement*, 281.

7. MacColl, *Roger Casement*, 279; Reid, *Lives of Roger Casement*, appendix A.

8. William York Tindall, *A Reader's Guide to James Joyce* (New York: Noonday Press, 1959), 252; Patrick McCarthy, "*Finnegans Wake*," in *A Companion to Joyce Studies*, ed. Zack Bowen and James F. Carens (Westport, Conn.: Greenwood Press, 1984), 609.

9. John Bishop, *Joyce's Book of the Dark: "Finnegans Wake"* (Madison: University of Wisconsin Press, 1986), does not take up these cases. Richard Brown, *James Joyce and Sexuality* (Cambridge: Cambridge University Press, 1985) says homosexuality in Joyce is "peripheral" (84) and does not mention Casement.

10. John Gordon, *"Finnegans Wake": A Plot Summary* (Dublin: Gill and Macmillan, 1986), 207, 83.

11. Enda Duffy, *The Subaltern Ulysses* (Minneapolis: University of Minnesota Press, 1994), 102, 108, 99.

12. Duffy, *The Subaltern Ulysses*, 103.

13. *JJII* 23; Roland McHugh, *Annotations to "Finnegans Wake"* (Baltimore: Johns Hopkins University Press, 1991), 311; Glasheen, *Third Census*, 52; MacColl, *Roger Casement*, 138–42, 120, 243, and passim; H. Montgomery Hyde, *Carson: The Life of Sir Edward Carson of Duncairn* (London: William Heinemann, 1953), 170–71. Ellmann's biography does not mention Casement; nor does his name appear in the three volumes of Joyce's letters.

14. I endorse Glasheen's suggestion, *Third Census*, xxxi, that the scene's women provide cover for the men's interest in each other.

15. Escape from impurity propels anthropologist Michael Taussig's argument in *Shamanism, Colonialism, and the Wild Man: A Study in Terror and Healing* (Chicago: University of Chicago Press, 1987). Taussig includes a study of Casement's Putomayo report.

16. *The Pound/Joyce Letters*, ed. Forrest Read (New York: New Directions, 1967), 255, 239.

17. This is the gist of Judith N. Shklar, *American Citizenship* (Cambridge, Mass: Harvard University Press, 1991).

18. Hyde, *Carson*, 171. For William Joyce, see Rebecca West, *The Meaning of Treason* (New York: Viking Press, 1947).

19. MacColl, *Roger Casement*, 288.

20. Edward W. Said, *Representations of the Intellectual* (New York: Pantheon Books, 1994), 17, 119.

21. Jean-Michel Rabaté, "On Joycean and Wildean Sodomy," in this volume, 41.

22. Rabaté, "Joycean and Wildean Sodomy," 43.

23. Seamus Deane, "Joyce the Irishman," in *The Cambridge Companion to James Joyce*, ed. Derek Attridge (Cambridge: Cambridge University Press, 1990), argues that for Joyce "transgression and betrayal is legitimized by . . . language itself" (50); "treachery . . . is fundamental to his . . . writing. . . . He saw it as the problem of his culture" (52). I try to develop Deane, and thereby to supplement Dominic Manganiello, *Joyce's Politics* (London: Routledge and Kegan Paul, 1980), where there is no mention of Casement.

24. Emer Nolan, *James Joyce and Nationalism* (London: Routledge, 1995), xiii, 158.

25. Robert M. Polhemus, "Pound's 'Instigations' of/and: The 'Lot Complex' in *Finnegans Wake*," paper presented at Modern Language Association Convention, San Diego, 1994.

26. Sheldon Brivic, *Joyce's Waking Women: An Introduction to "Finnegans Wake"* (Madison: University of Wisconsin Press, 1995), 16, 43, 108, 109; Lesley McDowell, "Daughter's Time: Issy's Problematics of Time in *Finnegans Wake*," in *"Finnegans Wake:" "Teems of Times,"* ed. Andrew Treip (Amsterdam: Rodopi, 1994), 93.

27. Ford Madox Ford, *It Was the Nightingale* (1933; rpt., New York: Ecco Press, 1984), 292.

28. MacColl, *Roger Casement*, 127. Kristoffer O. Jacobson called my attention to Casement's pen name and its ramifications. In the light of Shan Van Vocht's shared identity in *FW* with Cathleen Ni Houlihan, Grace O'Malley, and the Prankquean, all three, but especially the latter, might be conflated with Casement. McHugh, *Annotations to "Finnegans Wake,"* does not note that *quean*, spelled with an *a*, was "late C.19-20" slang for male homosexual. See OED; Paul Beale, ed., *Partridge's Concise Dictionary of Slang and Unconventional English* (New York: Macmillan, 1989); and Don Gifford with Robert J. Seidman, *"Ulysses" Annotated* (Berkeley and Los Angeles: University of California Press, 1988), entry on *U* 1.543–44 (17:36–37), 23.

29. For betrayal in homosexual fiction, see Leo Bersani, *Homos* (Cambridge, Mass: Harvard University Press, 1995), 151–81. Rebecca West, *The New Meaning of Treason* (New York: Viking Press, 1964) considers Cold War traitors who are gay and claims that treason has come to an end.

Confessing Oneself

Homoeros and Colonial *Bildung* in *A Portrait of the Artist as a Young Man*

Gregory Castle

I would like to start this essay with a remark made by Joseph Valente in the present volume, made originally in his contribution to the *James Joyce Quarterly* special issue that made this volume possible. Valente argues that the "homosocial energies" in *A Portrait* "are indissociable from Stephen's phobic denial of them; that this denial constitutes a *fundamental determinant* of the novel's basic narrative structure and hence of Stephen's destiny."[1] But that structure could also be defined more pointedly, as Valente suggests, with reference to the generic protocols of the bildungsroman and *Künstlerroman,* in which case the problem of gender destiny becomes tantamount to (perhaps identical to) the problem of world-historical socialization, of conscription into the normative patriarchal, heterosocial sphere as it is scripted in the bildungsroman genre. In this case, we could say, vis-à-vis the bildungsroman, that the homoerotic energies Valente posits as flowing into the novel from the autobiographical subject *were already there in the novel's form,* already codified in the history and law of (a) genre.

The autobiographical transference of homoerotic energies is preceded by the structural saturation of the bildungsroman with what Eve Kosofsky Sedgwick calls *homosocial desire.* The affective drives of homoerotic desire, rerouted from the kinds of transgression that might allow its fulfillment (the annihilation of constraints, the breaching of borders and boundaries), are recathected in triangular homosocial relations between two men in which a woman (or a "discourse" of "woman") stands as putative object of at least one of them.[2] Triangular structures arise whenever repression of homoeros necessitates obeisance to normative, compulsory heterosexuality, especially to the institution of marriage, which perfects the illusions of totality, normativity, and "naturalness"; at such times, according to Sedgwick, "the ultimate function of women is to be conduits of homosocial desire."[3] Needless to say, such relations need not be genitalized; in fact they are far more potent whenever the sexual element is sublimated in the pursuit of a heterosocial identity and the satisfaction of a heteroerotic desire (in all of its cognitive, ideological, and somatic appurtenances and valences) that represses and reroutes "deviancy" of all kinds. These fissures and re- and desublimations operate on (at least) two sociohistorical levels: on one level, we find "the transfer of sexual regulation from religious institutions and ideologies to a complex of secular institutions and ideologies such as the state and the sciences of medicine and individual psychology."[4] On this level, specific homosocial structures elicit homophobia as an institutionalized check on the return of repressed homoeroticism. In the logic of homosociality, women mediate and displace the "secret" or "illicit" desire of male authority— that which is grounded in homoeros, that dares not speak its name—and thereby construct "normative" relations in which male dominance over women guarantees the reproduction of both homosociality and the repressive mechanisms that maintain the ruse of heterosexuality. On a second level, a reaction among men leads to a variety of "changes in men's experience of living within the shifting terms of compulsory heterosexuality"[5]—a variety that in and of itself flouts heterosocial norms. Though homosociality is the space in which homoeros is sublimated or repressed, it is also the space and opportunity for revolutionary (re)action and (re)formation.[6]

Joyce's *Portrait of the Artist as a Young Man* dramatizes both the reproduction of homosociality and the reactions against such reproduction. The pathways of power are laid open for Stephen Dedalus at just those points where perverse (homo)erotic desire is sublimated and rerouted through various normative heterosexual relations. Dante's demand that the young Stephen apologize for desiring the Protestant Eileen might thus be seen as a coded affirmation of heterosexuality, all the more insidious coming in a negative form: though as a Protestant Eileen is the *im*proper object for libidinal cathexis, the ideal of marriage is implicitly reaffirmed (as it is when Dante excoriates Parnell for sinning against the sacrament of marriage in his affair with Kitty O'Shea). Something similar goes on in chapter 2, which narrates the leaps forward of adolescence, with its inevitable turbulence of sexual and social identities. When Stephen suffers an "agony of penetration" in his concourse with the prostitute, an agony that clearly denies a phallic identity in favor of a penetrable, even *rapeable,* femininity, we are tempted to regard Stephen's heterosexuality as suspect, barely able to contain the homoeroticism figured in this gender reversal.[7] Because their instrumentality is now directed toward justifying his famous boast to forge a racial conscience, Stephen's relations with women (Mercedes, the prostitute, the Virgin Mary, the bird-girl, E.C. of the villanelle) succeed less in facilitating than in distancing him irrecoverably from harmonious socialization. His mother, after all, packs him off for exile.

As we shall see, these sublimations are reinforced by the bildungsroman tradition, even as that tradition fails to represent adequately Stephen's colonial desire for freedom from the imperial culture of *Bildung*, with its coercive meta-narrative of bourgeois self-development.[8] At the same time, however, Stephen's development as an Irish colonial (non)subject, precisely because it deconstructs the imperial prerogatives of *Bildung* and of the *Bildungheld*, opens up the possibility of subjectivity and historical agency denied by classical *Bildung*. In what follows, I want to demonstrate that this deconstruction begins and ends in a critical appropriation and restaging of the sacrament of penance, particularly the first stage, confession. In *A Portrait*, Joyce exposes the homosocial structuration of the sacramental ritual of confession, unveiling the divine mediation that disguises the *human* relations between priest and penitent; on another level, this exposé leads to an exploration of the subterreaneous affiliations between the ancient notion of confession as a public *confession of faith* and the will to self-development narrativized in the modern bildungsroman. I argue that Stephen undergoes a series of confessions (sacred and profane) that constitutes not only a critique of confession as sacred ritual but also a critique of the secular concept of *Bildung*. Moreover, by unveiling the divine homosociality at the heart of confession, this critique seeks also to call into question the sexual politics of Irish Catholic education and mentorship. And while a critique of confession in this generic context is not by any means equivalent to a critique of colonial power and instrumentality, it nevertheless contributes to the liberation of the colonial (non)subject from oppressive categories of subjectivity and sociohistorical agency. In fine, I believe that Joyce's critique of *Bildung* is productive and issues in a hybrid discourse, what I call the colonial bildungsroman, in which the colonial (non)subject achieves a long-withheld subjectivity and historical agency, but always at the cost of the very metanarratives (the confession, the bildungsroman) that have traditionally defined and legitimized the "subject" in both sacred and secular history.

In the classical bildungsroman, homosociality is embodied in the apprentice/mentor relationship, in which the figure of woman plays a paradigmatic and instrumental role in facilitating the young hero's socialization. The rites of passage narrativized in the bildungsroman can thus be regarded as de(homo)-sexualized ceremonies of homosocial affiliation and consolidation that lay open for the young male hero—the bourgeois *Bildungheld*, for whom autonomy and wholeness, harmony and social integration are entitlements—the "ways of the world," the pathways of power and male privilege. Indeed, John H. Smith has argued that the "goal" of the bildungsroman is nothing less than ascension to male privilege and homosocial bonding, the representation of "the self's developmental trajectory within the bourgeois patriarchal order and thereby to expose the structuration of (male) desire."[9] The achievement of this goal takes place, as such things inevitably do in the classical bildungsroman, in the context of homosocial desire and the dialectical structures of mentorship it has reproduced and formalized. Further, the homoeroticism that makes these structures possible (in that they arise in the act of repression), is occluded and mystified in homosocial mentoring, in bonds of fraternity, of blood brotherhood, of aristocratic equality that guarantee the perpetuation of male authority and rule as well as the ruse of "natural" heterosexuality. When this trajectory moves through colonized space, it exposes the imperial nature of a *Bildung* plot constituted by homosocial relations that maintain the "bourgeois patriarchal order" in very much the same way colonial masters maintain order in the colonies: by repressive mechanisms that seek to do away with all deviance from compulsory norms. The desire for narrative structure, for the specific narrative structure of socialization enacted in the bildungsroman, is misunderstood by the hero as a desire for destiny, particularly that mythos of destiny that emerges out of neoclassical humanism, one that is both self-fulfilling and universal, artistic triumph coming out of willful compliance with the world-historical Spirit. It is this mythos that Joyce's bildungsroman seeks to demythologize, enacting a destiny that is both self-fulfilling *and* self-annihilating, artistic triumph coming out of willful error and the circumvention of normative self-development.

In the foregoing, I have used the phrase "colonial (non)subject" to indicate and re-mark the proximity of the subaltern space of colonial subjection with respect to the master's subjectivity. Homi Bhabha has called this kind of proximity "a form of colonial discourse that is uttered *inter dicta:* a discourse at the crossroads of what is known and permissible and that which though known must be kept concealed."[10] The "(non)" cancels this proximity without removing it, thereby revealing colonial "subjectivity" as the intrusive or perverse space of mimicry where the colonized "writes" and "speaks" and "represents" him-/herself in destabilizing parodies or restagings of imperial discourse. Through the agency of a travestied subjectivity, the (post)colonial writer produces identities (diasporic, exilic, cross-gendered) out of a constitutive internal division that the colonial (non)subject neither seeks to resolve nor to abandon. Lacking the subjectivity to enter into symbolic discourse as an enfranchised citizen, the colonial (non)subject will always be something of an alien.[11] The radical aspect of sexual deviance retrieved in colonial *Bildung*—only one valence of which is homoeros—is that which precedes the inscription of gender dimorphism and the law of genre that follows from it and institutes male privilege at the level of discourse. Colonial *Bildung* is not a transcendental metanarrative that hails or disavows subjects, nor is it an uncrowning of transcendence. It unsettles classical subject positions, developing in rebellion within them, never fully abdicating the "classical" inscriptions. It erupts into oppositional mimicry in which hierarchies are leveled, rituals travestied, subject positions inhabited in exorbitant and often violent ways, caricaturing the sovereign autonomy of the Western "subject" by fracturing it in every act of habitation. In this return of a repressed homoeros, in this radical ambivalence of the "proximate," colonial (non)subjectivity unseats the autonomous, essential, unitary self authorized by Enlightenment humanism, installing in its place multiple possibilities of identity formation. We do not discern the harmonious resolutions of classical *Bildung*—a normative process of self-development—only the temporal and temperamental agon (agonies, deconstructions) of colonial *Bildung.*

It is easy to see how the imperial disavowal of colonial subjectivity (disavowal in Freud's sense of an incomplete repudiation) is akin to what we find in the economy of homophobia—in both cases an insupportable *proximity* occurs, "in which the social and psychic are conjoined and in a way which transforms each as conventionally understood."[12] A trace of the subaltern's presence remains, a residue and reminder of what Marlow, in Joseph Conrad's *Heart of Darkness,* calls our "remote kinship with [a] wild and passionate uproar."[13] It is in this way that both colonial power and compulsory heterosocial behavior end up fearing the same "deviance," proximity to which can only fuel a panicky defense of empire in the name of bourgeois subjectivity—that is to say, in the name of "man"kind. In the recourse to mimicry, a new field of knowledge, a new space for *Bildung* opens up that enables the inscription of "aberrant" or subaltern desire as outside norm *and* deviance, *inter dicta.* The intersubjective relations set up in the colonial context of Stephen Dedalus's *Bildung* entail the desublimation of homoerotic desire that in various ways destabilizes strategies of narration used in the classical bildungsroman. And while the bildungsroman form is well suited to narrate the kind of socialization desirable in the colonies, it must contend with a force not met with in metropolitan contexts—colonial desire, which is always a desire for revolution or exile. Colonial desire seeks new avenues for the discovery and narration of self-knowledge and finds one of them in the internalization of the dialectic of knowledge and power—the dialectic of colonialism—that structures the classical bildungsroman. In this process, the harmony of inner and outer worlds desired in classical *Bildung* plots is displaced and refigured as an *inner split,* a dehiscence in the normative concept of *Bildung* and its dialectical will to harmony in which the two poles of the dialect (which Martin Swales denominates, following Hegel, the poetry of interiority and the prose of social life) render dialectical progression and synthesis radically ambivalent.[14] The concept of harmony is discombobulated in colonial *Bildung,* the disavowed subject speaking dissonantly from a fractured, nonuniversal perspective.[15]

This "failure" to achieve *Bildung* is simultaneously the formation of new modes of knowledge and *self*-knowledge in which the will to know (and what is known) issues from a mimicry of the old styles of knowing,[16] thus creating the very (non)subjectivity that makes the interior dehiscence possible. What makes this division productive of new knowledge is the refusal to see division as *divisive,* as the creation of an absolute "other" vis-à-vis some privileged and autonomous self (a move that would mean the near-fatal disavowal of *Bildung*). Colonial *Bildung* is thus predicated on the denegation of "the subject," a condition that, in its turn, becomes the ground for new subject positions (which are always mimic re-presentations of that bourgeois fetish, "autonomous individuality") and new perversions of narrative that underwrite "transculturated" *Bildung* plots.[17]

One of the productive "perversions" of narrative that open up the possibilities for self-development occurs in what I call *profane confession*. Understood as a kind of perversion,[18] profane confession desublimates the relations of power that characterize the "official" one-way dyad of sacred and secular confessions in which the priest, judge, or inquisitor hearing confession does not reciprocate with a narrative of disburdening. By so doing, the one-way structure of confession falls away to reveal the aleatory desire that canon law and church practice represses. Profane confession makes overt the homosocial desire (to repent, to absolve) between penitent and priest; it calls forth the triangular mediation of desire, displacing homoeros in the direction of pious adoration. The structure of confession, especially the absolute effacement of the priest in his role as substitute for Christ, occludes the mediation of desire by making Christ and the priest one pole of a dyadic structure. But the ruse of substitution marks the Divine Son as a third term, instrumental object of adoration masking the potentials for (homo)erotic bonds between priest and penitent. Further, Stephen Dedalus's confession, because it invokes the Virgin Mary (whose sodality Stephen headed at Belvedere) in an eroticized mediation involving marriage to E.C., adds a heteroerotic valence that underscores the homosocial structure of religious confession.

To confess is to acknowledge, to own, to avow; it is linked etymologically to the desire to utter, to declare, to disclose, to make manifest. In theological terms, confession is "the acknowledging of sin or sinfulness," specifically "the confessing of sin to a priest, as a religious duty"; in legal terms, it is an "acknowledgment before the proper authority of the truth of a statement or charge."[19] Other senses include "to disclose one's faults," "to unburden one's sins or the state of one's conscience to God or to a priest."[20] Official confession, whether conducted in the confessional, the docket, or the interrogation room, is essentially dyadic, a stylized and regulated speech-act that involves, usually, a one-way path of disburdening (on television, the police often remind suspects that *they* are asking the questions, an aspect of confession that emphasizes its coercive nature). In these normative contexts, the confession is a disavowal of a secret, a seeking after absolution for some transgression; it is, above all, a ceremonial or ritualistic attitude toward Law.

In the sacrament of penance, confession prepares the penitent for the Eucharist, offering an opportunity to cleanse the self of what the church believes deforms the soul and outrages God in order that the satisfaction of the penance and reconciliation through the Host can proceed smoothly. This operation is one-way in the sense that the priest, who is de-faced in his symbolic function as substitute for Christ, does not reciprocate by disburdening, does not enter into a dialogue with the penitent on the other side of the screen. Though historically the *confessor* referred to one who confesses his or her faith publicly, and though in contemporary dictionaries it covers "one that confesses" and "a priest who hears confession," church practice is to reserve the term for the priest who hears confession.[21] Nowhere is the borderline between penitent and confessor more pronounced and policed than in the sacrament of penance. Speech is conventional and scripted, depending for the most part on "generic" categories of venal and mortal sins and on prescribed formulas of absolution. In fact, "confessional knowledge" flows not between human subjects but between the human penitent and the dehumanized priest who can no longer know in *human* terms what is said in the confessional.[22] In this way only, in "the pious practice of frequent confession," as Pope Pius XII wrote in the encyclical *Mystici corporis,* "genuine self-knowledge is increased, Christian humility grows, bad habits are corrected, spiritual neglect and tepidity are countered, the conscience is purified, the will strengthened, a salutary self-control attained and grace increased by reason of the sacrament itself."[23] The "genuine" self-knowledge generated in the confessional can be regarded as a kind of self-disavowal, a submission of the self to the transcendent example of Jesus Christ and his earthly substitutes.

The erotic or desiring self, which canon law and papal encyclicals seek to expunge from the celebration of the sacrament of penance, turns out to be, at least according to M. M. Bakhtin, the element of confession that links it to narrative forms like the bildungsroman. Bakhtin speaks of an "internal dialogism leading to repentance" that characterizes "pagan" as well as Christian confession and that is exemplified by St. Augustine's *Confessions.*[24] He then adduces the example of Dostoyevsky to pose the "problem of *confession*" in terms of a philosophy of language: the problem of confession is "the problem of a thought, a desire, a motivation that is authentic . . . and how these problems are exposed in words." He then goes on to draw direct lines of filiation between the genres of confession and the bildungsroman: "Artistic prose, the novelistic element present in ethical tracts, especially confessions, may be quite significant—for example, in Epictetus, Marcus Aurelius, Augustine and Petrarch we can detect the embryonic beginnings of the *Prüfungs-* and *Bildungsroman.*"[25] Here, the "genuine" self-knowledge of the confessional begins to dovetail with the narrative logic of the classical bildungsroman, in which the pursuit of self-knowledge is grounded in a dialectical process that harmonizes that pursuit with the demands of social institutions. The structure of confession—with its one-way circuit of disburdening (met only with official dispensations of prescribed absolutions, not a counterdisburdening)—reinforces by finally marking as such the one-way circuit of homosocial relations, a reinforcement made concrete in the bildungsroman with its unidirectional power-knowledge flows, sweeping apprentice-hero up and carrying him or her toward "proper" mentors who, not surprisingly, have mapped out the pathways in advance and control all the sluice gates.

It should be no surprise, then, that confessions in Joyce's colonial bildungsroman have a strong profane character, for they have of necessity picked up on and developed the internal dialogism that Bakhtin adduces as a problematic of desire and language and that the church regulates as "genuine" self-knowledge or represses as sin. Profane confession, by so evading regulation and repression, evidences both a loss of faith in the necessity for absolution and a positive gain in the ability to recognize and affirm the self *in sin* rather than in sin's absolution. The ur-text for this profane mode of confession—one that looks back for its "origin" to Augustine even as it debunks the need for absolution and reformation—is, of course, Oscar Wilde's *De Profundis.* Though Wilde's confessional letter to Lord Alfred Douglas remains overtly nonreciprocal, Wilde does not *re*form or *trans*form himself so much as see more clearly the "natural" route of his self-development. This idea, found throughout *De Profundis,* suggests that the moment of repentance is less a matter of seeking absolution for sins than in affirming one's self and one's self-development; it is a confession of faith *in oneself.* Indeed, repentance is an initiation into oneself and "the means by which one alters one's past."[26] In a sense, the confessional becomes for Wilde what the mountaintop was for Zarathustra: a space for the unfolding and affirmation of the self in/as the will to Life, which is at the same time a refusal to *re*form or *trans*form the self (at least along traditional lines). In *A Portrait,* a similar dynamic takes place, with the crucial difference that Stephen forces a kind of reciprocity in his confessional relations; accordingly, the disburdening of taboo or secret knowledge reconfigures as self-knowledge, as a series of epistemological crises in which Stephen must assess both *what* he knows and *how* he has come to know it. It is precisely at these crisis points that confession intersects with and destabilizes (by unveiling) the homosocial economies of the bildungsroman that construct knowledge as a male privilege.

As Sedgwick demonstrates in her *Epistemology of the Closet,* "The *special* centrality of homophobic oppression in the twentieth century . . . has resulted from its inextricability from the question of knowledge and the processes of knowing in modern Western culture at large."[27] What Stephen knows and how he confesses knowledge of it are key considerations for understanding his relation to the homosocial order. We see in his quest for self-knowledge the potential for new knowledges that promise to open up aesthetico-pedagogic spaces outside the colonized homosociality of Dublin—or deep within it as a species of immanent critique, what Gayatri Spivak calls an "inaccessible blankness circumscribed by an interpretable text."[28] In *A Portrait,* Stephen's negation of colonial and nationalist domination is furthered not inconsiderably in his relations with alternative confessors, usually male, who allow him to sublimate homoerotic desire in the confession of a host of intellectual and moral "sins." Indeed, a sufficiently elastic generic conception would allow us to regard Stephen's theoretical monologues as forms of confession in which heretical views can be articulated as new knowledge. We note especially the role of Lynch, who serves as a conduit for an aesthetic theory that posits (in a mockery of bourgeois autonomy) the godlike capacity of the self-sufficient artist to forge a world of pure interiority (i.e., pure artistic apprehension), a world in which the dialectic of inner and outer is internalized and transformed into an "inner world of individual emotions mirrored perfectly in a lucid supple periodic prose" (*P* 164). These perversions of confession contrast sharply with the scenes of official Augustinian confession made to priests of the church. At the retreat narrated in chapter three, Stephen confesses certain general, "orthodox" sins ("He began to confess his sins: masses missed, prayers not said, lies"), but he does not name them (he speaks only of "Sloth" and "impurity" [*P* 144]); he certainly cannot utter "homoerotic desire." But even as he occludes the specificity of his sin (one form or another of outlawed sexuality) in the articulation of a generalized, orthodox confession, he names this sin (in the interstices of the retreat) through graphic counterimages contiguous with—*in proximity to*—the banalities for which he seeks absolution.

The frenzy to confess produced in Stephen by Father Arnell's sermon at the retreat, with its exorbitant imagery and horrifying conceptions of temporal and spatial interminability, is fueled in part by Stephen's imagination, which displaces homoerotic desire by rendering all desire as bestial, utterly improper yet not overtly homosexual (which is the zenith of improper sexual behavior or identity) or for that matter *hetero*sexual. The profane litany that follows indicates a range of sexual perversion that goes far beyond even the standard deviance of heterosexual relations:

> The sordid details of his orgies stank under his very nostrils: the sootcoated packet of pictures which he had hidden in the flue of the fireplace and in the presence of whose shameless or bashful wantonness he lay for hours sinning in thought and deed; his monstrous dreams, peopled by apelike creatures and by harlots with gleaming jewel eyes; the foul long letters he had written in the joy of guilty confession and carried secretly for days and days only to throw them under cover of night among the grass in the corner of a field or beneath some hingeless door or in some niche in the hedges where a girl might come upon them as she walked by and read them secretly. (*P* 115–16)

I cite this passage at length because its language of exorbitance—sordid orgies, monstrous dreams, apelike creatures, joys of guilty confession—suggests that Stephen's perverse heterosexual desire aligns itself with homoeroticism; the former is *proximate to* the latter rhetorically and imagistically.[29] Countering this litany of monstrous desires is a vision of absolution couched in the language of normative heterosexual union. The vision of proximation—in which "the outlaw turns up as inlaw, and the other as proximate proves more disturbing than the other as absolute difference"[30]—is dispelled by a reassertion of patriarchal authority that *re*marks all relations, all libidinal economies as *ap*proximations of the same. In the intercalation of the image of the Virgin Mary presiding over Stephen's imaginary marriage to Emma we find an inscription of approved, normative heterosocial relations that transform the "joy[s] of guilty confession" into *ceremonies of homosociality*. In a passage that sums up the enormity of his outlawed desire, Stephen suffers an image foisted upon him of the ideal heterosexual object: "The image of Emma appeared before him and, under her eyes, the flood of shame rushed forth anew from his heart. If she knew to what his mind had subjected her or how his brutelike lust had torn and trampled upon her innocence!" (*P* 115). Stephen's desire to confess to the Virgin defuses libidinal energies precisely by making the proximate *ap*proximate. The transformation of desire into approximations of convention motivates Joyce's narrative in chapter 3, which alternates between the retreat and the classroom and between these and Stephen's feverish daydreams, reinforcing the authority of the church fathers, whose homosocial bonding has determined Stephen's education from the start.

The homosocial nexus of priest and young male student, figured in terms of eroticized violence, has been discussed by others.[31] I would like to explore another set of relations with perhaps greater pertinence (because of its pedagogical force) for the fate of *Bildung* in a colonial setting—that is, the relations of schoolboys with each other, relations that, in normative *Bildung* plots, presage and prepare for the institutional obligations that cement forever the dynamics of homosociality, especially mentorship, at the level of homophobic reaction and violence. For example, just before the performance of the Whitsuntide play at Belvedere (*Vice Versa*, which Joyce subtly inscribes as a symbolic enactment of patriarchal and pedagogical violence), "noble Dedalus," that "model youth," is hailed by Vincent Heron, who can be effectively ignored until he touches on the subject of the Father, whose authority, in one form or another, Stephen seeks to circumvent. "Any allusion made to his father by a fellow or by a master put [Stephen's] calm to rout in a moment" (*P* 76). A "shaft of momentary anger" signals a change in Stephen's demeanor; an "old restless moodiness" from a previous night with E.C. permeates him and he realizes, epiphanally, the "growth and knowledge of two years of boyhood" (*P* 77). He becomes, in other words, self-conscious of his own development. When Heron forces Stephen to "admit" to his relationship with E.C.—to confirm (and affirm) the heterosocial structure of courting and "being found out"—Stephen responds by reciting the *Confiteor*, thus amalgamating the young men and their pranks with the priests and their sacraments. And though Stephen acknowledges the "playfulness" of Heron's "stroke," it nevertheless provokes a memory of the kind of pedagogical violence that the bildungsroman offers as a deepstructural analogue of colonial domination.

In the hypermasculine world of Catholic boarding school, the violence meted out by Heron is connected, through the pedagogical contexts in which it takes place, with a colonial relation in which the (non)subject is coerced into reeducation or, worse, denied education altogether. Heron here stands in for the colonial official who demands obedience on principle; his authority over Stephen reduplicates without mimicry the structures of imperial power, and all the more insidiously for being simultaneously an act of imperial coercion *and* an act of betrayal. Heron is, then, the personification of colonial ambivalence *that is unaware of itself as such*. In an inchoate way, Stephen is able to penetrate the "indulgence" of his schoolmates, to see a pattern of violence connected with the acquisition of knowledge, the implication always being in such circumstances that one disburdens oneself, one confesses not as the subject of history but rather as the object of its interrogations. Stephen resembles Albert Memmi's colonized, who is "out of the game" of history: "Of course, he carries its burden, often more cruelly than others, but always as an object. He has forgotten how to participate actively in history and no longer even asks to do so."[32] Or perhaps we might say, apropos Stephen, that the colonized can only know his own history, his own formation, can acquire knowledge only of himself. To be sure, Stephen cannot accede to his own life history as a viable alternative to world history by the conclusion of *A Portrait* and is certainly far from such a case in chapter 2. Nevertheless, we can see adumbrated in Stephen's reaction to Heron the kind of maneuvers he will have to master if he is to negotiate the tangle of homosocial relations that prevent him, netlike, from attaining the selfhood he only dimly foresees at this stage of development—a stage overdetermined by "foreknowledge," "premonition," "intuition" (*P* 64–65), forms of proleptic self-knowledge that can appear to the adolescent only as "a strange unrest" or as "monstrous images" (*P* 64, 90).

In reciting the *Confiteor*, Stephen is strangely calmed "amid the indulgent laughter of his hearers," and he wonders "why he bore no malice now to those who had tormented him" (*P* 82). His memory of their cruelty "called forth no anger from him" (*P* 82); and far from forgetting "that malignant episode," it is revisited and rewritten as a pivotal moment whose consequences only now crop up, a moment (both moments, the primal beating and its remembrance) after which the life of desire is demystified but not entirely understood:

> He had not forgotten a whit of their cowardice and cruelty but the memory of it called forth no anger from him. All the descriptions of fierce love and hatred which he had met in books had seemed to him therefore unreal. Even that night as he stumbled homewards along Jones's Road he had felt that some power was divesting him of that suddenwoven anger as easily as a fruit is divested of its soft ripe peel. (*P* 82)

The very withdrawal of anger that is meant to distance him from the cruelty of his male peers is figured by an image that feminizes it, the nonresistance of the fruit signaling the passive and somatic nature of Stephen's sense of himself *as a rapeable body*. If the general erotic cast of the images is not enough to suggest homoeroticism, we can consider that while Stephen does not forget "a whit" of the episode in which Heron serves as his confessor, he does forget E.C., his putative heterosexual "love" interest, the instrumental support of his *Bildung* plot: "He tried to recall her appearance but could not. He could remember only that she had worn a shawl about her head like a cowl and that her dark eyes had invited and unnerved him" (*P* 82). The general effect of this dominance of homosocial repression and heterosexual charade (nicely imaged in the cowl, which invokes both the monk's hood and the sublimation of homoeros) is to subject Stephen to a succession of possible mentors and social authorities—represented as voices in the gymnasium "urging him to be strong and manly and healthy," a din of "hollowsounding voices that made him halt irresolutely in the pursuit of phantoms" (*P* 83–84). His irresolution, his preference for the "company of phantasmal comrades" (*P* 84), marks his ambivalence, which is, in turn, figured paradoxically in the word *Foetus,* carved on a desk in a university lecture hall, a figure for heterosexual desire and normative productivity that unveils the proximity of his father's hypermasculinity to something dangerous and illicit—the monstrosities of his own "deviant" sexual desires somehow linked to the somatic strata of "proper" cathexes and sublimations. What we have here is not so much epiphany as incarnation: "the word and the vision [of his father's school days] capered before his eyes," and "his recent monstrous reveries came thronging into his memory" (*P* 90).

At this critical juncture in his *Bildung* plot, Stephen is coming to consciousness of his mentor-masters, at the same time glimpsing the (homo)sexual desire at the heart of his relations with them. The moment of equanimity, the "one rare moment" when Stephen "seemed to be clothed in the real apparel of boyhood" (*P* 85), the still point of ease in homosocial ceremony erupts into panic. He flees the theater and encounters the deleterious effects of his fall from innocence: "Pride and hope and desire like crushed herbs in his heart sent up vapours of maddening incense before the eyes of his mind" (*P* 86). He flees from homosociality into its heart, where he finds not a space of resistance but a soothing atmosphere of calm, the very somatic strata—of animality, corruption, illicit sexual desire, of his own monstrous images—that homosociality must conspire to hide. He is able to calm his fear of this desire by acceding to a displaced image of it. That Stephen desires a kind of proximity to unregulated libidinal flows is underscored by the *value* Stephen assigns to "piss and rotted straw": "It is a *good* odour to breathe" (*P* 86; emphasis added). By affirming and revaluing the bestial and the corrupt, Stephen covertly affirms and revalues the "monstrosities" that are emerging within him and that are linked to the unspeakable desire of homoeroticism.

Joyce has not left us with many choices. On the one hand, the affirmation of piss and straw confirms the homosocial order through metonymic displacement of homoeros onto the nonhuman material stratum. On the other hand, Stephen hears the murmur of a voice (dim echo of the voices of mentors that permeate the chapter), "suffer[s] the agony of its penetration" (*P* 100), swoons into the role of odalisque, a passive, pulpy fruit unpeeled by the prostitute who (by Stephen's own lights in *Stephen Hero*) performs, albeit in a meaner register, the same state function as marriage. Illicit though it is, Stephen's dalliance with the prostitute can be read as an entrée into the world of young Catholic men in Ireland, a world of male privilege that masks its own unnamed desire in heterosexual commerce and homophobia. In keeping with the bildungsroman tradition, he uses women to further his formation both as colonial (non)subject and as artist. E.C. is the "legitimate" object of his heterosexual masquerade, supplemented by the prostitute, that "illegitimate" object who enables Stephen's homoerotic cathexis under the guise of a heterosexual commerce with women.[33] In either case, Stephen's illegitimate libidinal investments form an interminable circuit of complicity, in which rebellion and deviance are prescribed, through a reappropriation and reinvestment of the structures of homosociality.

In view of this complicitous condition, it is supremely ironic that the first tremors in the smooth surface of homosocial bonding and displacement and the beginnings of an oppositional colonial *Bildung* occur in the pedagogical milieu surrounding the retreat. At one point, Stephen finds himself lulled by the vague bestiality of the boys, including the inevitable Heron, "talking" and "jesting" animatedly around him: "The voices that he knew so well, the common words, the quiet of the classroom when the voices paused and the silence was filled by the sound of softly browsing cattle as the other boys munched their lunches tranquilly, lulled his aching soul" (*P* 125). It is difficult to tell whether Stephen's soul aches because of his burden of sexual deviancy or because he cannot finally *belong* with these munching boys. The ambivalence increases when he calls upon the Virgin to intercede: "There was still time. O Mary, refuge of sinners, intercede for him! O Virgin Undefiled, save him from the gulf of death!" (*P* 125). From what, we might ask, is Stephen asking for salvation? His aforementioned sexual deviancy? or the munching boys? Are they one and the same? Does he recognize his own homoerotic desire here, lulled by the *proximity* of these boys to his own "monstrous desires"? Or does he carry on the displacement of desire, experiencing its effects in the classroom as the lulling, tranquilizing rituals of homosociality, repeating the equanimity, which we hear in the "pick, pack, pock, puck" (*P* 59) of water dropping into a brimming fountain, that concludes and defuses Stephen's triumphant mission to the rector's office?

If Stephen's desire for intercession responds to a recognition of homoerotic desire, it is not the kind of recognition the leads to self-knowledge, at least not yet. What might emerge as homoeros (or heterosexual perversion) is rerouted and regulated as heterosexual desire, conscripted into an idealized and normative, church-sanctioned conception of monogamous union. As a result, his recognition (if such it is) can lead only to the kind of official disburdening, nonreciprocal and univocal, represented by the confessional. At this stage of his development, priestly mentors model with absolute authority and assurance a homosocial relation that interdicts and sublimates taboo desire. Baffled and frightened by his own desire, Stephen turns to the confessional for relief:

> No escape. He had to confess, to speak out in words what he had done and thought, sin after sin. How? How?
> —Father, I . . .
> The thought slid like a cold shining rapier into his tender flesh: confession. But not there in the chapel of the college. He would confess all, every sin of deed and thought, sincerely: but not there among his school companions. Far away from there in some dark place he would murmur out his own shame: and he besought God humbly not to be offended with him if he did not dare to confess in the college chapel: and in utter abjection of spirit he craved forgiveness mutely of the boyish hearts about him. (*P* 126)

Note that Stephen promises he "would confess all, every sin of deed and thought, sincerely." But, of course, he doesn't do this, as we find out a few pages later when he falls back on the banalities that are coached out of him by the officious priest. The space of resistance here primed is marked by the exclusion of Stephen's specific desires, which, interestingly, the official confession (*P* 143–45) does not seek to uncover. Nevertheless, to refuse to name these desires is tantamount to refusing the demands of the sacrament, which requires complete abjection on the part of the penitent, the better to demonize and expunge all deviant behavior. This refusal to accede to the high-order abstractions of sin emptied of desire in the name of absolution, a refusal of the homosocial relations that triangulate penitent/Christ/confessor, is marked, paradoxically, by a displacement that enables transgressive utterance within the language of orthodox confession. "Far away from there in some dark place he would murmur out his own shame"—here we have a spatial displacement that prefigures Stephen's transvaluation of Christian concepts and rituals and a displacement of normative speech-acts, a murmuring that eroticizes and taps into the homoerotic tensions repressed by the divine homosociality of the sacrament of penance.

Just as Stephen says: No escape. For the very homoeroticism that homosociality is meant to keep repressed returns as a trope—the "cold shining rapier" recalling "the shaft of momentary anger" (*P* 77) that Stephen feels earlier when Heron speaks of Dedalus *père*. Confession is figured as homosexual penetration, undermining the sacrament of penance by exposing the repressed "secret" of official confession. Confession has thus implicated him, albeit in the sublimated form of religious rite, even further in the desire that he feels has rendered him unfit for God and the Virgin. What he thinks he cannot escape *from* (the monstrosity of his desire) turns out to inhabit his mode of escape (confession). The normative modes of heterosexuality in which Stephen is compelled to participate (e.g., his imaginary marriage to Emma), by offering themselves implicitly as the rewards of confession, encourage Stephen's further investment in the very homosociality, dominated by relations of confessors and penitents, that has enslaved him and the Irish generally.[34] In this network of complicities and betrayals we find a definitive example of how heterosexuality calls our attention to the very homoeroticism it masks.

Stephen's desire to confess in some "dark place" prefigures the greater displacement Stephen inaugurates in his meditations on the priesthood, when he "tries on" the identity of the priest, in a kind of cross-dressing that manifests a dangerous adjacency, one that codes the relations between confessor and penitent as *proximate:*

> He would know *obscure things,* hidden from others, from those who were conceived and born children of wrath. He would know the sins, the *sinful longings* and *sinful thoughts* and *sinful acts,* of others, hearing them *murmured* into his ears in the confessional under the *shame* of a *darkened chapel* by the lips of women and girls: but rendered immune *mysteriously* at his ordination by the imposition of hands his soul would pass again uncontaminated to the white peace of the altar. . . . He would hold his secret knowledge and secret power, being as sinless as the innocent. (*P* 159; emphasis added)

In the awakening and repression of a strong homoerotic desire for the (ambivalent) power of the confessor, Stephen mimes the orthodox homosocial ritual of confession by sexualizing both ends of the confessor/penitent dyad, the better to have, perversely, an *im*mediate relation with the desired other regulated by the sacrament of penance. His mimicry, like his perverse desire, becomes dangerous precisely in the sense of Jacques Derrida's "dangerous" supplement and Dollimore's "dangerous" proximity: in both cases, structure *as such* is undermined in the unveiling of a third term or operation that upsets dyadic relations and underscores the complete absence of self-presence as well as the hard necessity *to know* what is neither self nor "other." In both cases, a binary ground (presence/transcendence, straight/queer) is dissolved in the uncovering of a continuum, even an order of rank, that remakes the world in/as the misprision of representation.

Perverse desire is dangerous because it does not seek to annihilate norms but rather to gain knowledge by transgressing them. "If transgression subverts," writes Dollimore, "it is less in terms of immediate undermining or immediate gains, than in terms of the *dangerous knowledge* it brings with it, or produces, or which is produced *in and by* its containment in the cultural sphere." But he goes on to caution that such knowledge can also be co-opted by dominant groups, turning containment into a new form of repression. This knowledge must include, therefore, "an awareness of that always present, always potentially tragic dialectic between authority and resistance whereby instability becomes a force of repression much more than a force of liberation."[35] Another way of putting the problem is to regard the choices of the colonized as either a complicity without resistance or a complicity *that is a form of resistance.*[36] The latter makes possible oppositional subject positions within institutional structures; it also problematizes the (programmatically male) artist-hero of the colonial bildungsroman, who accedes to subjectivity only when he has broken the law of genre (specifically the "lawlike development" that Wilhelm Dilthey posits as the motive force of *Bildung*)[37] and thus rewritten the narrative of destiny scripted in classical *Bildung.*

Joyce's colonial bildungsroman is resistant and complicitous in just this way. The propulsion toward social maturity is interrupted and derailed by refusals and demurrals that weaken the dialectical hegemony of classical *Bildung*; but it is nevertheless shaped by and even contained within normative conceptions of spiritual and social development. Thus, though Stephen's desire for "secret knowledge and secret power" is played out in overtly heterosexual terms (he speaks of "women and girls"), it nevertheless imbricates rhetorically with the homoeroticism of the boarding school and the covert homosexual desire encoded in Stephen's confusion about "smugging": "What did that mean about the smugging in the square?" (*P* 42). Couched in the perceptions of a child, this question characterizes the calculated obliquity of Stephen's perceptions of the homoeroticism repressed but discernible behind the trappings and rituals of the church. His subsequent attempt to puzzle out the meaning of the episode, magnificently misunderstood as a "terrible sin" committed against the sacristy, looks forward not only to his misunderstanding of the priest's homosocial bond (which he pantomimes as heterosexual voyeurism) but also to his elaboration in chapter 5 of an aesthetics of impersonality that resolves libidinal energies at the abstract level of pure aesthetic forms, impersonal cathexes of homosexual desire.

However, something else is going on in Stephen's restaging of priestly rites. For the very "orthodox" ceremonial gestures that constitute the highly stylized homosocial rites of the church begin to approximate an oppositional "perverse" dynamic—akin though not analogous to what Bhabha describes as "colonial doubling," in which "disavowed knowledges return to make the presence of authority uncertain."[38] Stephen's restaging of priestly rites marks the mimic appropriation of sacral functions, thus furthering the production of a hybrid form of *Bildung* that turns back the gaze of the master/mentor and redeploys, in a carnivalesque upending, the orthodox generic categories of the conventional bildungsroman. One material sign of this production is the salacious desire that motivates Stephen to covet the absolute power of the confessor. But wouldn't this same salaciousness also neutralize opposition to homosociality? If we regard heterosexuality as the ruse of homosociality, as the displacement of taboo homosexual desire, if we see it as instrumental in maintaining homosociality and the *male* privilege of the priesthood, salacious desire would represent only an irritation to the norm, not a subversion of it. Even among priests, heterosexual desire is an acceptable deviation since it seals all the more tightly the ruse put in place to mask the homosocial essence of ecclesiastical authority.

What makes this salacious desire potentially oppositional is the extent to which it configures confession as an unstable mechanism within a colonial context. Let me be clear on this point: the relations set up in confession are not identical or analogous to colonial instrumentality (i.e., to the relations of colonizer/ colonized as theorized by Memmi or Bhabha); nor is Stephen's subversions of the sacrament of confession tantamount to an undoing of colonial structures or relations. The relations of the church to empire and colonial authority specifically are too complex to go into here; suffice it to say, that profane confession, regarded as part of a more general insurrectionary attitude taken by the colonized toward church authority makes it all the more difficult for the church to reduplicate or foster either colonial or nationalist hegemony. The instability of profane confession thus constitutes an opportunity. The penitent desires "secret knowledge and secret power," while the confessor is free, in his turn, to confess back. A one-way circuit begins to move two ways; the unthinkable violation of an inviolable sacrament, in which the subaltern penitent commandeers the confessional in order to push forward with *his or her own* desire for self-development, resembles the turning back on the master of the master's discriminatory gaze that constitutes the oppositional thrust in Bhabha's conception of mimicry. The one who would give up knowledge here takes it away, which can only be regarded by imperial and ecclesiastic officials as the most fundamental of perversions: an unnatural and profane reversal of roles. Hence the sense of savage betrayal on the part of the Catholic Church when revolt begins among those educated in the very forms and traditions (imperial and ecclesiastical) that undergo destabilizing mimicry.[39]

The one-way circuit of disburdening is confounded when the penitent, not satisfied with disburdening, seeks to transform confession into a dialogical mode of self-knowledge. The profane confessions Stephen makes to Davin, Lynch, and Cranly in chapter 5 mark crisis points of self-development and barely contain the homoeroticism that the sacrament of penance displaces and sublimates. By the end of *A Portrait,* confession has become for Stephen both self-critique (as in his often brutally candid diary entries) and self-development, as opposed to the abject disburdening of sin—indeed, disburdening of the self—that we find in official confession. Confessing oneself emerges as the strategy of choice for the colonial (non)subject who has failed in all other forms of mentorship, who in fact has transformed the structure of official confession by circulating his own desire through it, violating the inviolable and redefining sin as self-knowledge.

The boarding-school homoeroticism that is both disavowed and preserved as a kind of libidinal investment throughout chapter 4 of *A Portrait* must find new mechanisms of cathexis; the fully enfranchised imperial subject would find them in the normative relations of mentor/mentee, which subsume and defuse homoerotic desire. The colonial (non)subject cannot know these relations; indeed, mentorship in the colonies is unheard of precisely because mentoring requires intersubjectivity and the possibility (the inevitability) of the mentee or apprentice entering into full intersubjective and political enfranchisement. Ordinarily, this relation might approximate the Hegelian master-slave dialectic in which the slave can achieve self-consciousness and even mastery (if only of the material stratum); in the colonial context, it can reach at best the abject state of coercive classical *Bildung,* unanimated by the revolutionary energy of mimicry, that Memmi describes in *The Colonizer and the Colonized:*

> The revolt of the adolescent colonized, far from resolving into mobility and social progress, can only sink into the morass of colonized society—unless there is a total revolution. . . . Sooner or later then, the potential rebel falls back on the traditional values. This explains the astonishing survival of the colonized's family. The colonial superstructure has real value as a refuge. It saves the colonized from the despair of total defeat and, in return, it finds confirmation in a constant inflow of new blood. . . . Revolt and conflict have ended in a victory for the parents and tradition. But it is a pyrrhic victory. Colonized society has not taken even half a step forward; for the young man, it is an internal catastrophe.[40]

Falling back into an unreflective, passive acquiescence to imperial forms (for the colonized male, classical *Bildung*) leads only to a travesty of classical *Bildung* in which the colonized suffers an "internal catastrophe," an internalization of both the narrative logic of classical *Bildung* and the failure of this logic to apply in any relevant sense to the colonized. In these terms, Stephen would not be able to progress because he is not a subject of/in world history; his return from exile would thus be read as a return to the "morass of colonized society."

Despite all of this, Stephen's confessions to Davin, Lynch, and Cranly, motivated by a desire to repudiated colonial entrapments and the "internal catastrophes" they create, refigure the narrative desire endorsed by the classical bildungsroman in part by miming the authority of ecclesiastical mentors, in part by sliding between the penitent/confessor points of the triangle without repudiation or warning, in part by refusing to accede to the third term, the figure of woman (the figure for desire *as such*), who waits batlike in the shadows of every colloquy. In these ways, Stephen opens himself up to the ambivalence of profane confession, which seeks not absolution and reformation of the self but the production of selves (or of a split and contested "selfhood"). In the profane confessional he discovers the mode of intersubjective desire, of *psychic* catastrophe, that will permit him freedom and wholeness without tyranny.

Critics have long noted Stephen's narcissism, the solipsistic self-absorption that disallows any kind of apprenticeship to an authority other than himself (or "literature" in the abstract). Chapter 4 evidences the shift into "an inner world of individual emotions mirrored perfectly in a lucid supple periodic prose" (*P* 167); from this coign of vantage, a lull in the onset of "internal catastrophe," Stephen hopes to challenge the authority of imperial socialization, with its repressive homosociality and compulsory heterosexuality. Its justification, in chapter 5, is a theory of aesthetics and an aesthetic production that sanitizes and desexualizes both homo- and heteroerotic desire. But we might ask at this point if Stephen's artistic rebellion isn't merely a ritual of desacralization that further isolates, by transcribing into abstract, aesthetic categories, the homoeroticism he never ceases to deny. Are the opportunities for profane confession that Stephen creates to shape and test himself (as an artist, as a sexual being) effective in their goal to disentangle him from the nets of language, religion, and country? Or do these opportunities merely translate his involvement in the homosocial rituals of the church into a secular idiom? In each case the third term is openly questioned, the homosocial trinity of official confession (penitent/Christ/confessor) breaking down under the pressure of unsuccessful repressions and incomplete cathexes.

All of this, of course, stands in direct contrast to Stephen's reticence, in chapters 4 and 5, when in the company of priests, a reticence that signals a turn away not only from the subjection of "an acquired speech" (*P* 189) but also from the priesthood's generally coercive homosociality. That this is the case is evident in the sharper, more critical focus of Stephen's meditations in these chapters, which bear out Bakhtin's suggestion that confession has a latent self-reflexiveness:

> It is true that alongside [an] externally rhetorical approach to the unity of a human personality and its acts there existed as well a confessional, "repentant" approach to one's own self, an approach with its *own* scheme for structuring the image of a man and his acts (since the time of Augustine)— but this confessional idea of the interior man (and the corresponding structuring of his image) did not deeply influence chivalric romance or Baroque novels; it became significant only in modern times.[41]

The "'repentant' approach to one's own self " is represented in the interior realm (the "inner world" that Stephen posits) in which he (*and* Joyce) is able to fashion a space of critical acuity, a "text-inscribed" blankness at the heart of the homosocial rite of *Bildung*. Though putatively carrying out the demands of the *Bildung* plot—going to university, considering vocations, vying with Cranly for E.C.—his meditations increasingly confront the "outer" world with the indignation of his inner nature. It is in this space that he fashions the profane alternatives for ritual and ceremony that he still desperately needs to orient his self-development.

Stephen's fall from grace in chapter 4 coincides with the shift from sacred to profane confession, for here we watch as the fruits of his official sacred confession—the chance "to live in grace a life of peace and virtue and forbearance with others" (P 145)—slowly and subtly decompose. The question that concludes the first vignette, "I have amended my life, have I not?" (P 153), not only reveals by the very need to ask it the incomplete nature of his spiritual amendment but also adumbrates another uncertainty, this one about the possibility— *the chance*—of homosexual desire coming to the surface between himself and Cranly. "Of whom are you speaking?" Stephen asks, when Cranly has spoken vaguely of Stephen being "more than a friend" (P 247). These questions, both unanswered, both rhetorical in the classical sense of presupposing an answer that needn't be spoken (indeed, that *mustn't* be spoken), frame a sequence of scenes in which confession attains an increasingly profane character, beginning with Stephen's meditation on the priesthood and the "secrets" of the confessional, discussed above. At first, as in the scene following his interview with the director (P 158–61), the critical element of the mimicry is unformed; we find only a young man infatuated with ritual, actively exploiting the aesthetic thrills of inversion and desacralization, but unwilling to commit himself to overturning the structures of belief that authorize both the aesthetic thrills and the sacraments they simulate.

His refusal of the priesthood, his obedience to a "wayward instinct" (the same, though more refined, that earlier had produced "monstrous images"), is followed by an arguably brilliant act of self-confession, in which the shouts of boys and Stephen's realization of his "mild proud sovereignty" (P 168) suggest a kind of antiphonic ceremony over which he presides as confessor, his own thoughts framed and contextualized by the play of nude boys swimming and hailing him, attempting to conscript him in a ritual of homosocial bonding in which he is marked as the sacrifice ("Bous Stephanoumenos") (P 168). The "voices" that earlier had called him to official duties are here displaced by an inner call to life:

> His throat ached with a desire to cry aloud, the cry of a hawk or eagle on high, to cry piercingly of his deliverance to the winds. This was the call of life to his soul not the dull gross voice of the world of duties and despair, not the inhuman voice that had called him to the pale service of the altar. (P 169)

This voice, his own voice projected out into the world of hawks and eagles (the material stratum of bestiality that Stephen associates with "monstrosity"), comes back to him, to the "alter" of himself, that inner world where he confesses himself in "lucid supple periodic prose" and where he disburdens himself of the need to hear the dull gross voices of the world. At this pivotal, liminal point, his creative imagination pliable but curiously at rest, his boyhood falls away from him. Alone, near "the wild heart of life" (the world of beasts with which he has already identified his suppressed cry), Stephen accedes to his artistic destiny in a passage of auto/homoerotic energies, in which his communion with himself, mediated by the bird girl (a communion between his silent body, on which the social text inscribes itself, and his wild desire to cry out), translates the male homoeroticism associated with the church and the boyhood he has just passed beyond into something ambivalent, unfolding in the space between the masculine "indifferent dome" of the sky and the feminized earth "beneath him," a labial space into which he falls and disintegrates and into which he opens up phallically: "Glimmering and trembling, trembling and unfolding, a breaking light, an opening flower, it spread in endless succession to itself breaking in full crimson and unfolding and fading to palest rose" (*P* 172). We might regard the villanelle form (much analyzed in purely aesthetico-theological terms) as still another, high-handed sublimation of homoerotic desire. The villanelle form, with its structural rigidities, both articulates and contains, in a rhetoric at once sensuous and sacred, Stephen's encounter with the proximate; we see here that a fluid, labial, "liquid life" "enfolded him like water" (*P* 223). This enfolding rearticulates his surrender to desublimated libidinal drives in terms of orthodox structures of poetic and religious adoration summed up in the figure of the "temptress of his villanelle."

    As if to affirm the moment of profane surrender that concludes chapter 4, as if to take its measure as *the* measure of Stephen's destiny, a triumvirate of confessions structure chapter 5, each calculated to draw out the implications of his self-ordination as "a priest of eternal imagination" (*P* 221). Each offers him a possibility of self-knowledge through mimicry of classical homosocial desire, positioning, by turns, a figure of feminized Ireland (with Davin), a butcher's boy (with Lynch), and the phallic Mother (with Cranly) at the apex of an overtly triangulated structure. The objects Stephen and Lynch invoke in the pursuance of the former's aesthetic theory ("a basket which a butcher's boy had slung inverted on his head" [*P* 212]) regulate the libidinal flows between them, much as the figure of woman as a batlike soul mediates the desire flowing between Stephen and Davin. It is interesting to note that this abstract aesthetics of epiphanic wholeness only barely masks the homoeroticism at its core, the desire that necessitates homosocial regulation and that smuggles itself into the theory beneath the exemplary basket: the butcher's boy, one of the disavowed, sign of the improper *inversion* of desire. That Stephen displaces the iconic woman with an image barely masking homoeros signals a willingness to pierce the veil of homosocial regulation; but by retaining the triangular pathways of power and the crucial function of mediation, Stephen does not advance beyond the structure (or the erotics) of homosociality.

    "Let us eke go" Cranly says, as he takes Stephen away from the verbal jousting of the boys in the college grounds. The long scene with Cranly that follows approximates the dynamics of official confession, with Cranly as confessor and Stephen as penitent:

—And you made me confess to you, Stephen said, thrilled by his touch, as I have confessed to you so many other things, have I not?
—Yes my child, Cranly said, still gaily.
—You made me confess the fears that I have. But I will tell you also what I do not fear. I do not fear to be alone or to be spurned for another or to leave whatever I have to leave. And I am not afraid to make a mistake, even a great mistake, a lifelong mistake and perhaps as long as eternity too. (*P* 247)

Confession for Stephen has now become a fearless assertion of his own identity and destiny and his potential for Icarean error. In this restaging of the official confession, Stephen not only announces his intentions, confessing that he is confessing, he also undermines the official sacrament by unveiling what is occluded in scripted confessions and absolutions: (homo)erotic desire. Stephen is "thrilled" by Cranly's touch and alludes to "many other things" that he has confessed, thus creating, in the reciprocity of disburdening, an aura of homoerotic intimacy. His self-consciousness of the confessional nature of their colloquy is an important part of Stephen's acquisition of self-knowledge. Knowingly transgressing against destiny, he finds knowledge of himself not in the telos of a journey known in advance by masters or mentors, but rather in the process of willfully inhabiting and miming the dialectic of *Bildung* and mentorship, repeating and deregulating its ambivalence, the same ambivalence sequestered in the history and etymology of the "confessor." The nature of his confession—that he is not afraid to make a mistake, even to err willfully—covertly accedes to the homosexual desire whose ambivalence is captured in Stephen's crystalline awareness of his own incompletely repressed desire. Cranly alludes to one "who would be more than a friend" and Stephen wonders, "Had he spoken of himself, of himself as he was or wished to be?" When he asks, "Of whom are you speaking?" he refers as much to the duality of his own sexual nature as to the homoerotic dyad he might constitute with Cranly.

Though Stephen's ambivalent sexual identity is nicely captured in a carefully poised rhetorical question worthy of Yeats, we are reminded of Mario Mieli's "normal" ego, which is "largely determined by a series of abandoned homosexual object-cathexes, these being transformed into narcissistic libido and subsequently directed at heterosexual goals."[42] Does Stephen's question signal a moment of homoerotic abandonment, hovering at the brink of full confession? Does he accede to the oppressive heterosociality that governs the passage via the ghostly image of Woman? Shortly after Cranly invokes Stephen's mother and the certainty of "a mother's love" (*P* 241–42) (and thus of the normative relations of Oedipal desire), the song of a servant girl introduces an abstract analogue of the instrumental woman of classical *Bildung:*

> The figure of woman as she appears in the liturgy of the church passed silently through the darkness: a whiterobed figure, small and slender as a boy and with a falling girdle. Her voice, frail and high as a boy's, was heard intoning from a distant choir the first words of a woman which pierce the gloom and clamour of the first chanting of the passion. (*P* 244)

Aside from the iconic nature of this desexualized and fetishized figure of woman, we are struck with the confusion of gender and stages of development: the "figure" has the body and voice of a boy (the normative subject of classical *Bildung*), but the words are a woman's. The inversion here—the male occupying the position closest to the somatic level of existence, the female occupying the position of transcendence (i.e., of language)—signals once again the space of opposition both to the teleological pulsion encrypted within destiny as such and to the repressive mechanisms of homosocial relations of power that authorize the ideological fictions of harmonious *Bildung.*

Colonial *Bildung* short-circuits these relations of power not only by allowing banned homo/heterosexual desire to express itself in social relations that are predicated on its suppression but also by attaching a positive value to this short-circuiting, this "mistake" (in terms both of gender and genre), as Stephen styles it. By suggesting, in his grand artistic justification for exile, that the solitude attendant upon his "great mistake" will be productive of new knowledge, Stephen revalues mistakes as opportunities for new knowledge about himself and the world (not unlike the "errors of volition" for which he advocates in *Ulysses*).[43] His famous boast that he will "forge in the smithy of [his] soul the uncreated conscience of [his] race" (*P* 252–53) seems paradoxically to rely on the law of the father, but only if we ignore the illicit connotations of the desire "to *forge*" a racial conscience. With this in mind, we can conceive of his boast as a promise that new knowledge is in the offing—a promise that is left hanging at the conclusion of *A Portrait* and that deconstructs in *Ulysses.*

One way of talking about Joyce's bildungsroman is to say that *Bildung* in the colonies can unfold only under the aegis of homoeros; but because of Stephen's homophobia (never quite rooted out, even as he appears to accede to the *chance* of homosexual desire), the range of opportunities for discursive resistance is limited. The travesty of heterosexual relations that we see in *A Portrait* and that continues in *Ulysses* dramatizes both the failure of normative heterosocial and heterosexual relations *and* the force of Stephen's homophobic reactions. The irony, of course, is that the very thing he fears is the very thing that guarantees his "way" out: the homoeros of profane confession. Confessing oneself— through a displacement of the dialectic of desire and demand that makes of desire a demand, a displacement that internalizes and destabilizes dialectical progress and change—leads to a dangerous and hybrid self-knowledge. In his freedom from ecclesiastical domination, Stephen furthers the mimic reversal of colonial discrimination that necessitates and structures colonial *Bildung.*

Homoeroticism cannot become explicit—that is to say, Stephen cannot *act on* homosexual desire—for he is still bound up in the normative heterosexuality of the world he seeks to refuse. But though he never knows himself as homosexual, the dynamics of a subversive and covert homoeroticism serve him in articulating desire that is, in any case, far from normative. Heterosexual desire, the sign par excellence in the classical bildungsroman of a world-historical norm of power/knowledge, becomes in *A Portrait* a ruse, the mimicry of a signal (the sign of a covert mimicry), the mask (not quite separate from what it disguises) of homoerotic desire. Joyce's bildungsroman enacts both the disavowal of discriminated identities (the colonized as deviant or "queer") and the challenge to authority these identities issue in a *re*cognition, a new knowledge that threatens, if it does not yet topple, colonial authority. Opposing the traditional discourse of harmonious self-development in which self-knowledge coincides with what society already knows, Joyce's text offers new knowledges, new textual and social practices, new sites of contestation. Homoerotic desire in the colonial bildungsroman, in its perverse mimicry and internalization of the inner/outer dialectic of development, makes possible a mode of articulating colonial desire *as new knowledge* rather than as a transgression of what is already known.

NOTES

1. Joseph Valente, "Thrilled by His Touch: The Aestheticizing of Homosexual Panic in *A Portrait of the Artist as a Young Man,* in this volume, 49.

2. Eve Kosofsky Sedgwick, *Between Men: English Literature and Male Homosocial Desire* (New York: Columbia University Press, 1985), 21–27.

3. Sedgwick, *Between Men,* 99.

4. Ibid., 134.

5. Ibid.

6. For a discussion of the different "conditions" for and contexts of homosexuality, see Jonathan Dollimore, *Sexual Dissidence: Augustine to Wilde, Freud to Foucault* (Oxford: Oxford University Press, 1991), 192. Dollimore cites Freud's approval of the term *homoerotic* as more accurately reflecting the diversity of homosexuality—a diversity, I might add, that includes nongenital modes of homo-"sexual" communion. I tend to use *homosexual* with reference to sexual (i.e. genital) modes of expressing homoeros.

7. On the idea that imperial discourse represents its purity, intentions, and essence (and, though unwittingly, its vulnerability) in the iconic figure of the rapeable English lady, see Jenny Sharpe, "The Unspeakable Limits of Rape: Colonial Violence and Counter-Insurgency," *Genders* 10 (spring 1991): 25–46.

8. Theoretical definitions of the term *bildungsroman* vary, but most commentators agree that it should be distinct from other narrative forms of development, the most common of which are *Entwicklungsroman* and *Erziehungsroman.* The former concerns

personal development but does not emphasize self-discovery or the formation of personality—in short, it does not emphasize *Bildung* (an example familiar to Joyceans is Maria Cummins's *The Lamplighter*); the latter concerns education in the narrow sense, usually resulting in the "pedagogical novel" (an ur-text might be Rousseau's *Emile*). The term *Künstlerroman* refers to a novel dealing with the formation of the artist. For the purposes of this essay, I have subsumed it under the term bildungsroman, for Joyce, it seems to me, is writing against the general notion of *Bildung*.

9. John H. Smith, "Cultivating Gender: Sexual Difference, *Bildung*, and the *Bildungsroman*," *Michigan Germanic Studies 13*, no. 2 (1897): 215.

10. Homi Bhabha, *The Location of Culture* (London: Routledge, 1994), 89.

11. For a critique of the problem of (post)colonial "subjectivity" informed by Derrida's theories of *différance* and immanent critique, see Gayatri Chakravorty Spivak, "Can the Subaltern Speak?" in *Marxism and the Interpretation of Culture*, ed. Cary Nelson and Lawrence Grossberg (Urbana: University of Illinois Press, 1988), 271–313. On the diasporic subject, see Stuart Hall, "Cultural Identity and Diaspora," in *Identity: Community, Culture, Difference*, ed. J. Rutherford (London: Lawrence and Wishart, 1990).

12. Dollimore, *Sexual Dissidence*, 124.

13. Joseph Conrad, *Heart of Darkness: An Authoritative Text, Backgrounds and Sources, Criticism*, ed. Robert Kimbrough, 3d. ed. (New York: Norton, 1988), 38.

14. See Martin Swales, "Irony and the Novel: Reflections of the German Bildungsroman," in *Reflection and Action: Essays on the Bildungsroman*, ed. James Hardin (Columbia: University of South Carolina Press, 1991), 49–52.

15. It is useful to keep in mind that *dehiscence* carries two senses: both a splitting open along a natural line *and* the discharge of contents by so splitting.

16. See, for example, Marc Redfield, "Ghostly Bildung: Gender, Genre, Aesthetic Ideology, and *Wilhelm Meisters Lehrjahre*," *Genre* 26 (winter 1993): 377–407.

17. On the concept of transculturation, see Maria Helena Lima, "Decolonizing Genre: Jamaica Kincaid and the *Bildungsroman*," *Genre 26* (winter 1993): 431–59. Lima writes, "Regions which have undergone European colonization constitute particularly interesting sites to observe what I call generic transculturation since different cultures will transform the 'originary' genre to serve their particular needs. . . . Post-colonial writers have had to invent stories and allegories of 'self' and 'other,' mythologies of their own that begin to translate their complex heritage" (433). Lima regards the postcolonial bildungsroman as exemplary in bringing out this "new," resistant self.

18. Perversion, as it developed in both theology and the study of human sexuality, implies both the condition of presublimated libidinal energies (what Freud called the polymorphous perverse) and deviation from normative heterosexuality. In both cases, the perverse is eccentric with respect to the norm and is subject to repressions and sublimations. In part to recuperate the category of the perverse for a radical sexual politics, Dollimore has put forward the notion of a "perverse dynamic" that "is not an identity, a logic, or an economy, so much as an anti-teleological dialectic producing knowledge in opposition to destiny." It "transvalues sameness, abandoning self-identity for the unstably proximate"; it "reidentifies and exploits the inextricable connections between perversity, proximity, paradox, and desire" (*Sexual Dissidence*, 229–30).

19. *Oxford English Dictionary*, s.v. "confession."

20. *Webster's New Collegiate Dictionary*, s.v. "confession."

21. See the *New Catholic Encyclopedia* (New York: McGraw-Hill, 1967–79) 4:141–42; and the *Oxford English Dictionary*, s.v. "confessor."

22. See *New Catholic Encyclopedia*, 4:134.

23. Cited in *New Catholic Encyclopedia*, 4:133.

24. M. M. Bakhtin, *The Dialogic Imagination: Four Essays*, ed. Michael Holquist, trans. Caryl Emerson and Michael Holquist (Austin: University of Texas Press, 1981), 350.

25. Bakhtin, *The Dialogic Imagination*, 350.

26. Oscar Wilde, *De Profundis and Other Writings* (London: Penguin, 1986), 164, 179.

27. Eve Kosofsky Sedgwick, *Epistemology of the Closet* (Berkeley and Los Angeles: University of California Press, 1990), 33–34.

28. Spivak, "Can the Subaltern Speak?" 294.

29. See Dollimore, *Sexual Dissidence* (esp. 14–17, 43–48) on how the history of representation has deployed the "forbidden" or the "deviant" as a mark of homosexuality.

30. Ibid., 15.

31. See Valente, "Thrilled by His Touch"; and Vicki Mahaffey, "Père-version and Im-mère-sion: Idealized Corruption in *A Portrait of the Artist as a Young Man* and *The Picture of Dorian Gray*," in this volume.

32. Albert Memmi, *The Colonizer and the Colonized*, trans. Howard Greenfeld (Boston: Beacon Press, 1967), 92.

33. Here, I am indebted to Gayle Rubin's important essay, "The Traffic in Women: Notes on the 'Political Economy' of Sex," in *Toward an Anthropology of Women*, ed. Rayna R. Reiter (New York: Monthly Review Press, 1975), 157–210.

34. It is pertinent to note that the modern mode of penance, particularly the notion of a private or secret confession in which the priest is sworn not to reveal "confessional knowledge," is generally acknowledged to be of Celtic origin. See *New Catholic Encyclopedia*, 132.

35. Dollimore, *Sexual Dissidence*, 88–89; first emphasis added.

36. Dollimore notes the complicity built into most attempts to form what he calls a transgressive aesthetic. "[A]t certain historical conjunctures certain kinds of nonconformity may be more transgressive in opting not for extreme lawlessness but for a strategy of inclusion" (ibid., 51). Speaking of Wilde, he notes, "If his transgressive aesthetic anticipates post-modernism to the extent that it suggests a culture of the surface, the decentered and the different, it also anticipates modernism in being not just hostile to, but intently concerned with, its opposite: depth and exclusive integration as fundamental criteria of identity" (73).

37. Wilhelm Dilthey, "Friedrich Holderlin (1910)," trans. Joseph Ross, in *Poetry and Experience*, vol. 5 of *Selected Works*, ed. Rudolf A. Makkreel and Frithjof Rodi (Princeton, N.J.: Princeton University Press, 1985), 336.

38. Bhabha, *The Location of Culture*, 120.

39. This sense of betrayal is brought out more fully in *Stephen Hero*, where the Jesuit "ambassadors," who seek to gain Stephen's favor, and their motives are more fully drawn.

40. Memmi, *Colonizer and Colonized*, 99.

41. Bakhtin, *Dialogic Imagination*, 407; second emphasis mine.

42. Mario Mieli, *Homosexuality and Liberation: Elements of a Gay Critique*, trans. David Fernbach (London: Gay Men's Press, 1980), 34.

43. See the "Scylla and Charybdis" episode of *Ulysses:* "A man of genius makes no mistakes. His errors are volitional and are the portals of discovery" (*U* 190).

Joyce's Lesbian Other

"A Faint Glimmer of Lesbianism" in Joyce

Colleen Lamos

"Homosexuality in women," Freud remarks, "is certainly not less common than in men, although much less glaring."[1] Female homosexuality in Joyce's works is notable for its invisibility, appearing only as a half-guessed thought or a speculative conjecture. For instance, recalling an erotic moment she once shared with Hester Stanhope, her girlhood friend, Molly Bloom remembers that "we used to compare our hair. . . . we were like cousins what age was I then the night of the storm I slept in her bed she had her arms round me then" (*U* 18.638–42). Later, when Hester departed, "she kissed me six or seven times didnt I cry yes I believe I did or near it my lips were taittering when I said goodbye" (*U* 18.672–74). Despite its air of Victorian innocence, Marilyn French detects a "homosexual tinge" in the scene.[2] Although Joyce's works are colored by many tinges of male homosexuality, the fainter hues of lesbianism are barely distinguishable.

The glaring absence of female homoeroticism from Joyce's oeuvre is particularly puzzling in light of the fact that he was surrounded by lesbians in Paris. Indeed, by the 1920s the city had acquired the nickname of "Paris-Lesbos" by virtue of the public visibility of lesbians and their prominence in avant-garde literary culture.[3] Joyce's publishers—in France, Sylvia Beach, and in the United States, Margaret Anderson and Jane Heap—were openly gay, as were many of his acquaintances, such as Djuna Barnes. The bookshops of Beach and her lover, Adrienne Monnier, as well as the literary salons of Natalie Barney and Gertrude Stein were frequented by equally well-known lesbians such as Bryher, Hilda Doolittle, and Janet Flanner.[4] Not only was Joyce familiar with this lesbian milieu, but he depended for his livelihood upon the generosity of Harriet Shaw Weaver, a spinster whose biographers and critics have found it necessary to explain was *not* a lesbian.[5] Three days after arriving in Paris on 8 July 1920, Joyce met Beach and, through her and others, was quickly introduced to many of the

185

leading lesbian figures in the intellectual circles of the Left Bank. Moreover, he encountered them at a crucial moment in the composition of *Ulysses*. When he came to Paris, he had just begun work on "Circe" and in the following year and a half completed that episode and the rest of the novel and expanded the entire manuscript by about a third in his revisions of the printer's page proofs.[6] In total, he probably wrote about half of *Ulysses* after he had become acquainted with the lesbian literary culture of Paris.

Given Joyce's personal and professional relationships with lesbians, his interest in female sexuality, and his otherwise iconoclastic representations of perverse forms of sexuality, why did he fail to address explicitly in *Ulysses* sexual desire between women? To answer this question we must examine the ways in which lesbianism was known and not known—the epistemology of lesbianism, to rephrase Eve Kosofsky Sedgwick—in Joyce's oeuvre and in his society. Although he relied upon some of the members of the Parisian lesbian milieu, especially Beach, to sustain him, to publish his work, and to establish his literary reputation, the chief influence upon the portrayal of female same-sex desire in his writings up to and including *Ulysses* is the often contradictory set of discourses concerning homosexuality and female sexuality prevalent in modern Western culture. Joyce's encounter with Paris lesbians and the inscription of lesbianism in his work need to be examined within this troubled context.

The signs of lesbianism in Joyce's texts are indirect and marginal. Apart from *Finnegans Wake,* they appear principally in the "Penelope" episode of *Ulysses* and in the notes to *Exiles*. However, they raise far-reaching epistemological and interpretive problems concerning female (homo)sexuality. The indications of female same-sex desire in Joyce's texts are typically ambiguous, often notable for their ostensible innocence. Indeed, the signs of female same-sex desire in many modernist works are fully reversible, signifying either—or both—sanctified affection or corrupt perversion, pure friendship or impure lust. The double aspect of lesbian signs poses questions not only of their interpretation but of what constitutes a sign of lesbianism *as such* and for whom, including Molly, Joyce, and his readers.

Discerning the signs of lesbianism in Joyce's texts is especially difficult because, shrouded in shame and confusion, homosexuality calls for a definitional clarity that its very "unnatural" character precludes. Indeed, the perversity of homosexuality for those charged with policing (or expressing) it consists in its ability to camouflage itself. Particularly in male modernist texts, the signs of lesbianism are masked by women's presumed sexual ignorance and inability to distinguish between affectionate friendship and carnal lust, so that lesbianism is the male writer's or reader's dirty secret and, hence, always deniable. Consequently, lesbianism is notorious for its supposed invisibility. In *Ulysses,* for instance, Molly Bloom is shielded from realizing the damaging implications of same-sex desire, a cognizance reserved for the astute reader. By contrast, on the rare occasions when lesbianism is overtly depicted in male modernist texts and female characters are accorded knowledge of their condition, they are typically represented as depraved, as in D. H. Lawrence's "The Fox" and William Carlos Williams's "The Knife of the Times." In Joyce's novel, Bella/o Cohen with her "Gomorrahan vices" plays this role. Whether "innocent" or "guilty," though, female same-sex desire hovers on the boundary of knowability, and female characters who are allegedly unaware of such a desire are given the most amplitude to express it.[7]

In general, lesbianism thus appears as a more occluded secret than male homosexuality in modernist texts. While the putative knowledge of lesbianism may have escaped the notice of the young women who, at the time, were brought to doctors to be cured of their devoted admiration for other women, the lesbians in Joyce's circle lived in the shadowy epistemological realm that D. A. Miller calls the "open secret."[8] For women such as Bryher, Flanner, Barnes, and Beach, their sexuality was at once common knowledge and a private matter, suppressed in their public writings and, until recently, overlooked or veiled in so-called polite discretion by their biographers. Joyce colluded in this open secrecy by fictionally representing lesbianism as a hidden perversion.

The ambiguity of the signs of lesbianism in modernist texts is bound up with the uncertain status of same-sex desire. Since the late nineteenth century, homosexuality has been understood both as the condition of a minority and as a tendency to which everyone is susceptible. Sedgwick thus argues that, for the past century, the discourse about homosexuality has been locked in a "conceptual incoherence" marked by two major contradictions or "paradigm clashes."[9] The first clash is between minoritizing and universalizing paradigms. On the one hand, homosexuality is believed to be the plight of a certain group of people who are genuinely homosexual by virtue of a genetic, hormonal, or other constitutional defect. On the other hand, such inverts have the potential to seduce and infect normal people. Thus, Krafft-Ebing differentiated "*perversion* of the sexual instinct" (the disease of sexual inversion owing to a "hereditary taint") from "*perversity* in the sexual act" (the vices into which otherwise sound people sometimes fall).[10] His distinction between "acquired" and "congenital" inversion is repeated by Joyce and many of his critics. However, the presupposition that true homosexuality is a special case, distinct from the broader zone of liberating, polymorphous sexuality, is compromised by the lingering doubt that "real" lesbians, such as Emily Lyons, might lure a lonely girl like Bertha, as Joyce imagines in his notes to *Exiles*.

The second paradigm clash that Sedgwick observes in the modern discourse about homosexuality is between gender inversion and gender separation. In the first sense, same-sex desire is thought to be the result of a reversal of gender identity, so that a lesbian is revealed by her masculine manner. Cross-gender behavior is typically considered the surest sign of homosexuality, and transvestite women often fall under such suspicion. In the second sense, same-sex desire is believed to be motivated by rejection of the opposite sex and solidarity with one's own gender. Thus, lesbians are also conventionally understood as man-haters, even when their desires are attributed, as Freud does in "The Psychogenesis of a Case of Homosexuality in a Woman," to a "masculinity complex" motivated by penis envy. The most insidious form of lesbianism for psychologists and sexologists, and often the most seductive for contemporary male writers, is the feminine woman who desires another woman. The putative narcissism and autoeroticism of such women, like Molly, posed a fascinating challenge to modern male analysts, artists, and voyeurs.

The uncertain ontological status of same-sex desire and the secrecy in which it is obscured render the attempt to interpret lesbianism in male modernist texts caught in a dialectic of concealment and exposure. On the one hand, as a contingent, possible attribute, lesbianism bears an underground existence as any woman's possible desire, an interior alterity; on the other hand, as the determinate essence of a certain kind of woman, lesbianism is an exterior, abjected otherness. Within the terms of this antithesis, interpretation of the signs of same-sex desire inevitably takes the form of an exposé. Reading the marks of lesbianism in Joyce's texts therefore reiterates the scene in "Circe" in which Bella/o Cohen forces Bloom to "tell all." As Michel Foucault has argued, such "confessions of the flesh," combining elements of religious ritual and pornographic narrative, enjoin the penitent or initiate—or the literary text—to admit her guilty lusts and submit to the authority of the confessor-interpreter.[11] Reading Joyce's texts within a cultural context in which homosexuality is censored, it is impossible to examine the homoerotic implications of "Penelope," for instance, without in some sense seeming to "out" Molly Bloom and eliciting the pleasure excited by a forced confession. However, my intention is not to reveal Molly's true nature but to examine the ways in which signs of lesbianism are legible and the constraints under which a reading of them is possible.

Because lesbianism is so closely interwoven with other female relationships, there is no simple line to be drawn between it and same-sex friendships (or rivalries) or bisexuality. Indeed, the general heading of homosexuality is misleading insofar as it implies the dubious belief that same-sex desire is confined to those who are genuinely gay. On the contrary, I interpret the equivocal signs of lesbianism in Joyce's texts not as indications of a character's fundamental orientation but as part of a larger discursive struggle over the meaning of female sexuality. The fleeting glimpses of female same-sex desire in *Ulysses* and *Exiles* contrast sharply with the pervasive and phobic hints of male same-sex desire in both texts. Molly's affection for Hester Stanhope never raises for her the fears, for Stephen, attendant on the mention of Oscar Wilde's "love that dare not speak its name."

The appearance of female same-sex desire on the margins of *Ulysses* and *Exiles* reveals Joyce's participation in contemporary social, political, medical, and literary discourses concerning lesbianism that were often at odds with each other and issued in divergent understandings of female same-sexuality. His texts manifest the complex and shifting forces at work in the production of the modern "lesbian." This confusion regarding the definition of lesbianism and of female sexuality resulted from the confluence of feminist political ideologies, sexological and psychological explanations of sexual behavior, Victorian conventions of feminine purity, fin de siècle French decadent literary fantasies of feminine evil, and nostalgic, anthropological postulations of the primordial nature of female sexuality. Located at the crossroads of these competing ideas regarding female sexuality, Joyce's writings reflect their discord as well as the censorship of homosexual possibilities in colonial Ireland and modern Europe, including the gendered nature of that censorship.

As many critics have demonstrated, Joyce's understanding of female sexuality was informed by his reaction against yet his lingering involvement with the nineteenth-century Irish Catholic antinomy between women's purity and degradation, the virgin/whore dichotomy expressed by Stephen in *A Portrait.* Yet, influenced by Ibsen and motivated by his own ambivalent encounter with feminism but especially by his revolt against clerical and cultural authorities, Joyce famously rejected what he called, in a 1906 letter to Stanislaus, the "lying drivel about pure men and pure women and spiritual love and love for ever: blatant lying in the face of the truth" (*LII* 191–92). Facing the facts of carnal lust in the homosexual department proved to be a more difficult matter for Joyce, however. Despite his hostility to notions of sexual purity, the image of lesbianism that emerges most clearly in his texts up to and including *Ulysses*—the girlhood crush—is indebted to the Victorian belief that love between women is a sentimental, nongenital affair.

The assumptions regarding female same-sex eroticism that Joyce inherited are, broadly speaking, the twin concepts of sensuous sapphism and evil lesbianism. Although *sapphism* and *lesbianism* were used variously and sometimes interchangeably by contemporary writers, the terms serve to distinguish between two, sharply distinct conceptions of female homoeroticism. According to the sapphic model, friendship and passion between women in the nineteenth century coincided; this continuity between female desire and identification was subsequently ruptured by the reaction against feminism and the classification of lesbianism as a sexual perversion.[12] Before its pathologization as a medical or psychological disorder, romantic affection and some forms of sexual behavior between women were not only condoned but idealized as embodying a spiritual love, as opposed to the material investments of heterosexual marriage. In the twentieth century, such love is represented by Virginia Woolf in *Mrs. Dalloway* and in what she called her "Sapphic story," "Slater's Pins Have No Points," by H. D. in her poetry and prose, and by Barney in her literary and social practices. As a literary and erotic model, the figure of Sappho significantly shaped the self-understanding of many modern women writers.[13] Aligned with a feminine sensibility and often with feminist political goals, against putatively masculine values and genital aims, sapphic love was regarded by sex experts and

modernist writers, including Joyce, either as mere adolescent fumblings between girls, and thus as an apprenticeship to mature heterosexuality, or as an
obfuscation of the real facts of perversion.[14]

The other model of female homoeroticism that informs Joyce's texts derives from French decadent literature with its English and Irish crossovers. The
modern image of the alluringly wicked lesbian, exuding a licentious, exotic,
and even murderous sexuality, draws upon a large body of texts from Balzac,
Gautier, and Baudelaire to Swinburne and Pierre Louÿs, including the small but
influential works of Renée Vivien.[15] Like the figure of the lesbian vampire in recent American films, this seductive, evil woman terrified and transfixed the
modern imagination. Hating men but imitating them in her desires and dress—
or else appearing as hyperbolically feminine—such a woman was often decried
as the outcome of the modern confusion of sexual roles. Although this image of
the lesbian stems from a cultural tradition dating back to de Sade, her specter
came to represent the corruptions of modernity. The Reverend Pat Robertson's
charge in the 1980s that "the Equal Rights Amendment encourages women to
leave their husbands, kill their children, practice witchcraft, destroy capitalism,
and become Lesbians" resonates with similar accusations in the early years of
the century.[16] Her Irish incarnations include Sheridan Le Fanu's "Carmilla" and
George Moore's *A Drama in Muslin,* both depicting lesbians who prey upon innocent young girls. Often a whore and almost always engaged in a deadly orgy
of passion, such a lesbian is located, in *Ulysses,* in Bella/o Cohen's house of pros-
titution.

In a broad sense, Joyce's representation of female homoeroticism is
schematically divided between these contemporary images of sapphism as a
generalized female sensuality and lesbianism as a dangerously captivating decadence. The former is absorbed into Molly's affirmative flesh, while the latter is
abjected in the figure of the lubricous Bella/o. Yet, at bottom, they are two faces
of the same woman, a split version of female sexual agency whose desires are
ambiguously related to homoeroticism.

Heirs of the triumphant sexological division between homosexuality and
heterosexuality as mutually exclusive orders of sexual desire characterizing and
determining two distinct kinds of persons, we at the end of the twentieth century may find it difficult to recollect the moment of their scission. Joyce's texts
mark that moment; in certain respects, they do not present female same-sex desire as essentially different from "normal" female sexuality. The absence of a
clear distinction may be read either as his rejection of the authority of sex doctors or as his refusal to recognize a female sexual desire that does not parasitically derive from men. Joyce's ironic, double voice renders both conclusions
plausible. Yet what the figures of female homoeroticism in his texts do not admit is the appearance, in his day and in his most important personal relations,
of lesbians as independent women devoted to their careers and their lovers.
While he acknowledged that "the emancipation of women . . . has caused the

greatest revolution in our time in the most important relationship there is—that between men and women; the revolt of women against the idea that they are the mere instruments of men,"[17] such New Women, branded as or embracing the label of lesbian, fail to appear in his published writings. Instead, they reinscribe the contradictions in which female same-sex passion has so often been occluded. The confused, "open secret" of lesbian desire is perhaps most apparent in "Penelope."

Molly's graphic description of her bodily pleasures attests to her impeccable heterosexual credentials, yet those pleasures shade into the homoerotic. Indeed, she is the only one of *Ulysses'* main characters to admit to having had a homoerotic experience. Despite the visibility of her carnal desires and her voluble expression of them, the nature of her girlhood relationship with Stanhope is obscured by the commingling of female homosociality and homosexuality, a blurring that was both the enabling condition for same-sex passion and its limitation. Molly's emotionally intense bond with Stanhope could thus involve sleeping together, embracing, kissing, and playing with each other's hair, yet still be regarded by both of them, as well as by readers of *Ulysses,* as a harmless friendship. Her night with Stanhope retains the putative innocence of a slumber party but with the titillating suggestion of a soft-porn fantasy.

Although Molly betrays no consciousness of the erotic energies in her friendship with Stanhope, Joyce was aware of its homosexual implications. In the notes for *Exiles,* he imagines a similar relationship between the young Bertha and her departing friend, Emily Lyons. Before the latter leaves on a ship for America, the two "kiss and cry," and their longing for their lost, "girlish days" is marked by a "delicate sensuality." "A faint glimmer of lesbianism irradiates [Bertha's] mind" while thinking of Emily. The nostalgic "note of regret" that suffuses this scene is tempered by the ominous implication that the "dark" Emily is a "man-killer and perhaps also [a] love-killer." "They have no male lovers and are moved vaguely one towards the other. The friend is older, stronger, . . . a prophecy of a later dark male" in Bertha's life.[18] Her adolescent love for Emily has the familiar structure of the female romantic friendship as it was pathologized by modern sex experts. Joyce's remarks hint strongly at the hidden core of perversion within what had previously been considered pure love between women. Exposing the carnal desire at the heart of sapphic affection, his commentary on this scene of parting echoes sexological case studies of unsuspecting heterosexual girls who are attracted by virile (and "man-killing") women into dangerous and sterile ("love-killing") homosexual passion. In keeping with the long-standing habit of regarding female same-sex love as a faute de mieux substitute for heterosexuality or as, in Cleland's *Memoirs of a Woman of Pleasure (Fanny Hill)* and much modern pornography, a form of sexual initiation that whets a girl's appetite for the solid food of a man's penis, Emily Lyons is a supplement who temporarily fills in for "a later dark male."

By contrast, Molly, who is ignorant of what the doctors say about homosexuality, knows quite a lot about heterosexuality and speaks openly of it. Although some critics have described her as passive, her lively discourse is energized by her active sexuality, her transsexual fantasies, and her command of the gaze—attributes that have alternatively excited critical praise or condemnation. Less often noticed in the controversy concerning the display of Molly's body in "Penelope" is that she also has the power to look. Exercising what is commonly referred to as the male gaze, Molly's spectatorship suggests her possession of phallic agency rather than her representation of (or "being") the phallus, in Lacanian terms.[19] Her nominatively masculine visual pleasure takes us beyond the impasse of debates concerning her famously "feminine" narcissism and situates that pleasure within the problematic of same-sex desire.

Molly plays both the designated male and female sides of the gaze. Most often, she exhibits herself for men, yet she also looks at men, at women, and at herself. She views and compares her hair with that of other women, such as Mrs. Galbraith. Describing her voyeuristic enjoyment (and jealousy) at watching Galbraith, Molly notices the other woman's autoerotic gratification: "in Grantham street 1st thing I did every morning to look across see her combing it as if she loved it" (U 18.479–80). Proud that her bust is larger than that of Kathleen Kearney and other Irish actresses (U 18.885–86), Molly also gazes at her own breasts and delights in them. "I loved looking down at them," "shaking and dancing about in my blouse" (U 18.850–51); "so plump and tempting . . . they excite myself sometimes" (U 18.1378–79). Molly's autoerotic narcissism has been interpreted as a sign of her conventional femininity,[20] yet such desires were understood by contemporary commentators as a dangerous indication of latent lesbianism. Bernard Talmey's 1904 Woman: A Treatise on the Normal and Pathological Emotions of Feminine Love drew the connection frequently made between autoerotic practices and lesbianism: "The female masturbator . . . forms passionate attachments for other women" and develops contempt for men.[21] Same-sex love was considered an extension of self-love, and lesbian perversion (so-called mutual masturbation) was the natural outcome of self-abuse. Indeed, Molly's voracious sexual appetite could be read as a textbook case of the consequences of masturbation, which include, according to Talmey, "viraginity," the "hypertrophy of the clitoris," and weakened maternal feelings, as well as the temptation to try it with another woman.

Immediately after recalling the erotic stimulation of her own breasts, Molly's thoughts turn toward sex with a woman. Her fantasy mingles auto- and alloerotic excitement, the plumpness of her breasts sliding into the turgidity of a penis: "its well for men all the amount of pleasure they get off a womans body were so round and white for them always I wished I was one myself for a change just to try with that thing they have swelling up on you so hard and at the same time so soft" (U 18.1379–83). Molly's repeated lesbian fantasy—"I wouldnt mind being a man and get up on a lovely woman" (U 18.1146–47)—seems all in good fun, in keeping with her adventurous sexuality and contributes to the belief that she represents a polysexual plenitude. Although her carefree autoeroticism and homoeroticism appear poles apart from Bella/o Cohen's theater of transsexual, sadistic cruelty in "Circe," the parallels between Molly and Bella/o suggest that they are versions of the same phallic woman—in Richard Brown's words, "massive, potent and self-possessed."[22] The two women tap the same erotic current, yet they are kept sharply distinct in *Ulysses* in order that Molly remain an acceptable, largely nonthreatening object of the reader's and Bloom's desires. Nevertheless, the continuity between the abject Bella/o and the attractive Molly reveals the bivalent undercurrent of lesbianism that, in Joyce's time and ours, is constitutive of female sexuality as its latent possibility and threat.

Despite certain troubling ambiguities, the typical feature and revealing trait of homosexuality in the modern discourse of sexuality is gender transitivity. Inverts, in the medical idiom, are women trapped in the body of men or vice versa, constituting a hermaphroditic or "intermediate sexual form" and, hence, inclined to cross-dress.[23] By the early twentieth century, gender transitivity was linked to homosexuality and blamed on the feminizing effects of modern life (for men) or the virilizing influence of feminism (for women). Joyce's praise of Ibsen's "faint traces of femininity, his delicacy of swift touch," which he attributes to "a curious admixture of the woman in his nature" (*CW* 64), is cited in support of the argument that Joyce endorsed a bisexual or androgynous vision. Less widely recognized, though, is the way in which male effeminacy and female masculinity in Joyce's works are imbricated within the contemporary discourse of homosexuality. In "Circe," Bloom's womanliness and anal eroticism are attributed to congenital defects and his Jewishness. "[*V*]*irgo intacta*," with his "*fetor judaicus*" (*U* 15.1785–86, 1796) and malformed genitals, Bloom is a parody of the notions advanced by modern "sex specialists." Elsewhere, however, such as in his praise of Ibsen, Joyce echoes their ideas, including Otto Weininger's notion that everyone possesses, to some degree, components of the other sex and thus of homosexuality: "there is no friendship between men that has not an element of sexuality in it."[24] The theme of transvestism so prominent in *Ulysses* is bound up with Joyce's ambivalence toward homosexuality and the sexual discourse of his day.

Cross-dressing forms an important link between Molly and the gender-switching Bella/o Cohen. Although she never dresses up in men's clothes, she appears as such in Bloom's fantasies. Virag taunts him, "have you made up your mind whether you like or dislike women in male habiliments?" (*U* 15.2397–99); indeed, the night before, Bloom "dreamed . . . a strange fancy of his dame Mrs Moll with red slippers on in a pair of Turkey trunks" (*U* 14.508–9), literally and figuratively wearing "the breeches" (*U* 13.1241). *Ulysses* is populated with transvestite women, beginning with Mrs. Bandmann Palmer, the actress who plays Hamlet (*U* 5.195) and who provokes the question of whether "the prince was a woman" (*U* 9.519). Cissy Caffrey "dressed up in her father's suit and hat and the burned cork moustache and walked down Tritonville road, smoking a cigarette"

(*U* 13.276–77), while Mrs. Dignam wears her late husband's trousers and boots when she turns up in "Circe" (*U* 15.3841).

Molly's appearance in Bloom's dream recalls the notorious behavior of her girlhood sweetheart's real-life model, Lady Hester Stanhope. Before leaving England for the Middle East in 1810, Lady Stanhope had created a scandal by her licentious ways and habit of cross-dressing. Her adventures in the Orient, where she established herself as a prominent figure among the Turks, made her an international celebrity. According to a biographer, Lady Stanhope's "success" was due to "her masculine attitude to life, . . . which appealed to the ambidextrous sexuality so prevalent in the Turkish male."[25] Her usual outfit was what Bloom calls "Turkey trunks," embellished by a waistcoat, turban, and cartridge belt or silken sash, into which she would thrust a sword or a pistol. Whether she adopted such a costume out of "dire necessity" or a cunning wish to manipulate the "perverse tastes" of Turkish men, Lady Stanhope enjoyed the fact that, by her own account, the Turks "never looked upon her in the light either of a man or a woman, but as an *être à part*."[26] In the sexual economy of *Ulysses*, she represents the exotic eroticism, with its hint of homosexuality, associated with D. B. Murphy in "Eumaeus." Joyce's allusion to Lady Stanhope's exploits in what Richard Burton called the "Sotadic Zone" underscores Molly's potentially undomesticated, "Oriental" homoeroticism and reinforces her link with Bella/o.[27]

Bella/o Cohen manifests many of the standard features of the lesbian, particularly her representation in French decadent literature. Voluptuous yet virile, these femmes fatales exercised a horrifying charm over their male victims. In this tradition, lesbians were often depicted as whores; indeed, "lesbians and prostitutes," according to Elyse Blankley, were regarded "as twin exfoliations of the same root stock."[28] Strictly speaking, Bella/o is, of course, not a lesbian, but she is described in terms that have much in common with the portrayal of lesbians as sadistic seductresses prevalent at the turn of the century.[29] Moreover, as a Jew, Bella/o is sexually tainted. According to Weininger, Jewish men are "saturated with femininity," while Jewish women are viragos.[30] In the logic of modern anti-Semitism, Jews and homosexuals share a natural affinity as racial and sexual perverts, a logic that Proust examines in the analogies he draws between them as similarly "accursed races" and between the trials of Dreyfus and Wilde. In short, the ambiguity of Joyce's responses to homophobia and anti-Semitism is embodied in the figure of Bella/o Cohen.

By contrast, Molly's fantasy of "Gomorrahan vices" and her association with transvestism remain safely within a heterosexual context. In their letters, she and Hester address each other in Circean terms as "my dog" and "my dearest Doggerina," yet Molly's lusts (including her adulterous passions) are situated in the home rather than in the brothel. Her sexual appeal nevertheless derives from the way in which her desires allude to the latter while remaining protected from their degrading implications; she is a domestic version of Bella/o. The continuity between the two women undermines, while underscoring, Joyce's strategy for representing censored desires, especially homosexual ones, by splitting them between, on the one hand, characters such as Bella/o who possess sexual knowledge but who are homophobically abjected and, on the other hand, characters such as Molly who participate in such desires yet do not seem to know what they are doing. Molly's ignorance opens a fantasy space where same-sex desire and gender transgression can be tolerated.

Presented as a woman without secrets, Molly appears to tell all. Her easy revelations play upon the specter of perverse lesbianism as well as the putative innocence of sapphic love. Molly both raises and evades the question of homosexuality, at once expressing female same-sex desire and eluding its stigma. As a spectacle, Molly incites the reader's pleasure, yet the excitement of her frank disclosures is permitted by her peculiar blindness. As a reader of her own sexuality, she is at once worldly wise and resolutely naive. Her incomprehension of lesbianism allows her to engage in and imagine desires, the meaning of which she is unaware; by extension, they enable her more sophisticated readers to enjoy them voyeuristically (after all, we have been to the brothel) but also to forget, as it were, the implication of female same-sex desire. Molly's ignorance is a shield for what Joyce and perhaps his readers do not wish to admit that they know.

The paradoxical epistemology of female same-sex desire in Joyce's texts helps to explain his silence regarding his lesbian friends and associates. Brenda Maddox remarks that "the Joyces seemed not to notice homosexuality"; she claims that Joyce was "indifferent to it in their friends."[31] Because of his very close association with Sylvia Beach, Joyce's relationship with her is an index of his attitude toward lesbianism. Beach was extremely reticent concerning her sexual desires, which she considered a private matter. Although she did not hide her partnership with Adrienne Monnier, she was apparently unable to acknowledge her sexual desires except in a negative light.[32] Beach's parsonage decorum, discipline, and self-sacrifice led her to suppress her personal desires, which, in turn, permitted Joyce to ignore them. Covertly, she was interested in lesbian issues, such as the controversy over *The Well of Loneliness*, and was friends with other lesbians in Paris.[33] In keeping with her wish to conceal her own homosexuality, she thought that André Gide's coming out in *Corydon* "only made him ridiculous."[34] Beach's reluctance to make public her erotic desires played into Joyce's hands, and her refusal for ten years to notice her business and personal interests enabled him not to notice them as well. Yet Beach's internalized homophobia complicates the problem of Joyce's reaction to her sexuality and to lesbianism in general.

It was not until his break with Beach over the publication rights to *Ulysses* that Joyce made a recorded reference to her homosexuality, in a 22 December 1931 letter to Weaver. Six months before, during a protracted dispute over royalties, in which Joyce, worried about his financial situation and stung by Weaver's suggestion that he live within his means, became suspicious that Beach was withholding money from him, Monnier had written to him, charging him with exploiting her and Beach. According to Mary Colum, Monnier's letter "deeply wounded" Joyce, and Maria Jolas attributed Monnier's accusation to her green-eyed, "Sapphic heart," although Ellmann claims that Joyce "treated this attack with studied courtesy."[35] Writing to Weaver (a friend of Beach's), Joyce gracefully yet explicitly aligns Beach's lesbianism with inherited psychological disorders, in keeping with the common notion that lesbianism is a congenital taint, and insinuates Monnier's spell-binding power:

> in spite of her many kindnesses to me and her many charming qualities, of late years she has become an automaton under the influence of her more intelligent partner (in many ways a remarkable and charming woman too) . . . that both are abnormal (which doesn't matter much) but chiefly that Miss Beach is the daughter of a suicide, that her sister has been in an asylum and that she herself suffers periodically from very queer headaches.[36]

Apparently without regard to his daughter Lucia's schizophrenia—a congenital disorder that he actively refused to admit but which was very much on his mind at the time—Joyce depicts Monnier and Beach as sick lesbians whose "abnormality" is, in Beach's case, conventionally linked to mental illness and self-destructiveness, although the "queer headaches" (a reference to her migraines) is Joyce's own touch.

Whether he employed these homophobic stereotypes for the sake of a tactical advantage, manipulating Weaver in a typical attempt to triangulate his relationships, or whether he sought to rationalize his shabby treatment of Beach, having wrestled from her the rights to *Ulysses* that, a year before, he had contractually granted to her, Joyce's letter is remarkable for its simultaneous acknowledgment and denial of the significance of her lesbianism. Paralipsistically emphasizing while appearing to dismiss the importance of her "abnormality," Joyce's 1931 letter reiterates the "charming" ambiguity of female same-sex desire that he had inscribed in the double-edged depiction of lesbianism in *Ulysses*. His aside in this letter is an apt figure for his parenthetical, equivocal treatment of female same-sex desire in his work until *Finnegans Wake*. Djuna Barnes perhaps hit the mark when she observed, in 1922, that he seemed "a bit disinterested" in women, "a little skeptical of their existence."[37] Indeed, he ignored Barnes's lesbianism and treated her like the young men in his circle.[38] His behavior may have conferred an honorary masculine status on women like Barnes, Beach, and Weaver, but his disregard for their gender and sexuality also served his own interests in eliciting their personal and financial backing for his work.

Joyce's blindness to the sexuality of his friends and supporters in the early 1920s allowed him to maintain the phobic confusions of the modern understanding of female homosexuality. Although his failure to come to terms with female same-sex desire in his writings through *Ulysses* can be attributed to his lack of personal experience with lesbians before 1920, he nevertheless perpetuated the obfuscating contradictions between lesbianism as a pathological, minority condition and as a universal temptation, between lesbians as cross-dressing man-haters and as sexy seductresses, between the guilty desires of Emily Lyons and the innocent sapphism of Bertha, or, finally, between the virile Bella/o and the mythically feminine Molly. Participating in the multilayered contemporary discourses concerning lesbianism, Joyce's work also shares its incoherences. Rather than subjecting them to critical scrutiny, however, Joyce's texts exploit them, largely for the sake, in *Ulysses,* of presenting Molly as a figure for the supposedly primitive plenitude of women's flesh. The enabling condition for such a representation of female sexuality is Molly's covert, denied affiliation with the debased Bella/o. In a broader sense, the condition of possibility for modern female heterosexuality is likewise its disavowed continuity with homosexuality. The "dark" Emily is the shadow that foregrounds Bertha's normality, just as Bella/o's perversity renders Molly's desires an affirmation of heterosexuality. For Joyce, the empirical precondition for this game was his refusal to notice the lives of the women around him, such as Beach, including the profoundly damaging effects upon them of the homophobic construction of the modern lesbian. The double-voiced irony of *Ulysses* allows expression of censored lesbian desires, but at the price of playing upon their homophobic abjection. The "faint glimmer of lesbianism" in his works of this period illuminates the obscuration of female sexuality.

NOTES

1. Sigmund Freud, "Psychogenesis of a Case of Homosexuality in a Woman," in *The Standard Edition of the Complete Psychological Works of Sigmund Freud,* ed. and trans. James Strachey, vol. 18 (London: Hogarth Press, 1955), 147.

2. Marilyn French, *The Book as World: James Joyce's "Ulysses"* (Cambridge, Mass.: Harvard University Press, 1976), 249.

3. Michael Wilson, "'Sans les femmes, qu'est-ce qui nous resterait?': Gender and Transgression in Bohemian Montmartre," in *Body Guards: The Cultural Politics of Gender Ambiguity,* ed. Julia Epstein and Kristina Straub (New York: Routledge, 1991), 209.

4. Among the numerous accounts of this lesbian literary culture, see Shari Benstock, *Women of the Left Bank: Paris, 1900–1940* (Austin: University of Texas Press, 1986). Many of the published memoirs of lesbians of the period are virtually silent concerning their authors' sexuality.

5. Jane Lidderdale and Mary Nicholson, *Dear Miss Weaver* (London: Faber and Faber, 1970), 40; and Bonnie Kime Scott, *Joyce and Feminism* (Bloomington: Indiana University Press, 1984), 90.

6. A. Walton Litz, *The Art of James Joyce: Method and Design in "Ulysses" and "Finnegans Wake"* (London: Oxford University Press, 1961), 144.

7. See Eve Kosofsky Sedgwick, "Privilege of Unknowing," in *Tendencies* (Durham, N.C.: Duke University Press, 1993), 23–51.

8. D. A. Miller, *The Novel and the Police* (Berkeley and Los Angeles: University of California Press, 1988), 205–6.

9. Eve Kosofsky Sedgwick, *Epistemology of the Closet* (Berkeley and Los Angeles: University of California Press, 1990), 85–87.

10. Richard von Krafft-Ebing, *Psychopathia Sexualis,* trans. Franklin S. Klaf (New York: Stein and Day, 1965), 53–54, 188.

11. Michel Foucault, *The History of Sexuality,* vol. 1, *An Introduction,* trans. Robert Hurley (New York: Pantheon Books, 1978), 61–62.

12. See Carroll Smith-Rosenberg, "The Female World of Love and Ritual," in *Disorderly Conduct: Visions of Gender in Victorian America* (New York: Oxford University Press, 1985), 53–76; and Foucault, *An Introduction.*

13. See Susan Gubar, "Sapphistries," in *The Lesbian Issue: Essays from "Signs,"* ed. Estelle B. Freedman et al. (Chicago: University of Chicago Press, 1985), 91–110.

14. Havelock Ellis calls such "passionate friendships" between girls a "spurious kind of homosexuality" that they will grow out of and attributes them to "abnormal" sex segregation in educational institutions (*Studies in the Psychology of Sex* [1905] 3d ed., vol. 1, part 4, *Sexual Inversion* [New York: Random House, 1942], 215–22). Some lesbian critics agree with elements of these attacks on sapphic love, as the controversy over *The Well of Loneliness* attests (see Esther Newton, "The Mythic Mannish Lesbian: Radclyffe Hall and the New Woman," in *Hidden from History: Reclaiming the Gay and Lesbian Past,* ed. Martin Duberman et al. [New York: Penguin, 1989], 281–93).

15. See Lillian Faderman, *Surpassing the Love of Men: Romantic Friendship and Love between Women from the Renaissance to the Present* (New York: William Morrow, 1981), 254–94. By contrast, Karla Jay reads Vivien in terms of her identification with Sappho (*The Amazon and the Page: Natalie Clifford Barney and Renée Vivien* [Bloomington: Indiana University Press, 1988]). The decadent tradition was not solely a homophobic, masculine creation, and an important body of modern lesbian writers, including Djuna Barnes and H. D., has exploited its transgressive potential. See Cassandra Laity, "H. D. and A. C. Swinburne: Decadence and Sapphic Modernism," in *Lesbian Texts and Contexts: Radical Revisions,* ed. Karla Jay and Joanne Glasgow (New York: New York University Press, 1990), 217–40. These crossovers between the sapphic and lesbian models of female homosexuality point to the contradictions in the modern understanding of lesbianism, a paradigm clash parallel to the virgin/whore dichotomy as defining terms for women.

16. Ellis cautions that female homosexuality is not "a vice of modern refined civilization" but remarks that feminism and the economic independence of women "develop the germs" of sexual inversion and encourage female criminality and insanity (*Sexual Inversion,* 204, 262). Other sexologists, such as Iwan Bloch, drew a direct link between feminism, lesbianism, and man-hating.

17. Arthur Power, *Conversations with James Joyce,* ed. Clive Hart (New York: Barnes and Noble, 1974), 35.

18. James Joyce, *Poems and Exiles,* ed. J. C. C. Mays (Harmondsworth: Penguin, 1992), 349–50.

19. See Kimberly Devlin, "Pretending in 'Penelope': Masquerade, Mimicry, and Molly Bloom," *Novel* 25 (1991): 71–89.

20. Elaine Unkeless, "The Conventional Molly Bloom," in *Women in Joyce,* ed. Suzette Henke and Elaine Unkeless (Urbana: University of Illinois Press, 1982), 158.

21. Bernard S. Talmey, *Woman: A Treatise on the Normal and Pathological Emotions of Feminine Love*, 6th ed. (New York: Practitioners Publishing Co., 1910), 123.

22. Richard Brown, *James Joyce and Sexuality* (Cambridge: Cambridge University Press, 1985), 101. He describes Molly in these terms but does not link her to Bella/o Cohen.

23. The phrase is Otto Weininger's (*Sex and Character*, trans. from 6th German ed. [New York: G. P. Putman's Sons, 1906], 48) but the idea was common. Edward Carpenter's "intermediate sex" and Magnus Hirschfeld's "third sex" are echoed in Proust's account of the men-women of Sodom and Gomorrah. According to Ellis, "[t]here is . . . a very pronounced tendency among sexually inverted women to adopt male attire" (*Sexual Inversion*, 245).

24. Weininger, *Sex and Character*, 49.

25. Joan Haslip, *Lady Hester Stanhope* (New York: Frederick A. Stokes, 1936), 111.

26. Haslip, *Lady Hester Stanhope*, 121, 111. While detailing those similarities between the historical Lady Hester and the Stanhope figure in "Penelope" which could account for the latter's attractiveness to Molly, Michael Begnal denies "latent homosexuality on Molly's part." ("Molly Bloom and Lady Hester Stanhope," in *James Joyce and Popular Culture*, ed. R. B. Kershner [Gainesville: University Press of Florida, 1996], 68.)

27. In the "Terminal Essay" to his translation of the *Arabian Nights*, Burton describes the Eastern "Sotadic Zone" as a region where "there is a blending of the masculine and feminine temperaments, a crasis which elsewhere occurs only sporadically. Hence the male *féminisme* whereby the man becomes *patiens* as well as *agens;* and the woman a tribade, a votary of mascula Sappho, Queen of Frictrices or Rubbers" (quoted by Rudi C. Bleys, *The Geography of Perversion: Male-to-Male Sexual Behavior outside the West and the Ethnographic Imagination, 1750–1918* [New York: New York University Press, 1995], 217).

28. Elyse Blankley, "Renée Vivien and the City of Women," in *Women Writers and the City: Essays in Feminist Literary Criticism*, ed. Susan Merrill Squier (Knoxville: University of Tennessee Press, 1984), 48.

29. My discussion of Bella/o extends my previous reading of the part she plays in Bloom's helpless and unwitting indulgence in sodomical pleasures ("Signatures of the Invisible: Homosexual Secrecy and Knowledge in *Ulysses*," *James Joyce Quarterly* 31 [spring 1994]: 337–55). Her Circean brothel is the abjected scene of unacknowledged homoeroticism for both Bloom and Molly, although with differently gendered implications.

30. Weininger, *Sex and Character*, 306.

31. Brenda Maddox, *Nora: A Biography of Nora Joyce* (New York: Fawcett Columbine, 1988), 180.

32. Noel Riley Fitch observes that only once, in a suppressed portion of her memoirs, did Beach mention her sexual desires. Moreover, she did so in a peculiar fashion that emphasizes her passing fancy for a gay man rather than her long relationship with a woman and homophobically attributes the latter to fear of men: "My 'loves' . . . were Adrienne Monnier and James Joyce and Shakespeare and Company. And once I felt so drawn to Robert McAlmon that I wrote and told him so. . . . But by the time he [returned] my thirteen generations of clergymen had regained their ascendancy and to McAlmon's evident relief, we talked only of the weather. Adrienne used to call me *Fleur de Presbytère*—'Flower of the Parsonage.' Whether from my puritan ancestry or puri-

tanical upbringing—once when I was in my early teens my mother told me 'never to let a man touch me'—I was always physically afraid of men. That is probably why I lived happily so many years with Adrienne" (quoted in Noel Riley Fitch, *Sylvia Beach and the Lost Generation: A History of Literary Paris in the Twenties and Thirties* [New York: W. W. Norton, 1983], 367).

33. Sylvia Beach, *Shakespeare and Company* (1956; rpt. Lincoln: University of Nebraska Press, 1980), 115.

34. She expressed her opinion privately, in a letter to her mother (quoted in Fitch, *Sylvia Beach*, 194). Joyce was appalled by Gide's book (*JJII* 488).

35. Mary and Padraic Colum, *Our Friend James Joyce* (New York: Doubleday, 1953), 193–94; Maria Jolas, "The Joyce I Knew and the Women around Him," *Crane Bag* 4 (1980): 85; *JJII* 652. Monnier's unpublished letter of 19 May 1931 is in the Berg Collection of the New York Public Library.

36. Unpublished letter (British Library), quoted in Maddox, *Nora*, 275. Joyce's account of Beach's lesbianism resembles his explanation of Wilde's homosexuality, attributed to "heredity and the epileptic tendency of his nervous system" (*CW* 203).

37. Djuna Barnes, "James Joyce," in *Interviews*, ed. Alyce Barry (Los Angeles: Sun and Moon Press, 1985), 294.

38. Scott, *Joyce and Feminism*, 108.

In the Original Sinse

The Gay Cliché and Verbal Transgression in *Finnegans Wake*

Christy Burns

What is narcissistic art? Does it refuse to speak beyond its own hearing, murmuring to itself without regard for social reaction, resisting every interpretive foray or "curative" critical exercise set to draw it back into the normative circle? Perhaps the narcissist's (in)distinction, the wavering line between internal and external forms of communication, troubles the interpretive process, so that, with its challenge to binaristic forms of evaluation, narcissism becomes the supreme scapegoat of all forms of representation. In 1910, Freud aligned narcissism with homosexuality, arguing that its emphasis on sameness signals a self-enclosing circle of desire, unhealthy in its implications.[1] Such denigrations of same-sex love implicate the tendency toward nonreproductive pleasure in a mythos of egotism (Narcissus) that circulated in Joyce's various contexts even before his encounter with Freud's theories in his study of Leonardo da Vinci (1910).[2] In Joyce's writing, narcissistic forms of representation are repeatedly associated with homosexuality, both in the pleasurable engagement with sensate aspects of language and the "perverse" transgression of mimesis, itself a form of mirroring. Women's desires especially are cast in terms of narcissistic self-enrapture, whether on a homo- or heterosexual model. In contrast, whenever male homosexual desire is represented in Joyce's work, it circulates around a model of paranoia—yet another Freudian cliché—so that it slips through only in parapraxes that erupt as two men endeavor to repress any slide into homosexual desire. Freud not only identified homosexuality as the cause of paranoid anxiety, but he also linked that illness to narcissism, based on its self-enclosed view of the world as a reflection of its own self.[3] Such denigrative stereotypes of gay sexuality have recently been critiqued by Jonathan Dollimore, Michael Warner, and others.[4] With these revisionary readings in mind, I will be examining Joyce's recurrent use of clichés of homosexuality in the *Wake,* arguing that his deployment and subsequent disruption of these stereotypes are intertwined with his changing form of textuality.[5] As Joyce distinguishes his approach to male homosexuality and lesbian desire, he casts them on a continuum of two extremes. Lesbian language moves beyond simple narcissism in the *Wake,* opening onto a more "fertile" notion of the unforeclosable nature of wordplay and meaning, while the murmurings of gay desire are met by a violently doubled and repeatedly resplit mode of representation that threatens to break down Joyce's progressively more radical parody and shift his work to a defensive/aggressive form of textuality from which stereotypes repeatedly emerge. I will here be suggesting that a dialectic between the extremes of seduction and aggression—narcissistic pleasures and paranoid defensiveness—ultimately defines the parodic critique of stereotyping that undergirds the textual flow of *Finnegans Wake* more generally, placing the perverse language of sexually transgressive practices at the center of Joyce's avant-garde experiments with words.

Woman-as-narcissist is initially represented as a heterosexual construct in Joyce, where women are "guilty" of being either oblivious to social realities or to male desires. Joyce thus renders Gerty MacDowell as a sadly pathetic narcissist, engaged in denial of the bleakness of her romantic and marital outlook, whereas, in Molly Bloom's monologue, he turns narcissism toward a savvy awareness of the female body, which can transform into autoeroticism or even lesbian desire.[6] In *Finnegans Wake,* female narcissism slides between autoerotic focus and an older woman's desire for the younger woman, in whom she sees a former self. As this narcissism translates into language, women's words are often the softly erotic babble that renders little word-sense and much sensation. Male homosexual desire, in contrast, is met by homosexual panic and paranoid defense, and the language that circulates around these scenarios is often pressed—by Shaun and his associates in their moralistic stances—toward aggressive attempts to rigidify and control language. Both the repressed potential for homosexual desire and the parapraxes that reveal it are agents of betrayal for the Shauns of *Finnegans Wake,* and betrayal is, as Lacan notes, one of the key anxieties motivating the paranoiac.[7]

In simplest terms, paranoia designates a psychological delusion, a persecution complex in which a subject perceives behind the visible a web of maleficent meanings. On Freud's analysis, the paranoiac is unable to accept the interplay between the ego and super-egoistic functions, so that he or she externalizes fault and/or evaluative agency, displacing this sense of an internal split onto some "other"—a persecutor who is located radically outside the self.[8] Psychoanalyst François Roustang suggests that

the paranoiac is someone who, paradoxically, is threatened with losing his own limits. That is why he needs to provoke the other into becoming his persecutor. The other will thus protect him from the threat of dissipating like a liquid; he will set a border which the paranoiac must constantly confront in order to reestablish the certainty of his existence in a circumscribed physical or psychic space.[9]

If paranoia is linked to a variety of manifestations, such as erotomania, delusions of grandeur, and persecution scenarios, I will here be focusing on the paranoiac's compulsion to control and reduce language, texts, and any variety of forms in which meaning can occur. *Finnegans Wake* employs a structural use of paranoia, so that rigidly "paranoid" attempts to reduce language are loosened by their opposite—narcissistic language that fails altogether to return any rationalistically defined, containable, and communicable meaning. As Joyce integrates the gay clichés of lesbian-narcissism and gay-paranoia in his writing, he shifts language and its informing desires away from the very structures of cliché and containment, elaborating a textualizing web that plays between transgressive pleasures and interpretive allowance.

I will begin with Joyce's representation of lesbian desire in *Finnegans Wake*, where women's words are so readily identified with a verbal *jouissance* that plays upon aural and tactile sensations in language. ALP's and Issy's babble of words may disrupt normative approaches to interpretation, eschewing the categorical and definitive hierarchies of reference. Yet their associative words also threaten to remain a clichéd version of narcissistic language. Issy, who is most often engaged in seductive babble, is transformed into Izod in "The Mime of the Mick, Nick and the Maggies," where she is described as "a bewitching blonde who dimples delightfully and is approached in loveliness only by her graceful sister reflection in a mirror" (*FW* 220.7–9). Issy, Izod's prefiguration in the *Wake*, is notoriously schizophrenic, marking a contrast to the externalized, paranoid split between the male twins, Shem and Shaun. Thus the mirror that is externalized in their relationship is embedded within Issy's own mind. She talks to herself, constantly glancing at the mirror, the social image she has internalized. Whenever Issy's words extend outward, her audience appears to be either (or both) directed toward men and women. Initially, one notes that she enjoys tantalizing males, although she occasionally rebels. One of her most "wakean" modes of resistance is to slide into nonmeaning, into pleasurable sounds that are not necessarily directed toward men. Her language fades playfully into the indistinct as she lisps out her "vowelthreaded syllabelles," for example, "Have you evew thought, wepowtew, that sheew gweatness was his twadgedy?" (*FW* 61.6–7). The childish lisping plays on the seduction of indirect sound. Issy, however, achieves seduction only in and through the stereotypes that construct her as a childish nymphet, who again transgresses and subverts the stereotypes but leaves them in place. It is as if Joyce needs the recognition value of stark types to give force to the subsequent movement away from such containment in Issy's very words. Indeed, the women in the *Wake* speak an associative flow that is crucial to the move away from "controlling" words in that last text.

Issy often demonstrates a direct interest in her own sexual appeal and a cynical awareness of social codes—the necessity of attracting a male suitor. Her footnotes to the school lessons, in book II, chapter ii of the *Wake*, give glimpses of a playful boast of sexual awareness. "My six is no secret, sir," she laughs (*FW* 273.f7). And when the teacher describes "fickers who are returnally reprodictive of themselves," she footnotes, "I enjoy as good as anyone" (*FW* 298.17–18 and f.1). Both in terms of reproduction and reprodiction, Issy is prepared. She picks up on saucy allusions and is sassily scandalized by the lesson's reference to something that is "as plane as a poke stiff." "The impudence of that in girl's things!" she snaps (*FW* 296.29–30 and f.5). And much as Issy's sexuality appears to be defined toward men, she has no illusions about marriage. "One must sell it to some one, the sacred name of love," she thinks (*FW* 268.f1). If she is pubescent, like Nuvoletta or Gerty, Issy seems aware of her body as a tool of attraction and is far from abashedly modest, and the social parameters that direct her toward heterosexual relations are at points acknowledged with a somewhat cynical wink.

In the school lesson, Issy brags to a suitor that she has learned the language of love from her schoolmistress. As Issy taunts her love, whom she calls "smooth of my slate," to "eat my words for it as sure as there's a key in my kiss," she reveals that she has already learned the relation between words and desire, and she uses her banter as a form of sublimated exchange, likening the "verbe de vie and verve to vie." Complaining of her "intended, Jr, who I'm throne away on," she suggests that her "impending marriage" will be a subjection to the intention of another, even as it will be her social elevation. Most important, however, we learn that prior to her "fall," she has enjoyed some form of education—linguistic and perhaps also sexual—under to tutelage of an older woman. Teasing the object of her seduction, Issy brags about this experience: "I learned all the runes of the gamest game ever from my old nourse Asa. A most adventuring trot is her and she vicking well knowed them all heartswise and fourwords" (*FW* 279.f1). She knows the ruins of marriage, told by her old nurse Asa, as she also knows all the secrets ("run," in Old Norse) of it. The adventuresome "trot" (or whore) may very well, or *ficking* well, know all the arsewise and forward ways. Her name furthermore suggests that the nurse is associative in her very nature: "As a . . ." As Issy claims, at least, she now knows "the ruelles of the rut," whether they be directed toward homo- or heterosexuality. Rue-elles may signal a path (Fr. *rue* = street) or grief to come, or it may cast aspersions on the nature of her sexual experiences (streetwalker?). And "rut" may of course signal sexual experience as easily as it points to social containment.

Joyce seems to have acquired his notion of lesbian sexuality from the Victorian social codes, which allowed that a schoolgirl might engage briefly in "romantic friendships," so as to learn the ways of relating to some "other," necessarily male, companion to whom she would be wed when she reached maturity.[10] In "The Mime," however, Joyce inscribes various sexual ambivalences that potentially destabilize this model. As the children's play progresses and Izod's desires for male seduction are thwarted, one of the voices assures the reader with a prediction of her inevitable marriage:

> she'll meet anew fiancy, tryst and trow. Mammy was, Mimmy is, Minuscoline's to be. In the Dee dips a dame and the dame desires a demselle but the demselle dresses dolly and the dolly does a dulcydamble. The same renew. For though she's unmerried she'll after truss up and help that hussyband how to hop. (*FW* 226.14–19)

The voice predicts inevitable heterosexual bonding, so that women may have children—the dolly Issy desires. First, however, there is a chain of desire between women, where each older woman, in desiring to *be* her younger self, also actively desires another, younger woman with whom she can identify. Here we have the cliché of narcissism that Joyce takes up, with desire hinging upon a likeness to one's own self. Yet the "Dame" who "desires a demselle" (damsel or demoiselle) must be thwarted if propagation is to be carried through.[11] The closing parapraxes, however, suggest that she might teach hopping to a band of hussies, rather than to a "hussyband." Joyce leaves the heterosexual taboos on lesbianism in place, while also covertly pointing to their potential for instability.

In *Finnegans Wake*, as Issy, Nuvoletta, and ALP occasionally slip into narcissistic modes, their associative play allows noncompetitive relations between women, so that in contrast to paranoiacs, they refuse to draw boundaries while they likewise evade the controlling gesture toward language. This elision of competition between women in Joyce's model of lesbian desire marks the difference between agonistic and accretive forms of meaning in *The Wake*. Competition fails to take hold in relations between women in the *Wake*. Anna Livia Plurabelle negotiates the relations between her desire for her daughter, her sympathetic identification with her, and her awareness of the competition between herself and the young woman in the eyes of her husband, Earwicker. In her closing soliloquy, Anna Livia thinks of the way in which her husband—"wick dear," she calls him (*FW* 625.17)—may be turning his sexual desires toward a younger woman, one who is often, in the book, their daughter Issy:

> But you're changing, acoolsha, you're changing from me, I can feel. Or is it me is? I'm getting mixed. Brightening up and tightening down. Yes, you're changing, sonhusband, and you're turning, I can feel you, for a daughterwife from the hills again. Imlamaya. And she is coming. Swimming in my hindmoist. Diveltaking on me tail. Just a whisk brisk sly spry spink spank sprint of a thing theresomere, saultering. Saltarella come to her own. I pity

your oldself I was used to. Now a younger's there. Try not to part! Be happy, dear ones! May I be wrong! For she'll be sweet for you as I was sweet when I came down out of me mother. My great blue bedroom, the air so quiet, scarce a cloud. In peace and silence. I could have stayed up there for always only. It's something fails us. First we feel. Then we fall. And let her rain now if she likes. (*FW* 626.35–627.12)

"Acoolsha" is a term of endearment, which could be directed anywhere.[12] "Or is it me is?" she asks. Although it seems clear, from the more extended context, that Anna Livia is addressing her husband, suddenly identities become blurred. She might be herself changing, and she might be changing into Is, or Issy.[13] As in a dream, the references overlap and spread. From a momentary inability to distinguish between herself and the object of her affections, she reasserts that the "son/husband" is now turning toward a younger woman, an "Imlamaya," or perfect illusion.[14] Rather than fight her usurper, Livia can accede her position to the younger woman who might take her place in Earwicker's affections and desires. This because, in her thoughts, Anna Livia accepts an identification with the younger woman as a glimpse of her former self, when she too was a young virgin, her innocence or her "blue bedroom" like a womb. So rather than competing, erecting distinctions and boundaries, here a woman lays more emphasis on her bond to the daughter. The fall she seems to mourn, both in her own past and in her daughter's future, is the loss of the heavens and of the girlish idealization of love. In Joyce's construction of female identifications, narcissism, even in its altered form, eliminates the aggression implicit upon realizing the "alienation" or difference encoded within identification. Narcissism becomes the ability to simply embrace a contiguity, a similitude that links the distinct subjects. Rather than splitting off against her daughter in a competitive gesture, ALP accepts the difference and tunes her affection to an identification with her former self. When she says, of her potential rival, "let her rain now if she likes," of course she is allowing the younger rival to reign, but she is also aware that the younger one will "rain" or cry and fall from the clouds, and in this she recalls the earlier story in *Finnegans Wake* of the suicide of Nuvoletta, or "little cloud."

Joyce takes these clichés of lesbianism as self-absorbed interest in a former self (or, from the girl's point of view, as prepubescent sexuality being instructed), and he transforms the very process of verbal association upon which stereotyping can be based. That is, narcissism as cliché of the woman may be linked to lesbianism in the *Wake*, but the very construction of cliché is unraveled again by the language lesbians speak. As lesbian "assaucyetiams" fuel the associative pleasure of Joyce's own words, he textually derives inspiration from Proust's similar association of lesbian erotics and language.

Verbal association is explicitly linked to lesbian association in Marcel Proust's *Remembrance of Things Past*,[15] a subtext to Joyce's "The Mime of Mick, Nick and the Maggies." Proust published *A l'ombre des jeunes filles en fleurs* (*In a Budding Grove)* in 1919 and won the Prix Goncourt that year. The Joyces moved from Zurich to Paris during 1920 and must have been caught up in some news of its success. Describing a visit to the beach at Balbec, Proust recalls his intrigue upon seeing a beautiful group of young women traversing the beach. One day, as he waits before the Grand Hotel, he sees "at the far end of the esplanade, along which they projected a striking patch of colour . . . five or six young girls."[16] This group he variously describes as "a flock of gulls" with "birdish minds" (846), as "a luminous comet" (848), and as "young flowers" of various kinds (856). With their spectrum of colors they make up "a single warm shadow" (851) that attracts him singularly. Proust's rapture at their beauty emerges from his sense of an interplay between his ability to partially distinguish their separate identities and then see them again as a fusion of attributes:

> Although each was of a type absolutely different from the others, they all had beauty; but to tell the truth I had seen them for so short a time, and without venturing to look hard at them, that I had not yet individualised any of them . . . and when (according to the order in which the group met the eye, marvelous because the most different aspects were juxtaposed, because all the colour scales were combined in it, but confused as a piece of music in which I was unable to isolate and identify at the moment of their passage the successive phrases, no sooner distinguished than forgotten) I saw a pallid oval, black eyes, green eyes, emerge, I did not know if these were the same that had already charmed me a moment ago, I could not relate them to any one girl whom I had set apart from the rest and identified. (847)

The young women are identified as "types" that both differ and mingle in their impression. Likened to a rainbow or a series of musical phrases, the girls are remarkable to Proust at this moment just prior to individuation, in that his own inability to distinguish them "permeated the group with a sort of shimmering harmony, the continuous transmutation of a fluid, collective and mobile beauty" (847–48). Later, he likens the project of distinguishing them to "those too rapid readings in which, on the basis of a single syllable and without waiting to identify the rest, we replace the word that is in the text by a wholly different word with which our memory supplies us" (855). This combination of the various attributes of beauty—its range of types—excites Proust most for its interassociative possibilities.

In *Finnegans Wake*, Issy also splinters into a multitude of attributes, known as the "rainbow girls" in "The Mime," where Joyce parodies Freudian "cyclologi-cal" (*FW* 220.30–31) interpretations of childhood sexuality by interlacing his depiction of the child's game Angels and Devils (or colors), with sexually loaded parapraxes. This is where Joyce truly plays on the "Studium of Sexophonologis-tic Schizophrenesis" (*FW* 123.18–19). The children's play begins as the Floras

("Girl Scouts from St. Bride's Finishing Establishment") flirt with the boys, Glugg and Chuff. Or rather, Izod flirts with them. The text moves between descriptions of a group of girls and a single one:

> Aminxt that nombre of evelings, but how pierceful in their sojestiveness were those first girly stirs, with zitterings of flight released and twinglings of twitchbells in rondel after, with waverings that made shimmershake rather naightily all the duskcended airs and shylit beaconings from shehind him back. Sammy, call on. Mirrylamb, she was shuffering all the diseasinesses of the unherd of. Mary Louisan Shousapinas! If Arck could no more salve his agnols from the wiles of willy wooly woolf! If all the airish signics of her dipandump helpabit from an Father Hogam till the Mutther Masons could not that Glugg to catch her by the calour of her brideness! Not Rose, Sevilla nor Citronelle; not Esmeralde, Pervinca nor Indra; not Viola even nor all of them four themes over. But, the monthage stick in the melmelode jawr, I am (twintomine) all thees thing. (*FW* 222.32–223.9)

Minxlike and batlike, these so-jestive girls circle around (in rondel) in the descending dusk, beckoning each other behind (or "shehind") Glugg's back. At the moment of desire ("Sammy, call on!") and also of delayed verbal gratification (a pause: semicolon), Izod consolidates into a "she" who suffers from either dizziness or diseases. She seems to want Ark—Archangel Mick or the rainbow girls (Arc)—to save her (his "agnols," or lambs) from the wolf. Yet Glugg, for all the help of the alphabet, cannot name the right color and so win the sexual chase. In fact, the objection seems to be that Izod is not any particular shade of herself, but "all these things" at once. She is a self-enacted pantomime and a narcissistic self, caught up in the phrase "twintomine."

This (dis)identity in Izod extends as a representation of women throughout the *Wake*, as the Floras of Joyce's "Mime" make repeated appearances in various rainbowlike transformations. The lovely seaside girls of Proust's narrative are thus playfully translated, but in a manner that retains the same emphasis on their oddly nonindividuated, nonconsolidated status:

> And these ways wend they. And those ways went they. Winnie, Olive and Beatrice, Nelly and Ida, Amy and Rue. Here they come back, all the gay pack, for they are the florals, from foncey and pansey to papavere's blush, foresake-me-nought, while there's leaf there's hope, with primtim's ruse and marrymay's blossom, all the flowers of the ancelles' garden. (*FW* 227.13–18)

Here Joyce spells *rainbow* backward with the initials of the girls' names, and the "gay pack" is likened not only to flowers but to various attracting gestures, such as "flouncey" flirtation, or pandering to "true-papa's" blush, pleading with one's lover not to "forsake," the hopeful flower, springtime's ruse, the promise of mar-riage. All are flowers of a handmaid's *(ancille)* or whore's *(ancelle)* garden.[17] Joyce has already spelled "Raynbow" forward in an earlier passage, where the girls are likened to music ("cadenzando") and colors:

> Say them all but tell them apart, cadenzando coloratura! R is Rubretta and A is Arancia, Y is for Yilla and N for greeneriN. B is Boyblue with odalisque O while W waters the fleurettes of novembrance. Though they're all but merely a schoolgirl yet these way went they. I' th' view o' th'avignue danc-ing goes entrancing roundly. Miss Oodles of Anems before the Luvium doeslike. So. And then again doeslike. So. And miss Endles of Eons efter Dies of Eirae doeslike. So. And then again doeslike. So. The many wiles of Winsure. (*FW* 226.30–227.2)

Anna Livia Plurabelle is also here, associating her myriad identities with the rainbow of female attributes. Or is it also that she, by identifying with the schoolgirls, "does like" them, both in that she does things as they do, but also in that she is fond of them. The problem here is that one cannot distinguish be-tween associations and "assaucyetiams" that include sexually transgressive de-sires. Narcissism thus calls into question the distinction between self and other, and within Joyce's "narcissistic" language here, homo- and heterosexual forms of desire are overlapped, pressing on attempts to radically distinguish the two.

Within lesbian "narcissistic" pleasures, then, a noncompetitive element liquifies the binaries that create agonistic energy within Joyce's prose. Language flows erotically through a variety of associations that leave certainty and an-chored forms of interpretation aside. If these verbal associations are lesbian, and in a sense unreproductive, they are certainly repro*ductive* as they allow the elab-oration of several threads within one story. This noncompetitive form of asso-ciation and pleasure opens up the possibilities for autoeroticism as it grades into lesbian desire, emphasizing not so much an eroticization of "sameness," as Freud would argue, but more sympathetic connections and—at times—the abandon-ment to pleasure. Mature Livia takes pleasure in music that sounds like another reference to lesbian pleasures:

> For coxyt sake and is that what she is? Botlettle I thought she'd act that loa. Didn't you spot her in her windaug, wubbling up on an osiery chair, with a meusic before her all cunniform letters, pretending to ribble a reedy derg on a fiddle she bogans without a band on? Sure she can't fiddan a dee, with bow or abandon! Sure, she can't! Tista suck. Well, I never now heard the like of that! (*FW* 198.22–28)

Before all her "cunniform" or cunnus-form letters or progeny, she plays an erotic me-music, the pose of the muse who draws them away from definitive meanings as she plays upon her own pleasure. What is she doing, but playing a fiddle, or riddling with the (rain)bow of younger women? "Tista suck," she may well be. And if she plays with "abandon," we also hear echoes of Willingdon's urge to "get the band up," with regards to sexual activity, in book I. Music and sexual play both enfold and rupture the meaning-sense of language here. Auto-eroticism and narcissism are here indistinguishable, again playing on the clichés of sameness that supposedly construct homosexual desire. And yet Joyce's language—as ALP's desire—does not collapse into a single "sameness" or a homogeneous mass of nonmeaning. Meaning is alternately dispersed and extended by the cross-referentiality that resists attempts to separate autoeroticism from homosexuality and from heterosexual desires.

In contrast to Joyce's permissiveness toward lesbian desire, potentially erotic relations between men are continually subjected to separation, which is reasserted to a level of intensity where violence often erupts. Repeatedly, suggestions of male-male association meet immediate resistance, particularly where a mirror effect occurs. Twins and doubles react to a double threat, that which might belie individual uniqueness (so that sameness poses a threat of erasure or obfuscation of a distinctive personal identity) and that which might also suggest an erotic association, a narcissistic desire for the self mapped over the other. Narcissism, as a compelling sameness, is a nightmare between men in the *Wake*, and aggressive gestures throw up radical distinctions whenever such a possibility threatens. This is similar, and I am venturing historically related, to a phenomenon Eve Sedgwick has observed in Romantic novels, which she terms the "paranoid Gothic," where "a male hero is in a close, usually murderous relation to another male figure, in some respects his 'double,' to whom he seems to be mentally transparent."[18] In this scenario, homosexual panic transforms into a differentiating aggression, much as in *Finnegans Wake*, although Joyce plays less upon the problem of mental transparency between twins. Sedgwick rightly points out that critics need not read these moments as psychological clarifications of some "gay" consciousness (much as Freud seems to), but rather more fruitfully and historically should understand paranoia and homosexual panic as problems arising from "the entire spectrum of male homosocial organization" as it insists on heterosexuality and stakes itself in a polarization against homosexual relations.[19]

Two forms of aggression in the *Wake* most consistently allow male-male relations to maintain a repression of homosexual transfigurations: competition for female attention and war upon the father. In the *Wake*, homosocial tensions are even more closely linked to eroticism that troubles the line between hetero- and homosexual desires. In "The Mime," for example, while Chuff and Glugg compete for Issy's attentions, verbal innuendos mark the return of a repressed sense of homosexual possibility. If Chuff is yet another version of huffy Shaun, his name also invokes *chuff chums*, a term for homosexuals.[20] While the innuendoes accompanying Chuff and Glugg's competitions for the rainbow girls in "The Mime" suggest a homoerotic repression, this suggestion becomes humorously more pronounced through an excess of parapractic slips of the tongue in Shaun's telling of the tale of Burrus and Caseous in *Finnegans Wake* I.iv. These two figures, who are parodies of Brutus and Cassius, alternately sing the praises of one "sweet Margareen" and make war upon the father, temporarily bonding before their displaced desires return to resplinter them again.

As characterological constructs of Shaun and Shem—created within Shaun's defense against his double and brother—Burrus and Caseous show signs of homosexual panic, being repeatedly troubled by sexual innuendoes that Shaun seeks to suppress. The characters' overwrought doubling forms a manifest link between narcissism and strict interpretations of the mimetic project, so that the scenario functions as a model of aggressive and overreaching parody, in contrast to Joyce's own parodic gestures in the passage. Moreover, Joyce's association of agonism with homophobic anxiety functions as a nodal pressure point for the language of the *Wake*, where attempts to control "perverse" or transgressive language are undermined by the repeated parapraxes of Burrus' pronouncements in favor of traditional channels for sexuality—marriage and institutionally structured propagation (i.e., the family). As heterosexual desire is given a name, homosexual references undermine the implicit gesture of repression, and the line between hetero- and homoerotics is called into question, riveting the more general problem of distinctions and interpretation in the *Wake*. Faced with indistinction, the paranoiac steps up adamant claims of difference, reflecting on an inner failure to accept and comprehend the split within himself. On Lacan's analysis, paranoia therein becomes a representational problem:

> At the basis of paranoia itself, which nevertheless seems to us to be animated by belief, there reigns the phenomenon of the *Unglauben*. This is not the *not believing in it,* but the absence of one of the terms of belief, of the term in which is designated the division of the subject. If, indeed, there is no belief that is full and entire, it is because there is no belief that does not presuppose in its basis that the ultimate dimension that it has to reveal is strictly correlative with the moment when its meaning is about to fade away.[21]

Repeatedly in his works Lacan identifies a basic ambivalence within the subject, a split between that which is conscious and that which exceeds the subject's control and knowledge—the element of alienation within the self. Here, this split circulates around the tension between belief and uncertainty. Unable to accept the inevitability of some failing within belief, "the moment when its meaning is about to fade away," the paranoiac angrily reacts to destabilized language and representation. The pun, the split word, easing toward the arbitrariness of sound play, would therefore provoke in the paranoiac arguably the greatest distraction.

The split within desire is also, according to Freud, what so troubles the paranoiac. In the essay on Leonardo da Vinci, which Joyce owned, Freud argues that if a subject does not make a homosexual object choice he always either "still adheres to it in his unconscious or else protects himself against it by vigorous counter-attitudes."[22] As Sedgwick argues, however, this is more a symptom of the historical construction of sexuality that an abstract form of desire. In a homosocial culture that insists on male heterosexuality, any "betrayal" of desire might inspire a cycling escalation of phobia and insistence. In Shaun's stories and lectures, homosexual panic as a form of homophobia is confronted repeatedly by the parapraxes that suggest the ever-present possibility of homosexual desire. And the crucial tension that I am pressing here is that of whether the paranoiac is typed as homosexual or homophobic. For Freud, he is implicitly both, as the paranoiac's neurosis arises predominantly from *repression* of homosexual desire.[23] That is, some primary ambivalence, a split within the self that all subjects experience, antagonizes the paranoiac. For Freud (at times) this ambivalence is necessarily the undecipherable splinter of desire that shifts between hetero- and homosexual foci. For Shaun, this splinter functions as a form of internal betrayal, as he struggles to control his inner consciousness. The "betrayal" within language that Joyce so often marks is itself encoded within the division between twins, who function both as distinct characters and, at other times, as one mind divided against itself.

With the tale of Burrus and Caseous (and their love for Margareen), Joyce comically overlaps the story of Brutus and Cassius's conspiracy against Julius Caesar with culinary metaphors, punning Brutus into "Burrus" and Cassius into "Caseous," bringing out a story of butter (French *beurre*) and cheese (caseous: cheesy). Shaun, in his struggle to distinguish himself (as "pure" butter) from Shem (as gaseous, vile, and derivative) invokes, albeit messily, the law of the excluded middle, such that binaries must be distinct and free from any third space or hybridity:

> I cannot now have or nothave a piece of cheeps in your pocket at the same time and with the same manners as you can now nothalf or half the cheek apiece I've in mind unless Burrus and Caseous have not or not have seemaultaneously sysentangled themselves, selldear to soldthere, once in the dairy days of buy and buy. (*FW* 161.9–14)

The piece of "cheeps"—as cheap cheese in the pocket—has to persist by the law of the excluded middle, so that one cannot both have and not have it, just as one must either "half" it or leave it whole. Contrarily, however, Joyce fools this notion with its very language: he changes *and* to *or,* so that one cannot both have it *or* not have it. The binary is not so securely split; it is, rather, a choice that

Shaun lacks. And as Shaun attempts to deny any contiguity between himself and Shem, he is also endeavoring to excise the bit of Shem he finds in himself. But if Burrus, like Shaun, moralistically interrupts all potential fall into "low" and cheesy exchanges (with a kind of constant "but!"),[24] the two coconspirators Burrus and Caseous still have a hard time, being "seemaultaneously sysentangled themselves." The first level—the speaker's predominant meaning, prior to his parapraxes—is the thought that Burrus and Cassius might (or must) simultaneously disentangle themselves from one another. Nevertheless, they only "seem" to be simultaneous, or twinlike, just as they fail to disentangle identities, turning rather to integrate (Greek *sys* = together)[25] themselves. The language doubles irreconcilably here, just as Burrus and Caseous do. As Shaun fails to disentangle Shem's image from his own, references to a dreaded intimacy with Shem's (mirrorlike, male) body erupt on a latent level of reference. "Cheek" hits a first register with cheese, but it is also a crude term for buttocks, slipping into sexual innuendo.[26] To make matters worse, *cheese* is crude slang for the residue that clings under the foreskin: smegma.[27] If Caseous also echoes *gaseous* at moments, then Joyce is riddling the scenario with puns on the bodily grotesque, and Burrus, as "Butter," accrues the rather obvious (Butt) locus of one of Joyce's many physical preoccupations.

The revulsion is too much for Shaun, the doubling too terrible. He argues that if they are not wholly distinct, Burrus and Caseous operate much as an "original" and its parody might:

> Burrus, let us like to imagine, is a genuine prime, the real choice, full of natural greace, the mildest of milkstoffs yet unbeaten as a risicide and, of course, obsolutely unadulterous whereat Caseous is obversely the revise of him and in fact not an ideal choose by any meals. (*FW* 161.15–19)

Shaun may be feeling vulnerable in the rear—he even slips and refers to himself as "grease" (possibly Greek) and "milkstoffing," echoing *milksop*. Moreover, the metaphor of eating cannot but help Shaun's anxiety, and a paranoid struggle to both patrol his boundaries and distinguish his identity ensues. Is it surprising then that as Caseous is associated with gaseous Shem, the ever-perfect Shaun is, like Burrus, so inflexibly moral as to be near "risicide," or killed with self-parody (Latin *risus* = laugh)?[28]

The tension between twinned factions functions much like the troubled line between representation and its original. Shaun's attack on Shem echoes Plato's denigration of art as a mere copy of external likenesses that degrades the original, substituting a beautiful shell that lacks *eidos*, essence, idea, or—in language—original intention. With Shem and Shaun, the question may be which is the stable portrait and which the slide into denigrative parody. Here, Caseous is much like a parody of Burrus, cheese being a reworked revision of butter, never as "prime" or pure as his brother or partner, Burrus. As Shaun struggles to label Burrus "pure" and Caseous as secondary, verbal denotations and connotations intertwine, so that the reader must ask which is the primary meaning of Shaun's words, and wonder if homosexual innuendo might not supplant the more "innocent" or pure design.

And on an ever-more-thematic level, the scenario is shot through with this struggle to supplant (by betraying) an original authority—the calling into question of any "authorization." Burrus's "risicide" also refers to the regicide for which Brutus and Cassius were cast into hell and, in Dante's *Inferno,* condemned to be chewed in Satan's mouth. "It is why," Glasheen notes, "they appear as decently chewable foods—butter and cheese, Burrus and Caseous."[29] The murder of Caesar here transforms into a second form of binary aggression, where twins or coconspirators in the *Wake* often recombine in order to face off against the father.[30] Caesar here is "sisar," and he is cast as a main role in the family salad, made up of "Murphybuds" (potatoes) and "hot young Capels and Lettucia" (*FW* 161.29). "Pfarrer Salamoss" is attacked by Burrus and Caseous, who are rebelling against his authority. Within the family salad then, "there's many a split pretext bowl and jowl" (*FW* 161.31–32); so that what was perhaps once lying "cheek by jowl" in the womb or simpler terms of friendship and supposed unity is inevitably split and even warring. Here, the twins erase their difference (and mirrorlike eroticism) by momentarily facing off against Caesar, a tyrant said to be "unbeurrable" (*FW* 162.2) as a voice wonders if all authorities are sweet or foul ("brutherscutch or puir tyron," *FW* 163.8–9).

The problem arises, however, that any such conflict can soon be resolved, and after vanquishing the saladlike father, the two must again settle into the ill-ease of their proximity. Attempting to resign himself to an acceptance of contraries, Shaun momentarily allows,

> Thus we cannot escape our likes and mislikes, exiles or ambusheers, beggar and neighbour and—this is where the dimeshow advertisers advance the temporal relief plea—let us be tolerant of antipathies. *Nex quovis burro num fit mercaseus?* I am not hereby giving my final endorsement to the learned ignorants of the Cusanus philosophism. (*FW* 163.12–17)

McHugh notes the overlap of the last passage and the Latin phrase *ex quovis butyrum num fit merus caseous:* "from any butter there is not made pure cheese." *Nex,* however, means murder (Latin), suggesting that violence against the one (tyrannical Burrus? is he?) will not set the cheesy one right. Shaun, however, resists any suggestion that he "give an unconditional sinequam to the heroicised furibouts of the Nolanus theory" (*FW* 163.23–24). He thus turns to tackle Bruno of Nolan's theory that opposites combine. Joyce once summarized Bruno's work in a letter as "a kind of dualism—every power in nature must evolve an opposite in order to realise itself and opposition brings reunion etc etc." (*LI* 224–25). Shaun here lumps Bruno (the Nolan) with Nicholas of Cusa, since both adhered to the "coincidence of contraries" position, believing that opposites can combine into "one and the same person" (*FW* 354.8), and Cusa's work on the coincidence of contraries in God is believed to have influenced Bruno. If Shaun is notably ambivalent about Cusa's theory, that is because he fears that opposites might fuse into one complete whole. Shaun therefore humorously qualifies his concession to Cusa, saying that he hopes to eventually prove that "both products of our social stomach . . . are mutuearly polarised the incompatabilily of any delusional acting as ambivalent to the fixation of his pivotism" (*FW* 163.34–164.3). It is, in a sense, no use pretending an ambivalence about the fixation of Shaun's binary; he must radically distinguish himself from Shem. For Shaun, contraries do *not* combine; rather, they create a competitive ambivalence that must be controlled. This is accomplished not by associative acceptance, as in the case of Anna Livia and Issy, but by rigidifying hierarchical structures and aggressively denigrating Shem and elevating Shaun himself.

As soon as Shaun "resolves" his problem of contraries, temporarily accepting the combination but theoretically resisting, he has to introduce the next level of restorative heterosexual "fixation": "Positing, as above, too males pooles, the one the pictor of the other and the ombre the *Skotia* of the one, and looking wantingly around our undistributed middle between males we feel we must waistfully woent a female to focus" (*FW* 164.4–7). As he attempts to posit two male poles or opposites who mirror one another (like Narcissus to his pool), Shaun requires a female "to focus" what I am supposing is their (hetero-defined) identities. To oblige them, "the cowrymaid M.," otherwise known as "Margareen," appears. Music overhead plays "I cream for thee, Sweet Margareen . . . O Margareena! O Margareena! Still in the bowl is left a lump of gold!" (*FW* 164.18–20). She is, of course, fake butter, so a tricky substitute for Burrus. She will be later called "Margery," slang for an effeminate in the early twentieth century.[31] Moreover, there is some question as to Margareen's true sex. As a parenthetical aside assures us:

> (I am closely watching Master Pules, as I have regions to suspect from my post that her "little man" is a secondary schoolteacher under the boards of education, a voted disciple of Infantulus who is being utilised thus publicly by the *seducente infanta* to conceal her own more mascular personality by flaunting frivolish finery over men's inside clothes, for the femininny of that totamulier will always lack the musculink of a verumvirum. My solutions for the proper parturience of matres and the education of micturious mites must stand over from the moment till I tackle this tickler hussy for occupying my uttentions.) (*FW* 166.20–29)

As Jean-Michel Rabaté has pointed out, *Finnegans Wake* often works to blur sexual dichotomies and to frustrate attempts to demarcate male and female identities.[32] The reader is left with an uncanny uncertainty as to whether the object of voiced sexual desire is male or female, and here the figure in focus seems at times a female and at times male. "Master Pooles" may refer to those two who are "mutuearly polarised," the poles of Shem and Shaun in one here, but "Pooles" and "Pules" pun on *poule,* French for "hen," suggesting the twins' emersion in ALP's identity. And the figure who is apparently masculine is suddenly "her," if prior reference functions, and one gathers that "she" is the object of Burrus's and Caseous's attentions. They are a "little man"—a young boy she has seduced—who is used by her to hide her "more mascular" personality. She *or he* wears "frivolous finery" over men's underclothes. This casts aspersions on Margery's sex—is "she" really a woman? Are they/the "little man" really men? As the voice (perhaps Issy's) asserts, "the femininny of that totamulier will always lack the musculink of a verumvirum." This translates roughly into "the femininity of a complete woman (Latin *tota mulier*) will always lack the masculinity of a real man" (Latin *verus vir*).[33] My guess is that this is a suggestion that Margareena's femininity reeks of "mascular" airs, being too virile, in effect, not to be male. Still, the referent is uncertain and may undermine the masculinity of the twins, as a "masculink." What is clear, however, is that Margareen (Margery) blurs the very sexual dichotomy that the twins are struggling to hold in place, and she thus cannot help Burrus and Caseous (much less Shaun) ward off homosexual panic. At this crisis, their emotions transform into an anxious and competitive aggression.

Margareen may, in fact, be "The Very Picture of a Needless Woman" (*FW* 165.15–16), if her presence is necessary more as mediation of desire. Sedgwick points out that "'to cuckold' is by definition a sexual act, performed on a man, by another man" and she argues that its central position in a piece of literature "emphasizes heterosexual love chiefly as a strategy of homosocial desire."[34] Where women are sometimes celebrated with apparent appreciation, misogyny is still a component, and here it quickly breaks out. Margareen is promptly stereotyped as a whore, "whose types may be met with in any public garden" (*FW* 166.5–6), and her fickleness provides the core of triangulation: "Margareena she's very fond of Burrus but, alick and alack! she velly fond of chee" (*FW* 166.30–31). Her split affection instigates yet another conflict between the co-conspirators, who now turn on one another in a competitive gesture. When the two fight over her, Shaun eventually reclaims his word (and wife-*as*-word) as "sacred" and unchanging. Shaun's voice ends the episode with a lecture on the necessity of controlling one's words and women: "My unchanging Word is sacred. The word is my Wife, to expose and expound, to vend and to velnerate, and may the curlews crown our nuptias! Till Breath us depart! Wamen. Beware would you change with my years" (*FW* 167.28–31). Shaun's concluding lecture—to the rainbow girls—asserts the necessity of consolidating authorial position over the word *and* women. The tension between women's associative unravelings of "productive" forms of meaning, and the subsequent disruption of the interpretive attempt to "control" and possess language, is thus answered, in Joyce's parody, by a paranoiac insistence on absolute control.

As the troubled tension surrounding the (non)differentiation between homo- and heteroerotics is repeatedly refigured in Joyce's writing, so too does his experiment with parody pull more radically against the paranoiac's attempt to delineate boundaries. I am suggesting that in *Finnegans Wake* narcissistic models of a psychologically inflected mimesis work in radical contradistinction to a paranoid mode of textuality, where single meanings are insisted upon, desires denied, and identities fixed. The paranoiac resists any social attempts at objectification, much as in *Finnegans Wake* HCE resists society's move to assess, judge, and assign a representation to him. As the paranoiac anxiously endeavors to evade social judgment (and the pain of his own superego, in a sense), he himself becomes aggressively certain of his own assessments. Recall Roustang's characterization of the paranoiac as one who needs a persecutor to secure his own boundaries. If establishing the certainty of one's own existence is the primary goal of paranoia, the paranoiac's most likely opponent would be that which lies opposite of certainty—the possibility of chance and arbitrary occurrence. Just as paranoiacs cannot accept subjective transience, they cannot likewise mime the necessary shrug that pays tribute to chance. Anything that evades logic or reason would therefore threaten the paranoiac, even as, paradoxically, he/she requires this threat to establish his/her identity.

Paranoia may therefore be understood not only as a mental illness caught up in issues of control and defense, but also as a form of textuality that repeatedly and compulsively stresses the intentionalistic and interpretive control of each word and belief issued forth. Working to press language toward its more logical or rational potential, the paranoiac turns away from a word's playful and coincidental effects, just as he/she might try to fix representation as a stable, objective form. Likewise, as literary interpretation and forms of analysis slide away from more flexible forms of mediation, they run the risk of falling into paranoid extremes.

The undecidability that haunts the paranoiac therefore transmutes into a distrust of representation. Lacan's analysis of the splinter within belief translates into a problem of interpretability, such that the paranoiac insists upon the certitude of his interpretation (as paranoids classically do) in a gesture that marks the denial of arbitrariness, pure sensate pleasure, and nonmeaning. In this manner, paranoia also functions as the structural opposite to a key term in Joyce's aesthetic practice—parody. Both words take their initial stem, *para-*, from the Greek for contiguity (alongside another), while paranoia's second root, *nous* (mind), specifies that one is in a sense beside oneself mentally, not fully centered nor clear of boundaries. The subject is in effect doubled or blurred. Parody, on the other hand, indicates a critical contiguity of one text (or subtext) to another, such that identities are overlapping without full distinction nor collapsible into sameness.

Joyce's radical experiment with language and forms of historical narration in *Finnegans Wake* might then be implicated in the struggle against paranoid control of his medium. Indeed, representations of homophobic patrol of physical and psychic boundaries function as a critical hinge in his move away from univocal forms of narration and into the textual *jouissance* that circulates around Anna Livia's and Issy's words and has been so famously celebrated by Kristeva, Cixous, and others. The loosening of control, however, threatens to dissolve an identifiable position for the "other," potentially resulting in a narcissistic form of communication that never extends beyond a benign, self-fulfilling interpretation. The narcissistic text cannot be opened through interpretation, just as the paranoid form resists any reading but the author's own (which can never be surrendered to the reader for judgment). Narcissism and paranoia thus define the extremes of Joyce's representational experiment, and the *Wake* moves between invoking stereotypes and pressing toward verbal transgression.

In III.iii, when asked by the four judges whether "any orangepeelers or greengoaters appear periodically up your sylvan family tree" (*FW* 522.16–17),[35] HCE responds "Buggered if I know!" While on the surface the judges seem merely to be asking if there are any Protestant constabularies (orange-peelers)[36] or naive fools (since *green* meant naive from eighteenth century, and to "Play the goat" is to be a fool), they may also be wanting to know if there were any lesbians, *orange* being slang for female pudenda from the Restoration period, or if there are not also Irishmen interested in "goaters" or posteriors. HCE responds with his own double language:

> —It all depends on how much family silver you want for a nass-and-pair. Hah!
> —What do you mean, sir, behind your hah! you don't hah to do thah, you know, snapograph.
> —Nothing, sir. Only a bone moving into place. Blotogaff. Hahah!
> —Whahat?
> —Are you to have all the pleasure quizzing on me? I didn't say it aloud, sir. I have something inside of me talking to myself. (*FW* 522.18–26)

The *blot* was low slang for the anus, by the 1930s, and HCE teases the tribunal by pimpingly pressing for how much "family silver" they will offer for a nice pair ("nass-and-pair"), before shifting to references to the "bone" (penis) and ass. But more troubling still to the tribunal is the difficulty HCE has in telling any direct "truth." Engaged in a "narcissistic" form of self-directed talk, HCE refuses to make the judges the sole reason for his words. His own pleasure counts at least as much. This self-directed pleasure is rewarded then with the usual stereotypes in return:

> —You're a nice third degree witness, faith! But this is no laughing matter. Do you think we are tonedeafs in our noses to boot? Can you not distinguish the sense, prain, for the sound, bray? You have homosexual catheis of empathy between narcissism of the expert and steatopygic invertedness. Get yourself psychoanolised! (*FW* 522.27–32)

The one who cannot keep "the sense" and "the sound" separate must be guilty of homosexuality, that which "murmurs" at the margins and in the parapraxes. HCE is said to be guilty of stereotypical invertedness, or rather "steatopygic," which is defined as "abnormal protuberance of buttocks." What would be hidden comes to view, and what the judges wish rather to comprehend ("What do you mean, sir, behind your hah!") fails to arrive.

Textual perversity is here sketched out as a kind of self-enclosed pleasure, the game of the narcissist. Homosexuality is taken as a way in which one lacks distinctions and turns language narcissistically in on itself. By weaving "gay clichés" into the *Wake,* Joyce is thus addressing the potential critique of "narcissistic" art, which uses the mirror only to reproduce the self, and which can never "speak" beyond the economy of its own pleasure. What is troubling about narcissism, in the strictest sense, is that, as a form of self-love turned inward, it avoids the social relations, is more imaginary than reality-based in its affections, feeding its own desires without need of external input. Narcissistic art would be fantasy, escapism, utopia, in that it would seek its ego ideal by mapping it over the other, never truly seeing or encountering the other. Homosexuality/heterosexuality has been thus construed along the axis of imaginary/real, an axis crucially problematized by *Finnegans Wake.* The text plays out Joyce's own sometimes private pleasure; but language itself, wrought as it is with unconscious desires and swerves, pursues its own sensate association, as it were. *Finnegans Wake* in that sense allows language to rise off the canvas in the intensity of its own effects. If one were "to communicake with original sinse" (*FW* 239.1–2), one would perhaps reclaim some original intent or purer form of language. But the terms are already adulterated, and to press for such "original *sinse*" commits the sin of performing an aggressive separation from and exclusion of the sensate, disruptive elements of language that make up its medium. And it would be also to exclude laughter, that which shakes the boundaries between self/other, will/desire, meaning/pleasure, and a range of separations. If "this kissing world's full of killing fellows" (*FW* 248.24–25), Joyce parodies such a bond, adding in both humor and pleasant non-sense in an oscillation between aggressive attempts to crystalize patterns into stereotypes (and words into clichés) and the movement toward release of competitive boundaries, so that he may, in that sense, "entwine our arts with laughters low!" (*FW* 259).

NOTES

1. See Sigmund Freud, "Five Lectures on Psycho-Analysis," in *The Standard Edition of the Complete Psychological Works of Sigmund Freud,* trans. and ed. James Strachey, 24 vols. (London: Hogarth Press and the Institute of Psycho-Analysis, 1953–74), 11:3. This work was published just before Freud's study on Leonardo da Vinci, which also discusses homosexuality. See also Freud's more extensive discussion, "On Narcissism," *Standard Edition,* vol. 14.

2. Richard Brown demonstrates Joyce's familiarity with Freud's notions of perversion and homosexuality in *Psychopathology of Everyday Life*, Freud's essay on Leonardo da Vinci, and Ernest Jones's interpretation of *Hamlet*. See *James Joyce and Sexuality* (Cambridge: Cambridge University Press, 1985), 83.

3. Sigmund Freud, "Introductory Lectures on Psycho-Analysis," *Standard Edition*, 16:424.

4. Jonathan Dollimore, *Sexual Dissidence: Augustine to Wilde, Freud to Foucault* (Oxford: Clarendon Press, 1991), 174–76n.; and Michael Warner, "Homo-Narcissism; or, Heterosexuality," in *Engendering Men: The Question of Male Feminist Criticism*, ed. Joseph A. Boone (New York: Routledge, 1990).

5. In the late 1970s, Colin MacCabe commented on the link between sexual and textual perversity in Joyce's writing, just as, more recently, Jean-Michel Rabaté has noted that the slippage into nonmeaning in *Dubliners* functions as the opposite of orthodoxy and opens a certain "perversity" of nonmeaning. See MacCabe, *Revolution of the Word* (New York: Barnes and Noble, 1979), 111–29, and Rabaté *James Joyce, Authorized Reader* (Baltimore: Johns Hopkins University Press, 1991), 20–26.

6. See my article "An Erotics of the Word: Female "Assaucyetiams" in *Finnegans Wake*," *James Joyce Quarterly* 31 (spring 1994): 315–35.

7. Jacques Lacan, *The Four Fundamental Concepts of Psycho-Analysis*, trans. Alan Sheridan (New York: Norton, 1966), 238.

8. Freud, "Introductory Lectures on Psycho-Analysis," 16:429.

9. François Roustang, "How Do You Make a Paranoiac Laugh?" *Modern Language Notes* 102, no. 4 (1987): 715.

10. Ruth Frehner, at the Zurich James Joyce Foundation, brought to my attention this intersection with Victorian notions. See Martha Vicinus, *Independent Women: Work and Community for Single Women, 1850–1920* (London: Virago Press, 1985), 34–35.

11. Later in "The Mime," Joyce additionally drops an allusion to Freud's study of Dora's affection for Frau K., mentioning a "Dodgesome Dora for hedgehung sheolmastress" (*FW* 228.16–17). Freud initially believed that Dora displaced her desire for her father to the figure of Herr K. As Jacques Lacan has noted, Freud is misled in this assumption by his own identification along lines of sex; he identifies with the father's desire and cannot see Dora's homosexual attraction (*Ecrits: A Selection*. trans. Alan Sheridan [New York: Norton, 1977], 92–93). Freud's study of Dora's homosexuality was published in 1905. Dora became attached to a Mrs. K, with whom she read books, and so, in a sense, "studied" with her as well.

12. Roland McHugh identifies this as a reference to the Anglo-Irish word *acushla*, "my pulse." She might then be referring to a rhythmic identification with Earwicker and any other associations the thought of him brings, whether of former lovers or her own identification with him. See *Annotations to "Finnegans Wake*," rev. ed. (Baltimore: Johns Hopkins University Press, 1991), 626.

13. Just a few pages earlier, Issy has been referred to as "Is is" (*FW* 620.32).

14. If the daughterwife comes from Himilayas, McHugh, *Annotations to "Finnegans Wake*," also finds biblical words *Imla*, meaning "fullness," and *maya*, Sanskrit for "illusion."

15. Joyce drops numerous hints in "The Mime" that he is using Proust's *Remembrance of Things Past* as a subtext. In the description of Hump's role (played by Humphrey Chimpden Earwicker), the patriarch is said to have partially recovered from "recent im-

peachment"—one of Finn's many falls—and he is "studding sail once more, jibsheets and royals, in the semblance of the substance for the membrance of the umbrance with the remnance of the emblence" (*FW* 220.31–33). The allusion to *Remembrance of Things Past* emerges here, along with Joyce's play on linguistic rhythms. Further on, when Chuff and Glugg fight, the text shrugs off their aggression with a simple, "We've heard it aye since songdom was gemurrmal." *Sodome et Gomorrhe* was the fourth installment of Proust's novel to appear, and its depictions of homosexuality scandalized Europe in the early 1920s. The allusion of greater weight to the question of lesbian eroticism, however, is Joyce's reference to the rainbow of "Floral" girls as "the youngly delightsome frilles-in-pleyurs," who "are now showen drawen, if bud one, or, if in florileague, drawens up consociately at the hinder sight of their commoner guardia" (*FW* 224.22–24).

16. Marcel Proust, *Remembrance of Things Past*, trans. C. K. Scott Moncrieff and Terence Kilmartin, vol. 1 (New York: Random House, 1981), 845.

17. McHugh, *Annotations to "Finnegans Wake,"* 227. The first is archaic English, the second French slang.

18. Eve Sedgwick, *Epistemology of the Closet* (Berkeley and Los Angeles: University of California Press, 1990), 186n.

19. Eve Sedgwick, *Between Men: English Literature and Male Homosocial Desire* (New York: Columbia University Press, 1985), 115–16 and passim. Sedgwick clarifies this concisely in *Epistemology of the Closet:*

> The result of men's accession to this double bind [of the basically homosocial and heterosexual codes within mentorship, male friendship, and rivalry] is, first, the acute *manipulability*, through the fear of one's own "homosexuality," of acculturated men; and second, a reservoir of potential for *violence* caused by the self-ignorance that this regime constitutively enforces. The historical emphasis on enforcement of homophobic rules in the armed services in, for instance, England and the United States supports this analysis. In these institutions, where both men's manipulability and their potential for violence are at the highest possible premium, the *pre*scription of (the remarkably cognate) "homosexuality" are both stronger than in civilian society—are, in fact, close to absolute. (186)

20. Eric Partridge, *A Dictionary of Slang and Unconventional English*, ed. Paul Beale (New York: Macmillan, 1984).

21. Lacan, *Four Fundamental Concepts*, 238.

22. Sigmund Freud, *Standard Edition*, 14:191.

23. Sigmund Freud, "Some Neurotic Mechanisms in Jealousy, Paranoia and Homosexuality," *Standard Edition*, 18:225 and passim.

24. "But!" and also Butt (of Butt and Taff), who likewise have an episode of homosexual panic and ensuing aggression (*FW* 338–54 and passim). Moreover, Adaline Glasheen identifies Burrus with Butt (from Butter) (46). See *A Third Census of Finnegans Wake* (Berkeley and Los Angeles: University of California Press, 1977).

25. McHugh, *Annotations to "Finnegans Wake."*

26. Partridge, *A Dictionary of Slang.*

27. Late nineteenth–twentieth century (Partridge, *A Dictionary of Slang*). It is, in fact, the first meaning he lists.

28. McHugh, *Annotations to "Finnegans Wake."*

29. Glasheen, *Third Census*, 41.

30. The Oedipal scenario that Joyce employs here may replay Freud's conscious attempt to establish the priority of a heterosexual family romance, but the undercurrent indicates as well the subversive potential of homosexual desires repressed. The Oedipal scenario sets up aggression against the father as a reinforcement of heterosexuality, which is replayed within the sons' competition for the female, so that the family romance generally functions as a suppression of homosexual desire. As Jean Laplanche and J. B. Pontalis summarize it, it is "a desire for the death of the rival—the parent of the same sex—and a sexual desire for the parent of the opposite sex" (*The Language of Psychoanalysis*, trans. Donald Nicholson-Smith [New York: Norton, 1973], 283). While it can also be cast as desire for the same-sex parent and aggression against the other, Laplanche and Pontalis note that this is treated as a "negative" form in Freud. Dollimore, however, observes that "perversion proves the undoing of the theory which contains it" (*Sexual Dissidence*, 197), for the more Freud uses the Oedipal scenario to insist on the "naturalness" of heterosexuality, the more he must work to maintain the line between the object of desire and that of identification. Readings of Freud, like Warner's in "Homo-Narcissism; or, Heterosexuality," now use homosexuality as the term that introduces—and necessitates—this subtler understanding of cross-identifications and multiplied roles, such that any simple binary between the parent desired and the one resisted is denied (Dollimore, 198). It is more the very repression of such multiple and ambivalent desires that creates the tensional binary that irrupts into violence. Joyce thus employs Freudian cliché, but the parody in this scenario clues the reader in to the fractures within his binaristic construction of Oedipal relations as purely heterosexual in their "positive" definition.

31. Partridge, *A Dictionary of Slang.*

32. Jean Michel Rabaté, *Joyce upon the Void: The Genesis of Doubt* (London: Macmillan, 1991), 154f.

33. McHugh, *Annotations to "Finnegans Wake."*

34. Sedgwick, *Between Men,* 49.

35. McHugh, *Annotations to "Finnegans Wake,"* glosses the orange versus green, "The Peeler and the Goat" (a song), and greengrocers.

36. Partridge, *A Dictionary of Slang. Peeler* is Irish policeman, from mid-eighteenth century.

Recent Controversies

Beyond "Syphilisation"

Finnegans Wake, AIDS, and the Discourse of Contagion

Marian Eide

"Until I was twenty-five, I was the only man I knew who had no story at all. I'd long since accepted the fact that nothing had ever happened to me and nothing ever would. That's how the closet feels, once you've made your nest in it and learned to call it home."[1] Paul Monette's powerfully resonant description of life in the closet amplifies his experience as an adolescent in which the central secret of his queer desire cast a silence over all the other stories that might otherwise have shaped a life into a narrative. Approximately a century earlier, Oscar Wilde expressed a similar silencing of homosexual desire during his trial when he defined Lord Alfred Douglas's "love that dare not speak its name" as the love of an older man for a younger man.[2] In *Finnegans Wake*, Joyce recognizes the silence that surrounds queer desire and responds by creating a complex, associative language that expresses unauthorized pleasures. Through the complexity of his own language, Joyce encodes both the obscurity surrounding desires difficult to name or discuss and the potential for eloquently expressed desire.

Finnegans Wake presents an interior landscape in which exposing desires (without the protection of such psychological barriers as denial or repression) feels terribly dangerous. The text pairs the experience of pleasure with the social punishments leveled on those subjects who are fluent in the explicit expression of desire. Responding to an increasingly repressive political atmosphere in his own time and anticipating the horrors of the AIDS crisis, Joyce suggests the ways in which disease is as much a social phenomenon constructed as a punishment for the exposure of unauthorized pleasures as it is a biological fact of the body. In *Ulysses*, Joyce articulates this idea through the citizen's punning reference to British "syphilisation." The citizen equates British difference from Irish culture with disease; disease is also presented as a form of punishment for that difference. (I will return to this moment in *Ulysses*.) In a surprising response to the discursive construction of disease as divine punishment, Joyce chooses a verbal form of contagion by employing the virulent discourse of rumor to express the contours of desire. This contagious language provides an encouraging model for a changeable and responsive discourse of sexual pleasure.

In *Finnegans Wake*, homoerotic desires serve a double function: these desires disrupt static sexual categories in order to expand the array of possible pleasures; and they also interrupt the rote transmission of information, transforming cliché into the mutable and suggestive forms of rumor. Rumor is the genre for information that cannot be entered into the official discourse; it is the genre for the unmentionable pleasures whose names cannot be spoken. The information transmitted by rumor is as changeable as Humphrey Chimpden Earwicker's sexuality. When HCE is described by other characters in a homoerotic situation, such as his encounter in the park in the second chapter, the rumor serves to place stable categories of sexuality in question. Joyce chose Oscar Wilde as one of the figures on whom he would pattern HCE and in doing so reflected both the complexity and variation of Wilde's sexuality and the degree to which he was shunned and persecuted for his perceived sin. Like Wilde's, HCE's much-discussed "sin" engages both homoerotic pleasures and a love for a younger person (sometimes figured as his incestuous desire for his daughter and sometimes for a younger man who may be a version of his sons). HCE is also modeled on the heterosexual Charles Stewart Parnell, whose reputation (like Wilde's) was ruined by rumors of his sexual engagements.[3] In order to reflect the complexity of desire, *Finnegans Wake* complicates the categorical discourse of sexual identity. Characters in this text do not have static identities. Rather, they participate in a series of changeable exchanges of pleasure. Homoerotic references and narratives are often indicators of both actual homosexual exchanges and of a proliferation in possible expressions of pleasure. For this reason, I will often describe these moments as "posterior pleasures," both for their male homoerotic references and also for their implication of changeable pleasures.[4]

HCE's sexual encounters are figured as hidden and socially unacceptable through their association with the lower, hidden, and posterior regions of the body. But these regions and these pleasures are also figured as revolutionary in their potential to produce multiple possibilities from singular acts. This constellation of conceptual associations is condensed in the word "aposterioprismically" (*FW* 612.19), which combines the posterior with the prism to indicate that the posterior realm is the locus of multiplicity where the singular input of light is multiplied by the prism into many colors. The posterior, which is also often represented in *Finnegans Wake* as the male homoerotic region of the body, is the gateway for this multiple experience of pleasure. In representing sodomy as the locus of multiplying desires, Joyce reverses the shift that narrowed the definition of sodomy to anal penetration from its initial ecclesiastical definition as any act performed for sexual pleasure without the intention of procreation.[5] Joyce represents posterior pleasures as revolutionary by pairing internal experiences of "unmentionable" desires with external revolutionary events, such as the conversion of the Druids to Christianity (the word "aposterioprismically" comes from the section of the *ricorso* in which that event is narrated), the Crimean War, in which Buckley shoots the exposed Russian General, and the Easter Rising (I will return to these moments near the close of this essay). Posterior pleasures are linked both to political revolutions and to social revolutions that are perceived to be as threatening as their political counterparts. In representing that threat, Joyce draws on the origins of the term *bugger* (used to refer to a homosexual), which arose from slang references to heresy as Bulgarian (bugger derives from *Bulgarus*).[6] Writing about homoeroticism, he emphasizes the relationship between unsettling ideas, or heresies, and disruptive sexual pleasures.

HCE is perceived by the gossips who narrate his story as a source of contagion, both biological and cultural. The gossips describe him as both diseased and an agent of disease (not just Earwicker but a bug, in effect), and as such he is the cause of dis-ease. His behavior is the subject of gossip and rumors that are constantly evolving and being transmitted in incessant talk that seems contagious. Joyce's exploration of changes and mutations in the language of rumor might be understood through an analogy to his description of biological contagion in sexually transmitted diseases. The disorder in *Finnegans Wake*'s language is associated with disorders of the body, with disorders of social expectation, and with HCE's disorderly sexual desires.

A virus, which etymologically means poison (or slimy liquid) and is often referred to colloquially as a *bug,* models just such a disordering in the body and in culture. This word spans the genetic alterations that cause disease and the social alterations that encompass cultural poisons such as rumors, which are often described as *virulent.* The viral association I explore here works both to address Joyce's social critique and his linguistic play. It engages the significance of mutability in the organization of individual words and letters and also in the organization of social relations. *Finnegans Wake,* as I will argue, intertwines destructive and creative forces in language and in culture to show that social control, like intellectual understanding, is always partial and shifting.

Finnegans Wake also reflects an understanding of pleasure as a mutable form by representing it in an analogously mutable discourse. Joyce chooses rumor as one form that, because it is fundamentally altered with each telling or each hearing, reflects the nature of desire. He develops a written form that will work according to the same mechanism as rumor: it will alter with each reading and alter each reader to reflect the changeable nature of the desires it represents. In I.iv, HCE is put on trial for his rumored posterior pleasures. An incriminating letter dug out of the midden heap by the little hen is introduced into the evidence against him, along with a history of where the letter had been before it arrived in court.

> Wind broke it. Wave bore it. Reed wrote of it. Syce ran with it. Hand tore it and wild went war. Hen trieved it and plight pledged peace. It was folded with cunning, sealed with crime, uptied by a harlot, undone by a child. It was life but was it fair? It was free but was it art? The old hunks on the hill read it to perlection. It made ma make merry and sissy so shy and rubbed some shine off Shem and put some shame into Shaun. (*FW* 94.5–12).

Each member of the Earwicker family has read this letter and has responded to it or been affected by it. HCE, the "old hunks" on Howth hill, has "read it to perlection" or perfection, while reading it made ALP merry and Issy shy. Shem either looses some shine (Shaun), by having it rubbed off, or becomes increasingly shiny (having rubbed some shine on) as a result of his reading: he becomes both more and less like Shaun. Shaun, in turn, begins to resemble Shem: it puts some "shame" (Shem) into him. Members of the family have in turn affected or altered the letter. HCE's wind has broken it, ALP's waves have borne it, and Shaun the post has run with it. But Shem's alteration of the letter is the most interesting. Shem, referred to here as "Reed" or a reader and a pen made from a reed, writes of it, an alteration that is equated, by its place in the sequence, with the more physical alterations made by the rest of the family. The process of interpretation, a process in which readers write, has fundamentally altered the text of the letter as readers of *Finnegans Wake* are guided to alter Joyce's text through the act of reading.

The interdependence of reading and writing is also explored in relation to Shaun, who is questioned about writing during his *via crucis*.[7] At the last station of the cross, he is asked: "Still in a way, not to flatter you, we fancy you that you are so strikingly brainy and well letterread in yourshelves as ever were the Shamous Shamonous, Limited, could use worse of yourself, ingenious Shaun, we still so fancied, if only you would take your time so and the trouble of so doing it" (*FW* 425.4–8). Though Shaun is merely a "well letterread" (illiterate) postman, he is also "brainy" and well read, a man of letters, well lettered. The interlocutor wonders why Shaun cannot do as well as Shem ("Shamous Shamonous") if he were to choose to write himself.

Shaun replies that if he chose to, he could write as well as his brother. Though he is illiterate, he would dictate to a scribe, "I'd pinsel [pencil, write] it with immenuensoes [amanuenses, innuendo]" (*FW* 425.18). Like the rumors or innuendoes circulating about his father's disease, Shaun's writing would be subject to changes and distortion in the transmittal process. The first reader would be the amanuensis, the person who listened to Shaun's dictation. That reader would also in the most literal sense be the writer of Shaun's text. In the gap between listening and recording, reading and writing, there is always ample room in the world of the *Wake* for distortion and alteration.

Shaun, however, ultimately dismisses the possibility of writing, comparing the activity to contagious disease. "I would never for anything take so much trouble of such doing. And why so? Because I am altogether a chap too fly and hairyman [In Dublin slang, both *fly* and *hairy* indicate cunning][8] for to infra-dig the like of that ultravirulence" (*FW* 425. 332–35). Shaun envisions writing as a disgusting undertaking, a conclusion not surprising given his brother's practice of writing on his body with his own excrement. Shaun finds this filthy activity completely beneath him in part because he imagines that writing might be quite dangerous, poisonous, contagious, or "ultravirulent." Shaun's description of writing as viral implicitly defines textual production as a combination of reading and writing that creates a mutable language, one that is constantly in the process of alteration and as such is both undesirable and virulently dangerous. Responding in this way, Shaun takes up his typically conservative position in response to his brother's more revolutionary disposition. Shaun's fear of Shem's writing is a version of the fear of posterior pleasures. Shem's source of creativity is heterodox and revolutionary, as indicated by the fact that he gets his ink from his posterior.[9] Creativity, then, is figured as a revolutionary force analogous to the sexual revolution posed by homoerotic expression.

The writing Shaun refuses as disgusting and virulently contagious is also viral, in that it is tropic or heavily metaphorical, relying on associative links between disparate ideas. It is also tropic in the viral sense in that these links produce alterations in each of the component parts. Just as a virus alters to fit (to be tropic to) the host cell it enters, this language alters with the associations it compiles. The analogy between tropism in language and in viruses can be located in the mechanics of viral infection and replication.

Viruses are unique among biological parasites in that they lack the structures necessary for sustaining or reproducing themselves. A virus consists solely of a strand of genetic material, either DNA or RNA, and a surrounding envelope of protein or lipoprotein. In order to replicate itself, a virus must invade a host cell and commandeer its structures for reproduction. The ability of a virus to attach to a host cell depends on tropism. Tropism indicates an inclination or turning; a virus might be said to incline toward a certain host cell.[10] Tropism has the same etymological root as the trope in language (a turn, in language a turn of phrase, or figure of speech). Tropism is also a helpful way to imagine the mechanism of desire in the *Wake*. Desire is figured as a changeable and responsive system much like the tropic system of the virus or the tropism of language, in which pairings are based on partial and shifting similarities. Joyce makes the analogy between biological and literary tropisms differently. His image for this relation is the heliotrope, a flower that inclines toward light and that figures desire in the *Wake*.

The tropism of viruses is often explained through the metaphor of a lock and key. Just as each key fits into and opens only one kind of lock, viruses are tropic to particular kinds of cells that "recognize" their exterior envelopes and allow them to bind onto the cell's surface, to enter, and to reproduce using the cell's own machinery for replication. For the most part, the cell itself is treated opportunistically as a machine that will produce replicas of the virus through the mechanisms with which the cell more usually reproduces itself. Often the host cell is destroyed entirely after replication takes place. Joyce recognized that the official discourse of most Western legal and religious bodies demands that sexuality be tropic in this particularly predictable way: that each lock fit only one key. But he also recognized the limitations of this orthodoxy. Desire is shifting and changeable, and human tropisms resist both prediction and regulation. Joyce envisioned sexual desire in a manner I would compare to the tropism of a nonequilibrium virus for its host cell. New viruses, like HIV, are in a constant state of alteration that makes the particular fit between the virus and its host cell variable and shifting. And though HIV is always tropic to the immune system's T cells, the particular way it fits those cells changes so frequently that antibodies cannot guard against the joining of HIV to a T cell. To pursue the analogy with human sexuality, even when the partners stay the same, the desires shift and alter.

Once allowed inside a cell, retroviruses, the family of viruses to which HIV belongs, replicate themselves quite differently from other viruses. This difference arises from the fact that the genetic material of a retrovirus is RNA (single-strand chromosomes) rather than DNA (which is double). Accordingly, retroviral RNA can act as a template to perform a different kind of replication in the cells to which it is tropic. Rather than remaining fairly separate from the host and merely making use of the cell's reproductive facilities, the retrovirus actually inserts itself within the host cell's genes (inserting its altering phrase in the host cell's sentence, in effect),[11] forming a template within the existent and now altered genome.

The replication of the retrovirus parallels the mechanisms of rumor in that rumor also functions as an intrusive phrase in the sentence of official discourse. It is a phrase that, though it remains relatively hidden, can change official views just as HIV changes the functioning of the host cell. The scandal of Oscar Wilde's unlicensed pleasures, as Ed Cohen effectively demonstrates, substantially altered public conceptions of homosexuality.[12] Yet the specificities of his love were hidden in rumors of the "unspeakable"; the particulars could not be entered into official history.

I make the specific comparison between rumor and retroviruses because other viruses are far more independent from their hosts. Retroviruses, however, actually integrate themselves into the host's genes. Rumor, I am arguing through this retroviral analogy, has an equally subtle and insidious effect on official language. It shifts public perception while itself remaining both integral and relatively obscure.

Until recently, certain cancers were the most commonly recognized retro-viral products; the rapidly spreading cancer is comprised of the altered host cells that reproduce themselves though they no longer have the same cellular functioning. In the last decade, however, HIV has become the most widely recognized and researched retrovirus. The tragedy of HIV is that the cells with which it is tropic are the helper T lymphocytes. More commonly referred to as T cells, these cells are a part of the immune system whose function it is to recognize foreign agents within the body and disable them. Yet, HIV is tropic to these T cells. In other words, the structure of HIV's key fits perfectly into the T cell lock and finds immediate access. Not only do these viruses foil the T cell's ability to expunge them, but by altering those cells in order to reproduce themselves, they prevent the T cells from carrying out their immune function, from recognizing any other foreign agents. The HIV retroviral alteration of the T cell cripples the innermost defenses of the immune system. This situation can be tragic ultimately for the parasite as well as for its host, for without the host's continued health, the parasite cannot survive.

To make a slightly irreverent, but for me quite illuminating, comparison, retroviruses function in the biological system of the genetic code much the way I participated as a child in a game I called Telephone but many children refer to as Gossip. Readers may be familiar with this verbal game, which works much like a rumor. The object is both to concoct a message that is difficult to say and to have it return to its sender exactly as it was sent. This procedure is close to the process that drives the replication of cells based on their genetic code; the aim is to repeat the code without alteration from cell division to cell division. The game is more fun, of course, if the message gets garbled along the way. As a child, I habitually cheated to achieve this affect. I inserted an inappropriate word in the message, a word that I wanted to spark laughter at the end of the transmission. HIV, in a considerably less amusing version of my childhood strategy, inserts itself in the message of genetic code and significantly alters the end result of the code's transmission.

HIV, like influenza and ebola, is a nonequilibrium virus in that it is not sufficiently "evolved to coexist with humans" and can therefore be "strikingly lethal to us."[13] Because the nonequilibrium virus has not evolved a stable or mutually beneficial relationship with its host, the virus itself is in a constant process of mutation and selection. A nonequilibrium virus continuously evolves until it achieves compatibility with its host, this rapid alteration makes it impossible for the host's antigen system to recognize or disable the virus. And the infectious disease that results is therefore highly unstable and unpredictable. HIV's process of change and alteration is part of what makes it so difficult for physicians to treat or cure AIDS, the disease that results from the virus's incursions. During the adaptation process, which HIV is still undergoing, the virus is more likely to harm and even kill its host.

The nonequilibrium phase is a revolutionary stage in viral development in which the effort to foster a new biological system has the violent effects of disease. In this way nonequilibrium viruses have an influence similar to the revolutionary force of sexual desire Joyce explores. The nonequilibrium virus is a new combination of familiar genetic material that disrupts a physiological system in equilibrium. The interaction of the nonequilibrium virus and the defenses of the immune system (in the case of HIV) produce the occasion for disease. Similarly, the posterior pleasures Joyce explores in *Finnegans Wake* are merely new combinations of existing verbal and sexual practices that enter an orthodox legal and social environment defended against heterodox desires. The place of meeting between the orthodox and the heterodox is similar to the interaction between the nonequilibrium virus and its host where disease is a by-product. The by-products of evolving heterodox practices within orthodox environments are dis-ease, gossip, shunning, and punishment.

There are, however, a number of viruses, some of them retroviral, that have reached equilibrium with their human hosts and are completely unthreatening in their parasitism. Occasionally, these viruses develop a mutually beneficial form of symbiosis. (In much the same way, the critical examination of sexual orthodoxies through the introduction of posterior pleasures is necessary to the continued health of a social system that otherwise suffers from the problems of hypermasculinity, patriarchy, and homophobia.) Because medical research tends to focus on viral agents of disease, we are less familiar with these beneficial viruses. The current concentration of research in virology (due in large part to the damage wrought by HIV) and the mapping of the human genome, however, are bringing these beneficial viruses into sharper focus. In a recent issue of *Virology,* for example, Venables and his coauthors speculate that an endogenous retrovirus (in other words, a retrovirus present in the human genome from birth) may provide the mechanism that allows women to carry embryos within their bodies in pregnancy (unlike other species such as birds or fish whose progeny gestate outside the body). Though research on this retrovirus, ERV-3, is still in its initial stages, the authors speculate that ERV-3 has a beneficial function for its host because it has been conserved throughout primate evolution. Additionally, the site of its expression in the placental cell layer that separates mother from child and its similarity to other immunosuppressive agents suggest that "ERV-3 may serve to protect the fetus from immune attack by the mother."[14] In other words, this retrovirus may interfere with the immune response that would otherwise expel the fetus as a foreign agent within the woman's body. The fact that humans can carry progeny to term within the body increases the likelihood of survival exponentially both for us and for the retrovirus we carry.

The ambiguous potential of the virus to assist either creation or destruction parallels the possibility that radical changes in the social structure (such as how we understand sexuality) will be viral. On the one hand, by breaking down the immune system of social control, these changes leave the body politic open to disturbing alterations, as the physical body is open to debilitating contagion.

This interpretation is the one that motivates the rhetoric of conservative political movements. But there is also the alternative possibility that the increased openness wrought by lowered defenses will create the opportunity for creativity in much the same way ERV-3 promotes procreation by disabling a part of the immune system. *Finnegans Wake* clearly advocates the condition of increased openness, and in doing so anticipates the experience of the AIDS crisis, in which we have discovered that silence is the most debilitating of the symptoms of this disease and that the disease can also give voice to a number of new modes of expression.

The contagious disease that most preoccupied literature at the beginning of the twentieth century was the bacterial illness syphilis. Joyce incorporates some of the social fear of this disease quite explicitly in *Ulysses* with the citizen's punning "syphilisation" and implicitly in *Finnegans Wake* as a "vile disease."

In a drunken interlude in the "Cyclops" episode, the citizen is heard pontificating on the necessity of a nationalist movement in Irish politics. His objective is to police Irish culture and protect it from the incursions of contaminating British influence. To indicate these dangers, he implies that, along with their culture, British colonists brought syphilis to Ireland. The citizen equates foreign civilization and foreign disease in his punning reference to British colonial influence as their "syphilisation" (*U* 12.1197).[15] Recognizing the violent incursions of colonial culture, but in partial contrast to the citizen's more bigoted views, *Ulysses* advocates the benefits of exposure to difference, making a connection between hybridity and civilization through the hybridized figure, Leopold Bloom. Disease is one harmful by-product of this mingling between cultures; political repression is another. But the products of the Irish literary renaissance might also be seen as the creations of this hybrid.

The citizen's statement reflects a static (or orthodox) definition of cultural identity based on purity, a definition that has its parallel in an orthodox understanding of sexual identity. But his pun on civilization as "syphilisation," with its mixture of two words, also reflects the colonized nation, with its mixture of two incommensurably different worlds. Advocating a return to the purity of Irish language and Irish sport, the citizen's politics do not tolerate the hybridity wrought by colonial culture or reflected in his pun. His position contrasts sharply with Joyce's interest in double, versatile, ambiguous, and even contaminated subjects. *Finnegans Wake* presents the English language as inherently impure, diseased by the agents of other languages such as Latin, Greek, and German. The citizen's political vision, in contrast, idealizes an identity based on purity, on categorical divisions in which difference is not to be allowed. The equation of disease and difference in the word "syphilisation" is an equation commonly applied to sexual difference. The citizen's "syphilisation" operates in the realm of national identity as both the symptom of cultural contamination and its punishment. His suspicions about national contamination are often repeated in the realm of orthodox sexual identity politics, where disease is figured as both the symptom of, and the retribution for, contaminated sexual "purity." Even before the tragedy of AIDS, as *Finnegans Wake* makes clear, stereotyping made it possible to equate unlicensed sexual love in general, and homosexual love specifically, with disease.

In the *Wake*, as in *Ulysses*, Joyce explores the cultural assumptions and stereotypes linked to disease, opening the space for my argument against an ideology that would address a chance biological occurrence as a moral indicator. *Finnegans Wake* explores contagion through its preoccupation with rumor and also through its thematic focus on HCE as the host for a parasite, the earwig evoked by his last name, Earwicker. (Earwigs get their name from the once common belief that they entered the brain through the ear and lived there parasitically.) The operation of contagion in the text, as both a biological and a cultural phenomenon, serves to anticipate our contemporary concerns with the AIDS pandemic. At the beginning of the AIDS crisis the disease was dubbed with the inaccurate and unfortunate tag "the gay plague." Of course HIV is transmitted by the mingling of bodily fluids no matter the circumstance for their mingling. Nonetheless, verbal exchange or rumor at the beginning of the AIDS crisis (rumor that has remained unnervingly resilient in the face of contrary medical evidence) ascribed a kind of moral intentionality to the biological accident or happenstance of infection. The bigoted cultural link between homosexual intercourse and the scourge of AIDS has been instrumental in prolonging the crisis; and a pernicious suppression of information and refusal to educate in the most basic ways about prevention has insured the spread of the virus, whereas spread of information, an infection in discourse, would have prevented some physical contagion.

In chapter 2 of *Finnegans Wake* the connection between sexuality and disease is made explicit in rumors about HCE. The association between his status as a bug and his catching a bug, in the sense of becoming infected with a disease, is implicit. In this section, Earwicker's putative sin is reintroduced and circulated without being specifically named. (The very unspeakability of the event connects it to Wilde's "love that dare not speak its name.") In the course of a discussion about his sin, the rumor circulates that HCE has contracted a disease.

A baser meaning has been read into these characters the literal sense of which decency can safely scarcely hint. It has been blurtingly bruited by certain wisecrackers (the stinks of Mohorat are in the nightplots of the morning), that he suffered from a vile disease. Athma, unmanner them! To such a suggestion the one selfrespecting answer is to affirm that there are certain statements which ought not to be, and one should like to hope to be able to add, ought not to be allowed to be made. Nor have his detractors, who, an imperfectly warmblooded race, apparently conceived him as a great white caterpillar capable of any and every enormity in the calendar recorded to the discredit of the Juke and Kellikek families, mended their case by insinuating that, alternately, he lay at one time under the ludicrous imputation of annoying Welsh fusiliers in the people's park. (*FW* 33.14–27)

The gossips, drawing on the same posterior source of creativity as Shem "(the stinks of Mohorat are in the nightplots of the morning)," speculate that HCE has contracted a disease, or bug, and that he is a bug. They describe him as a great white caterpillar, a characterization that coincides with Lady Campbell's description of Oscar Wilde. Like Wilde's detractors, HCE's believe him capable of every enormity, equating him with the American Juke and Kallikek families who were hereditary degenerates;[16] they believe, in other words, that he suffers from a genetic disorder. Because syphilis can be hereditary, the gossips' implication connects a sexual "sin" with biological retribution in the form of disease.

Spreading a rumor based on their interpretation of HCE's character(s) (and perhaps specifically the character *E*, which stands for Earwicker, earwig, i.e., bug), the gossips speculate that his "vile disease" (which might be condensed into the characters *VD* and stand for venereal disease) was contracted while "annoying Welsh fusiliers in the people's park." The habitual connection in the book between shooting and shitting implies HCE's enjoyment of a posterior pleasure. The gossip's interpretation involves a literal reading ("literal sense") that is bad enough that decency forbids its discussion; and a "baser meaning" may also be derived (a meaning more basic or deep but also more base or indecent). The very fact that the gossips avoid literal reference to HCE's "sin" evokes the silencing of desire and implies that his transgression is sodomy, the unnameable sin: "The Latin designation for sodomy was *crimen non nominandum inter christanos*—the crime not to be named among Christians."[17] Ed Cohen notes that "sodomy had been defined in ecclesiastical terms as one of the gravest sins against divine law whose name alone proved such an affront to God that it was often named only as the unnameable."[18]

Defending HCE against these "ludicrous" charges, this narrator reinscribes the crime by forbidding its utterance and proclaiming that there are "certain statements which ought not to be, and one should like to hope to be able to add, ought not to be allowed to be made." In censuring the gossips, the narrator echoes Joyce's critic Shane Leslie, who in a review of *Ulysses* wrote: "There are some things which cannot and, we should like to be able to say, shall not be done."[19] Leslie's response to *Ulysses* reinforces the ideology that would silence the discourse of desire and repress loves by silencing their names and their stories. Joyce returns Leslie's critique by altering the code slightly, as a retrovirus or bug might alter the genetic code, in order to create a more flexible language that can express desire. The discussion of whether to name indecencies allows the gossips to participate in a licentious verbal exchange, which this narrator would curtail for reasons of "purity."

Inserting their phrase, the rumored version of the story, into the sentence of received wisdom, HCE's detractors also act in the manner of retroviruses, altering the information they receive in order to create something new. HCE's sexual practice and contracted disease is their conception; it is both their thought or interpretation and simultaneously their creation, the idea to which they give birth. Their "base" meaning is the basic text we read, Joyce's writing; but they also interpret just as Shane Leslie, in his role as critic, interprets the "base" meaning of *Ulysses*. In the act of interpretation, these gossips create something new. Deducing a "base" meaning from the text, they in turn create a new text, a bug that, like a computer virus, infects future versions of the code in which it intervenes.

Among the characters who gossip about HCE's fall is his daughter, Isabel, who appears in the guise of Sylvia Silence, the girl detective. She is identifiable through a link to "Doveland" and through her lisp, gorgeously described as "her vowelthreaded syllabelles" (*FW* 61.6). She comments: "Have you evew thought, wepowtew that sheew gweatness was his twadgedy? Nevewtheless accowding to my considewed attitudes fow this act he should pay the full penalty, pending puwsuance, as pew Subsec. 32, section 11, of the C.L.A. act 1885, anything in this act to the contwawy notwithstanding" (*FW* 61.6–11). Issy's comment is characteristically double and ambivalent in perfect accord with her multiple personalities. She expresses sympathy in proposing that sheer greatness was her father's tragedy, but it is the sort of punitive sympathy that assumes every rise (or arousal) must be punished with a fall. She associates her father with Oscar Wilde, suggesting that HCE be tried under the law that sent Wilde to prison. But by adding the disclaimer, anything in this act to the contrary notwithstanding, she both sounds a harsh note that would ignore any possible exceptions within the law and also allows for the possibility that there might be something in HCE's act that would contradict rumor and make the act of 1885 an inappropriate law under which to judge him.

Section 11 of the Criminal Law Amendment Act of 1885 prohibited "indecent relations between consenting adult males."[20] Passing this criminal act was an important event in defining official legal and penal attitudes toward sexuality because it marked the first time in the British Empire that homosexual pleasure as such was prohibited by statute. The law "defined new statutory limits on male sexuality," Ed Cohen notes; "as amended in order to include the now infamous section 11, also known by its author's name as the 'Labouchere amendment,' it also became the occasion for reclassifying the legal status of sexual acts between men for the first time since 'sodomy' was made a civil offense in Britain in 1533."[21] Under the law enacted by Henry VIII, sodomy alone was a capital offense and was not defined exclusively as a homosexual activity. Rather, the law made death the penalty for any act of "Buggery committed with Mankind or Beast." The law was most famously used in defense of women sodomized by their husbands in the course of gross domestic sexual abuse. Section 11 altered that law to reflect a homophobic ideology in that it altered the prohibition of one specific activity in order to legislate against all sexual relations between men.[22]

Writing about desire several decades after the passage of this law, Joyce responds to a situation in which homosexual erotic activity has been explicitly and completely censured throughout the British Empire. As he finished *Finnegans Wake,* Joyce saw the rise of a regime in Germany that labeled homosexuals with armbands, sent them to work camps, and ultimately murdered many. By associating homoerotic arousal with political revolution, Joyce signals a belief in the systemic similarity between oppressive national politics such as fascism and imperialism and the social politics of sexual control and suppression. He responds to the resurgence of such repressive politics through his subversive discourse of desire. In *Finnegans Wake,* the discourse of sexuality is located both in official languages of suppression (such as the 1885 law) and also in unofficial exchanges of gossip, rumor, riddles, and banter in which the judgment implied is matched by the enjoyment of discussing posterior pleasures. Sexuality finds its way into language whether it be the discourse of regulation and judgment, or of suggestion and pleasure. Silence, as a moment within that discourse, becomes a marker of the closet, of the condemnation expressed in official discourses, and also a marker of the place where language has gone underground into the contagious discourse of the erotic that *Finnegans Wake* re-creates.

The varying associative connections between homoerotic desire, contagious disease, and the mutable language of rumor are gathered in Earwicker's name. His name is illuminated, in the perverse logic of this book, through a riddle. In a dialogue concerning the encounter between Buckley and the Russian General (an encounter that replicates HCE's experience in the park), Taff proposes a riddle to Butt: "my farst is near to hear and my sackend is meet to sedon while my whole's a peer's aureolies" (*FW* 340.35–341.1).

The clearest answer to the riddle is HCE's name: Earwicker. The first part sounds like hear and has the same function: *ear.* The second is made to sit on as *wicker* is made into a chair on which to sit. Together they form a *perce oreille,* French for "earwig." This first answer to the riddle highlights ears and hearing or listening. An alternative answer to the puzzle might highlight the piercing of the rear. *Hear* also sounds like *rear,* and "sackend" carries within it the sound of an end or rear end. Another possible answer to the second clue might be that an arse is made to sit on. The whole is a pair of aureoles, haloes that might be imagined as a pair of globes, or an arse. The word "peer's" suggests the penetration of the arse through the sound association with piercing in English and *perse* in Estonian, which means arse.

HCE's name pairs posterior pleasures and listening. The earwig pun suggests a penetration of the ear, bringing together the motif of sexual, and specifically anal, penetration and a motif of verbal exchange. The Earwicker name also prompts the idea of the distortions of gossip or rumor in that its meaning can be altered by every interpretation of the riddle to reveal the association to the earwig as an emblem of listening (penetration of the ear) or buggery (penetration of the arse). The riddle also has national political implications, if we are to hear in "peer's auriolies" the names of Easter Rising soldiers Patrick Pearse and Michael Joseph Rahilly[23] or the Irish Republican Brotherhood ballad writer John Boyle O'Reilly.[24]

The same cluster of associations between the Easter Rising and homoerotic arousal is condensed in "The Ballad of Persse O'Reilly," which contains another version of HCE's rumored sexual encounter in the park.

> He was joulting by Wellinton's monument
> Our rotorious hippopopotamuns
> When some bugger let down the backtrap of the omnibus
> And he caught his death of fusiliers,
> > (Chorus) With his rent in his rears.
> > Give him six years.
>
> <div align="right">(<i>FW</i> 47.7–12)</div>

The beginning of the verse is replete with images recalling HCE's encounter. The image of the Wellington Monument situates a reader both at the scene of a battle (with its reference to the soldier who defeated Napoleon) and at the "scene of the crime" in Phoenix Park. The monument has obvious phallic overtones. The description of HCE as a "bugger" who let down his "backtrap" recalls the variant associations in HCE's name with sodomy, insects, disease, and penetration of the ear, or listening. The result of the encounter, "he caught his death of fusiliers" (a repetition of the earlier rumor concerning HCE: that he was "annoying Welsh fusiliers in the people's park" [*FW* 33.26–27]) emphasizes the relations between a public uprising and private arousal through associations between shitting, shooting, and ejaculation.

The choral section of this verse recalls the situation of the Irish tenant farmers whose plight was one impetus for Irish resistance to British imperial rule. Forced to pay rent during unproductive years and even during famine, tenants often fell behind in payments and found their rent in arrears ("With his rent in his rears"). In extreme cases, they were jailed ("Give him six years"). Joyce links this history of oppressive economic control with sexual control through the double implication of "rent"; for the chorus also describes the rent in HCE's rear, his openness to posterior pleasures, an openness that could also be punished by jailing.

Joyce charts a complex connection between language and sexuality in which the obscurity of his language mirrors the hidden territories of sexual desire. He makes this suggestion in part by presenting verbal activity (writing text, gossiping, listening) as another form of bodily activity with relations to sexual enjoyment and also to the effects of disease. The body becomes a text in *Finnegans Wake*.

HCE serves as a cipher for common perceptions of homosexuality and buggery that are themselves diseased (and uneasy), and that project that disease onto the homosexual. Joyce heard "vir" in "virus" and tried to redefine a particular notion of masculinity, virility, rather than homosexuality, as a virulent category only partially susceptible to control. The emergence of HIV after *Finnegans Wake* was written complicates and emotionalizes Joyce's project to an almost unbearable degree. The dynamic of the contagious discourse employed in the *Wake* is exactly the dynamic employed by HIV in its incursions into the human immune system, where it inserts its phrase into the host's sentence. Joyce adopts the strategy not so much to expose the body or the consciousness to incursions from outside that will cripple it, but rather to create a "rent" in the "rear," a backdoor through which new possibilities can enter.

NOTES

1. Paul Monette, *Becoming a Man: Half a Life Story* (New York: Harcourt Brace Jovanovich, 1992), 1–2.

2. "The 'Love that dare not speak its name' in this century is such a great affection of an elder for a younger man as there was between David and Jonathan, such as Plato made the very basis of his philosophy, and such as you can find in the sonnets of Michelangelo and Shakespeare. It is that deep, spiritual affection that is as pure as it is perfect. It dictates and pervades great works of art like those of Shakespeare and Michelangelo, and those two letters of mine, such as they are. It is in this century misunderstood, so much misunderstood that it may be described as the 'Love that dare not speak its name,' and on account of it I am placed where I am now. It is beautiful, it is fine, it is the noblest form of affection. There is nothing unnatural about it. It is intellectual, and it repeatedly exists between an elder and a younger man, when the elder man has intellect, and the younger man has all the joy, hope and glamour of life before him. That it should be so the world does not understand. The world mocks at it and sometimes puts one in the pillory for it." Quoted in Richard Ellmann, *Oscar Wilde* (New York: Random House, 1984), 463.

3. I am indebted to Vicki Mahaffey for her understanding of this pairing of Wilde and Parnell in the person of HCE. See her chapter in this volume.

4. My focus on homoeroticism in this essay is entirely skewed to male models, though it would certainly be possible to derive similar ideas from lesbian erotic references surrounding Issy by examining her sexualized relations to her other selves (the rainbow girls or Nuvoletta).

5. Ed Cohen, *Talk on the Wilde Side: Toward a Genealogy of a Discourse on Male Sexualities* (New York: Routledge, 1993), 117.

6. Oxford English Dictionary.

7. In his correspondence (*LI* 214, 216), Joyce remarks that he is constructing chapter 13 of the *Wake* on the framework of the *via crucis*, the path Jesus journeyed when he carried his cross to his own crucifixion. Shaun follows the same path, and at each of the fourteen traditional stations along the way, he is asked a question.

8. Roland McHugh, *Annotations to "Finnegans Wake"* (Baltimore: Johns Hopkins University Press, 1980), 425.

9. A more orthodox metaphor for the writing process might make the expected corporal equation between a pen and the phallus.

10. Robin Morantz Henig provides a clear explanation of viral tropism in *A Dancing Matrix* (New York: Alfred A. Knopf, 1993): "The way a virus causes disease depends on tropism, or movement toward a particular host cell. . . . The rhinovirus is tropic for the lining of the nose and throat; it kills the cells there, and you have the miserable symptoms of the common cold" (75).

11. I borrow this metaphor from Lee Edelman. who, in "The Plague of Discourse: Politics, Literary Theory, and AIDS," also explores the connection between language and disease and the contagions that link them. Comparing the mechanics of viral infection to the rhetoric surrounding AIDS, Edelman describes the retrovirus HIV as a phrase that inserts itself in the host cell's sentence. See Lee Edelman, "The Plague of Discourse: Politics, Literary Theory, and AIDS," *South Atlantic Quarterly* 88 (1989): 301–17.

12. Cohen, *Talk*, 97.

13. David Baltimore, "The Enigma of HIV Infection," *Cell* 82 (July 1995): 175.

14. Patrick J. Venables, Sharon M. Brookes, David Griffiths, Robin A. Weiss, and Mark T. Boyd, "Abundance of an Endogenous Retroviral Envelope Protein in Placental Trophoplasts Suggests a Biological Function," *Virology* 211 (1995): 592.

15. While the citizen's specific example of syphilis importation might not be easily documented, the problem to which he refers was widespread. European colonial occupation brought with it, intentionally or accidentally, diseases for which indigenous populations, previously unexposed, had little immune defense. The most familiar example of this phenomenon is the devastating effect smallpox had on native populations in North and South America.

16. McHugh, *Annotations to "Finnegans Wake,"* 33.

17. Cohen, *Talk*, 240.

18. Cohen, *Talk*, 103.

19. Quoted in McHugh, *Annotations to "Finnegans Wake,"* 33.

20. Quoted in Ellmann, *Oscar Wilde*, 409.

21. Cohen, *Talk*, 72.

22. Cohen, *Talk*, 92.

23. For more on Patrick Pearse and Michael Joseph Rahilly see R. F. Foster, *Modern Ireland: 1600–1972* (London: Penguin Books, 1988), 449 and 473.

24. McHugh, *Annotations to "Finnegans Wake,"* 44.

Paring His Fingernails

Homosexuality and Joyce's Impersonalist Aesthetic

Tim Dean

I refuse to consider Art a drain-pipe for passion,
a kind of chamberpot, a slightly more elegant
substitute for gossip and confidences. No, no!
Genuine poetry is not the scum of the heart.
——Gustave Flaubert

"Joyce incarnates the enormous authority of sublimation in our culture," cautions Leo Bersani in his devastating critique "Against *Ulysses*," adding, "*Ulysses* is modernism's monument to that authority."[1] I would like to address this aspect of modernist literary authority, as Bersani formulates it, by considering how the project of "queering" Joyce might diminish or, on the other hand, secure the cultural authority that his fiction allegedly embodies. While it certainly would be plausible, given the current state of the humanities, to conceive of queering Joyce as simply the latest strategy in consolidating his cultural authority by updating his academic cachet, I prefer to argue that in fact we miss out on Joyce's true perversity if, as has recently been the case, we inflect Bersani's critique in more overtly sexual terms by attempting to unmask Joyce's rationale for aesthetic impersonality as nothing more than a sophisticated ruse of the closet. Whereas the conventional sublimation of homosexual into homosocial liaisons tends to reinforce the closet and its homophobic discipline, Joycean impersonality countersublimes a perverse *jouissance*, as even the initial censors of his work obscurely intuited. In order to make the case for a more thoroughgoing perversity in Joyce's writing, I shall review Bersani's critique and its implicit development—via Eve Kosofsky Sedgwick's epistemology of the closet—in recent Joyce scholarship, before outlining an alternate account of aesthetic impersonality that I shall argue provides access to a much queerer Joyce, one whose writing involves a distinctly antiauthoritarian mode of sublimation and there-

fore wields a very different kind of cultural authority. In proposing this reinter-
pretation of Joyce's impersonalist aesthetic, I offer the following account as a
preliminary intervention in the ongoing debate over the politics of Anglophone
literary modernism, since virtually all the high moderns subscribed to the doctrine of impersonality in one way or another.[2]

In "Against *Ulysses*" Bersani criticizes the premier novel of high modernism in
order to expose the redemptive principle animating modernist aesthetics in
general. In so doing, he develops Richard Poirier's earlier polemic, in *The Renewal of Literature,* against modernism's institutionalization of "difficulty" as a
historical necessity, which Poirier views as "an attempt to perpetuate the power
of literature as a privileged and exclusive form of discourse."[3] It is worth noting
that the critique mounted by Bersani and Poirier represents something considerably more significant than the standard academic complaint that modernism
is elitist in its demands on the reader (although Poirier does characterize modernism as "a snob's game").[4] Instead, by arguing principally with Eliot and Joyce,
Poirier aims ultimately to discredit "the notion that the writing and reading of
literature have a culturally redemptive power"[5]—exactly the notion that Bersani
attacks with equal vigor in *The Culture of Redemption.* The basic problem with
the idea that literature redeems life, according to Poirier and Bersani, is that this
assumption simultaneously devalues historical experience while normalizing
the modes of representing experience; as Bersani puts it, "The catastrophes of
history matter much less if they are somehow compensated for in art, and art
itself gets reduced to a kind of superior patching function."[6]

Although this redemptive aesthetic is far from new, the modernist locus
classicus to which it may be traced is Eliot's 1923 essay on *Ulysses,* which adver-
tises the "mythical method"—following Joyce's manipulation of "a continuous
parallel between contemporaneity and antiquity"—as "a way of controlling, of
ordering, of giving a shape and a significance to the immense panorama of futility and anarchy which is contemporary history."[7] Infamous Eliot sentences
such as this one clearly imply that "contemporary history" would remain mean-
ingless without the forms imposed on it by art, specifically art that follows the
mythical rather than the "narrative method." And just as clearly, Eliot is using
the occasion of Joyce's novel of 1922 to justify tactics employed in his own poem
of the same year, *The Waste Land,* whose commitment to a redemptive aesthetic
("These fragments I have shored against my ruins") has never been in doubt.[8]
These tactics and the displaced rationale that accompanies them indicate what
we might call Eliot's—and, by extension, Joyce's—nonmimetic realism, as distinct from the realism that dominated the nineteenth-century novel and that
Eliot's essay on Joyce declares outmoded. By *nonmimetic realism* I am referring
to Eliot's commitment to representing "contemporary history"—or, as he put it
in his manifesto for poetic difficulty two years earlier, "our civilization, as it ex-

ists at present"—indirectly and allusively. In this respect, the mythical method provides for fiction what "difficulty" provides for poetry.[9]

The problem with Eliot's advocating the mythical method as the only way to distill meaning and value from "the immense panorama of futility and anarchy which is contemporary history" lies not only in the devaluation of "contemporary history" that accompanies any redemptive aesthetic, but also in Eliot's less conspicuous revaluation of contemporary *literary* history.[10] By advancing such hyperbolic claims for the mythical method ("It has the importance of a scientific discovery"), Eliot converts formal innovations into historical necessities, thereby naturalizing as ineluctable the kind of aesthetic practices exhibited by *The Waste Land* and *Ulysses*. It is Eliot's nonmimetic realism, coupled with his presenting literary historical negotiations under the guise of historical exigencies equivalent to wartime fallout, that permits him to say about *Ulysses*, "I hold this book to be the most important expression which the present age has found; it is a book to which we are all indebted, and from which none of us can escape":[11]

> Mr. Joyce's parallel use of the *Odyssey* has a great importance. It has the importance of a scientific discovery. No one else has built a novel upon such a foundation before: it has never before been necessary. I am not begging the question in calling *Ulysses* a "novel"; and if you call it an epic it will not matter. If it is not a novel, that is simply because the novel is a form which will no longer serve; it is because the novel, instead of being a form, was simply the expression of an age which had not sufficiently lost all form to feel the need of something stricter. . . . The novel ended with Flaubert and with James. It is, I think, because Mr. Joyce and Mr. [Wyndham] Lewis, being "in advance" of their time, felt a conscious or probably unconscious dissatisfaction with the form, that their novels are more formless than those of a dozen clever writers who are unaware of its obsolescence.[12]

In this passage Eliot exercises the rhetorical ploys to which, in their different but related ways, Bersani, Poirier, and Guillory all object. However, my point in examining Eliot's advertisement for Joyce is to show how it might be viewed not only as a prime example of the redemptive aesthetic (one committed to repairing historical catastrophes, such as World War I, through new forms of art) but also as a strategy for securing Eliot's own position in *literary* history and its attendant institutions by means of a displaced emphasis on "*contemporary* history." If the mythical method can be understood better as a disguised form of self-promotion than as a cornerstone of the culture of redemption, then are we left with no option other than the reduction of modernist aesthetics to solely self-serving terms? While it is clear that the high moderns encouraged one another to believe, write according to, and even institutionalize Eliot's principles, the heroic prowess and redemptive power implicit in the "mythical method" nevertheless fail to fully account for high modernist aesthetics, as even Eliot himself was dimly aware. Rather than viewing critical rationales such as the mythical method, "difficulty," and impersonality as so many ill-constructed masks donned by modernist writers in order to camouflage their remarkably successful bids for cultural and institutional power, I think we should understand these rationales symptomatically, as conflicted critical responses to the queer energies unleashed by certain forms of modernist writing. I would like to suggest that instead of manifesting a will to power tinged with remarkably sexual overtones, as Poirier characterizes the impetus at work in *Dubliners* and *Portrait of the Artist*,[13] Joyce's impersonalist aesthetic generates a self-shattering sexual power that lends his writing a perverse exemplarity for queer sublimation.

As readers of Bersani's work will be aware, *self-shattering* is his term for the salutary ego-disrupting effects that stem from aesthetic—as well as from masochistic sexual—impulses. The salience of *The Culture of Redemption* for readers of Joyce (and many others besides) lies in its demonstration that sexual self-shattering is virtually synonymous with a kind of aesthetic power. Having discussed Bersani's account of sexuality elsewhere, I'd like here to consider further his argument about art, one that is not so much a supplement or analogue to his thesis on masochism as it is the indissociable obverse of his more familiar, if still poorly grasped, account of sex. Extrapolating from Freud's intuition that sexuality, in its capacity to undo the coherent ego, may be considered a tautology for masochism, Bersani locates the same renunciation of authoritative selfhood in "art," which he identifies with those moments of textual collapse when aesthetic self-implosion compels literature to withdraw from any pretension to rhetorical efficacy.[14] Paradoxically, art becomes compelling for Bersani when it ceases attempting to compel us into specific actions, when it gives up trying to persuade us to behave in predetermined ways. In such moments, Bersani hypothesizes, "art could be put on the side of sexuality in the Freudian opposition between civilization and pleasure."[15] The significance of this Wildean realignment of art lies partly in the political implications of what, elsewhere in *The Culture of Redemption,* Bersani calls "the errance of the imaginary"; speculating on the antiredemptive energies of Flaubert's *Bouvard et Pécuchet,* Bersani claims, "The incoherence of Flaubert's bonshommes is perhaps the novel's most precious achievement, for it suggests that the *errance* of the imaginary dissolves the identities that coercive strategies must assume in order to be effective. . . . [I]t proposes the aesthetic as a strategy for eluding definitions and identifications, and in so doing it suggests, paradoxically, the political uses of art's uselessness in any struggle for a free society."[16] In this way art is itself redeemed through its renunciation of all redemptive intent—a point to which I shall return.

Reconceptualizing both sexuality and art by counterposing to Freudian orthodoxy the more disturbing findings of psychoanalysis, Bersani considers which texts serve the culture of redemption (Freud's "civilization") and which ones undermine it. His critique of aesthetic practices organized on redemptive principles focuses most sharply on the myth of the coherent self, from which flows, he persuasively argues, the authority of art to redeem and coerce: "[T]he culture of redemption itself depends on even more fundamental assumptions about authoritative identities, about identity *as* authority."[17] Although I concur with Bersani's general critique of the culture of redemption, I wish to demur from his positioning of *Ulysses* within this redemptive aesthetic, since I read Joyce's novel as one of Bersani's best allies. And while he is concerned above all to question the cultural authority of art as it is commonly understood, Bersani's critique of *Ulysses* is aimed less at those readers who venerate Joyce's work as a sacred text or fetish than at the novel's own aesthetic strategies, which he credits with effectively promoting such an approach to art.[18] *Ulysses* is modernism's principal literary endorsement of sublimation, according to Bersani, because by inundating us with figures of its own ideal reader, Joyce's novel positions us as exegetes subordinate to its own authority. Referring to Joyce's practice of citation, Bersani argues that "Western culture is saved, indeed glorified, through literary metempsychosis: it dies in the Joycean parody and pastiche, but, once removed from historical time, it is resurrected as a timeless design. Far from contesting the authority of culture, *Ulysses* reinvents our relation to Western culture in terms of exegetical devotion, that is, as the exegesis of *Ulysses* itself."[19]

The issue of authorial control over the encyclopedic array of materials that *Ulysses* assembles is as crucial to Bersani's critique as it was to Eliot's advertisement for Joyce. Whereas Eliot attributes the novel's authority to Joyce's use of the mythical method, Bersani effectively ascribes authority to Joyce's impersonal aesthetic: "*Ulysses* indulges massively in quotation—quotation of individual characters, social groups, myths, other writers—but quotation in Joyce is the opposite of self-effacement. It is an act of appropriation, which can be performed without Joyce's voice ever being heard."[20] This question of authority—whether authorial, narratorial, or cultural—surfaces consistently in Joyce criticism, owing to the difficulty of locating in his work a unifying consciousness conventionally understood to be the author's.[21] And because this question of authority is for modernity inevitably a political as well as a hermeneutic concern, high modernists' efforts to eliminate authorial consciousness from their works (rationalized through the doctrine of impersonality) tend increasingly to be viewed with suspicion, as if impersonality were simply an ingenious ruse for consolidating mastery and authority. Thus, for example, Maud Ellmann concludes that "subjectivity is never more indelible than in its passion for its own extinction. . . . the doctrine of impersonality was born conservative."[22]

Must quotation always amount to an appropriation of the other's discourse, an insidious form of linguistic colonialism? I don't think so. Bersani's claim that "quotation in Joyce is the opposite of self-effacement" harks back to

Eliot's doctrine of impersonality, which holds that "[t]he progress of an artist is a continual self-sacrifice, a continual extinction of personality."[23] The paradox of this doctrine is that the originality—and hence authority—of the artist's voice increases in direct proportion to his or her self-effacement: "[N]ot only the best, but the most individual parts of his work may be those in which the dead poets, his ancestors, assert their immortality most vigorously," maintains Eliot in "Tradition and the Individual Talent."[24] From this perspective, quotation and allusion are employed almost identically in *Ulysses* and *The Waste Land;* and Joyce and Eliot would appear to have sacrificed themselves in favor of "Western culture" and "the mind of Europe," respectively. Yet this self-sacrifice—of which the preponderance of quotations and allusions is the sign—can easily be construed as part of the redemptive aesthetic, with modernist artists occupying the position of the martyr-hero Christ. Hence Bersani's conviction that quotation in *Ulysses* represents not self-effacement but its reverse, a subtle form of self-aggrandizement.

However, several fundamental distinctions are necessary at this point. Eliot's comment about "the dead poets, his ancestors, assert[ing] their immortality most vigorously" is just one of many such remarks scattered throughout his early work in which Eliot betrays his seduction by the occultist prospect of a thoroughgoing poetic atavism that would indeed require self-effacement, and in which massive indulgence in quotation would signify not so much acts of appropriation—as Bersani claims of Joyce—but rather acts of mediumistic channeling, an almost supernatural accessing of the voices of the dead. While I cannot begin to do justice here to the occultist Eliot, I want to distinguish Joyce's use of quotation from both Eliot's shamanism and Bersani's understanding of quotation as appropriation. Whereas Bersani's pointed reference, in the passage quoted above, to "literary metempsychosis" may suggest that Joyce's impersonalist aesthetic is cognate with what I am designating Eliot's shamanism, the terms in which Joyce introduces this aesthetic should dissuade us from too readily assimilating it to Eliot's. Rather than a form of literary metempsychosis, Joycean impersonality is associated, at least in *A Portrait of the Artist as a Young Man,* with a form of homosexual *jouissance* accessible primarily to Joyce's readers. And therefore the hermeneutics of suspicion that has dominated advanced literary criticism for the past couple decades, whether in its poststructuralist or historicist variants, misleads us when it encourages an understanding of aesthetic impersonality as merely camouflage for the modernist will to power—including, most recently, a sexual camouflage or a form of the homosexual closet.

The mistake entailed in demystifying impersonality as nothing more than a means to omnipotence lies partly in the fact that this demystification derives as much from Joyce as from postmodern debunkers; indeed, it forms a central part of Stephen Dedalus's aesthetic theory. In chapter 5 of *Portrait of the Artist,* in the process of admonishing his foil Lynch on the superiority of dramatic over lyric and epic literary forms, Stephen declares:

The dramatic form is reached when the vitality which has flowed and eddied round each person fills every person with such vital force that he or she assumes a proper and intangible esthetic life. The personality of the artist, at first a cry or a cadence or a mood and then a fluid and lambent narrative, finally refines itself out of existence, impersonalises itself, so to speak. The esthetic image in the dramatic form is life purified in and reprojected from the human imagination. The mystery of esthetic like that of material creation is accomplished. The artist, like the God of the creation, remains within or behind or beyond or above his handiwork, invisible, refined out of existence, indifferent, paring his fingernails.

—Trying to refine them also out of existence, said Lynch.

A fine rain began to fall from the high veiled sky and they turned into the duke's lawn to reach the national library before the shower came.

—What do you mean, Lynch asked surlily, by prating about beauty and the imagination in this miserable Godforsaken island? No wonder the artist retired within or behind his handiwork after having perpetrated this country. (*P* 207–8)

How we interpret Joyce's cultural authority or his relationship to the modernist doctrine of impersonality depends, I submit, on how we read this image of the artist "paring his fingernails."

Considering this passage first in its immediate context, we may be led to suppose that Lynch's comic deflation of Stephen's aesthetic idealism indicates Joyce's own demystification of impersonality. Lynch delivers his skeptical interpretation of the image of the artist "paring his fingernails" as the two characters approach the *national library,* and in so doing he draws attention to the nationally marked material conditions of literary production that Stephen's ideology would conceal: "What do you mean . . . by prating about beauty and the imagination in this miserable Godforsaken island? No wonder the artist retired within or behind his handiwork after having perpetrated this country." Lynch's demystification of impersonality gathers its animus from the puns on "Godforsaken island," a common enough phrase that evokes not only the cultural, colonial, and religious dimensions of Ireland's insularity, but also the ironic correlation between a "priestridden" (*P* 33) and a "Godforsaken" nation. The play on "Godforsaken" allows Lynch to restate Stephen's idea of the artist as a deity "refined out of existence" in terms of the death or disappearance of God and the consequent deracination of redemptive institutions: the artist as deity is not so much hovering, godlike, above his creation as he is completely vanished, having judiciously abandoned this "miserable island," just as Joyce himself did in choosing exile.

In adjudicating this tension between Stephen as a mouthpiece for Joyce's impersonalist aesthetic and Lynch as a mouthpiece for the materialist demystification of that aesthetic, we need to find the means for evaluating which character—and therefore which position—represents the primary target of Joyce's irony. The first part of the passage quoted above, in which Stephen argues for the advantage of dramatic over lyric and epic forms, comes almost verbatim from two sources, Joyce's 1900 paper "Drama and Life" and his Paris notebook entries on aesthetics, dated March 1903 (*CW* 38–46 and 141–48, respectively). Immediately before the passage in question, Stephen applauds epic for its approach to impersonality:

> The simplest epical form is seen emerging out of lyrical literature when the artist prolongs and broods upon himself as the center of an epical event and this form progresses till the centre of emotional gravity is equidistant from the artist himself and from others. The narrative is no longer purely personal. The personality of the artist passes into the narration itself, flowing round and round the persons and the action like a vital sea. (*P* 207)

While it is possible to track these sentiments from their source in Joyce's notebooks, through *Stephen Hero*, to *Portrait*, the elevation of aesthetic impersonality to the status of divine creation must be traced to Flaubert's letters. Responding to an inquiry from one Mademoiselle Leroyer de Chantepie concerning his composition of *Madame Bovary*, Flaubert famously explained in a letter of March 18, 1857:

> *Madame Bovary* has nothing "true" in it. It is a totally invented story; into it I put none of my own feelings and nothing from my own life. The illusion (if there is one) comes, on the contrary, from the *impersonality* of the work. It is a principle of mine that a writer must not be his own theme. The artist in his work must be like God in his creation—invisible and all-powerful: he must be everywhere felt, but never seen.[25]

Joyce's borrowing from Flaubert this image of the artist as God (and the impersonalist principle it represents) is especially resonant for us because one of the main antiredemptive narrative strategies that Bersani contrasts to that of Joyce is Flaubert's. Whereas Bersani in *The Culture of Redemption* directly counterposes *Bouvard et Pécuchet* to *Ulysses*, Ezra Pound, writing seventy years earlier, explicitly aligns the aesthetics of these two novels, claiming that in *Ulysses* Joyce "has done what Flaubert set out to do in *Bouvard and Pécuchet*, done it better, more succinct."[26] In this disagreement I find myself siding with Pound, although paradoxically for reasons made available by Bersani, in that the effect of impersonality in *Ulysses* is ultimately antiredemptive, or more queerly redemptive, as I shall demonstrate.

If in advocating aesthetic impersonality Stephen silently quotes both Flaubert's letters and Joyce's own notebooks, his image of the artist "paring his fingernails" generates an intratextual allusion whose homosexual connotation is crucial to Joyce's aesthetic. By providing such a distinctly feminine image—"paring his fingernails"—for the ostensibly invisible artist, Stephen alludes to Tusker Boyle, one of the schoolboys who is caught smugging in the novel's opening chapter and who is nicknamed Lady Boyle "because he was always at his nails, paring them" (*P* 38). Since paring his nails earns this boy a mockingly grand female title and, moreover, Stephen intuits this femininity as somehow responsible for, or at least connected to, the sin of smugging, then the image of the impersonal artist "paring his fingernails" takes on the tint of homosexuality as surely as the green rose—on which Stephen meditates in the novel's opening pages—conjures Oscar Wilde's green carnation or, before that, Walter Pater's green tie, which, in Peter Ackroyd's unequivocal formulation, "was equivalent to wearing a dress."[27]

Now the point of wearing a green tie in fin de siècle England (or, half a century later, a red one) is just that such tints are *not* equivalent to wearing a dress. A man in a dress is a dead giveaway to even the most casual, untutored observer, whereas a man in a green tie signals his homosexuality only to fellow initiates and the rather more urbane heterosexuals, fellow sophisticates. Homosexual signs such as color-coded accessories—or, in the world of *Portrait,* the trope of "paring his fingernails"—possess the double function of simultaneously revealing and concealing. Such subtle, minimal signs reveal one's nonnormative sexuality to those who share it, thereby alerting potential sexual partners and initiating a subcultural bond predicated on shared minority identification; yet at the same time such signs conceal, however imperfectly, one's divergence from the norm, thereby functioning as protection against the guardians of sexual orthodoxy. The prospect of Joyce's generating a homosexual code at this crucial point in his novel by referring to the impersonal artist "paring his fingernails" seems to provide unexpected support for Poirier's contention that Joyce's "repeated condescensions about failed or stunted sensibility are a reminder that only he is the calculating master of the codes, only he can break them and release them onto the page."[28] Joyce's invention of a homosexual code could indeed be understood as enhancing his literary prowess; yet on the other hand, this invention also potentially impugns his prowess by casting over it the shadow of too much familiarity with homosexual semiotics. Rejecting both of these options, I would argue instead that it is more accurate to interpret his introduction of this homosexual code as a sign of Joyce's familiarity with a set of mainstream cultural conceptions of homosexuality, including the idea that its association with concealment means that homosexuality is most effectively, albeit paradoxically, denoted by means of connotation.

The connection between "paring his fingernails" and "smugging" makes more sense in light of this interpretation, since smugging is surrounded with uncertainty not only for Stephen but also for the critics. An obsolete dialect term of uncertain etymological origin, *smugging* is thrice euphemized by R. B. Kershner, the editor of my critical edition of the novel, who glosses *smugging* as "[p]robably a mild sort of homosexual play."[29] In the qualification *probably* we may read a form of the deniability that characteristically attends homosexuality, particularly since in the qualification *mild sort* we hear echoes of the conventional excuse for homosexuality—that it is "just a phase" or merely a "tendency"—and in the phrase *homosexual play* we witness an effort to desexualize homosexuality, to convert it from sex into little more than a schoolboy game.[30] Yet although such euphemisms conjure a conventionally homophobic conception of homosexuality, Kershner's hesitation is attributable also to the term's inscrutability, since its primary meanings aren't, in fact, sexual (they concern theft, secrecy, and plagiarism), and the *OED* supplement that offers a sexual meaning for the term cites as its evidence the line from *Ulysses* in which Joyce repeats the word; and so for our purposes the sexual meaning of smugging, while hardly in doubt, is derived somewhat tautologically.[31] In this difficulty of translating the term *smugging* into anything but a range of relatively indeterminate sexual associations, we may discern an allegory of homosexuality's resistance to the denotative and its correlative identification with the connotative.

According to the history of sexuality outlined by Foucault and elaborated by Eve Kosofsky Sedgwick, among others, this connection between homosexuality and the connotative is both pervasive and historically specific, insofar as it forms a defining feature of the epistemology of the closet. In her book of that title, Sedgwick argues that "by the end of the nineteenth century, when it had become fully current—as obvious to Queen Victoria as to Freud—that knowledge meant sexual knowledge, and secrets sexual secrets, there had in fact developed one particular sexuality that was distinctively constituted *as* secrecy: the perfect object for the by now insatiably exacerbated epistemological/sexual anxiety of the turn-of-the-century subject."[32] In light of Sedgwick's influential argument, it would seem plausible to construe Joycean impersonality as *not* "simply one among many possible disguises . . . in narration," as John Paul Riquelme would have it,[33] but rather as a specifically sexual disguise. If impersonality is understood as a mode of concealment, then after Sedgwick it inevitably becomes legible as sexual concealment, a subterfuge of the closet. Even more than Joyce's, Eliot's impersonality has been interpreted as a form of sexual dishonesty.[34] And more recently, we have witnessed—in the words of *James Joyce Quarterly* editor Robert Spoo—"Stephen's emergence . . . as a kind of conflicted antihero of the closet."[35]

Applied to Joyce, the Sedgwickean line of reasoning certainly generates some original readings; for instance, it authorizes our interpretation of the homosexual code embedded in Stephen's description of the impersonalist aesthetic as revealing a portrait of the artist as a young homosexual. Indeed, Joseph Valente concludes what seems to me the most powerful of these new readings by extending Sedgwick's epistemology to Joyce himself:

The unstable differential equation between Stephen and Joyce, wherein the protagonist conceals the author by standing for him, means that self-portraiture is its own refuge, requiring no deliberate forms of secrecy. All of the disclosures that Joyce might have packed or wanted to pack into his depiction of Stephen, including the display of homoerotic desires and discomforts, ultimately prove indistinguishable from the exercise of poetic license as a mode of denial. That is to say, regarding such things as erotic preferences, the ontology of self-portraiture makes the candor Joyce demanded of authors easy because it makes the credulity of the reader impossible. A portrait of the artist is an open closet.[36]

My enthusiasm for such readings is qualified by both my sense that Sedgwick's epistemology is fundamentally flawed and my conviction that we misconstrue Joyce's aesthetic by reducing it to a form of evasion or hypocrisy. I have discussed elsewhere the illegitimate totalizing impulse in Sedgwick's theory, but I would like to emphasize here that although I am persuaded that "by the end of the nineteenth century . . . there had in fact developed one particular sexuality that was distinctively constituted *as* secrecy" (as Sedgwick claims), I find implausible the subsequent deduction that all textual hints of secrecy refer back to homosexuality.[37] By mapping the hetero- /homo- binary onto that of knowledge/ignorance, Sedgwick aligns homosexuality and the closet with ignorance as such and then interprets all sites of ignorance as indicative of cultural anxieties surrounding homosexuality. And while this overly schematic epistemology opens up some novel interpretations, it also introduces all sorts of unnecessary problems, such as insensitivity to historical nuances and cultural differences.

More particularly, the Sedgwickean obsession with secrecy distracts us from other cultural associations borne by homosexuality, associations that prompt an alternate interpretation of the trope of "paring his fingernails." Rather than reading this homosexual code in terms of the psychology of literary character and viewing Stephen as a closet case, I would argue that Stephen's image of the artist homosexualizes the impersonal aesthetic in a more significant—because less psychologistic—way. Joyce identifies his aesthetic with homosexuality not out of homosexual panic or a desire for the closet, but because—in accordance with turn-of-the-century representations of the homosexual as both artistic and hypersexed—he associated homosexuality with a radical enjoyment or *jouissance.* As Ed Cohen has argued, this association is historically quite specific: following Oscar Wilde's public trials in 1895, aestheticism and the pursuit of art gained connotations not only of effeminacy but also of homosexuality.[38] Hence the trope of "paring his fingernails" conjures not merely "Lady Boyle" (effeminacy or gender inversion) but also the more sexually charged act of smugging (homosexuality or sexual perversion). Indeed, in a pioneering account of gay semiotics, Harold Beaver identifies art and especially the adjective *artistic* as privileged codes for homosexuality. Discussing gay vernacular, Beaver argues that "queens are all accomplices in the art of fiction. Deprived of their own distinctive codes, homosexuals make art itself into their distinctive code. Aesthetic absorption is all."[39]

Before situating Bersani's work within this modern aestheticist tradition that so strongly connects sexuality and art, we need to examine Joyce's motive for figuring aesthetic impersonality in terms of homosexuality. I would describe this motive as culturally rather than psychologically derived and would point for evidence to the historical association of homosexuality with what turn-of-the-century sexologists called hyperesthesia and what we might gloss in terms of *jouissance*. While in Western modernity artistic tendencies and intensified susceptibility to aesthetic sensations have always been viewed as sexually suspect, this suspicion fastened particularly firmly to the emergent figure of the homosexual at the turn of the century. Yet as I shall argue in the final section of this paper, the double association of homosexuality with art and *jouissance* implies a rather different conception of sublimation than the normative psychoanalytic understanding of sublimation that Bersani claims *Ulysses* embodies.

One of the most influential arguments for identifying homosexuality with privileged access to artistic creativity may be found in Edward Carpenter's *The Intermediate Sex,* a pioneering treatise on sexual politics first published (in London) in 1906. Although it is not clear whether Joyce actually read any of Carpenter's work, Richard Brown has documented Joyce's interest in—and ownership of books by—nineteenth-century sexologists and psychiatrists, such as Havelock Ellis and Krafft-Ebing, whom Carpenter cites extensively in *The Intermediate Sex* and, indeed, whose work he helped publicize.[40] Unfortunately, the title of Carpenter's book, together with the author's propensity for using as synonyms terms that today we would be more likely to differentiate more clearly (inversion, homosexuality, "the homogenic tendency," "the intermediate type," Uranianism), has misled Brown and others into assuming that Carpenter's principal focus is androgyny rather than homosexuality—and into subsequently claiming that therefore Joyce's aesthetic should be understood as androgynous rather than as homosexual or perverse.[41] However, while Carpenter retains Karl Heinrich Ulrichs's mid-nineteenth-century term "Urnings" (or "Uranians") to designate persons defined by same-sex object choice, he largely rejects Ulrichs's popular explanation of male homosexuality in terms of a "feminine soul enclosed in a male body *(anima muliebris in corpore virili inclusa)*";[42] and the focus of his study is firmly on homosexuality, not androgyny.

Carpenter's work is dedicated not only to removing the stigma of pathology from homosexuality, but also to promoting the inherent cultural superiority of the homosexual or "intermediate type," a superiority that he claims lies partly in the intermediate type's combination of masculine and feminine features. Carpenter's view of homosexual superiority, for which he amasses considerable documentation, comes through most clearly toward the end of *Intermediate Types among Primitive Folk* (1914):

> The double life and nature certainly, in many cases of inverts observed today, seems to give to them an extraordinary humanity and sympathy, together with a remarkable power of dealing with human beings. It may possibly also point to a further degree of evolution than usually attained, and a higher order of consciousness, very imperfectly realised, of course, but indicated. This interaction in fact, between the masculine and the feminine, this mutual illumination of logic and intuition, this combination of action and meditation, may not only raise and increase the power of each of these faculties, but it may give the mind a new quality, and a new power of perception corresponding to the blending of subject and object in consciousness. It may possibly lead to the development of that third order of perception which has been called the cosmic consciousness, and which may also be termed divination.[43]

The idea of perception intensified to the point of divination is very close to Stephen Dedalus's identification of aesthetic impersonality with divine creation; likewise, the "higher order of consciousness" that Carpenter attributes to homosexuality resembles Stephen's description of "[t]he personality of the artist pass[ing] into the narration itself, flowing round and round the persons and the action like a vital sea," in which we are given an image for what Carpenter calls "the blending of subject and object in consciousness." Furthermore, the thesis of *Intermediate Types*—namely, that "unusual powers of divination and prophecy were to be found in homosexual folk"[44]—extends Carpenter's earlier characterization, in *The Intermediate Sex*, of "the more normal type of the Uranian man" as grounded in "the artist-nature, with the artist's sensibility and perception."[45] Enumerating a number of authorities on this topic, Carpenter explains in *The Intermediate Sex*:

> [Otto] de Joux, who speaks on the whole favorably of Uranian men and women, says of the former: "They are enthusiastic for poetry and music, are often eminently skillful in the fine arts, and are overcome with emotion and sympathy at the least sad occurrence. . . ." And in another passage he indicates the artist-nature, when he says: "The nerve-system of many an Urning is the finest and the most complicated musical instrument in the service of the interior personality that can be imagined."[46]

These passages allow us to supplement the standard Joycean interpretation of art in religious terms with the more suggestive interpretation of both art and priestliness in terms of homosexuality. Thus Stephen's self-representation as "a priest of the eternal imagination" (*P* 213) should be read in light of Carpenter's observation that "the frequency with which accusations of homosexuality have been launched against the religious orders and monks of the Catholic Church, the Knights Templars, and even the ordinary priests and clerics, must give us pause."[47]

The fact that the "type" of figure we've come to know as "homosexual" has historically been closely associated with priestly functions, as well as with artistic creativity, supports our reading of the impersonal artist "paring his fingernails" in a cultural rather than a psychological framework. It is not so much the fictional character of Stephen Dedalus or the historical figure of Joyce who is to be considered homosexual (or closeted), as it is the impersonal aesthetic as such. And the Sedgwickean emphasis on homosexuality's historical association with secrecy provides little help in understanding these other historical connections. Beyond its connotations of subterfuge, homosexuality was identified at the turn of the century with artistic creativity, priestliness, and, finally, with privileged access to extreme sexual enjoyment. Through the trope of "paring his fingernails," Joyce is drawing into his aesthetic all these cultural associations attaching to homosexuality.

Now although Carpenter's idealization of homosexuality's cultural superiority paradoxically entailed his minimizing the erotic dimension of same-sex relations, contemporaneous experts, such as Viennese psychiatrist Krafft-Ebing, were only too ready to identify homosexuality, or "contrary sexual instinct," with disproportionate increases in sexual desire and enjoyment. In the canonical psychiatric work of the period, his *Text-Book of Insanity,* Krafft-Ebing—by way of classifying an enormous range of pathologies, both mental and organic, in terms of their deviation from the norm—regularly had recourse to the notion of "hyperesthesia," a category that designates pathology in purely quantitative terms as an abnormal increase in sensitivity to stimuli. Before examining "hyperesthesia sexualis" and connecting it with homosexuality, Krafft-Ebing introduced hyperesthesia in relation to *aesthetic* sensitivity—although without registering the redundancy implicit in the category of "esthetic hyperesthesia," both of whose terms share a single etymological root in the Greek word for sense perception. Nevertheless, anticipating both Carpenter's and Joyce's conceptions of the artist as hypersensitive to the point of clairvoyance, Krafft-Ebing defined esthetic hyperesthesia as "intensified feelings of pleasure in art, persons, and things, and consequent sympathies, antipathies, and idiosyncrasies."[48] In a diagnosis that recalls Stephen Dedalus's susceptibilities and his fluctuations of consciousness throughout *Portrait,* Krafft-Ebing asserted, "With continuance of this abnormal increased impressionability of the emotions the mood is constantly changing, and with each new idea a related and adequate state of feeling is induced."[49]

Having discussed esthetic hyperesthesia under the rubric of "elementary psychic disturbances," Krafft-Ebing classified sexual pathologies under the rubric of "disturbances of the motor side of mental life (impulse and will)," thereby betraying what Arnold I. Davidson has shown to be a typically pre-Freudian conception of sexual instinct.[50] However, the conceptualization of sexuality in *Text-Book of Insanity* is essentially modern in its assumption that sexuality—and, especially, sexual abnormality—defines or grounds human subjectivity. As Krafft-Ebing argues, "[A]nomalies [of the sexual instinct] are very important elementary disturbances, since upon the nature of sexual sensibility the mental individuality in greater part depends; especially does it affect ethic, *esthetic*, and social feeling and action."[51] Yet Krafft-Ebing's classification of these anomalies, in which hyperesthesia and perversion form two of the four principal subdivisions, is likely to strike the post-Freudian reader as oddly skewed in its emphases:

> The anomalies of the sexual instinct may be classified as follows: *(a)* It is lessened or entirely wanting (anesthesia); *(b)* abnormally increased (hyperesthesia); *(c)* it is perversely expressed: i.e., when the manner of its satisfaction is not directed toward the preservation of the race (paresthesia); *(d)* it manifests itself outside of the period of anatomico-physiologic processes in the generative organs (paradoxia).[52]

Paresthesia, Krafft-Ebing's term for perversion, is itself subject to further subdivision, insofar as "[t]he perverse sexual impulse may be directed (1) toward the opposite sex or (2) toward the same sex"; and *paresthesia sexualis* is introduced with the reminder, "This anomaly is of the greatest clinical and forensic importance, especially as it is frequently associated with sexual hyperesthesia."[53] Defining paresthesia in terms of the sexual instinct's deviation from its putative natural function of species propagation, Krafft-Ebing's subclassifications of perversion in fact provide an important source for Freud's enumeration of sexual aberrations via the four major categories of sadism, masochism, fetishism, and homosexuality in the first of his *Three Essays on the Theory of Sexuality*.[54] And referring to Carl Westphal's famous essay of 1870, "Contrary Sexual Instinct," Krafft-Ebing decisively links homosexuality with the excesses of receptivity and appetite denoted by hyperesthesia.[55] Conceding that in homosexuals "the genitals are normally developed, the glands are normal in function, and the sexual type is completely differentiated," he nonetheless asserts, "Very frequently contrary sexual feeling is accompanied by hyperesthesia sexualis."[56]

From Krafft-Ebing's precise differentiations in *Text-Book of Insanity* we may conclude that it is not merely the case that, at the turn of the century, homosexuality was associated with abnormality and excess; but, more specifically, that the emerging psychiatric conceptualization of homosexuality associated it with both sexual and aesthetic hyperesthesia in a way that conforms almost exactly to Joyce's vision of the artist in *Portrait*. One dimension of this psychiatric conceptualization was popularized by writers such as Carpenter; the other dimension Joyce may have gleaned from his own reading of Krafft-Ebing; and both dimensions are involved in his conception of the impersonal artist "paring his fingernails."

In order to illuminate Joyce's cultural motive for associating the impersonal aesthetic with sexual perversion—and, by extension, with intensified sexual enjoyment—I have elaborated Krafft-Ebing's notion of hyperesthesia sexualis and emphasized his connecting it with homosexuality. However, at this point I should indicate that my understanding of the kind of enjoyment that Joycean impersonality entails also depends upon Lacan's seminars on Joyce, whose significance has been largely misconstrued, despite valiant attempts by Joyceans to turn Lacan's difficult writing on Joyce to good account. Whereas Krafft-Ebing treats hyperesthesia sexualis as simply one among many nascent diagnostic categories, Lacan treats *jouissance*—which, famously untranslatable though this French term is, might be permitted to gloss *hyperesthesia sexualis*—as a category central to both his description of symbolic subjectivity in general and his reading of Joyce in particular. Indeed, in his address to the fifth international Joyce symposium, at the Sorbonne in 1975, Lacan coined the neologism *joyceance* to suggest how Joyce's writing inspired a crucial revision in French psychoanalytic theory. Noting that, through the cognate *joy,* Joyce's patronym "echoes that of Freud" (the German noun *Freude* approximates the French *jouissance*), Lacan rhetorically aligns Joyce with Freud.[57] By punning on Joyce's patronym and the French word for primordial enjoyment, Lacan draws attention to the unique relationship in Joyce's writing between *jouissance* and oedipal prohibition, which the patronym is symbolically supposed to secure.[58] That is, for Lacan the symbolic function known as the Name-of-the-Father, which conventionally forecloses access to enjoyment, operates quite differently in Joyce's case.

Before unpacking this formulation and elaborating its implications for both a theory of literary sublimation and our understanding of Joyce's impersonalist aesthetic, I would like to consider the epistemological status of the rhetorical strategy through which Lacan develops this point about Joyce. I am aware of the temptation to dismiss Lacan's coinage of *joyceance* as simply a bad pun, typical of his overwrought style.[59] Yet Joyce and Lacan represent two of our century's most ardent proponents of the heuristic—and even libidinal—value of punning. Furthermore, as the Latin root of the term *homonymy* suggests, puns bring together two like elements that should remain semantically separate; similarly, homosexuality could be understood as designating a coming together of two bodies that appear alike but that are supposed to stay sexually apart. Both homonymy and homosexuality threaten confusion in the symbolic order; the prejudice against the former—made explicit once we acknowledge that any reference to "a bad pun" is entirely redundant—could conceivably be related to the prejudice against the latter.

Lacan's pun *joyceance* is significant for the revision it prompts in Lacanian theory and for the notion of sublimation it implies with respect to Joyce's writing. While it is not possible here to trace the complete development of the term *jouissance* in Lacan's work,[60] we may begin by observing that it is the term through which Lacan designates that privileged sexual pleasure enjoyed by the mythic father of the primal horde, as imagined by Freud in *Totem and Taboo*. Glossing the function of myth as "a story to illustrate a structure," Lacan interprets the narrative of the primal horde and its founding parricide as an allegory of the symbolic order's effects on the human subject, who gains access to culture's symbolic circuits only by forfeiting primordial enjoyment.[61] This structural forfeiture, in which an alien force intervenes to prohibit enjoyment, is also figured through the myth of Oedipus. Lacan's axiom intended to encapsulate this structural law is that *speech kills jouissance:* the symbolic order cuts us off, once and for all, from complete satisfaction. *"[J]ouissance* is forbidden to him who speaks as such," Lacan insists.[62] And significantly for our understanding of the effect of *jouissance* in Joyce, Lacan describes the constitutive loss of *jouissance* brought about by the symbolic order as a sublimation: "To introduce as primordial the function of the father represents a sublimation."[63] Furthermore, he adds that this originary sublimation is necessary for "the normalization of desire."[64] In this way Lacan revises—by hugely expanding—the psychoanalytic notion of sublimation (which remains notoriously undertheorized in Freud) to encompass *all* verbal activity, not just socially esteemed artistic and intellectual enterprises, as the conventional definition of sublimation would have it.[65]

This reconceptualization of sublimation to include all symbolic activity, including aspects of everyday speech, becomes especially significant in Joyce's case because, according to Lacan, Joyce uses his writing precisely to gain access to, rather than forfeiting, *jouissance:* "this *jouissance* is the only thing that his text traps for us," Lacan maintains.[66] This is the central point of Lacan's seminars on Joyce. It is Joyce's play with language that grants his writing this privileged status; and it prompts Lacan to revise his own account of *jouissance* by means of another pun, *jouis-sens,* or enjoy-meant, which designates a second-order, semiotic *jouissance.*[67] This pun *jouis-sens* suggests the potential for a particularly skillful technique of language-use to *materialize* enjoyment, to capture and encrypt *jouissance* in the text, rather than losing enjoyment through language. We might note that, from this perspective, Joyce's writing captures *jouissance* at the surface of the text, not via thematic or referential means. It is not so much his ebulliently groundbreaking representations of sexual and other bodily functions that enable Joyce to materialize *jouissance,* as it is what we might call his text's *joie-de-langue,* which exploits the homophonic and other acoustic properties of language to ever-increasing degrees.[68]

Since Joyce's materialization of *jouissance* is resolutely superficial, any passage selected to illustrate this effect will seem arbitrarily chosen. However, we

may observe Joyce creating the effect of *joyceance* in his descriptions of Stephen's aesthetic responses—as, for example, when Stephen remembers some lines from Yeats:

> A soft liquid joy like the noise of many waters flowed over his memory and he felt in his heart the soft peace of silent spaces of fading tenuous sky above the waters, of oceanic silence, of swallows flying through the seadusk over the flowing waters.
> A soft liquid joy flowed through the words where the soft long vowels hurtled noiselessly and fell away, lapping and flowing back and ever shaking the white bells of their waves in mute chime and mute peal and soft low swooning cry. (*P* 218)

In this intensified registration of aesthetic sensation we see a perfect illustration of the artist's hyperesthesia; and although Joyce may be ironizing the Paterian idiom in which he formulates Stephen's response, he is nonetheless clearly committed to making "a soft liquid joy flow . . . through the words" of his own fiction. He achieves this effect in the passage quoted above by exploiting features characteristic of poetic language—the use of various schemes of repetition to create a hypnotic rhythm, the heavily alliterative diction, the assonant power of "soft long vowels." These heightened acoustic effects not only subordinate the words' referential function to their material dimension, but also gesture toward the noiseless words—the oxymoronic "mute chime and mute peal"—that represent the nonmimetic effect these sounds are supposed paradoxically to produce. The paradox lies in the impossibility of representing *jouissance*—what, in his Paris notebooks, Joyce calls "the feeling of joy . . . proper to comic art"—except by directly reproducing it in the representational medium. That is to say, *joyceance* can be represented only by being performatively produced through an articulation of the specific mode of its resistance to representation. The oxymoronic figures of "mute chime and mute peal" serve here to articulate that impossibility. Thus while at one level Joyce may be ironizing Pater, at another level he is distancing himself from Yeats as a poetic precursor by implying that the capacities of dramatic prose supersede those of lyric poetry. Since the passage quoted above follows Stephen's completion of his villanelle, the contrast between that poetry and Joyce's own prose may be intended to assert allegorically a more general aesthetic superiority of fiction over other literary forms.

Yet once one has begun exploiting these material dimensions of language in order to capture "joy," it would be hubristic to suppose that he could completely control their reverberations—such, indeed, is perhaps the most unfortunate myth even in *Wake* criticism.[69] I refer to this embarrassing aspect of sophisticated critical writing on Joyce in order to emphasize that our enjoying Joyce in the sense I have outlined does not by any means entail our attributing to him absolute mastery of his words. This qualification returns us to the question of Joyce's authority and the issue of sublimation with which, apropos of Bersani, we began. Alluding to Lacan's expansion of the category of sublimation, I quoted his remark about the patronym's role in "the normalization of desire" to suggest that the symbolic order's evisceration of *jouissance* gives us the model for normative sublimation. In Lacan's view, Joycean sublimation is fundamentally perverse. To specify what, in this context, perverse sublimation involves will enable us more accurately to evaluate Bersani's critique of Joyce.

The concept of sublimation warrants our attention here not only because it represents the central term through which Bersani reproaches *Ulysses,* but also because Freud's major work on sublimation, his study of Leonardo da Vinci, explicitly connects artistic production with homosexuality. Since we know that Joyce read *Leonardo da Vinci and a Memory of His Childhood,* it is reasonable to suppose that Freud's 1910 "portrait of the artist as a young man" furnished Joyce with additional motivation for associating homosexuality and aesthetics in his 1916 novel.[70] And no doubt Freud's study of Leonardo—a *Künstlerroman* in reverse, as it were—also fueled Joyce's reluctance to undertake psychoanalysis himself, since *Leonardo* famously reduces art to the level of the symptom. Yet while Freud's contribution to aesthetic theory lies primarily in the account of literary effects that he provides in his essay "The 'Uncanny'" (1919), his account of textual production in *Leonardo* may still yield subtler insights than those generally available through psychobiography, with its crude epistemology of historical and literary character.

The idea of sublimation underpins the culture of redemption insofar as it rationalizes a diversion of gross sexual impulses into the more refined spheres of artistic creation and scientific investigation. By transforming the ephemeral materiality of sex into the permanence and ideality of art or intellection, sublimation performs a virtually religious operation of transubstantiation, effectively redeeming sexuality from any unmediated expression save what is required for species propagation. It is fairly evident how this understanding of sublimation implies a devaluation of sexuality. Furthermore, according to Bersani, by justifying the culture of redemption this notion paradoxically minimizes or misconstrues the significance of art to boot, despite the cultural premium conferred on art. Yet two aspects of sublimation complicate this mechanism's redemptive function. The first is that sublimation bypasses repression; the second, that the process of sublimation makes use primarily of polymorphously perverse impulses.

Distinguishing sublimation from idealization, Freud explains, "In so far as sublimation describes something that has to do with the instinct and idealization something to do with the object, the two concepts are to be distinguished from each other. . . . As we have learnt, the formation of an ideal heightens the demands of the ego and is the most powerful factor favouring repression; sublimation is a way out, a way by which those demands can be met *without* involving repression."[71] And sublimation's capacity for "evad[ing] the fate of repression" characterizes Leonardo's "special disposition," claims Freud.[72] If sublimation designates a mode of satisfying sexual drives without the intervention of repression (which would result in a symptom or other compromise formation), then sublimation also necessarily avoids the paternal prohibition essential to "the normalization of desire." And if sublimation is to be distinguished properly from idealization, it may in fact indicate an expression of sexuality that is far from redemptive. Insofar as it achieves satisfaction outside the oedipal economy instituted through the patronym, sublimation appears potentially perverse.

This presents us with a major paradox, which we may approach, if not completely resolve, by considering Freud's insistence that sublimation exploits "what are known as the *perverse* elements of sexual excitation"[73]—an insistence that reaches back to the second of his *Three Essays on the Theory of Sexuality:*

> It is possible further to form some idea of the mechanism of this process of sublimation. On the one hand, it would seem, the sexual impulses cannot be utilized during these years of childhood, since the reproductive functions have been deferred—a fact which constitutes the main feature of the period of latency. On the other hand, these impulses would seem in themselves to be perverse—that is, to arise from erotogenic zones and to derive their activity from instincts which, in view of the direction of the subject's development, can only arouse unpleasurable feelings.[74]

On the one hand, Freud's reference to "the direction of the subject's development" gestures toward the normative developmental program described—and to some degree endorsed—in the third of his *Three Essays*. This points the way to normative sublimation. On the other hand, by making use of polymorphously perverse drives, sublimation may be understood as involving not so much the redemptive desexualization of sexuality as its potentially subversive *degenitalization*. Here we see the basis for a distinction, which is elaborated in Laplanche's seminar, between normative and perverse sublimation:

> The major problem in Freud's *Leonardo*, from the viewpoint of sublimation, is that although two activities (painting and intellectual investigations) are presented to us, both sublimated and struggling against each other, sublimation is also, and most frequently, evoked only for the intellectual activity, and the struggle between the two activities is in the end an inability to "desublimate," to return, even partially, to the instinctual—to the point that the pictorial activity becomes something much closer to the instinctual, to what Freud calls "enjoyment of life," than to intellectual activity.[75]

One of the chief contributions of Laplanche's seminar lies in this pluralization of sublimation, which allows us to grasp that the perverse variant of sublimation implies not that (culturally valued) art substitutes for (culturally devalued) homosexuality, as Freud initially seems to be saying in *Leonardo,* but rather that normative development consists in successfully eradicating at the same time homosexual *and* artistic impulses, since both indicate a failure to subordinate polymorphous perversity to the rigors of reproductive genitality.

Sublimation is able to obtain "the satisfaction of the drive with a change of object, that is, without repression," as Lacan emphasizes in his seminar on sublimation, because the drive has no predetermined object or aim.[76] The paradox of sublimation is that its mechanism involves diverting the sexual drive in order to reach satisfaction, yet without this detour passing through either repression, idealization, genitality, or even an object relation.[77] In other words, the paradox of sublimation leads us to what Bersani calls "this peculiar idea of a sexuality independent of sex"[78]—or what Lacan names *jouissance.*

This is exactly what Joyce aims for in his writing, according to one of his best-known Paris notebook entries, dated 13 February 1903. Distinguishing between art that inspires desire and art that inspires a joy—or *joyceance*—indicative of the kind of satisfaction implicit in perverse sublimation, Joyce writes:

> An improper art aims at exciting in the way of comedy the feeling of desire but the feeling which is proper to comic art is the feeling of joy. Desire, as I have said, is the feeling which urges us to go to something but joy is the feeling which the possession of some good excites in us. Desire, the feeling which an improper art seeks to excite in the way of comedy, differs, it will be seen, from joy. For desire urges us from rest that we may possess something but joy holds us in rest so long as we possess something. Desire, therefore, can only be excited in us by a comedy (a work of comic art) which is not sufficient in itself inasmuch as it urges us to seek something beyond itself; but a comedy (a work of comic art) which does not urge us to seek anything beyond itself excites in us the feeling of joy. (*CW* 144)

As with Lacanian *jouissance* and Bersanian self-shattering, the value of Joycean "joy" resides in its inherent solipsism, its resolute recoil from use: this art "does not urge us to seek anything beyond itself." As a recommendation of "art for art's sake," Joyce's aestheticism could easily be read, in accordance with postmodern clichés about high modernism, as apolitical or, worse, politically conservative. By discouraging the reader from seeking anything beyond itself, Joyce's art seems to advocate a quietism that necessarily prohibits the kind of action required to effect social change—for example, to intervene in the colonial exploitation of Ireland.

Yet I would argue that the opposite is true. Inhibiting us from seeking anything beyond itself (by satiating us with "joy"), the Joycean text actually implies a mode of being that is profoundly resistant to exploitation. The *joyceance* that compels a recoil from use is exactly homologous to—in fact, it derives from—sexuality's constitutive recoil from its object. Following Laplanche's account, in

Life and Death in Psychoanalysis, of sexuality's reflexive origin in autoeroticism, Bersani develops Freud's radical insight that "the sexual instinct is in the first instance independent of its object."[79] In so doing, Bersani makes available a new politics of solipsism that both he and Joyce connect with homosexual aesthetics.[80] And since Joyce inherits his commitment to aestheticism in part from homosexual aesthetes such as Pater and Wilde, we can locate Joyce as the missing figure in a tradition of queer aestheticism that runs from Pater and Wilde to Bersani and Beckett (the latter of whose work Bersani has recently promoted as rigorously antiredemptive and therefore politically salutary).[81]

Joyce suggests the difficulties involved in this project by offering us, in the early *Dubliners* story "An Encounter," an allegory of "improper art." In "An Encounter" we witness a mode of sublimation that incites desire rather than joy, and which therefore opens the way to just the kind of exploitation that "proper art" is meant to forestall. While I find utterly convincing Margot Norris's careful demonstration, in "A Walk on the Wild(e) Side," of the complex set of doubling, mirroring, and surrogacy relations of homosocial identification and homophobic disidentification in "An Encounter," I would qualify her characterization of the story's old man as "the sadistic homosexual pervert," since this figure is neither homosexual nor heterosexual. He's simply perverse—although insufficiently solipsistic in his perversion.

Several critics have interpreted this anonymous pervert as a reincarnation of Father Flynn, whose death in "The Sisters" initiates the story that immediately precedes "An Encounter." This connection between priestliness and perversion confirms Edward Carpenter's observation in *Intermediate Types,* while also retrospectively associating religious texts with the "improper art" embodied by the pervert, who is represented as performing a perverse sublimation and achieving sexual gratification through language:

> He began to speak to us about girls, saying what nice soft hair they had and how soft their hands were and how all girls were not so good as they seemed to be if one only knew. There was nothing he liked, he said, so much as looking at a nice young girl, at her nice white hands and her beautiful soft hair. He gave me the impression that he was repeating something which he had learned by heart or that, magnetised by some words of his own speech, his mind was slowly circling round and round in the same orbit. At times he spoke as if he were simply alluding to some fact that everybody knew, and at times he lowered his voice and spoke mysteriously as if he were telling us something secret which he did not wish others to overhear. He repeated his phrases over and over again, varying them and surrounding them with his monotonous voice. (*D* 26)

The repetition in this passage may be read as a discursive version of the rhythmic beating that the old man speaks of when discoursing—at equal length and with equal intensity—on the "nice warm whipping" he wishes to mete out to boys. As the narrator reports, "[I]f a boy had a girl for a sweetheart and told lies about it then he would give him such a whipping as no boy ever got in this world. He said that there was nothing in this world he would like so well as that" (*D* 27). Far more than either whipping boys or looking at girls, the old man enjoys talking about these things, caressing them with his voice.[82] In obtaining *jouissance* through language, this pervert represents a negative type of the Joycean artist, who also aims to reach a perverse, solipsistic joy through elaborate patterns of verbal repetition. However, the narrator's recoil from the pervert is complicated by an identification with him, since the beating fantasies that the old man elaborates are mirrored not only by his own beating off, as it were, at "the near end of the field," but also by the narrator's repeatedly mentioned beating heart and the beating rhythms of his own verbal style. This constellation of beating fantasies is represented in *Portrait* through the pandying scenes, whose framing as paradigmatic instances of injustice supports my claim about Joyce's wariness of involving the other in what ideally remains a solipsistic experience. The problem with the old man of "An Encounter" is that he's not solipsistic enough. Attempting to draw the other into his *jouissance,* this "queer old josser" stands finally as an allegory of the colonizer—and therefore as a monitory figure for the impersonal artist.

Joyce's ethics of impersonality anticipates Harold Beaver's claim that for gay men, "[a]esthetic absorption is all." To the postmodern, antiaesthetic objection that for many gay men *politics* is—or should be—all, we can now reply that aesthetic absorption, which Joyce terms *joy,* offers a potentially queerer form of politics. Far from the aestheticization of politics that Walter Benjamin identified with fascism, this represents the politics of aestheticism, one that refuses the customary underestimation—prevalent even in contemporary English departments—of the radical power implicit in certain aesthetic experiences. What we might call the politics of joy is more perverse than conventional gay politics, because it harnesses the historical connections between aberrant sexuality and an aberrant commitment to art for the purpose of thwarting any exploitative or appropriative movement. Insofar as art can induce "joy," it can thereby inhibit the various instrumentalist modes of colonization through which people exploit others for their own ends. And it is in this respect that, as Bersani says of Flaubert's *Bouvard et Pécuchet,* "art could be put on the side of sexuality in the Freudian opposition between civilization and pleasure." If art is thus redeemed by its renunciation of redemption and becomes politically useful through its very recoil from use, then the artist's role as agent of social change is paradoxical indeed. Joyce's term for this paradoxical role is impersonality.

NOTES

1. Leo Bersani, "Against *Ulysses,*" in *The Culture of Redemption* (Cambridge, Mass.: Harvard University Press, 1990), 176.

2. An early version of this essay was presented at the "Joyce and Modern Culture" conference, Brown University, June 1995. While the present version is, in part, a response to the special issue of *James Joyce Quarterly* on "Joyce and Homosexuality," it also forms part of a larger project on "Modernism and the Ethics of 'Impersonality,'" one chapter of which has appeared as "Hart Crane's Poetics of Privacy," *American Literary History* 8 (spring 1996): 83–109. For advice and help I would like to thank Colbey Emmerson, Gary Handwerk, Shannon McRae, Margot Norris, Mark Schoening, Joe Valente, and especially Jason Friedman.

3. Richard Poirier, *The Renewal of Literature: Emersonian Reflections* (New York: Random House, 1987), 98.

4. Ibid.

5. Ibid., 9.

6. Bersani, *The Culture of Redemption*, 1.

7. T. S. Eliot, "*Ulysses,* Order, and Myth," in *Selected Prose of T. S. Eliot,* ed. Frank Kermode (New York: Harcourt Brace Jovanovich, 1975), 177.

8. See, for example, Calvin Bedient, *He Do the Police in Different Voices: "The Waste Land" and Its Protagonist* (Chicago: University of Chicago Press, 1986), which shares Eliot's commitment to a redemptive aesthetic and argues that throughout *The Waste Land* "Eliot's 'allegorical style' displays an intelligent economy of language that moves to check—by its chastity, its formal arrangements—the forsaken babble of historical discourse" (xi).

9. Writing in 1921 in "The Metaphysical Poets," Eliot outlines his rationale for difficulty in realist terms: "[I]t appears likely that poets in our civilization, as it exists at present, must be *difficult.* Our civilization comprehends great variety and complexity, and this variety and complexity, playing upon a refined sensibility, must produce various and complex results. The poet must become more and more comprehensive, more allusive, more indirect, in order to force, to dislocate if necessary, language into his meaning. . . . Hence we get something which looks very much like the conceit—we get, in fact, a method curiously similar to that of the 'metaphysical poets'" (*Selected Prose,* 65). Whereas the novelist has recourse to parallels drawn from classical antiquity in order to redeem contemporary history, the poet has recourse to allusiveness in general and the form of the conceit in particular, in order to effect a similar redemption.

10. Here I'm drawing on John Guillory's account of Eliot in chapter 3 of his brilliant critique, *Cultural Capital: The Problem of Literary Canon Formation* (Chicago: University of Chicago Press, 1993). As will become clear, I am persuaded by Guillory's principal thesis, just as I am in sympathy with the general drift of Bersani's and Poirier's critiques; but I disagree with all these critics' understandings of modernist impersonality.

11. Eliot, *Selected Prose,* 175.

12. Ibid., 177.

13. Contrasting what he describes as Eliot's putatively homosexual "yearning for a nature more masculine, at least more traditionally masculine, than he could find in himself" with Joyce's "flamboyantly, altogether more psychological, sexual assurance," Poirier argues that "to read [Joyce] properly one has to have a taste more for displays of authorial power than for sentiment. Joyce took a sadomasochistic pleasure in the fact that figures like Stephen and Gabriel could be forced by him to confront and to be intimidated by the energy, the exuberance, the virtuosity (however prefabricated) that is implanted in the suffocatingly programmed or encoded life which he himself has mastered. His re-

peated condescensions about failed or stunted sensibility are a reminder that only he is the calculating master of the codes" (*The Renewal of Literature*, 109–10).

14. As Bersani puts it in *The Freudian Body: Psychoanalysis and Art* (New York: Columbia University Press, 1986), "The artefacts of art are material metaphors for moves of consciousness which do not intrinsically 'belong' to any particular cultural domain but rather transversely cross, as it were, the entire range of cultural expression" (5). By "art" Bersani refers not to a culturally sequestered category of representation, but rather to various representations of consciousness in crisis, especially "disabled consciousness" (6), which draw his attention because they reproduce the self-destructive *jouissance* of masochistic sexuality: "If the sexual is, at the most primitive level, the attempted replication of a shattering (or psychically traumatizing) pleasure, art . . . is the attempted replication *of* that replication" (111).

15. Bersani, *The Culture of Redemption*, 134.

16. Ibid., 133.

17. Ibid., 3.

18. It is striking that although "Against *Ulysses*" had an independent life (*Raritan* 8 [fall 1988]: 1–32) before becoming part of *The Culture of Redemption*, Bersani's polemic generated virtually no public response from the Joyce community. The main exception to this peculiar silence is Denis Donoghue, "Is There a Case against *Ulysses*?" in *Joyce in Context*, ed. Vincent J. Cheng and Timothy Martin (Cambridge: Cambridge University Press, 1992), 19–39, which fails to grasp Bersani's argument.

19. Bersani, *The Culture of Redemption*, 170.

20. Ibid.

21. The best account of the ruses and subversions of authority in Joyce is provided in Vicki Mahaffey, *Reauthorizing Joyce* (Cambridge: Cambridge University Press, 1988). These questions of Joyce's narrative authority, his gendered authority, and his position at the center or the margins of the cultures he inhabited could fairly be understood as constituting the principal topoi of Joyce criticism, whether in its formalist, narratological, poststructuralist, psychoanalytic, feminist, historicist, materialist, or postcolonialist modes.

22. Maud Ellmann, *The Poetics of Impersonality: T. S. Eliot and Ezra Pound* (Brighton: Harvester, 1987), 198.

23. Eliot, *Selected Prose*, 40.

24. Ibid., 38.

25. Gustave Flaubert, *The Letters of Gustave Flaubert, 1830–1857*, ed. and trans. Francis Steegmuller (Cambridge, Mass.: Harvard University Press, 1979), 229–30. The standard account of Joyce's relation to Flaubert is provided in Richard K. Cross, *Flaubert and Joyce: The Rite of Fiction* (Princeton, N.J.: Princeton University Press, 1971); a more eccentric and insightful account, which does not, however, discuss the issue of impersonality, is provided in Hugh Kenner, *The Stoic Comedians: Flaubert, Joyce, and Beckett* (London: Allen, 1964). A more subtle analysis of Joyce's analogy of artistic to divine creation may be found in Marguerite Harkness, *The Aesthetics of Dedalus and Bloom* (Lewisburg, Pa.: Bucknell University Press, 1984), who situates this analogy in the tradition of Irish aestheticism, principally that of Wilde and Yeats. However, the best account of Stephen's aesthetic theory in *Portrait* is given by Ian Crump, "Refining Himself Out of Existence: The Evolution of Joyce's Aesthetic Theory and the Drafts of *A Portrait*," in Cheng and Martin, *Joyce in Context*, 223–40, who situates impersonality more firmly in the French

ascetic tradition running from Flaubert and Mallarmé through Barthes and Blanchot. Having painstakingly elaborated Joyce's development of the impersonal technique, Crump concludes, "By using this authority-less technique, he succeeded, after ten years, in producing a novel which no longer permits us, its readers, to receive the author's univocal or definitive message, but rather forces us to apprehend, or interpret, the multiple, and often conflicting and unconscious, messages that emanate from Stephen's unstable authority. Joyce worked so long to restructure literary authority in *A Portrait* . . . because he believed that the Irish could only achieve true political independence once they had achieved their independence as readers" (235).

A complete account of Flaubert's impersonalist aesthetic would need to consider his explanation of the composition of *Madame Bovary* in relation to his famous comment that "Madame Bovary, c'est moi." While I am unable to provide such an account here, I would refer the reader to Joseph Valente's *James Joyce and the Problem of Justice: Negotiating Sexual and Colonial Difference* (Cambridge: Cambridge University Press, 1995), chap. 3, for a brilliant account of the cross-gender identifications at stake in the composition of *Giacomo Joyce*. Valente's account of this transitional Joyce text corroborates and supplements Crump's account of the stages involved in Joyce's development, over a number of years, of his impersonalist technique.

26. Ezra Pound, "Joyce" (1920), in *Pound/Joyce: The Letters of Ezra Pound to James Joyce, with Pound's Essays on Joyce*, ed. Forrest Read (New York: New Directions, 1967), 139. Pound repeats this judgment aligning Joyce with Flaubert at various point in his essays, reviews, and letters. Comparing Joycean impersonality with its Flaubertian predecessor, Bersani argues to the contrary:

> In *Bouvard et Pécuchet* we have seen another encyclopedic novel that appears to indulge in massive quotation. But the intertextuality of *Bouvard et Pécuchet* is highly deceptive: the textual act of quotation is simultaneously a disqualification of the citational process. Flaubert erases our cultural memory at the very moment he awakens it. The mutations of epistemological discourses in *Bouvard et Pécuchet* remove the novel from the cultural history it nonconnectedly absorbs. Nor does the work's intratextuality create connective designs or structures; each section repeats a process of solipsistic play that cuts it off from the other sections echoed in the repetition. Finally, not only does the work of art *know nothing*, but in its incommensurability with all cultural discourses of knowledge, it can only exist in a continuous anxiety about its capacity to sustain itself, perhaps even to begin itself. For Joyce, on the other hand, art is by definition the transcendence of any such anxiety. (*The Culture of Redemption*, 163)

27. Peter Ackroyd, "Pomp and Circumstances," review of Denis Donoghue, *Walter Pater: Lover of Strange Souls* (New York: Knopf, 1995), *New Yorker*, May 15, 1995, 88. In "Thrilled by His Touch: Homosexual Panic and the Will to Artistry in *A Portrait of the Artist as a Young Man*," in this volume, Joseph Valente notes Wilde's green carnation. In "A Walk on the Wild(e) Side: The Doubled Reading of 'An Encounter,'" her contribution to this volume, Margot Norris notes the homosexual connotations of the color green. Of course, this homosexual association with greenness complicates considerably the national color of Ireland, exacerbating the color's political significance.

28. Poirier, *The Renewal of Literature*, 109–10.

29. James Joyce, *A Portrait of the Artist as a Young Man,* ed. R. B. Kershner (Boston: Bedford, 1993), 49.

30. Vicki Mahaffey's somewhat rambling discussion of the word *smugging,* in "Père-version and Im-mère-sion: Idealized Corruption in *A Portrait of the Artist as a Young Man* and *The Picture of Dorian Gray,*" in this volume, is both informative and symptomatic of the term's unspecifiability. See also David Norris's uncertainty in the face of this word: "I cannot authoritatively state precisely what smugging consisted of, other than that it was most definitely sexual and perhaps approximates what Wilde described as 'spooning' or heavy petting between males, probably involving an element of mutual masturbation" ("The 'Unhappy Mania' and Mr. Bloom's Cigar: Homosexuality in the Works of Joyce," *James Joyce Quarterly* 31 [spring 1994]: 367).

31. In "Cyclops" the anonymous narrator describes Bob Dornan "[b]lind to the world up in a shebeen in Bride street after closing time, fornicating with two shawls and a bully on guard, drinking porter out of teacups. And calling himself a Frenchy for the shawls, Joseph Manuo, and talking against the Catholic religion, and he serving mass in Adam and Eve's when he was young with his eyes shut, who wrote the new testament, and the old testament, and hugging and smugging. And the two shawls killed with the laughing" (*U* 12. 802–8). In his annotation for *smugging* in both *Portrait* and *Ulysses,* Don Gifford refers to Joseph Wright's turn-of-the-century *English Dialect Dictionary* and glosses the word as "toying amorously in secret" (*Ulysses Annotated: Notes for James Joyce's Ulysses,* 2d ed. [Berkeley and Los Angeles: University of California Press, 1988], 340). Of course, the range of actions covered by the verb *to toy* remains open to interpretation, especially given the contrasting contexts involved—adult heterosexuality and adolescent homosexuality. The *OED* did not include a sexual meaning under its definitions of smugging until the supplement of 1986, where its example is the *Ulysses* reference.

32. Eve Kosofsky Sedgwick, *Epistemology of the Closet* (Berkeley and Los Angeles: University of California Press, 1990), 73.

33. John Paul Riquelme, *Teller and Tale in Joyce's Fiction: Oscillating Perspectives* (Baltimore: Johns Hopkins University Press, 1983), 131.

34. See, for example, James E. Miller, *T. S. Eliot's Personal Waste Land: Exorcism of the Demons* (University Park: Pennsylvania State University Press, 1977), esp. 10 and 36; Poirier, *The Renewal of Literature,* 102; and Wayne Koestenbaum, *Double Talk: The Erotics of Male Literary Collaboration* (New York: Routledge, 1989), 112.

35. Robert Spoo, "Preparatory to Anything Else . . . ," *James Joyce Quarterly* 31 (spring 1994): 136. For especially cogent applications of Sedgwick's theories of homosociality and the closet, see the contributions to this special issue by Valente ("Thrilled by His Touch") and Colleen Lamos, "Signatures of the Invisible: Homosexual Secrecy and Knowledge in *Ulysses,*" *James Joyce Quarterly* 31 (spring 1994): 337–56.

36. Joseph Valente, "Thrilled by His Touch: Homosexual Panic and the Will to Artistry in *A Portrait of the Artist as a Young Man,*" *James Joyce Quarterly* 31 (spring 1994): 186–87. He has extended and modified these remarks in the revised essay in this volume.

37. See Tim Dean, "On the Eve of a Queer Future," *Raritan* 15 (summer 1995): 116–34.

38. Ed Cohen, *Talk on the Wilde Side: Toward a Genealogy of a Discourse on Male Sexualities* (New York: Routledge, 1993), 136: "The supplementing of 'aesthetic' effemi-

nacy with connotations of male sexual desire for other men is, I would argue, one of the consequences of the newspaper representations of the Wilde trials." Cohen's whole fifth chapter is especially useful for detailing the historical process that linked aestheticism with male-male sexual desire.

39. Harold Beaver, "Homosexual Signs," *Critical Inquiry* 8 (autumn 1981): 106.

40. Richard Brown, *James Joyce and Sexuality* (Cambridge: Cambridge University Press, 1985), esp. 106–7.

41. This misguided emphasis on androgyny mars David Weir's otherwise useful account of the "larger alignment of aesthetics and sexuality in Joyce's work," in "A Womb of His Own: Joyce's Sexual Aesthetics," *James Joyce Quarterly* 31 (spring 1994): 207–31.

42. Edward Carpenter, *The Intermediate Sex, Selected Writings*, vol. 1, *Sex*, ed. David Fernbach and Noël Greig (London: Gay Men's Press, 1984), 190–91.

43. Ibid., 276.

44. Ibid., 260.

45. Ibid., 197.

46. Ibid., 197–98.

47. Ibid., 272.

48. Richard von Krafft-Ebing, *Text-Book of Insanity, Based on Clinical Observations: For Practitioners and Students of Medicine*, trans. Charles Gilbert Chaddock (Philadelphia: Davis, 1905), 52–53. The first edition of this work appeared in German in 1879 and was regularly revised up until its author's death in 1902.

49. Ibid., 52.

50. Arnold I. Davidson, "Closing Up the Corpses: Diseases of Sexuality and the Emergence of the Psychiatric Style of Reasoning," in *Meaning and Method: Essays in Honor of Hilary Putnam*, ed. George Boolos (Cambridge: Cambridge University Press, 1990), 295–325. Reprinted in *Homosexuality and Psychoanalysis*, ed. Tim Dean, forthcoming.

51. Krafft-Ebing, *Text-Book of Insanity*, 81; emphasis added.

52. Ibid.

53. Ibid., 83.

54. Sigmund Freud, *Three Essays on the Theory of Sexuality*, in *The Standard Edition of the Complete Psychological Works of Sigmund Freud*, ed. and trans. James Strachey, 24 vols. (London: Hogarth Press and the Institute of Psycho-Analysis, 1953–74), vol. 7 (1901–1905), esp. 153–60.

55. Carl Fredrich Westphal, "Die conträre Sexualempfindung, Symptom eines neuropathischen (psychopathischen) Zustandes," *Archiv für Psychiatrie und Nervenkrankheiten* 2 (1870): 73–108. Michel Foucault cites Westphal's article as the pivotal text in the historical emergence of homosexuality as a discrete ontological identity, in *The History of Sexuality*, vol. 1, *An Introduction*, trans. Robert Hurley (New York: Pantheon, 1978), 43.

56. Krafft-Ebing, *Text-Book of Insanity*, 85.

57. Jacques Lacan, "Joyce le symptôme I," in *Joyce avec Lacan*, ed. Jacques Aubert (Paris: Navarin, 1987), 27. In this context we might recall that Abraham A. Brill, one of Freud's first translators and the principal early popularizer of Freudian thought in the United States, named his daughter Gioia, the Italian translation of Freud's patronym. Cited in Paul Roazen, *Freud and His Followers* (New York: New York University Press, 1984), 381.

58. In his brilliant *James Joyce, Authorized Reader* (Baltimore: Johns Hopkins University Press, 1991), Jean-Michel Rabaté examines the theoretical and historical significance of Joyce's concern with his patronym and with paternity in general. Noting (12) that Joyce was fully aware of how his name translated into German as *Freude* and was pronounced in French as *jouasse*, cognate with *jouissance*, Rabaté points out that "if we can see in *Ulysses* the paradigm for a modernity defined by a new conception of textuality, there is nevertheless no denying that the novel keeps returning to a central issue of paternity: the question of the origins and the endless aporias of artistic self-begetting" (50).

59. In *The French Joyce* (Ann Arbor: University of Michigan Press, 1990), Geert Lernout offers a very foolish and reductive account of Lacan's seminars on Joyce, aiming his critique principally at Lacan's homonymic style (71–83). Elsewhere Lernout's polemic against Lacan consists in identifying the French psychoanalyst with Hitler: "Lacan chose the path that Hitler took (is there a more impersonal biography [*sic*] than *Mein Kampf*?): he refines himself out of existence" ("Joyce or Lacan," *James Joyce: The Augmented Ninth*, ed. Bernard Benstock [Syracuse: Syracuse University Press, 1988], 200). By thus rhetorically associating Lacan with both Hitler and Joyce's impersonal aesthetic in a clumsy attempt to discredit Lacan, Lernout reveals his failure to grasp not only Lacan's writing but also Joyce's.

60. For such an account see Nestor Braunstein, *La jouissance: Un concept lacanien* (Paris: Point Hors Ligne, 1992).

61. Although for many years it was customary to note that *jouissance* could not be translated adequately by one English word alone, more recently Slavoj Žižek has instituted the convention of using the word *enjoyment* to translate *jouissance*. In what follows, *enjoyment* should be taken to connote far more than it usually does in English, including the dimension of suffering implicit in *jouissance*. *Jouissance* implies suffering because it designates what Bersani means by self-shattering, a form of sexual intensity that is intolerable to the coherent self. Since *jouissance* is the category through which Lacan elaborates the Freudian death drive, *jouissance* should be understood as *beyond* the pleasure principle. In this sense *enjoyment* is far from being all fun.

62. Jacques Lacan, "The Subversion of the Subject and the Dialectic of Desire in the Freudian Unconscious," in *Écrits: A Selection*, trans. Alan Sheridan (New York: Norton, 1977), 319.

63. Jacques Lacan, *The Seminar of Jacques Lacan*, book 7, *The Ethics of Psychoanalysis, 1959–1960*, ed. Jacques-Alain Miller, trans. Dennis Porter (New York: Norton, 1992), 143.

64. Lacan, *The Ethics of Psychoanalysis*, 181.

65. A useful synopsis of the canonical psychoanalytic understanding of sublimation is provided by Jean Laplanche and Jean-Bertrand Pontalis in *The Language of Psychoanalysis*, trans. Donald Nicholson-Smith (New York: Norton, 1973), 431–34. Laplanche and Pontalis conclude pointedly, "The lack of a coherent theory of sublimation remains one of the lacunae in psychoanalytic thought"—a lacuna that Lacan and Laplanche himself have attempted to redress at some length. Lacan's *Ethics* seminar (1959–1960) develops a theory of sublimation that has been especially invigorating for cultural studies in recent years—for example, in Joan Copjec's *Read My Desire: Lacan against the Historicists* (Cambridge, Mass.: MIT Press, 1994). Laplanche also conducted a yearlong Paris

seminar on sublimation, published in 1980 as *Problématiques III: La Sublimation* (Paris: Presses Universitaires des France). The other main psychoanalytic school to pursue significantly the theory of sublimation—specifically, in terms of reparation—is, of course, the Kleinian one: see, for example, Melanie Klein, "Infantile Anxiety-Situations Reflected in a Work of Art and in the Creative Impulse" (1929), in *Love, Guilt, and Reparation and Other Works, 1921–1945* (London: Virago, 1988), 210–18. In *The Culture of Redemption,* Bersani brilliantly examines Freudian, Kleinian, and Laplanchian theories of sublimation, but alas, not Lacan's theory.

66. "Joyce le symptôme I," 27: "[C]ette jouissance est la seule chose que de son texte nous puissions attraper." Here Ellie Ragland-Sullivan's gloss is useful: "Lacan views Joyce as handling the letter outside its effects as signified, in a search for a pure *jouissance* (both enjoyment and suffering)" ("More French Connections," *James Joyce Quarterly* 26 [autumn 1988]: 116).

67. Jacques Lacan, *Television/A Challenge to the Psychoanalytic Establishment,* ed. Joan Copjec, trans. Denis Hollier et al. (New York: Norton, 1990), 10: "[T]hese [signifying] chains are not of meaning but of enjoy-meant [*jouis-sens*] which you can write as you wish, as is implied by the punning that constitutes the law of the signifier."

68. The failure to grasp that *jouissance* emerges primarily metonymically—in the arabesque movements of the Joycean text's reflexivity, rather than in the metaphoric or mimetic dimension of its thematization—mars Garry M. Leonard's provocative account of *jouissance* in Joyce (*Reading "Dubliners" Again: A Lacanian Perspective* [Syracuse: Syracuse University Press, 1994], esp. 95–112). The tendency to treat *jouissance* thematically also limits Patrick McGee's argument in *Paperspace: Style as Ideology in Joyce's "Ulysses"* (Lincoln: University of Nebraska Press, 1988). Jean-Michel Rabaté is much closer to Lacan's conceptualization of how *jouissance* functions in Joyce: "[I]f we agree that we find at the same time a continuous 'joyceance' of language to be reenacted through Joyce's signature and a perpetual indecidability of meaning, is it not a proof that there lies the only way out of a possible psychotic closure of the system of symptoms? There, Lacan's reading of *Exiles* takes on its full significance. . . . The cloud of doubt which wraps up the entire play does not prevent people from suffering on stage or among the audience, but it does prevent the audience from taking a perverse pleasure in any represented suffering, and it opens the path for an enjoyment of language, a language still to be re-created" ("Discussion," in Benstock, *James Joyce,* 206).

69. Lacan makes this point through the following felicitous formulation: "The discovery of the unconscious . . . is that the full significance of meaning far surpasses the signs manipulated by the individual. Man is always cultivating a great many more signs than he thinks" (*The Seminar of Jacques Lacan,* book 2, *The Ego in Freud's Theory and in the Technique of Psychoanalysis, 1954–1955,* ed. Jacques-Alain Miller, trans. Sylvana Tomaselli [Cambridge: Cambridge University Press], 1988, 122). For Joyce to count as a subject—that is, for him to have an unconscious—means that his mastery of language remains incomplete. The troubling impulse to mythify Joyce as master—a tendency he himself often encouraged—is, unfortunately, repeated with respect to Lacan in much of what passes for Lacanian criticism. In the face of such transferential, mythmaking impulses, we should bear in mind the distinction between discerning significance in a discourse and projecting an other as sole origin of that significance.

70. For a useful discussion of the relation between Freud's "portrait of the artist"

and Joyce's, see Jean Kimball, "Freud, Leonardo, and Joyce: The Dimensions of a Child-hood Memory," in *The Seventh of Joyce,* ed. Bernard Benstock (Bloomington: Indiana University Press, 1982), 57–73.

71. Sigmund Freud, "On Narcissism: An Introduction," *Standard Edition,* vol. 14 (1914–1916), 94–95.

72. Sigmund Freud, *Leonardo da Vinci and a Memory of His Childhood, Standard Edition,* vol. 11 (1910), 80.

73. Sigmund Freud, "'Civilized' Sexual Morality and Modern Nervous Illness," *Standard Edition,* vol. 9 (1906–8), 189.

74. Freud, *Three Essays,* 178.

75. Jean Laplanche, "To Situate Sublimation," trans. Richard Miller, *October* 28 (spring 1984): 12.

76. Lacan, *The Ethics of Psychoanalysis,* 293.

77. This notion of sublimation as involving no detour via an object-cathexis is complicated by Freud's theory of the ego, introduced in 1914 in "On Narcissism," which conceptualizes the ego as a privileged *object* in the psychic economy and maintains that libidinal cathexis of the ego desexualizes or sublimates the drive. Bersani discusses the implications of this complication in chapter 2 of *The Culture of Redemption* and chapter 2 of *The Freudian Body.* A further point of clarification: Lacan's redefinition of sublimation, in his *Ethics* seminar, as "raising an object to the dignity of the Thing" does not, in fact, contradict Freud's distinction between sublimation as involving the instinct and idealization as involving the object. In order to refine the distinction between sublimation as a vicissitude of the drive and repression as that which produces desire and its object, Lacan elaborates the concept of the Thing, which may as well result from demonization as from idealization.

78. Bersani, *The Culture of Redemption,* 32.

79. Freud, *Three Essays,* 148.

80. See Jean Laplanche, *Life and Death in Psychoanalysis,* trans. Jeffrey Mehlman (Baltimore: Johns Hopkins University Press, 1976); Leo Bersani, *Homos* (Cambridge, Mass.: Harvard University Press, 1995); and Tim Dean, "Sex and Syncope," *Raritan* 15 (winter 1996): 64–86. Given Bersani's pursuit throughout his work of what is essentially a single problematic—one that accords substantial, if not ultimate, privilege to non-normative manifestations of sexuality—it is striking that his critique of Joyce touches on the question of homosexuality only parenthetically and in relation to Lacan. Developing an invidious distinction between Joycean impersonality and other modernists' narrative strategies, Bersani argues that a

> whole set of conventional psychological and moral significances coexists quite comfortably in Joyce with a radical skepticism concerning the validity of any move whatsoever beyond the line of the signifier. (This cohabitation is quite familiar to us today. The Lacanians' ritualistic repetition of the word *signifiant* as the key to Lacan's radical rethinking of the Freudian unconscious has, for example, in no way affected the normative status, in their thought, of the psychologically and morally specific referent of a phallocentric heterosexuality.) The perception of human reality as a language effect has generally had the curious consequence of forestalling, of leaving no terms available for, the criticism of psychological, moral, and social

orders elaborated by the quite different view—now seen as epistemologically naive—of language as essentially descriptive of a preexistent real. (*The Culture of Redemption*, 174)

As I hope to have at least begun showing, Lacan and Joyce are both concerned more with the effects of *jouissance* than with purely linguistic effects, and it is in this concern that their political promise lies.

81. See Leo Bersani and Ulysse Dutoit, *Arts of Impoverishment: Beckett, Rothko, Resnais* (Cambridge, Mass.: Harvard University Press, 1993).

82. In "A Love Letter" Lacan confirms that "speaking of love is in itself a *jouissance*" (*Feminine Sexuality: Jacques Lacan and the Ecole Freudienne*, trans. Jacqueline Rose, ed. Juliet Mitchell and Jacqueline Rose [New York: Norton, 1982], 154).

Afterword
"The Vehicle of a Vague Speech"

Christopher Lane

There is, I feel in the words, some goad of the flesh driving him into a new passion, a darker shadow of the first, darkening even his own understanding of himself.

—James Joyce, *U* 9.461–64

You have homosexual catheis of empathy between narcissism of the expert and steatopygic invertedness. Get yourself psychoanolised!

—James Joyce, *FW* 522.30–32

Is lesbian and gay studies—or even queer theory—able to address the full dynamism of sexuality in Joyce's work? I suspect that it is not, in part because the terminology these critical fields adopt generally obscures the radical doubt informing all sexual desire and intimacy in his fiction.

Another way of presenting my question would be to ask whether Joyce's oeuvre can comply with a project aimed at "recovering" homosexual desire from overlooked, even suppressed passages. Like many of the contributors to this collection, I shall argue that Joyce's work is designed to revoke this possibility, given its author's doubt that one can satisfactorily alight on the meaning of sexual intimacy. To address this skepticism, we could invoke biographical evidence suggesting that Joyce was ill at ease with homosexuality and homosexuals (see Valente, "Thrilled" 73n. 26). Many of Joyce's observations (some apparently earnest, others frivolous) seem to document this unease. Yet the contributors to this collection importantly remind us that the task of weighing these statements against passages in Joyce's texts presents us with insurmountable difficulties, not least the possibility that attribution of meaning to Joyce can foster more violence to meaning than the sexual and psychic difficulties he adumbrates. In light of this dilemma, our "hermeneutics of suspicion" might ultimately prove fruitless (though not entirely groundless), generating profound doubt about the nature of our quest and the basis of our interpretive demands.

This collection's strength lies in its willingness not to subordinate textual passages to contemporary hermeneutic and political demands. The contributors realize that Joyce is neither homophobic nor entirely amenable to what we might call radical sexual politics. *Quare Joyce* is compelling because it engages Joyce in the mode in which Joyce himself engaged sexuality—a mode, if the paradox can stand, that is "faithful" to the vagaries and enigmas of human passion.

Before engaging some of the essays in this collection, I want to underscore this point by turning to several passages in *A Portrait of the Artist as a Young Man*. The passage from which I take my title, "the vehicle of a vague speech," occurs at the end of *A Portrait*'s second chapter and describes a moment of sexual intimacy between Stephen Dedalus and an unnamed prostitute ("A young woman dressed in a long pink gown laid her hand on his arm to detain him" [*P* 100]). Although I realize the likely provocation of beginning a "queer" afterword with this incident, I want to consider whether "sexual intimacy" adequately describes the moment; such considerations profoundly affect how we interpret Joycean sexuality:

> With a sudden movement she bowed his head and joined her lips to his and he read the meaning of her movements in her frank uplifted eyes. It was too much for him. He closed his eyes, surrendering himself to her, body and mind, conscious of nothing in the world but the dark pressure of her softly parting lips. They pressed upon his brain as upon his lips as though they were the vehicle of a vague speech; and between them he felt an unknown and timid pressure, darker than the swoon of sin, softer than sound or odour. (*P* 101)

Can this passage, about a heterosexual encounter, help us appraise "quare" Joyce? Stephen's "surrender" to the prostitute implicitly feminizes him, leaving the woman in control, but this is hardly queer. We might also note that the woman's body is represented only by fragments—that is, as "frank uplifted eyes" and "softly parting lips"—and that "the meaning of her movements" becomes clear only when Stephen "read[s]" them. But what does he *understand* by this reading? The passage is intriguing and brilliant (though I could hardly call it "queer"), because it illustrates a profound default in human relations and consciousness. The narrative reveals a yawning gap between the prostitute's intention to "seduce" Stephen and Stephen's own bid to comprehend and *not* understand this event.[1] To complicate matters further, we cannot confirm that Stephen is properly this woman's "object" (a formulation that doesn't capture fantasy's impalpable elements, as Joyce realized); nor can we say everything about her motives by stating that she is driven purely by poverty and destitution. Such factors may be sufficient to understand most of this scene, but the narrator suggests that more and less is going on here, due in part to Stephen's and the prostitute's psychic asymmetry. In what respect, then, can we say this pair is "intimate"?

Hugh Kenner has usefully remarked on *A Portrait's* sensory disseverations: "The audible soothes: the visible disturbs," he notes, adding, "Smell is the means of discriminating empirical realities . . . , sight corresponds to the phantasms of oppression, hearing to the imaginative life. Touch and taste together are the modes of sex."[2] The passage above begins with Stephen closing his eyes, a gesture implying he rids himself of "the phantasms of oppression." However, he is merely substituting one reality for another. Additionally, the "phantasms of oppression," which sight signifies, become more acute and recriminative when detached from the external world, as Stephen later discovers. The gap created by this substitution, which might endorse the literal and figurative distance between Stephen's brain and lips, is surely the narrator's interest here and elsewhere, in part because it generates immense doubt about the sexual event. This gap highlights the conditions of possibility and impossibility affecting every couple's chances of intimacy in Joyce's work.

Since we know only how Stephen perceives her, we cannot be certain of the prostitute's intention—and I don't mean to be facetious in stressing this. However, we must consider why his grasp of this scenario is vague and imprecise. The woman's "softly parting lips" press upon Stephen's "as though they were the vehicle of a vague speech." (A similar idea, detached from this sexual cause, recurs at the end of the novel in Stephen's diary: "Vague words for a vague emotion" [*P* 251].) We can doubt the success of this communication, but we cannot ignore the contingency and psychic associations operating here, the woman's lips serving as a conduit and pretext for fantasies to which she is only tangentially connected. Into what does Stephen therefore fall in his "swoon of sin"? *A Portrait* asks this question repeatedly in its third and fourth chapters, which ruminate on Stephen's internal "unrest." But if the narrator of this novel seems incapable of representing this "fall" *without* religious and other symbolic allusions, the novel also signifies what must fall away from representation to give it at least a suggestion of sexual truth.

This emphasis on allusion—typical of Joyce—differs from claims that Joyce presents homosexuality (indeed, all sexuality) as an "open secret." We owe this latter formulation to D. A. Miller's final chapter of *The Novel and the Police*, "Secret Subjects, Open Secrets,"[3] though it actually surfaces in E. M. Forster's posthumous novel *Maurice*, where the narrator refers to "laughing open secret."[4] Yet Joyce is not a simple theorist of secrecy. We cannot unveil subplots or even substantive knots in his work by calling their difficulty "homosexual" or "queer," as many contemporary theorists now use the latter word. Joyce conceives of sexual desire for both sexes with and without their accompanying objects. The result is not conventionally "gay affirmative," but it is also neither phobic nor heterosexist. Joyce's redefinition of desire and objects is, paradoxically, what makes his writing so complex and "queer"—that is, sexually difficult rather than strategically coherent or politically insubordinate. I am pushing for this invigorated meaning for *queer* because I think Joyce represents all desire as odd and unruly. For this reason, it is neither accurate nor politically helpful to call Joyce's representations of homosexuality simply queer; ultimately, such assumptions normalize his conception of fantasy, passion, and intimacy.

It might seem ironic that I am using *queer* to convey a crucial and often ignored gap between sexuality and identity; gay and lesbian theorists often associate this word with the radical turbulence of homosexual desire. However, the gap I am invoking distinguishes the object of desire from the aim of the subject's drives in ways that manifest the "queerest" dimension of Joyce's sexual representations. In raising this distinction, which I take from Freud's "Instincts and Their Vicissitudes," published the year after Joyce's *A Portrait* first appeared in the *Egoist* (1914), I want to stress that the union of psychic aims and objects— regardless of the object's gender or sexual preference—is, from psychoanalytic and Joycean perspectives, a conservative appraisal of human sexuality.[5] "Union" confirms an illusion that subjects routinely combine psychic objects with aims, a premise erroneously implying lasting satisfaction. Joyce reminds us that sexuality is resistant to meaning, given its unconscious determinants. However, the discourse of "getting what one wants," which conceives of satisfaction as a dimension of egoic demand, ignores the randomness of this satisfaction. Owing to proliferating impediments and displacements, "getting what one wants" is nothing short of miraculous. Sexuality is contingent on numerous factors, many of them unconscious, yet Joyce repeatedly shows us how fantasy tries to conceal this contingency, granting the ego the comforting illusion that its objects of desire are predetermined by God or fate.

One of the most interesting aspects of *A Portrait* is its grim insistence that few objects—parents, women, friends, poems, or religion—sustain the ego with lasting satisfaction. As several contributors to *Quare Joyce* observe, Joyce "denatures" sexuality by uncoupling desire from reproduction and by adding a dimension of contingency—and thus *uninterest*—to the conventional pursuit of heterosexual objects (see Valente, "Thrilled," 60; Rabaté, 40; Dean, 246 and 261; Leonard 79 and 90). Arguably, this experiential distress—the sense that no object makes Stephen entirely happy—leads him to vacillate between idealizing women (Mercedes, E. C.) and loving other men (for instance, Cranly), before rejecting both options in his exile.

Perhaps we can grasp the psychic implications of exile and its consequent rejection of male and female objects only by asking how queer we would find an alternative conclusion to *A Portrait*. Imagine that Stephen, on hearing Cranly's cautionary words, realizes that he has loved him for years and then has an emotional and sexual affair with him that lasts, to mimic the conclusion to

Forster's contemporaneous novel *Maurice*, "for the ever and ever that fiction allows."[6] This, however, is how *A Portrait* draws to a close:

> —Alone, quite alone. You have no fear of that. And you know what that word means? Not only to be separate from all others but to have not even one friend.
> —I will take the risk, said Stephen.
> —And not to have any one person, Cranly said, who would be more than a friend, more even than the noblest and truest friend a man ever had.
> His words seemed to have struck some deep chord in his own nature. Had he spoken of himself, of himself as he was or wished to be? Stephen watched his face for some moments in silence. A cold sadness was there. He had spoken of himself, of his own loneliness which he feared.
> —Of whom are you speaking? Stephen asked at length.
> Cranly did not answer. (*P* 247)

This passage is remarkable for its ability to convey the burden of unexpressed—and perhaps inexpressible—longing. If we discount the fragments of Stephen's diary following this conversation, "Cranly did not answer" would be the novel's final words. The affective complexity of Stephen and Cranly's relationship dissipates, however, if we argue that Cranly, as a latent homosexual, had desired Stephen all along. To sustain this second reading, which Leonard persuasively critiques (see 79 and 86), one would have to read the two men's intellectual rivalry and sexual jealousy for E. C. as symptoms alternately blocking and fulfilling their mutual physical desire, which does little justice to the enigmas and vicissitudes of their friendship. Nonetheless, *A Portrait* does not entirely rescind this reading; the novel simply prevents this reading from being "gay affirmative" by emphasizing the *nonreciprocal* basis of Stephen and Cranly's relationship. The incongruence of the men's aims and intentions makes their inability to become lovers poignant and astutely drawn. Perhaps we learn more from the fact that this friendship is not consummated than we do from Forster's insistence, in the terminal note of *Maurice*, "A happy ending was imperative. I shouldn't have bothered to write otherwise. I was determined that in fiction anyway two men should fall in love and remain in it for the ever and ever that fiction allows."[7]

Is Joyce's suggestion that there is no sexual relation more "gay affirmative" than Forster's "imperative" that his protagonists find eternal happiness? Perhaps we can answer this provocative question by turning to Jacques Lacan, whose formulation "*il n'y a pas de rapport sexuel*" I am invoking.[8] Lacan's argument is not erotophobic, implying that people do not or cannot have sex; his claim is erotophilic by stressing that desire paradoxically obtains from the absence of reciprocity. Deriving from the structural effects of sexual difference, this nonreciprocity draws on fantasy to suture the psychic gap separating men from women, men from men, and women from women. To clarify this point, we may recall

René Magritte's famous painting *The Lovers* (1928), in which we see a man and woman kissing, though each face is invisible, covered by a piece of cloth. Magritte's tragicomic point is that the man's inability to see the woman, and vice versa, does not impede the couple's passion; it intensifies and even *causes* it. Lacan endorses this point by arguing that the subject's "lack-in-being" engenders its imaginary shift from insufficiency to anticipation: "Being of non-being, that is how *I* as subject comes on the scene"[9] For Lacan, the subject strives constantly to forget its castration by fantasizing a replete and lasting rapport with the object, while sexuality and sexual intimacy are constant reminders of this castration, highlighting the subject's dependence on fantasy as a support for its identifications and pleasures.

Dean's essay, "Paring His Fingernails" usefully clarifies Lacan's interest in Joyce's work; it also proposes a number of ways to interpret Joycean sexuality. Dean resists conceptualizing Joycean sexuality as a palpable form that Joyce can "closet"; nor does Dean suggest that Joyce unthinkingly inherits from fin-de-siècle sexologists a single conceptual model of homosexuality. Instead, like Leonard, he reads homosexuality in Joyce's texts (and Joycean sexuality in general) as an effect of the symbolic structures in which Joyce was writing. Arguably, this perspective is more historically attentive to diverse turn-of-the-century accounts of homosexuality than are Miller's and Eve Kosofsky Sedgwick's claims that late-nineteenth-century European societies constituted homosexuality only as a secret.[10] Like Dean, I think these suggestions of "closeted" sexuality in Joyce's and others' writing are inaccurate and misleading, in part because they often enlist psychobiographical evidence to support their contentions and speak of the closet only in terms of content. These suggestions also argue that homosexuality represented *the* secret in fin-de-siècle Euro-American literature;[11] any reader of Thomas Hardy, for one, could correct this false claim.[12] As Dean cautions, "[W]e misconstrue Joyce's aesthetic by reducing it to a form of evasion or hypocrisy" (251). His concerns about the parameters of "gay affirmative" readings, which to him miss the radicalism of Joycean sexuality, do not thereby make his account "degaying" or sexually nonspecific; nor indeed is his reading historically imprecise. If we can represent Forster's note to *Maurice* as exemplary of the "gay affirmative" position (I have argued elsewhere that, despite its author's claims, the novel ultimately is not so),[13] we can see why Forster's effort to unite Maurice and Scudder "for the ever and ever that fiction allows" represses the sexual dynamism exciting the two characters' previous trysts. We might be pressed to find Scudder's interest in "sharing" with Maurice erotic (this is Scudder's euphemism for having sex),[14] but we can argue that the couple's "imperative" to find "happiness" ultimately is desexualizing because it tolerates only conscious and harmonious same-sex desires that resurface with greater narrative turbulence and critical interest in Forster's posthumous *Life to Come* collection.

Joyce was clearly suspicious of such claims of interpersonal harmony, yet I am not suggesting that he has no interest in genitality and thus in representing same-sex desires—a caution I would bring to Leonard's sometimes unclear distinction between "homosecrecy" and "heterosecrecy." Rather, like Dean, I contend that Joyce's greater interest in unconscious and psychically "perverse" formations of desire—which results in greater tolerance for the vicissitudes of desire itself, something generally working in homosexuality's favor—often makes his accounts of passion more interesting than contemporaneous accounts of homosexuality in, say, Forster's or Radclyffe Hall's fiction. I would read these two writers' work against the sexual trajectory we find in Joyce because while Forster and Hall were similarly indebted to turn-of-the-century sexology and psychology, they generally did not share Joyce's interest in sexual fantasy. Rather, they strove so earnestly for homosexuals' acceptance as congenitally disposed and creatively talented that they often downplayed the very desire they defended. We might refine this argument by observing that as homosexuals (it seems anachronistic to call Forster a "gay man"), Forster and Hall had more at stake than Joyce in their representations of homosexuality. We could also highlight all of the places in which Forster's and Hall's works are erotically disposed despite themselves;[15] but the point is less to assert the superiority of one writer over another, and more to stress the conceptual implications of their varying notions of desire, fantasy, and intimacy.

This leads me to an historical argument about competing conceptualizations of male and female homosexuality at the turn of the last century. Again, Dean's essay helpfully underscores that while Edward Carpenter's *The Intermediate Sex* interpreted homosexuality on the basis of categorical distinctions, Richard von Krafft-Ebing's formulation of "hyperesthesia" in 1892 and Freud's essays of 1905 on sexuality ultimately refute such notions of sexual typology, instead defending homosexual desire on the basis of psychic conditions and identifications. While Joyce read many—if not all—of these sexological and psychoanalytic arguments and inherited at least the context of Carpenter's and Karl Heinrich Ulrichs's claims about congenital predispositions and sexual types, his greater interest lay in theories about the vicissitudes of psychic drives.

In this respect, I support this collection's fundamental premise that readers cannot grasp Joyce's radical conception of sexual desire without appreciating his narratives' fundamental *distrust* of successful object relations. This distrust inevitably creates difficulties when we ruminate on the basis of sexual desire in Joyce's work. Thus I find it unsurprising that several contributors to this volume begin by asking substantive questions about Joycean sexuality, seemingly intent on clarifying the mystery of this phenomenon—such tensions among curiosity, doubt, and certainty probably recur at some point for every reader of Joyce. Margot Norris asks, "What, precisely, is that 'enormity' [to which Joyce refers in "An Encounter" in *Dubliners*], and what is its ethical status if the story's publication depends on, and the author relies on, its expected and desired invisibility?" (19). Similarly, Valente questions Joyce's reticence about Oscar Wilde's 1895 trials: "What could account for this unwonted circumspection from a man long since resigned to offending hypocritical sensibilities with his writing?" ("Thrilled,"47). Both questions are necessary to ask—indeed, it would be remiss to avoid asking these questions altogether—yet Norris's reading of "An Encounter" and Valente's reading of *A Portrait* derive their strength by suggesting that no single answer can sate our curiosity. Posing such questions in the hope of resolving Joyce's enigmatic relation to Wilde or Proust (as Caserio argues concerning the latter, 153) merely generates fresh uncertainty about our ability to conquer mystery.

Perhaps for this reason, Norris follows her question by quoting Joyce's words to his editor, Grant Richards, which also conclude with a question: "Many of the passages and phrases over which we are now disputing escaped you: it was I who showed them to you. And do you think that what escaped you (whose business it is to look for such things in the books you consider) will be surely detected by a public who reads the books for quite another reason?" (*SL* 88). Joyce seems to refer to a technique of concealment here, invoking phrases whose meaning either "escape[s]" the reader or suffers detection. I am reminded of Marlow's claim, in Joseph Conrad's *Heart of Darkness*, that in recounting his experiences with Kurtz, he could not avoid "step[ping] over the threshold of the invisible."[16] For when Marlow alights on what he believes is the "riddle" of Kurtz and life in general, he acknowledges "with humiliation that probably [he] would have nothing to say."[17] We can use this paradox in Conrad's novel to ask, with Dean and Leonard, whether Joyce's suggestion of concealment is equivalent to our contemporary attempts to clarify and resolve secrets. *Secretion* and *secret* are etymologically entwined (Latin *secretus,* from *se* + *cernere,* to sift apart), yet these words suggest different hermeneutic principles: *Secretion* denotes a leak and a failure to contain, while *secret* implies the reverse.

These moments in Norris's and Valente's essays alone suggest that *Quare Joyce* radically departs from conventional gay and lesbian studies collections. These often bind such enigmas to gaps in the author's biography, which the critic in turn tries earnestly to resolve. Given Joyce's complicated relation to Wilde and probably to Sir Roger Casement (Valente, "Thrilled"; Rabaté; Mahaffey; and Caserio), his supportive relation to Paris's lesbian subculture in the 1920s and 1930s (Valente, "Joyce's (Sexual) Choices"), his knowledge of (though not agreement with) sexology and psychoanalysis (Dean; Valente, "Thrilled"; and Leonard), and his acute notion of the vagaries of textual and sexual meaning (Rabaté, Dean, and Valente, "Thrilled"), it would be absurd to reduce all of these factors to suggestions of a homosexual secret. If Wilde understood the unconscious only in its Gothic conception, as a repository of ontological truth (for me, such claims simplify Wilde's notion of secrecy in *The Picture of Dorian Gray* and elsewhere), Joyce does not conceptualize repression or secrecy in this way. As Mahaffey implies, Joyce conceptualizes this relation by analogy and association—by recourse to the signifier to identify where the signifying chain fails—which means that while he inherited Gothic conceptions of the unconscious (a legacy Freud and Wilde also arguably rejected), he modified Gothic ideas about secrecy by insisting that a subject's "secret" is often, paradoxically, that it hasn't one.

This realization is surely the strength of Valente's closing remarks on the "open closet" (see also Leonard 87 and 93). Valente modifies Miller's formulation of the "open secret" by moving his interpretation from a substantive concern (the hermeneutics of secrecy) to a conceptual and psychic question (of what can sexuality consist when it represents "an open closet"? see "Thrilled" 69). It is surely historically anachronistic to associate the signifier *closet* with homosexuality; this connection arose from the 1960s and 1970s North American and European lesbian and gay liberation movements, which saw "coming out of the closet" as a sign of sexual honesty, hope, and integrity. I obviously don't dispute the importance of living as closely as possible to one's psychic and sexual fantasies, but it seems to me doubtful and unwise to imply (as Miller and Sedgwick do) that these notions of sexual dishonesty and integrity existed *as such* when Dickens and Henry James were writing. "The open closet" is a different proposition, though, in part because it casts doubt on the importance and reliability of object choice and suggests that sexuality represents less a substance (i.e., a secret) than a warning of subjective incompletion, psychic inconsistency, and alienation. If the "open secret" shores up an idea of ontological deceit and sexual integrity, the "open closet" (like Joyce's work) revokes the idea that closets *contain* sexual meanings. Dean's, Leonard's, and Valente's psychoanalytic emphases are thus invaluable because while these critics argue that Sedgwick's conception of closets ultimately is not Joycean, they also show that Joyce's conception of sexuality is remarkably close to Freud's arguments about the drives. For this reason, Dean claims that Joyce's interest in impersonality should be understood in terms of impersonality's providing access to "a perverse *jouissance*" (241). This claim is enlightening because *jouissance* is not reducible to authorial blind spots (for example, Joyce's fascination with homosexual seduction and lesbianism or his occasional and alleged homophobia) or even the properties of Joyce's characters (Cranly's silence, Bloom's ambiguous paternalism, and the "queer old josser" in "An Encounter"). In this respect, Dean's reading of *jouissance* partly resembles Wyndham Lewis's thoughts about the repressive dimension of personality in "Analysis of the Mind of James Joyce." Lewis remarks,

> "Personality" . . . is clearly the wrong word [to represent the prevailing "sex-war" because] its sentimental use falsifies what is happening. But it is the *abstraction*, of course, that is required, today, of every human being. To "develop the personality" is an alluring invitation, but it invariably covers some process that is guaranteed to strip a person bare of all "personality" in a fortnight. . . . I am only pointing out that this excellent result is obtained by fraud. So we must not take that fraud too seriously, however much we may applaud its aims.[18]

Lewis claims that personality "turn[s] people's minds away from sex altogether eventually.... The family['s] ... expensive ecstasies and personal adornments must go in the end. The supposed encouragement of them today is illusory."[19] The corollary to this argument, which Dean and Joyce usefully adumbrate (contra Lewis's thoughts about the latter's alleged perspective on sexuality), is that *jouissance* shatters "personality" by encouraging impersonal aspects of sexual fantasy and desire to prevail. Perhaps for this reason, Forster claimed that Joyce's *Ulysses* (1922) degenerates into a "joyless orgy."[20]

Although such observations are conceptually fascinating, revealing Forster's stubborn aversion to sexual desire, *jouissance* arises in various forms and does not manifest itself consistently in Joyce's writing. I would therefore supplement Dean's account of perverse *jouissance* in *A Portrait* by suggesting that a different type of *jouissance* emerges in Joyce's astute observation that a "howl of puritanical joy" accompanied Wilde's persecution in Britain (*CW* 204). This account of *jouissance* could be read as a comment on many Britons' gleeful enjoyment of Wilde's hubristic failure. By advancing this perspective, Joyce not only demonstrates a profound grasp of Wilde's humiliation, but also highlights a politically valuable understanding of how groups and communities struggle to maintain their identities, a perspective invaluable when considering Ireland's relation to Britain, and Joyce's relation to both.

If Wilde recorded this principle of *jouissance* in his epigrams for *The Picture of Dorian Gray* ("Those who go beneath the surface ... [and] read the symbol do so at their peril"; "It is the spectator, and not life, that art really mirrors"),[21] Joyce repeated this principle in many of his fictional accounts of sexual intimacy. Reading Levine's account of the "Eumaeus" section of *Ulysses,* for example, I am struck by not only Joyce's attentive grasp of homosexuality's different manifestations in Britain and Europe, but his interest in recording the ego's internal apprehension of desires that might also be "alien" to it.[22] Levine argues, "There is a sly humor at work in every sentence [of this section]: a rhetoric of innuendo that makes connections furtively, but with a knowing wink" (101). Such arguments might swiftly return us to "restoring" homosexual semantics, yet in quoting the following passage from *Ulysses,* Levine registers not only the impossibility of this adequate "restoration," but also the ego's contradictory reactions to homosexual desire:

> Briefly, putting two and two together, ... he reflected about the errors of notorieties and crowned heads running counter to morality such as the Cornwall case a number of years before under their veneer in a way scarcely intended by nature, a thing good Mrs Grundy, as the law stands, was terribly down on though not for the reason they thought they were probably whatever it was except women chiefly who were always fiddling more or less at one another it being largely a matter of dress and all the rest of it. Ladies who like distinctive underclothing should, and every welltailored

man must, trying to make the gap wider between them by innuendo and give more of a genuine filip to acts of impropriety between the two. (*U* 16.1195–1210)

Levine brilliantly detects many of the allusions in this passage, such as the "Cornwall case," which could refer either to the 1884 Dublin Castle scandal in which two officials, Cornwall and French, were discovered to be publicly "involved in an extensive homosexual circle," or to "the 1870 divorce suit at which Edward VII, then duke of Cornwall, was called to the witness stand because two of his friends were named as correspondents" (111). Yet she does not fully attend to the remarkable turns in the narrative itself, which, in typical stream-of-consciousness style, track Bloom's muddled responses and associations with assiduous care. Let us therefore dwell on these turns by identifying, somewhat crudely, their semantic breaks and psychic displacements. We would read, "he reflected about the errors of notorieties and crowned heads running counter to morality . . . / under their veneer / in a way scarcely intended by nature, / a thing good Mrs Grundy, as the law stands, was terribly down on/ though not for the reason they thought / they were probably / whatever it was / except women chiefly who were always fiddling more or less at one another / it being largely a matter of dress." These displacements are fascinating, not least because they illustrate a psychic oscillation from curiosity ("they were probably") to ambivalence ("whatever it was") to rationalization ("except women chiefly"). The narrative appears to avert the question of what physically ensues ("whatever it was") by displacing undressing for sex onto tailoring ("women . . . were always fiddling more or less at one another"), before seeming to conclude with the subject entirely changed ("it being largely a matter of dress"). Amusingly, though, the narrative demonstrates that the issue is not settled, for it cannily highlights the return of curiosity, as if catching the drive in its attempt to enter consciousness: "Ladies who like distinctive underclothing should, and every welltailored man must, / trying to make the gap wider between them by innuendo / and give more of a genuine filip to acts of impropriety between the two, / she unbuttoned his and then he untied her, / mind the pin, / whereas savages in the cannibal islands, say, at ninety degrees in the shade not caring a continental" (*U* 16.1207–1212).

Affect is surely the critical interpretive issue here. What matters is less our ability to attribute these thoughts to Joyce, or indeed Joyce's ability to authorize his representations, than his *characters'* response to the enigma of their desires, which variously precipitate anxiety, distress, joy, fury, and phobia—often simultaneously. As Levine astutely notes, "though the question 'is Murphy [one of this section's protagonists] a homosexual?' seems both unanswerable and somewhat beside the point . . . he is undeniably the focus for Bloom's anxieties" (113). The question is "beside the point" because, as Levine remarks, the passage suggests an "easy slide from heterosexual to homosexual possibilities and back again" (110). This argument, while unable to read Murphy (or Bloom) as homosexual, nonetheless points to homosexuality as a sexual possibility that crucially—perhaps violently—affects these character's identities. In this way, Murphy "sets off some internal alarm" in Bloom (103):

> Because of this centrifugal movement, [Murphy] seems to illustrate the more general semiotic point about character: that a Murphy (like a Stephen or a Bloom) . . . is most properly understood as a set of attributes temporarily clustered around a proper name. When Stephen asks, "What's in a name?" (*U* 16.364), his question resonates in similar ways. No inherent truth, is his implicit answer—just a process of imposture, of standing in for the thing itself, as signifiers stand in for and inevitably betray what they might wish to signify. (103)

This argument could quickly advance poststructuralist claims about subjective and sexual performativity, in which characters seem to blend and separate according to the vagaries of their desires. However, I don't think this is Joyce's or Levine's intention. Since as Levine notes, Murphy sets off some internal alarm in Bloom, the affect we witness as readers inadvertently becomes a "guide" to Joycean characterization. Such affect need not be consistent (and thus supportive of a unified ontology), though the idea of affective repetition in this passage suggests more than "a series of attributes temporarily clustered around a proper name." As Levine observes, "Of all the characters that he replicates, Murphy has his most complex relationship with Bloom—not only because of the various ways in which he is like him but also because of the intensity of Bloom's reaction to him" (103).

Margot Norris's fine reading of "An Encounter" reiterates a comparable argument about homosexuality. She contends that Joyce's story resists the idea of coherent sexual orientations, instead "serv[ing] the heuristic function of demonstrating under what conditions the homosexual text seduces, incriminates, and invites punishment" (21). Some readers might think this argument lets Joyce too quickly off the authorial hook, for it could suggest that Joyce serves only as the conscious betrayer of others' phobias while seeming to possess none of his own. But perhaps we don't need to push the argument quite this far; in doing so we inevitably raise questions about what we should attribute to Joyce and what to turn-of-the-century Ireland, et cetera. While seeming to release Joyce from these problems of attribution, Norris's claims about his enlightened betrayal in fact veer toward restoring the problem of these enigmas in another form: in this reading Joyce's radical strategy of betrayal seems to be decisive and deliberate.

What matters, ultimately, I think, is less where we find Joyce in all this and more what we consider to be the conceptual implications of desire and seduction in "An Encounter." As Norris notes, "The collapse of the homosexual and the pervert into a universal immoral type fits neither Joyce's treatment of Wilde nor . . . Stanislaus Joyce's account of the original 'encounter'" (20); nor, we can add, does it fit Joyce's thoughts about sexual knowledge and education. "An Encounter" provides access to this knowledge by allowing us to see, through the eyes and verbal exchanges of two boys, "a queer old josser" probably masturbating in front of them after befriending them. Yet as Norris remarks, the story allows us to comprehend its events "[o]nly in retrospect" (22); this makes us profoundly aware of the complex stakes of manipulation, consent, and seduction. Since the narrator "deliberately defers information that would have protected us against shock and trauma" (22), he highlights the acts of judgment accompanying every act of narrative interpretation. We cannot limit these judgments to those who seem sexually manipulative; nor can we exonerate the "innocent" by inferring that sexuality divides neatly between the guilty and the pure. Joyce does not let us forget the older man's responsibility (though he does invite us to ask, Responsible for what, precisely, and with what effect?), but he also prevents us from *limiting* the story's sexuality to the man's onanism; we understand his actions as masturbation only through the observing boys' eyes ("I say! Look what he's doing! . . . I say . . . He's a queer old josser!" (*D* 26; qtd. in Norris). At this point, we might recall Stephen's encounter with the prostitute in *A Portrait*, and we might also invoke T. S. Eliot's suggestion in "The Hollow Men," "Between the idea / And the reality / Between the motion / And the act / Falls the Shadow."[23] All of these claims about enigmas usefully highlight sexuality's vanishing points; they ask us to ruminate carefully on what constitutes the precise *encounter* in Joyce's story.

To some, this story might seem suspiciously to withhold the knowledge we need to establish motives and acts, but it does so, as Norris usefully observes, to pressure the reader "to supply a meaning at the risk of self-incrimination" (27). There is an "affective and ethical discrepancy" here that, in Norris's words, "subjects the reader['s] response to ethical scrutiny [because an] erotic discourse has a profoundly more disturbing effect than the representation of an actual violence and cruelty" (31). I am reminded of Jacqueline Rose's cogent argument about the sexual resonance of the primal scene—one that, properly understood, does not exonerate adults from sexual manipulation, but rather identifies sexuality in the gap between adults' and children's asymmetrical worlds: "The sexuality lies less in the content of what is seen than in the subjectivity of the viewer, in the relationship between what is looked at and the developing sexual knowledge of the child."[24]

Does the sexuality of "An Encounter" therefore "escape us," as Joyce implied to his editor, because we grasp it only when the story has finished? Perhaps this elision of meaning—which differs greatly from an evasion of facts—might infuriate us, especially given today's hypervigilant scrutiny of adult-child relations. When defining contemporary parameters, many are relieved to substitute *power* and *abuse* for *fantasy* and *desire* because the first two words seem, at first glance, to limit sexuality to the world of adults, leaving children sexless and pure. Yet if, as Eliot reminds us, there is shadow "between the idea and the reality," and "between the motion and the act," there is also a crucial interval between what is seen and understood, perhaps especially between the "act" and its signifier— for instance, *molestation, abuse, indecent exposure,* or simply *seduction.* Such points enhance, rather than allowing us to forget, the more obvious argument that Joyce's "reality" in *Dubliners* is virtual rather than literal or historically exact, a point we could easily forget when claiming that Joyce's text is geographically "specific," reducible to the inhabitants of one city. Following Norris's suggestion of a discrepancy between affect and ethics in "An Encounter," I suggest that this interval between the act and its signifier is the "queerest" dimension of Joyce's story, for it indicates how sexuality gets "constructed," in the most conventional sense, and how sexuality goes hopelessly wrong in this and other Joycean texts—failing to sustain meaning, for instance, but also creating misunderstandings that highlight the fragile bases of every type of communication in which his characters engage.

These complex valences of sexuality and sexual realism recur in Robert Caserio's essay on Casement, Joyce, and Pound. Arguing against Enda Duffy's claim that the sexual content of Sir Roger Casement's *Black Diaries* is "trite and mundane," Caserio remarks that Duffy's claim is "apparently realistic about sex, rather than repressive. But in this argument it is hard to tell the difference" (144). Apparent realism about sex is, I think, the issue here. In addition to Caserio's compelling questions about Joyce's relation to Casement's homosexuality, politics, and execution for treachery, what interests me is the suggestion that Casement and Joyce were more committed to sexual realism than are many contemporary critics struggling to make sense of these writers' textual and sexual politics. In their commitment to reading Joyce's puns in the grain of their (generally) sexual meaning, rather than of the type of politics they would prefer Joyce to have adopted, however, Caserio and Dean come closest, I think, to capturing the semantic exuberance *and* turbulence of Joycean sexuality.[25] For this reason, we can counterpoise Pound's comments to Robert McAlmon— "have we had enough of the pseuderasts and the Bloomsbuggers? Enough, enough, we have had quite enough" (qtd. in Caserio 147)—with the Butt-Taff-Buckley episode in *Finnegans Wake:* "We want Bud. We want Bud Budderly. We want Bud Budderly boddily" (337.32–33), as well as with the following, remarkable passage: "the hissindensity buck far of his melovelance tells how when he was fast marking his first lord for cremation the whyfe of his bothem was the very lad's thing to elter his mehind" (*FW* 350.13–16, qtd. in Caserio).

As Caserio observes, the meaning of this passage hinges on the pun "cremation/creamation," for the drama of proximity among men (which Valente and Leonard underscore in their readings of *A Portrait*) seems to determine whether homosexuality will foster group stability (which Caserio calls "Homo

Rule") or political diffusion and anarchy (which he calls "Casement-inspired Homo Unruliness" [146]). For Caserio, both of these conditions betray the violence and passion of Joycean sexuality (in *Wake*-ese, "Homo Rule" has an "abnihilising force" [146]), though the outcome—like Joyce's relation to homosexuality—seems impossible to determine or predict. "[I]s Homo Rule a worthy or an unworthy imagination for postcolonial community?" Caserio asks, adding, "We can tolerate Joyce's dream of a new political rule by same-sex 'creamation,' if we are in queer studies. But for all studies, Casement-inspired Homo Unruliness in Joyce leaves disturbing abnihilisations in its wake" (146). This passage raises a valid complaint that lesbians and gay men often are not included in our imagined communities. I can also see how "same-sex creamations" would be attractive for those working in queer studies. Yet such creamations, as the pun on orgasm and death indicates, exist in a volatile relation to "sameness" *and* "differences," in Caserio's essay sometimes shoring up a monopoly of the proximate ("Joyce's dream of a new political rule by same-sex 'creamation'"—i.e., Homo Rule), an idea Hélène Cixous has called *L'Empire du Propre* ("The Empire of the Selfsame");[26] sometimes representing a benign addition to the existing order ("differences that are equalized); but most often seeming to disband sociality altogether ("Casement-inspired Homo Unruliness in Joyce leaves disturbing abnihilisations in its wake").

These motifs recur in countless studies of homosexuality. Indeed, the diversity of same-sex desires is partly responsible for the fact that few ultimately can decide whether homosexuality is socially conservative (for instance, Luce Irigaray's definition of "hommosexuality," the defining principle of patriarchy)[27] or more closely aligned with anti-identitarian politics as the single most important factor informing society's death drive and its ability to redefine love (Bersani's account of "homo-ness").[28] These conceptual extremes manifest themselves on either side of the vast divide between the Log Cabin Republicans (arch-assimilationists) and the now-defunct Queer Nation (a group committed to overhauling all sexual and social relations). In light of these extremes, however, and the possibility of idealizing or denouncing homosexuality on the basis of either option, Rabaté helpfully reminds us that Aquinas defined similitude as an opportunity for not only (in Rabaté's words) "a pleasure in closeness and near identity" but also "another extreme, namely hatred" (37). If the line between love for the same (homoeroticism) and fear of the same (homophobia) is socially and psychically nebulous, we cannot limit the ensuing conflict to "homosexual panic" in heterosexual men. Rabaté raises a wider point about affect and idealization that prevails in and beyond Joyce's work, irrespective of object choice.

How, then, can we unpack these complex nuances of similitude, proximity, and difference to clarify homosexuality's impact on narrative meaning? Like Dean, Caserio, and Valente, Rabaté negotiates carefully between particularity and generality, arguing finally for a rapport between sexuality and narrative indeterminacy that engages homosexuality as society's surplus *and* constitutive element, rather than a redundant or even unwelcome dimension of masculine identification:

> Something resists comprehension in the transmission of an unnameable sin chaining father and son together but in an absolute void. The central element to be stressed here is obscurity, not the precisely homoerotic factor (which is always to be avoided at any cost) in and of the structure.
>
> It took many years before Joyce could simply face the fact that what he was exploring was precisely the obscurity that surrounds sin and paternity alike. (40)

Reframing the question of homosexuality and secrecy, Rabaté modifies our discussion of closets to produce a more interesting, if vexed, question about homosexuality's relation *to* meaning, a question quite different from presumptions of homosexuality *as* a meaning that is concealed or locked away. Whether discussing sin, desire, or love, Rabaté and other contributors to *Quare Joyce* invite us to conceive of desire's transmission as a cause of error, distress, and hilarity in Joyce's works. In other words, by addressing "the *vehicle* of a vague speech," rather than the most evidential effects of this speech, these critics help us alight on the truly perverse dimensions of Joyce's writing.

NOTES

1. Wyndham Lewis advanced a related point in his "Analysis of the Mind of James Joyce" when describing *A Portrait* as "cold and priggish" (see *Time and Western Man* (1927) [Santa Rosa, Calif.: Black Sparrow, 1993], 73). As I shall demonstrate below, however, Lewis arguably misread Joyce when claiming that his work is "much less psychological" than Gertrude Stein's (73).

2. Hugh Kenner, *Dublin's Joyce* (Bloomington: Indiana University Press, 1956), 114.

3. D. A. Miller, "Secret Subjects, Open Secrets," in *The Novel and the Police* (Berkeley and Los Angeles: University of California Press, 1988), esp. 195.

4. E. M. Forster, *Maurice: A Romance* (1913–14; 1971) (Harmondsworth: Penguin, 1987), 179. We note too that in *On Heroes, Hero-Worship and the Heroic in History* (1841), Thomas Carlyle writes: "Literature, so far as it is Literature, is an 'apocalypse of Nature,' a revealing of the 'open secret'" (ed. Carl Niemeyer, Lincoln: University of Nebraska Press, 1966), 163.

5. Freud, "Instincts and Their Vicissitudes" (1915), in *The Standard Edition of the Complete Psychological Works of Sigmund Freud,* ed. and trans. James Strachey, 24 vols. (London: Hogarth Press and the Institute of Psycho-Analysis, 1953–74), 14:122–23.

6. Forster, terminal note to *Maurice,* 218.

7. Ibid.

8. Jacques Lacan, "L'Étourdit," *Scilicet* 4 (1973): 13.

9. Lacan, "The Subversion of the Subject and the Dialectic of Desire in the Freudian Unconscious" (1960), in *Écrits: A Selection,* ed. Jacques-Alain Miller, trans. Alan Sheridan (New York: Norton, 1977), 300.

10. Eve Kosofsky Sedgwick, *Epistemology of the Closet* (Berkeley and Los Angeles: University of California Press, 1990), 1 and 73.

11. Sedgwick's claim that "one particular sexuality [homosexuality] . . . was distinctively constituted *as* secrecy" occurs in *Epistemology of the Closet,* 73. See Dean's critique of this claim in this volume, 250.

12. In *The Mayor of Casterbridge* (1886), Michael Henchard tells Susan, the wife he sold many years earlier at a country fair, that he wants to remarry her in order to maintain a secret that "would leave my shady, headstrong, disgraceful life as a young man absolutely unopened; the secret would be yours and mine only" (Hardy, *The Mayor of Casterbridge* [Harmondsworth: Penguin, 1985], 144). Later believing that Henchard is father, Elizabeth-Jane tells her friend Lucetta Templeman, "Ah—you have many many secrets from me!" (271). The narrator adds that Elizabeth strove to "keep . . . in all signs of emotion till she was ready to burst" (271) and, subsequently, to "cork . . . up the turmoil of her feeling with grand control" (290). Such signs of turmoil and anguish anticipate Hardy's later novel *Tess of the d'Urbervilles: A Pure Woman Faithfully Represented* (1891), in which Tess suffers extreme isolation while keeping secret the fact that Alec d'Urberville preyed upon and then abandoned her.

13. See chapter 6 of *The Ruling Passion: British Colonial Allegory and the Paradox of Homosexual Desire* (Durham, N.C.: Duke University Press, 1995).

14. Forster, *Maurice,* 181.

15. I read Forster in this way in "Betrayal and Its Consolations in Forster's *Maurice,* 'Arthur Snatchfold,' and 'What Does It Matter? A Morality,'" in *Queer Forster,* ed. Robert K. Martin and George Piggford (Chicago: University of Chicago Press, 1997), 167–91. See also John Fletcher, "Forster's Self-Erasure: *Maurice* and the Scene of Masculine Love," in *Sexual Sameness: Textual Differences in Lesbian and Gay Writing,* ed. Joseph Bristow (New York: Routledge, 1992), 64–90.

16. Joseph Conrad, *Heart of Darkness* (1899; 1902) (Harmondsworth: Penguin, 1983), 101. Earlier, Marlow remarks: "It is impossible to convey the life-sensation of any given epoch of one's existence—that which makes its truth, its meaning—its subtle and penetrating essence. It is impossible. We live, as we dream—alone" (39).

17. Ibid., 101.

18. Lewis, "Mind of James Joyce," 78–79.

19. Ibid., 79.

20. Forster, *Aspects of the Novel* (1927) (Harmondsworth: Penguin, 1990), 114.

21. Oscar Wilde, *The Picture of Dorian Gray* (1890) (Harmondsworth: Penguin, 1982), 6.

22. I am alluding here to Freud's claims that certain thoughts are "entirely alien" to consciousness. For elaboration, see Freud, *The Ego and the Id* (1923), *Standard Edition,* 19:16n.

23. T. S. Eliot, "The Hollow Men" (1925), in *The Complete Poems and Plays of T. S. Eliot* (London: Faber, 1969), 85. Consider also Eliot's famous statement in *The Four Quar-*

tets: "Words strain, / Crack and sometimes break, under the burden, / Under the tension, slip, slide, perish, / Decay with imprecision, will not stay in place, / Will not stay still" (ibid., 175).

24. Jacqueline Rose, *Sexuality in the Field of Vision* (London: Verso, 1986), 227.

25. Closer, for instance, than Richard Brown ultimately gets in *James Joyce and Sexuality* (Cambridge: Cambridge University Press, 1985), esp. 78–88, and 126–64.

26. Hélène Cixous with Catherine Clément, *La jeune née* (Paris: Union générale d'éditions, 1975), 144.

27. Luce Irigaray, "Des marchandises entre elles," in *Ce sexe qui n'en est pas un* (Paris: Minuit, 1977), 187–94.

28. See Leo Bersani, *Homos* (Cambridge, Mass.: Harvard University Press, 1995), 10, 41, and 76. "My argument," Bersani claims, "presupposes a desiring subject for whom the antagonism between the different and the same no longer exists" (59–60). I interpret this claim at greater length in "Uncertain Terms of Pleasure," *Modern Fiction Studies* 42, no. 4 (1996): 807–26.

Contributors

Christy Burns is Assistant Professor of English at the College of William and Mary. She has published articles on Virginia Woolf, Vladimir Nabokov, Jeanette Wintersen, and James Joyce. Her current project is entitled "Gestural Politics: Parody and Stereotype in the Writings of James Joyce."

Robert L. Caserio directs graduate studies in English literature at Temple University. His essay is from a work in progress entitled "Citizen Queen: Gay Fictions and Democratic Dogmas."

Gregory Castle is Assistant Professor of British and Irish literature at Arizona State University. He has published numerous articles on Joyce and other Irish writers and has recently completed a study entitled "Celtic Muse: The Ethnographic Imagination in Modern Irish Writing."

Tim Dean is an Assistant Professor of English at the University of Illinois, Urbana-Champaign, and currently a Fellow at the Stanford Humanities Center, where he is working on a book to be titled "Modernism and the Ethics of Impersonality." His most recent book is *Beyond the Couch: Lacan Meets Queer Theory*. He has also edited a collection, *Psychoanalysis and Homosexuality*.

Marian Eide is Assistant Professor at Texas A&M University. She has an article on *Finnegans Wake* forthcoming in the *James Joyce Quarterly* and is currently at work on a book entitled "Legible Virus: Joyce, Rushdie, and the Ethics of Interpretation."

Colleen Lamos is Associate Professor of English at Rice University. She is the author of *Modernism Astray: Gender Errancy in Eliot, Joyce, and Proust* and is a coeditor of "Joycean Masculinities," a forthcoming issue of *European Joyce Studies*.

Christopher Lane is Associate Professor of English at Emory University. He is the author of *The Ruling Passion: British Colonial Allegory and the Paradox of Homosexual Desire* and editor of *The Psychoanalysis of Race*. *The Burdens of Intimacy: Psychoanalysis and Victorian Masculinity* is forthcoming.

Garry Leonard is Associate Professor of English the University of Toronto, Scarborough. He is the author of *Reading Dubliners Again* and *The New (Improved) Testament: Joyce and Commodity Culture.* He is also a coeditor of "Joyce and Advertising," a special issue of the *James Joyce Quarterly,* and "Queer Utilities," a special issue of *College Literature.* His current project is entitled "Making It New: The Cinematic City, Modernity, and Modernism."

Jennifer Levine teaches Literary Studies and English at the University of Toronto. Her work on Joyce has appeared in *PMLA, The Cambridge Companion to James Joyce,* the *James Joyce Quarterly,* and *Novel.*

Vicki Mahaffey is Professor of English at the University of Pennsylvania. She is the author of *Reauthorizing Joyce* and *States of Desire: Wilde, Yeats, Joyce and the Irish Experiment.* Her current project is entitled "Fairy Tales and Feminine Acculturation."

Margot Norris is Professor of English and Comparative Literature at the University of California, Irvine. Her books include *The Decentered World of Finnegans Wake, Beasts of the Modern Imagination: Darwin, Nietzche, Kafka, Ernst, and Lawrence,* and, more recently, *Joyce's Web: The Social Unraveling of Modernism.* She is currently finishing a book entitled "Writing War in the Twentieth Century."

Jean-Michel Rabaté is Professor of English at the University of Pennsylvania. He has published several books on Joyce, including *James Joyce: Authorized Reader* and *Joyce upon the Void: The Genesis of Doubt.* He has also published books on Ezra Pound, Samuel Beckett, Thomas Bernhard and the aesthetics of modernism and postmodernism. His most recent book is *The Ghosts of Modernity.* He has also edited *Roland Barthes and the Arts of Seeing* and *L'Ethique du Don: Jacques Derrida and the question du don.*

Joseph Valente is Associate Professor of English and Interpretive Theory at the University of Illinois, Urbana-Champaign. He is the author of *James Joyce and the Problem of Justice: Negotiating Sexual and Colonial Difference.* He has also edited "Joyce and Homosexuality" and coedited "Joyce and the Law" (forthcoming), both special issues of the *James Joyce Quarterly.* His current project is entitled "Contested Territory: The Conception of Manhood in (Post)Colonial Ireland."

Name Index